LATE MEDIEVAL MYSTICISM

Department of Religious Studies
Moore Reading Room
University of Kansas

THE LIBRARY OF CHRISTIAN CLASSICS

ICHTHUS EDITION

LATE MEDIEVAL MYSTICISM

Edited by

RAY C. PETRY, Ph.D., LL.D.

PHILADELPHIA

THE WESTMINSTER PRESS

Published simultaneously in Great Britain and the United States of America
by the S.C.M. Press, Ltd., London, and The Westminster Press, Philadelphia.

First published MCMLVII

Library of Congress Catalog Card No. : 57–5092

9 8 7 6 5 4 3 2 1

Typeset in Great Britain
Printed in the United States of America

GENERAL EDITORS' PREFACE

The Christian Church possesses in its literature an abundant and incomparable treasure. But it is an inheritance that must be reclaimed by each generation. THE LIBRARY OF CHRISTIAN CLASSICS is designed to present in the English language, and in twenty-six volumes of convenient size, a selection of the most indispensable Christian treatises written prior to the end of the sixteenth century.

The practice of giving circulation to writings selected for superior worth or special interest was adopted at the beginning of Christian history. The canonical Scriptures were themselves a selection from a much wider literature. In the Patristic era there began to appear a class of works of compilation (often designed for ready reference in controversy) of the opinions of well-reputed predecessors, and in the Middle Ages many such works were produced. These medieval anthologies actually preserve some noteworthy materials from works otherwise lost.

In modern times, with the increasing inability even of those trained in universities and theological colleges to read Latin and Greek texts with ease and familiarity, the translation of selected portions of earlier Christian literature into modern languages has become more necessary than ever; while the wide range of distinguished books written in vernaculars such as English makes selection there also needful. The efforts that have been made to meet this need are too numerous to be noted here, but none of these collections serves the purpose of the reader who desires a library of representative treatises spanning the Christian centuries as a whole. Most of them embrace only the age of the Church Fathers, and some of them have long been out of print. A fresh translation of a work already

9

translated may shed much new light upon its meaning. This is true even of Bible translations despite the work of many experts through the centuries. In some instances old translations have been adopted in this series, but wherever necessary or desirable, new ones have been made. Notes have been supplied where these were needed to explain the author's meaning. The introductions provided for the several treatises and extracts will, we believe, furnish welcome guidance.

JOHN BAILLIE
JOHN T. MCNEILL
HENRY P. VAN DUSEN

CONTENTS

11

page

PREFACE

This volume presents a collection of sources marking the cul-
mination of mystical thought within medieval Christianity.
These works are supplied from already existing, reputable translations appropriately acknowledged throughout the book. The
chief editorial objective has been a distinctive resetting, in
clarified historical perspective, of the richly varied, but closely
related, texts of late medieval mysticism. The volume editor
has attempted a fresh orientation of representative sources with
regard to each other and to the long ages of the mystical tradition that preceded them. An extensive general introduction has
been followed by brief biographical data, crisp annotations of
source-secondary literature, and terse summations of the more
characteristic thought prefatory to the writings of each mystic.
Biblical translations are integrated in each case with the entire
source text. Though free of copyright restrictions, they are not
reducible to the usage of one or even a few versions. In the more
crucial notes, there are references to both the Vulgate and
Protestant numberings when these are divergent.

I am deeply indebted to the General Editors for encourage-
ment and assistance, as I am also to the Duke University Research Council for grants-in-aid making possible European and
domestic researches. The examination of manuscripts and
printed texts most essential for editing each of the mystical writings was facilitated by especially gracious and extended help
from the authorities of the Bibliothèque Nationale in Paris, the
Vatican Library in Rome, and the British Museum in London.
Help was likewise freely given by the Biblioteca Communale of
Siena, the Bibliothèque Royale of Brussels, and the university
libraries of Florence, Heidelberg, Louvain, Oxford, and Cam-

bridge. Prof. Dr. L. Reypens, S.J., and his associates of the Ruusbroec-Bibliotheek in Antwerp showed me unrepayable kindnesses. I acknowledge a rapidly accruing debt of gratitude to the Duke University libraries, especially to Mr. Donn Michael Farris, Librarian of the Divinity School, and to Miss Doralyn Hickey. I wish also to recognize Mr. Robert Beach and his associates of the Union Theological Seminary library, as well as the assistance of the Columbia University libraries. My thanks go to Mrs. Donald Roettger and Mrs. Louis Hodges for patient and efficient stenographic services. My wife has given me unstinting help for which I can say no sufficient word of thanks.

RAY C. PETRY

Duke University Divinity School

General Introduction

THE PROVINCE AND CHARACTER OF MYSTICISM

THE TERM "MYSTICISM" HAS LENT ITSELF HISTORI-cally to an accumulation of highly divergent usages. This confusing multiplicity of meanings has almost blotted out any clear, authoritative connotation, for our age, of expressions like "mystic" and "mystical." Such terms have, at their root, a reminder of undoubted association with the early Greek mysteries and their initiatory rites. The unknown Eastern writer of about A.D. 500 now customarily referred to as Pseudo-Dionysius the Areopagite utilized the title *Mystical Theology* for one of his most influential books. The terminology normally employed in the Latin church, however, was not "mysticism" but "contemplation."[1] Historical surveys of mystical experience in the period leading up to, and through, the era of this anthology frequently employ a variety of entries under such captions as "contemplation" and "the contemplative life." This is true of the *Dictionnaire de spiritualité*, upon which the present volume draws so heavily.[2] The connotations of such terms have a precision throughout the Middle Ages that is now largely buried under a welter of modern ramifications.

Some of the varied attempts to locate the core of mystical or contemplative experience have been itemized by W. R. Inge.[3] These tend to focus, as do the interpretative analyses of A. B.

---

[1] Dom Cuthbert Butler, *Western Mysticism*, 2d ed., E. P. Dutton & Co., Inc., London, 1926, p. 4.
[2] Ed. by M. Viller *et al.*, Vol. 2, Paris, 1953. See cols. 1643–2193 for the article "Contemplation." Abbreviated hereafter as DS II, 1643–2193, etc.
[3] Originally in his *Christian Mysticism*, London, 1899, 6th ed., 1925, ch. 1 and pp. 335–48, and later in his *Mysticism in Religion*, University of Chicago Press, 1948, pp. 25–29.

Sharpe, Evelyn Underhill, Rufus Jones, and others, the contemplative's supreme claim, rather than isolated definitions of mysticism.[4] Dom Cuthbert Butler finds this mystic thesis significantly stated for succeeding generations of contemplatives in Augustine's words: "My mind in the flash of a trembling glance came to Absolute Being—That Which Is."[5] Put over against the modern assessments of mysticism, this admirably prefigures the delimiting usages of Sharpe, Underhill, and Jones—not to mention a considerable body of definitions assembled by Dr. Inge. Sharpe's emphasis falls upon the soul's direct contact, in full awareness, and with an objectively intellectual intuition, of "transcendental reality." This, as Butler observes, accords significantly with Underhill's "conscious relation with the Absolute" and Jones's stress upon "the soul's possible union in this life with Absolute Reality." Dr. Jones, in another significant directive on the type of religion connoted by mysticism, stresses "immediate awareness" in the relationship with God and "direct . . . intimate consciousness of the divine Presence."[6] Margaret Smith considers the mystic's goal to be the setting up of "a conscious relation with the Absolute" wherein is found "the personal object of love."[7]

Such considerations of the nature and meaning of mysticism, as of the "mystical doctrine, or teaching on contemplation," lead naturally into analyses, like those by Underhill, of mysticism's distinctive characteristics. In the early chapters of her greatest work she discusses mysticism's eminently "active and practical" qualities; its "wholly transcendental and spiritual" aims; its accent on the reality of the One as "being a living and personal object of love"; its living union with this One; and its inescapable corollary of self-surrender.[8] This call to renunciation echoes throughout the centuries of contemplation, even as it receives emphasis today by students of mysticism as diversified

---

4 Butler, *op. cit.*, p. 4, makes especial use of statements from A. B. Sharpe, *Mysticism, Its True Nature and Value*, London, 1910, pp. 74, 96; E. Underhill, *Mysticism*, p. 97 (cf. the 12th ed., Dutton, 1930, p. 72); and R. Jones in James Hastings, *Encyclopedia of Religion and Ethics*, Vol. 9, pp. 83 ff. See also almost any of his fifty-odd books on mysticism, especially his *Studies in Mystical Religion*, London, 1909.
5 *Confessions*, VII, xvii, 23; also Butler, *op. cit.*, pp. 4, 31–32.
6 Butler, *op. cit.*, pp. 4–6 and notes; Jones, *Studies*, p. xv.
7 *Studies in Early Mysticism in the Near and Middle East*, The Sheldon Press, London, 1931, p. 3; *An Introduction to the History of Mysticism*, S.P.C.K., London, 1930, p. 3.
8 *Mysticism*, pp. 70–94.

in view as Margaret Smith and Joseph Maréchal. In the Latin and Eastern Christian tradition of the contemplative pilgrimage, as in many distinctively Oriental faiths, renunciation does hold the key to the mystic way. To be sure, there are overtones of positive life affirmation for the Christian fellowship not connoted for at least some non-Christian associations.

Father Maréchal's psychological analysis of the renunciation of the "I" has reverberations throughout this anthology.[9] So, likewise, has the insistence of Margaret Smith that mysticism's passion for direct association of the soul with God was fostered through ascetic regularity and monastic discipline. Implicit in this were the self-conquest and renunciatory devotion that lead most directly to the mystic vision. Her contention that mystics were, quite understandably, to be found, therefore, "among the ascetics and in the monasteries" is a commonplace as easily documented as it is frequently ignored.[10]

The ascetic workshop throughout our period of late medieval mysticism is, more often than not, the atelier of the regulars—the monastic laboratory in which asceticism is ordered to the purpose of self-renunciation. This end is the vision of God, that is, communion with the Divine. For the end which renunciation serves as a means is fellowship with Deity; and the means employed to that end are renunciatory dedications. These are not spasmodic sentiments, but well-schooled, habitual exercises for removing the self from the place of honor ascribable only to God.

Oscar Hardman's analysis of the role of asceticism in voluntary renunciation mounts to the point of his quoting, not unsympathetically, a sentiment to which Dom Ursmer Berlière could certainly have no objection, namely, that in every mystic there is an ascetic, and that asceticism is, one might say, at the very source of mysticism.[11] If there is no justification for saying that mystics cannot be produced outside monasticism, there is even less reason for ignoring the obvious fact that most medieval mystics were monastics. Dom Ursmer Berlière and others of his order, together with non-Benedictines, demonstrate how conjoined to mystic contemplation is regularized renunciation, whether of Bernard and the Cistercians or of Francis and the

9 *Études sur la psychologie des mystiques*, Paris, 1938, Vol. I, pp. 192–95.
10 *Early Mysticism*, p. 47.
11 *The Ideals of Asceticism*, London, 1924, pp. 114–15. Cf. Dom U. Berlière, *L'ascèse bénédictine des origines à la fin du xiie siècle*, Paris, 1927.

Mendicants. If mysticism and monasticism are not as insepa-rable as H. Leclercq makes asceticism and cenobitism, they are, at least, practically mutualizing and reinforcing.[12]

The monastic life of the Middle Ages lent itself to the cultiva-tion of a varied spirituality. F. Vernet and P. Pourrat would scarcely attempt, any more than the collaborative histories of spirituality, to identify the fruits of monasticism with contem-plative fruition, alone. No more would they equate all the clerical virtues with monastic disciplines and/or mystical ex-periences. In the larger reaches of spirituality associated with the late medieval period, there are certain spiritual norms, however, that have significant bearing for contemplative lives. Pourrat, in his over-all classification of monastic spirituality, thinks in terms of the speculative, with emphasis on the reason and on intellectual theories; of the affective or practical, with the focus on the sentiment of the heart and on love as the way of being, feeling, and knowing; and of the sometimes insepa-rable combination of the affective and speculative, of sentiment and reason. In so doing he is using terminology that is recur-rently useful in interpreting the late medieval mystics.[13]

The Victorines were certainly more speculative, in last analy-sis, than they were affective. Bernard was admittedly more affective than speculative. The Franciscans had, in the person of their founder, a true contemplative of severely limited, specu-lative sympathies. In Bonaventure these speculative tendencies were habitually joined to affective experiences as they were, also, in Anselm of Canterbury, and in Ramon Lull. The Domin-icans who produced such marked speculatives as Eckhart also gave rise to a Suso and to a Catherine of Siena. In her, however, speculative instincts are by no means lacking, even as Suso is a troubadour of love almost as much as Ramon Lull or Richard Rolle. The fact is that such apparently predominant specula-tives as the secular Nicholas of Cusa are full, also, of affective instincts; and the hermit affective, Rolle, has far more of the speculative in him than at first meets the eye. Here, again, in Cusa as in Rolle, reactions to the monastic institution conduced to and threatened mystical insights beyond the mere exercise of Cusa's secular priesthood and Rolle's criticism of the regulars.

---

12 *Dictionnaire d'archéologie chrétienne et de liturgie*, Vol. 2, pt. 2 (Paris, 1907), cols. 3048 ff.; Berlière, *op. cit.*, pp. 100 ff., 219, 220 ff.
13 F. Vernet, *La spiritualité médiévale*, Bloud and Gay, Paris, 1929; P. Pourrat, *Christian Spirituality*, London, 1924, Vol. II, pp. v ff.

Perhaps of more working validity than the speculative-affective character is the applicability of the threefold way to the mystic experience. Underhill's classic work, as indeed almost every book on the contemplative life, is developed about the triple mystic route of purgation, illumination, and union.[14] This classification antedates Christian contemplation. It is often suggested, and sometimes explicitly stated, in Platonic and Neoplatonic thought. The Pseudo-Dionysius utilizes it throughout his corpus.[15] So, likewise, do a majority of the authors in our book of contemplative readings. It is well to be forewarned, however, that an infinite variety of gradations are interlocked with such relatively simple classifications of the mystic ascent or development. Ladders or scales, degrees, and the like do not, however, denature, in the main, the hoary associations of the triple life. Generally in relation to the triple way, though not uniformly so, our authors treat a somewhat common body of frequently recurring aspects. These are, among others, awakening or conversion; self-knowledge or purgation; illumination with its attendant voices and visions; surrender and, on occasion, the dark night; finally, union, that is, consummation, or contemplation in its specialized sense. This last, carrying the soul to the apogee of spiritual experience, is referable, also, in terms of Underhill's organization, to that introversion which involves recollection and quiet as the anteway to contemplation; to introversion considered as contemplation, with its ecstasies, raptures, and dark nights; and to the consummately unitive life.[16]

The interpretation of mysticism has been facilitated by the more specialized, psychological investigations of Maréchal and A. Saudreau.[17] It has profited from the philosophical-theological bent of Dr. Inge, especially where applied to Plotinian areas. The bearing of ascetic-monastic regularity for mystic

[14] *Mysticism*, especially pt. II, pp. 167 ff.; Smith, *History of Mysticism*, pp. 7 ff.; *Early Mysticism*, pp. 6 ff.

[15] The recurrence of this triple approach in Plato, Philo, Plotinus is documented in DS II, 1719 ff., in Inge, *Christian Mysticism*, pp. 9 ff., in K. F. Riedler, *Das Buch vom vollkommenen Leben*, Thalwil-Zurich, 1947, p. 166. In Dionysius see, for example, *Hiér. eccl.*, ch. V, pt. I, sec. 3—M. de Gandillac, *Œuvres complètes du Pseudo-Denys l'Aréopagite*, Aubier—Paris, 1943, pp. 295–96; DS II, 1888 ff.; *Hiér cél.*, ch. X, Gandillac, *Œuvres*, pp. 221–23.

[16] *Mysticism*, pt. II, chs. 6–10.

[17] *Les degrés de la vie spirituelle*, 6th ed., 2 vols., Paris, 1935; *L'état mystique . . .*, 2d ed., Paris, 1921, etc.

spirituality has been admirably assessed by Pourrat and Berlière. The translations and commentaries of Butler, as well as the
singular irenicity of Jones, have likewise advanced the necessary
reorientation and modification of thought concerning the role
of mysticism in the total Christian tradition.

At this juncture it should be recorded how nobly the *Dictionnaire de spiritualité*, *La vie spirituelle*, and the *Dictionnaire de théologie catholique*, among numerous others, have served the cause of
interpreting specific mystical figures and of depicting large
movements and basic spiritual trends from a Catholic perspective. The article on "Contemplation" in the *Dictionnaire de
spiritualité* is particularly noteworthy.

To Dom Butler goes the credit for having set in clearer focus
the early and medieval Christian tradition as it strove to establish the balance between contemplation and action. With basic
orientation to Augustine, Gregory the Great, and Bernard of
Clairvaux, together with a rich assortment of other medieval
contemplatives, his book *Western Mysticism* translates in context
some classic primary sources.[18] Making quite clear that the
mystic in general, and the monastic mystic in particular,
acknowledges no such activist preoccupation as our secularized
Western society now demands, Butler shows much more. He
clearly demonstrates that the mystics were generally better
actives, not in spite of, but because of, their prior dedication to
God in worship as the end of all life. One aspect of the present
anthology that speaks largely for itself is this peculiar equipoise
of medieval contemplation and action with its major response,
however admittedly a by-product, to human need in the name
of the Divine.

THE SETTING FOR LATE MEDIEVAL
MYSTICISM

It is completely infeasible here to summarize, however super-
ficially, the beginnings and early development of the contemplative tradition. One cannot so briefly assess non-Christian,
Hebrew, and early Christian thought on mysticism as it leads up
to the immediate province of this anthology. The undoubtedly

---

[18] The present editor's article "Social Responsibility and the Late Medieval
Mystics," *Church History*, Vol. 21, no. 1 (March, 1952), pp. 3–19, develops
this theme of balanced contemplation and action for most of the mystics
in the anthology with extended source references.

mystical portions of the Old and the New Testament, particularly of the psalms, the Pauline letters, and the Johannine literature, have been succinctly analyzed by Miss Margaret Smith in her *Introduction to the History of Mysticism*, already noted. Detailed analyses are available, for instance, in the *Dictionnaire de spiritualité*.

More immediately necessary for this volume, however, is a short résumé of the major influence on medieval mysticism exerted by non-Christian Greek thinkers in relation to the early Christian Fathers. Especially significant for late medieval mysticism were the Platonic and Neoplatonic currents, particularly the thought of the Pseudo-Dionysius, as well as the influence of Augustine, John Cassian, and Gregory the Great. Also indispensable is a brief recapitulation of the predominantly monastic spirituality characteristic of the period extending from the sixth to the twelfth century.

PLATO (427–347 B.C.)

Plato, ever mindful of Socrates' sense of kinship with the Divine, sees in the soul a being of divine origin. In it is the longing for reunion with the eternal Being. Having lived, before its temporal birth, in the presence of pure Being and the contemplation of eternally unchanging reality, the soul still possesses the power to recognize and apprehend this true reality.

From the *Phaedo, Phaedrus, Banquet, Republic*, and other writings of Plato, one may gather his chief contemplative views. True knowledge finds its object, not in visible things, in their constitutive elements, or in their ordering, but in the invisible world of essences. Contemplation is a rare, sudden experience predicated on hard, purificatory effort. It presupposes maximum bodily detachment and the soul's living progressively in self-revelatory loneliness. It brings disciplined, dialectical consideration to objects regarded in their intelligible purity. Following this preparatory stage a sudden, clear illumination emerges. The veil is torn from that Beauty in itself which is true reality. The soul thus given new vision is bemused as in marriage under the spell of a joyous, almost foolish abandon.

Such contemplation beholds that immutable reality apart from which all sensible things would be but deceptive appearances. It looks upon reality itself, upon that divine Beauty which is pure and uncorrupted in its truth. This reality is given orderly disposition in the world of Ideas, that is, of forms, or veritable essences. The organ of this contemplation is the pilot of the soul, the nous. To it alone true Reality is accessible. These Ideas are contemplation's object to the extent that they are clarified "by the Sun of the intelligible world." This very principle of Truth and Beauty, albeit transcendent to both of these, is the Good itself. Even as it transcends all things, the Good is, in a sense, immanent in them. The soul, with affinities for the world below as also to the intelligible order, aspires to the higher world and to the Good. Uniting itself to that order, it finds its happiness at last, therein.

The soul, having pre-existently beheld the true Being and absolute Truth, now seeks to regain this vision. To that end, sense passions must be abased with the aid of reason. The soul's educated eye, its spiritual sense, now eschews all earlier darkness. The "Sun of Truth" is insatiably sought. New light falls gradually upon the world of nature. The soul finally looks upon the Good itself in its very essence, over and beyond its reflection in natural phenomena. Everything beautiful in the visible and in the invisible world alike is seen to emanate from the absolute Beauty.

The soul is guided all the way in its homeward itinerary by an intermediary, that "great demon love." Through it, communication is established between the divine and the mortal world. Through it, the soul is uplifted from terrestrial to celestial things. Far from being a mere conducer to the contemplative vestibule, this love is at once a moving principle and an occasion of knowledge. Within it, doing and knowing are joined. However unsynthesized and ambiguous the mystical and the more learned aspects of Plato may be, these qualities are not opposed. It is in the mystical Plato that Plato the scholar finds his light.

ARISTOTLE (384–322 B.C.) AND PHILO (30 B.C.–A.D. 50)

Aristotle and the Peripatetics, generally, think of the perfect man as being concerned contemplatively with metaphysical matters while given actively to practical issues. *Theōria* and pure thought, however delightful, yield finally to a kind of praxis, that is, to a daily activity wherein the human stays well within itself. Contemplation, or *theōria*, viewed as a union with pure act is thought illusory.

The Stoic ideal emphasizes the logical life. The life of action led forth in reason finds the divine Logos immanent in daily things, not detached from the sensible world. The conduct of the practical life is the Stoics' preoccupation. Actually they emphasize detachment from sheer things and attachment to the role of superior reason.

For Philo, contemplation is a matter of knowing God. This is not merely in terms of his rationally deduced existence as creator. Rather, the soul takes leave of everything, the body and its very self included, under the rapturous possession of the Divine. Contemplation such as this is, therefore, possible only through God's communication of himself. In the present life, action understood as prayer and liturgical chant leads normally to contemplation. Mediating between the God who is immanent in man and the universe are divine agencies, or Logoi. The supreme Logos, who is "the Word and the Image of God," assists man in his contemplative solitude and in his striving toward that loving, virtuous service of others that is prosecuted in oneness with the Divine. There is here an ascetic conquest of the lower passions. Knowledge is found in the victory over sense and in the ecstatic "going out of oneself." Finally, building upon the purgative and illuminative steps, the soul comes to the unitive experience. Herewith the vision of God is granted, with mystical ecstasy following upon the soul's self-transcending withdrawal from all finitude. The mind, mastered at last by the divine love, light, and joyousness, knows the contemplative love of God fully joined to active service for man. One thinks of Ruysbroeck, for example, when observing Philo's insistence upon "the 'universal life,' lived Godwards and manwards."

PLOTINUS (A.D. 204–269)

Plotinus finds the soul driven by an insatiable desire to seek out its first principle and its last end, namely, the supreme Good. This desire is the all-motivating end of action. It is, likewise, the condition for that living contemplation which is the intelligence. Those possessed of this intelligence preserve no static experience but rather seek the Good, further, under the energizing dynamic of love. "Those who contemplate are the ones who truly love." Eros, always oriented to a beauty beyond itself, becomes the intermediary between the desiring subject and the desired object. Thus love becomes, for the lover, the eye by which he beholds his beloved. No selfish passion, this desire for the Good seeks, in union with the supreme Good, its own perfection.

The soul and the nous—that organ of higher contemplation—move by this dynamis toward union with the supreme Good. This assumes in the contemplative an affinity with its end and in the nous a trace of the One. The nous bears in itself a likeness to the first principle from which it comes. In the soul's hidden depths is an image of the One and of the Good. Imperfect though the resemblance be, it makes possible the seeking and finding of the first principle by the intelligence. Likeness is attracted to its like even as the eye, comprising luminous elements, goes toward the light. The eye inclines toward the sun in conformity with it. The soul sees the beautiful in so far as it becomes beautiful. Let him who would contemplate God and Beauty become comformable to God and to the Beautiful.

Contemplation is conditioned on the purification of the nous. The nous renounces all, itself included, in order to become, in its action, only a trace of the One within it. Since we truly are that which we are in act, and since activity at its best is contemplation, we become that which we contemplate. In the act of self-renunciation, the nous gives itself up to a higher action. It falls under the benignant operation from above which makes mystical union possible. Denying, in a sense, that to see God is to die, Plotinus believes that one may see God even in this life. But the intelligence, in the process of rendering this possible, so far ceases to be itself as to find in the ecstatic vision a kind of death—a separation more radical than that of body from soul.

The soul and the nous realize in this self-renunciation a true conversion, a genuine, receptive turning to the first principle. Here, ensuing on purification, is the gift of illumination, an influx of love, an incomparable fecundity, a possession by the Divine, a virtual ravishment. The nous finds union with the One only if, and when, the One illumines, fortifies, and fructifies it. In contemplative experience the mystic is passive under the divine action. Only by God's initiative does one see God.

At the contemplative summit there suddenly appears a presence, as of a great light. This is all-encompassing as if to blot out the separateness of see-er opposed to that which is seen. One is reminded of a fully absorbed reader, not reflectively conscious of his reading. Presence here transcends knowledge. Contemplation at the peak is unknowing and unconscious. It is not so by default but by an all-encompassing self-comprehension which transcends further objectivizing and multiplying of data and goals. It is beyond further need such as the thinking nous customarily knows.

Here, then, is a union where two are truly one without confusion of identity. Plotinus is not properly interpreted as teaching a flat absorptionism, an identification of the One and the soul. He here focuses a relational sense of presence, a banishment of sheer otherness in a true, living union of the contemplative with the One. This is not identity, then, but union. The mystic, far from being annihilated, is possessed by the Divine. The soul having reached the end of its ascensional pilgrimage has come to joyous beatitude. This is a repose, not of inactivity, but of fructifying action. Herein the supreme Good—always distinct from other beings—continues to stimulate and elicit a loving, responsive commerce. Here, then, is the Platonic return to original purity and active conformity with the One. This is intimate union unseparated from the One. This is that godly life of godlike men, that world-renouncing "flight of the alone to the alone." [19]

AUGUSTINE OF HIPPO (354-430)

Most authorities probably agree that Augustine's teachings on mystical theology and contemplation have to be gleaned from relatively limited sections incorporating basic elements but no didactic synthesis.[20] In addition to prime sections that he emphasizes, Butler, for example, has translated some fairly extended passages.[21]

[19] The foregoing treatment is reconstructed from the excellent, source-based analysis of DS II, 1716–42, with literature, col. 1742. There is a lucid, brief exposé in Smith, *An Introduction to the History of Mysticism*, chs. 2 and 4. Consult W. R. Inge's authoritative *The Philosophy of Plotinus*, 2 vols., 2d ed., London, 1923. *Plotinus: The Enneads* is translated by Stephen Mackenna, 2d ed., Faber & Faber, Ltd., London, 1956. See E. Gilson, *A History of Christian Philosophy in the Middle Ages*, Random House, Inc., New York, 1955, by index.

[20] Butler, *Western Mysticism*, p. 20; DS II, 1919.

[21] Such as *Confess.*, VII, x, 16; xvii, 23; IX, x, 23–25; *Enarratio in Psalmum*, 41 (Heb., 42); *De quantitate animae*, 74–76, etc.; the *Enarratio*, rather lengthy and translated by Butler, *op. cit.*, pp. 21 ff. Compare *Augustine: Confessions and Enchiridion*, ed. by A. C. Outler, Library of Christian Classics series, Vol. VII, The Westminster Press, Philadelphia, 1955, especially p. 151, note 39; also texts of the *Confessions* and literature cited on pp. 17–23, 413. Note the significant evaluations of mystical experience in *Augustinus magister: Congrès International Augustinian*, Paris, 21–24, September, 1954, 2 vols.

Contemplation, it there appears, is primarily the lot of the blessed in heaven. Though properly belonging to the future life, some beginnings of it, some passing glimpses or foreshadowings of divine things, are possible here below. In his early work on the *Quantity of the Soul*, Augustine provides a deservedly famous analysis of seven grades or degrees in the soul's functioning.[22] These steps introduce the fundamental consideration, not only of purgation, but of illumination and union as well. Thus the more remote preparation for the contemplative life is found in purification which is tentatively mentioned in relation to the fourth grade. More specifically, the last three grades deal with the threefold way. In the fifth station, the soul finds tranquillity in the face of the passions, as well as a veritable cleansing and reformation actually begun in the fourth. Apropos of the sixth stage there is the *ingressio*, that is, the leading into or the approach of the soul to contemplation; even as the seventh is contemplation itself, here described as the soul's feeding or sustenance. That is, in the fourth and fifth degrees, the soul's ethical refurbishing or transformation is being effected, its purity established and sustained, its purgation and reformation are being wrought by God. This cleansing and healing of the soul having been achieved by him, he then leads the soul in, illuminating it in the sixth stage, by way of preparation for the seventh, or unitive, level. At this last station he feeds it.

Here, then, is the purification of the soul and its affections with the peace of soul that virtue gives; a heightening of its desire to know God, together with its entrance into light; and, finally, the contemplation of divine things.[23] In *The Lord's Sermon on the Mount* (I, iii, 10)[24] as in the so-called contemplation of Ostia, from the spiritually autobiographical *Confessions* (IX, x–xi, 23–27), ascending levels mark the soul's development. This progression passes through (1) poverty of spirit, (2) piety in receptiveness to the Sacred Scripture, (3) knowledge of one's own miserable defection from God, (4) hard-working, painstaking cultivation of the hunger and thirst for righteousness, (5) further openness to God's gracious mercy proved by

---

22 *De quantitate*, 79, 80; also 70–75; Butler, *op. cit.*, p. 28.
23 Pourrat, *Christian Spirituality*, Vol. I, p. 212.
24 As translated in *Ancient Christian Writers*, Vol. 5, by J. J. Jepson, from *De sermone domini in monte* (MPL 34: 1229–1308), The Newman Press, Westminster, Maryland, 1948. Cf. DS I, 1113.

one's own mercy extended to others in need of help, (6) a clean-hearted, pure-minded, self-liberating preparation for the contemplative vision and, finally, (7) wisdom, wherein the purified intelligence contemplates truth and the divine perfection even as it comes to experience true peace and a genuine similitude with God. In the second and third degrees, the study of Scripture is basic even as this accompanies all the other steps. Coming out of the fourth degree, the soul orients itself contemplatively, having already had a foretaste of union. It advances with a dual propulsion of purification and Godward attention. In the work of purification, love of neighbor exercises a large role, actually a dominant one in the fifth degree.[25]

The proximate readying of the soul for contemplation may be said to inhere in the processes of recollection and introversion.[26] Here recollection is much more than mere remembering. It is more properly the galvanizing of the mind's forces in fullest concentration. With images, sensuous creatureliness, and externalities all banished, with the intellectual processes stilled and the mind itself emptied, introversion may begin. In other words, the entering of the mind into itself, the mind's concentration on its deepest or highest part, is at hand.

The soul's return to God is, as Bishop William Bernard Ullathorne of Birmingham says, predicated on its entry, first, into itself. God communicates with man only at his soul's center. To this point Augustine speaks in his eloquent Book X (viii, 12 to xxvii, 38) of the *Confessions* (see VII, x, 16). As observed by Underhill, it was the tragedy of many mystics in the Middle Ages to have veered away from the appreciation of introversion, even as it was the higher glory of Ruysbroeck and others to have rejoined Augustine in stressing it.[27] Augustine did, indeed, find God "more inward" than his "most inward part," "higher than [his] highest." [28]

Augustine having sought God across the different reaches of consciousness entered at last "into the very seat of the mind." One cannot easily contest the assertion that whatever the term applied to Augustine's personal contemplation, one must acknowledge the accentuation of the intellectual character in it. In him the living light is, as it were, an ensemble binding with

---

[25] DS I, 1114; *De quantitate*, 79–80; 73–75.
[26] Butler, *op. cit.*, p. 29.
[27] E. Underhill, *Ruysbroeck*, London, 1914, pp. 152–53; also J. A. Bizet, *Ruysbroeck; œuvres choisies*, Aubier, Paris, 1946, p. 64.
[28] *Confess.*, III, vi, 11; Butler, *op. cit.*, p. 30.

it, in a Christian synthesis, the insights toward which the non-Christian influences of his pre-Christian philosophizings had inclined him. Augustine's mysticism is oriented to admiration and joyous regard for the divine graces, as it is also characterized by an intellectual and spiritual humility far removed from Neoplatonic subtleties.[29]

This is not to deny the obvious indebtedness of Augustine to Plotinus, for instance. Butler, in surveying the crucially autobiographical passages, notes the strongly Plotinian coloring. He remarks how Augustine pays his due to the Platonists who had urged him to return to himself. In the Ostian passages of the *Confessions* and elsewhere in it, as also in the *Enarration on Psalm 41*, there is, at times, an undoubtedly Plotinian contour of contemplative language and idea. Certainly, in a way not characteristic of many Western mystics with their prayerful absorption, Augustine's contemplation is mainly "an intellectual process."[30]

There is more than a little question about Augustine's highly intellectual contemplation. Is it actually mysticism or Platonism? Butler readily answers that this is genuine mysticism and valid contemplative experience. Beginning with what at first seems the sheerest Platonism, it develops into the highest type of mysticism. Augustine may admittedly diverge from the mystical itinerary that is today deemed classic. He has not been less favored than other contemplatives, on occasion at least, with the graces of infused contemplation.[31]

Aside from Maréchal's debatable attempt to capitalize Augustine for the defense of a possible vision of God while yet in this life, there is in the learned Jesuit's researches a significant reinforcement of Augustine's contemplative character.[32] In reply to the skeptical queries of E. Hendrikx, it has been reiterated that Augustine is indeed a mystic: "His serene luminous mysticism impregnates the Plotinian dialectic of which he is the tributary and permits the emergence in unequivocal terms of a highly personalized experience characterized by an uncommon, supernatural passivity."[33]

In the balance of the contemplative and the active, there is in

---

29 DS II, 1919–20.
30 *Confess.*, VII, x, 16; xvii, 23; IX, x, 23–25; Butler, *op. cit.*, pp. 31–34, 21–24; Gilson, *History*, p. 70.
31 Butler, *op. cit.*, pp. 20–24, 40–62; DS II, 1919–20; *Confess.*, X, xl, 65; *Enarr. in Ps.* 41: 9–10.
32 *Études*, Vol. II, pp. 180–84; DS II, 1920.
33 DS II, 1920.

Augustine, as later in Gregory and Bernard, an incitement to Christian service and social responsibility that inspired the whole of the Middle Ages.[34]

JOHN CASSIAN (d. 434)

John Cassian (d. 434) is closely associated with Augustine's contemplative impact. He has left a discernible mark on virtually every school of Western spirituality.[35] His emphasis on the capital vices came, through Gregory's modifications, to be a dominant motif in the ethical speculations of medieval thinkers. Occidental spirituality likewise reflected his analytics of the two ways. These distinguished the practical life (the *vita actualis*, or *ethica*) and the life of contemplation (the *divina* or *spiritualis contemplatio*) as well as his double reference to the sciences. They concerned his classification of "actual," and "theoretical" or "spiritual," knowledge. They also focused the ends to which these ways and types of knowledge lead. Final objectives are purity of heart (*puritas cordis*, or *apatheia*) and pure, perpetual prayer (*pura et iugis oratio*).[36] Like many others, he experimented extensively with the eremitic life only to adopt by choice that cenobitic renunciation whose reform principles entered into the lasting contribution of Benedict of Nursia and his Rule.[37]

Cassian is more explicit in his spiritual teachings than Augustine. The essential qualities of the Eastern tradition are adapted from Gregory Nazianzen and from Evagrius, especially, into a presentation that is much more practical than speculative. The insight of the experimentalist, more than the recapitulation of the Fathers, characterizes this popularizer of renunciatory asceticism.

The approach of Cassian to supernatural contemplation is,

---

[34] DS I, 1124–26.

[35] See M. Cappuyns, "Cassien," *Dictionnaire d'histoire et de geographie ecclésiastiques*, ed. by A. Baudrillart *et al.*, Vol. II (Paris, 1939), cols. 1319 ff., 1346 ff.; DS II, 223 ff., 1921–29.

[36] The analysis of this section follows the line of the foregoing and of F. Cayré, *Patrologie*, 4th ed., Paris, 1947, Vol. I, pp. 581 ff., together with O. Chadwick, *John Cassian*, Cambridge, 1950, chs. 5 and 6 especially. Key references to the *Conferences* and *Institutes*, impossible to document in detail here, may be found in the above according to the editions of the *Corpus scriptorum ecclesiasticorum latinorum*, Vols. 13 and 17.

[37] P. Schmitz, *Histoire de l'ordre de Saint-Benoît*, 2d ed., Maredsous, 1948, 1949, Vol. I, p. 34, and Vol. II, p. 359; also Benedict, *Reg.* 73; Berlière, *L'ascèse*, pp. 3–4.

then, from the vantage ground of the inner kingdom of God. It stresses spiritual knowledge, pure prayer, and the "place of God." The monastic life seeks to foster that spiritualization so indispensable to the soul's unity with God. This is the way of "renunciants" who solicit divine union via knowledge and the intellectual virtues in an interchange where "like recognizes like."

Cassian's first *Conference* posits contemplation as the goal of the truly religious life. The monastic way leads the soul by purity of heart and perfect love to the anticipation of that beatitude which inheres in the inner kingdom of God. Consummated only in the future life, it may be possessed here, in a measure, by every righteous soul through the working of the Holy Spirit by way of contemplation.

Such perfection is frequently checkmated by obstacles such as concupiscence and the eight principal vices as well as by manifold temptations and the devil himself. These may be countered by prayer, especially, as well as by penitence, fasting, mortification, and the ascetic's renunciation of all worldly supports, his very self included. The virtues help demolish obstacles to perfection even as they accent the way of corporate obedience and the soul's orientation to the good. Supernatural peace which crowns the virtues is the effect of love and the gift of God conditioned by prayer.

In prayer the mystic gifts complete what was launched in ascetic dedication. Perpetual prayer is not acquired without the virtues. Without prayer the virtues would not come to perfection. Contemplation is not the result of a natural dialectic. "Spiritual knowledge" is the contemplation of the hidden mysteries couched under the letter of Scripture. The Holy Spirit by its light confers this spiritual knowledge upon the pure of heart. It is a gift, not the result of a facile or even methodical exercise of natural capacities. The monastic common life does favor contemplation in that its devotion in all its forms is a purification which prepares the way for spiritual knowledge.

Three stages of prayer culminate in a fourth, that is, perfect or pure prayer, a prayer of fire. Wholly gratuitous and superior to all human effort, it is transitory and occasional at best—an interior *élan*, but fugitive. This is a prayer of silence and may extend to the point of ravishment. It is the condition of a fully renounced soul, one having invoked the way of apathy by overleaping not only the vices but also every possessive instinct. Under this reign of despoilment new spiritual sensibilities are, by way of charity, substituted for the old, natural ones. The soul knows internal tears, not merely external ones, that are at once the fruit of compunction and the joy that God alone bestows.

For Cassian, spiritual knowledge is inseparable from prayer. Furthermore, pure prayer is not dissociable from the contemplation which Cassian calls perpetual prayer, or *oratio iugis*.

Moral purity and the renounced life of the virtues (*apatheia*) conduce, then, to theoretical purity (*theōria*) at the summit of contemplative experience. The monastic life is characterized by pure, perpetual prayer because it unites, indissolubly, *theōria* and *apatheia*.

DIONYSIUS THE AREOPAGITE (c. 500)

To exaggerate the role of Dionysius the Areopagite in medieval mysticism would be difficult indeed. Through the mediating influence of such men as Hilduin, John Scotus Eriugena, and Hugh of St. Victor, he entered the mystical tradition of the later Victorines, Bonaventure, the Rhenish mystics, Cusa, Ruysbroeck, and the *German Theology*.[38]

Dionysius goes farther and deeper in his search for mystical reality than the cultivation of spirituality in general. In the larger sense, the whole arena of theology is mystical, since it emphasizes scriptural initiation and revelation as transmitted by God's own oracles to his properly designated, earthly hierarchs. The Areopagite, however, neither derogates ecclesiastical authorities nor sets them up as a privileged coterie. True mysticism focuses the mysterious decoding of the Christian allegories that the angels know so well. Through the angelic beings

[38] The ensuing treatment follows closely the good brief discussion of M. de Gandillac, *Œuvres*, pp. 31 ff., with its complete modern edition of the primary sources. It is also oriented to the massive source analyses with exhaustive literature given by R. Roques in DS II, 1885 ff., and III, 244 ff. The *Dionysiaca*, ed. by Dom Ph. Chevallier *et al.*, Paris, 1937, 2 vols., is indispensable for the entire Dionysian corpus. See also the older edition of Migne, *Patrologia Graeca*, Vol. III, Paris, 1856. Quite useful studies are G. Théry, *Études Dionysiennes*, Vols. I and II, Paris, 1932, 1937, and V. Lossky, "La notion des 'analogies' chez Denys le Pseudo-Aréopagite," *Archives d'histoire doctrinale et littéraire du moyen âge*, Vol. 5 (1930), pp. 279–309; also his *Essai sur la théologie mystique de l'église d'orient*, Aubier, Paris, 1944. In addition to providing a good introduction, C. E. Rolt, *Dionysius the Areopagite*, London, 1920, translates the *Divine Names and the Mystical Theology*. Sharpe, *Mysticism*, translates the second of these. Consult Maréchal, *Études*, Vols. I and II, by index. Cf. Gilson, *A History of Christian Philosophy*, pp. 81–85, 597–98.

and in the line of proper ecclesiastical tradition, we may come to know the allegories also. The contemplative life with its purgation, illumination, and union is open, therefore, to the totality of holy people and not to specialized renunciants alone, whether lay, clerical, or monastic. This is not some rarified experience with Deity in the Plotinian or even Eckhartian sense. Rather, that which characterizes Dionysian *theōria* or contemplation inheres in the symbolically interpreted, Christian liturgical rites. The illumined ones are concerned with a mystical theology which, in its sacramental and hierarchical reaches, provides, first, an intelligible, decipherable symbolism of the traditional allegories.

In the introductory procedure of the *Divine Names*, Dionysian exegesis utilizes, first, the method of affirmation or *cataphase*. The myriad degrees of reference incident to considering the Universal Cause in all its ramifying effects conduces to endlessly diversified inadequacies of imagination, denomination, and description. The opposite approach through negation or *apophase* involves a contrasting brevity. Here, the divine essence gets its only definition in terms of the ruthlessly constricting denial of all names, however remote or intimate, usually held applicable to God.[39]

The *Mystical Theology* proper is not content even with such progressive negations as are held necessary to the liberation of Deity from banal definition and description. True, symbolic initiations, holy rites, and the double use of *cataphase* and *apophase* all have their respected roles. But all must finally be transcended in that realm of "darkness clearer than light" hitherto penetrated by Moses only. Here all oppositions are transcended; not only those of intelligence and intelligibles, of being and nonbeing, but also of "yes" and "no."

In the realm of luminous shadow which both hides and reveals the divine mysteries, those who are free, whether of things seen or things seeing, advance into the true, mystical darkness of ignorance. Considerations of intelligence and essence alike having been abandoned, one enters into a union of ignorance with one who is beyond all essence and all knowledge. Renouncing all things and oneself utterly, the mystic comes, by the elevation of pure ecstasy, into the resplendent darkness of the divine superessence. Through a repudiation of all knowledge, he gains a knowledge that surpasses his understanding. It is into

---

[39] Gandillac, *Œuvres*, p. 34; *Mystical Theology*, ch. III, ch. I, 3.

this realm of learned ignorance—entered only by Moses, who himself saw not God but only the place where he dwelt—that Eckhart, Cusa, and others inquire.[40]

Perhaps the approach to this mystical summit appears to sever the direct continuity of spiritual hierarchy. It certainly stands accused of introducing an exceptional degree of union only slightly different from that accorded Moses and Paul. Actually, Dionysius carefully refrains from considering this contemplative mount as attainable under the circumstances of man's limited perfection. His references to that relative perfection here attainable accent the degree of the soul's dedication rather than actual ascent to the unitive peak. Each one of the "holy people," or contemplatives, stops short of the mystical zenith. How near, under God's solicitation, he comes, depends on the measure of his powers and his divinely enabled merits.[41]

Dionysius puts a curious emphasis upon the word "Eros," or amorous desire, which he places above "Agape," or charitable love. This love is more than the lure drawing each being toward perfect Beauty and that which lies beyond beauty. It is, already in God, the always superabundant source of an infinitely outgoing bounty. Here, also, the term "Eros" implies ecstasy. It impels all loving beings to go out of themselves. It constrains God to produce the universe. By it, superiors are led to guide inferiors. Under its spell, equals unite themselves one with the other, and inferiors raise themselves toward those who participate more fully in the divine love. Love is a universal phenomenon. The deifying union is only one example of it.[42]

What in the entire Dionysian corpus seems least Christian is the concept of hierarchy. This is less a product of pure Platonism, perhaps, than it is a mark of "Neoplatonic decay." At first glance the hierarchical concept appears to picture a set of concentric circles barring out all possibility of relation between the human and divine person. Apparently, the expansion of charity and the great duty of dispensing the light have here been estopped. Hierarchy seems too much for the love motif of "Eros." Against the profane, Dionysius carefully closes the door to the sanctuary. Is this a veiled hint of clericalist privileges and abuses? Closer scrutiny tends to allay our fears. The initial view, the classical image of the universe of stairs, is largely neutralized

---

[40] *Mystical Theology*, chs. I, V; on *theōria* and "ecstasy," cf. DS II, 1894–1911.
[41] Gandillac, *Œuvres*, p. 35.
[42] *Divine Names*, IV, 12, 13; *Œuvres*, 709 B, 712 A, pp. 106–107, 38. On Dionysian ecstasy in detail, cf. DS II, 1894–1911.

by the Plotinian "image" of spokes of a wheel all of which touch equally at their engendering, unifying center.[43]

Himself antecedent to all being, God is present in each being. Thanks to the immanence of the transcendent, each participates in all. The worth of the person is not only preserved, but extended, since God lives in each to the degree that each, according to his measure or fashion, is able to live in God.[44]

"Each according to his measure, or fashion" is the whole secret of the Dionysian hierarchy. As Lossky has so well seen, this notion of analogy is central for Dionysius.[45]

Analogy, however, does not have for Dionysius its later scholastic meaning. The Dionysian analogy signifies "according to the measure of powers or merits in each." Each properly restricts his operations to the functions assigned him on the basis of his abilities and limitations.[46] It is thus that one's place in the hierarchy is determined. This is not a case of spatial distances. Saying that the orders which live nearer to God are more conformed to him than those farther from him, does not imply that proximity means space; rather, proximity here connotes the greatest aptitude for receiving the divine graciousness.[47]

But does this susceptibility in any way result from an arbitrary degree? No! Dionysius insists on human freedom. This is the single cause of evil in the world—of the revolt of angels and men. This is less the attraction of nonbeing or the seduction by a bad principle than it is the meager participation in divine things.[48]

The *Divine Names* may be cited as authority for analogical premises. It is in the measure that free beings apply themselves, to the degree that they receive in their plasticity the multiple imprints of the pure, original seal, that they share in ordered mobility and arrange themselves hierarchically.[49] It is the privilege of the Universal Cause, this totally transcendent good, to invite beings into common with it. The gracious likelihood is

---

[43] *Divine Names*, V, 6; *Œuvres*, 821 A, pp. 132–33. On the reconciliation of love, ecstasy, and hierarchy see DS II, 1908 ff., III, 264–280.

[44] *Ibid.*, V, 5; *Œuvres*, 820 A, p. 131; *Divine Names*, I, 4; *Œuvres*, 592 C, p. 72; DS II, 1891. See the excellent articles by R. Roques, "La notion de hiérarchie selon le Pseudo-Denys," *Archives*, Vol. 17 (1949), pp. 183–222; Vol. 18 (1950–1951), pp. 5–44.

[45] See note 38.

[46] Letter, VIII, 1; *Œuvres*, 1089 D–1092 A, p. 341.

[47] *Ibid.*, VIII, 2; *Œuvres*, 1092 B, p. 342.

[48] *Divine Names*, IV, 19–20; *Œuvres*, 716 C–D, 717 C, pp. 111–13.

[49] *Ibid.*, II, 6, IV, 2, 28; *Œuvres*, 644 B, 696 A, 729 A–B, pp. 83, 95, 121–23.

held out that even the humblest will become, in his own way, a co-operator with God.[50]

This is not all. Within each degree or rank, men as well as angels have a double mission. While tending toward the highest communion possible, they likewise assist their inferiors to elevate themselves to their own rank.[51]

The precedent power and example of the *Celestial Hierarchy* prepare us to understand the language of the *Ecclesiastical Hierarchy*. It declares that "the common end of all hierarchy consists, then, in that continuous love of God and of the divine mysteries which produces righteously in us the unifying presence of God himself." But in order to attain to this "presence it is first necessary to pass by total deprivation, and without return, from all that which makes itself an obstacle." [52]

We see, then, the place of charity in a system that at first appeared to subordinate everything and everybody to an ensemble of fiats and interdicts. The ecstatic *eros* is not just an inclination to idealized beauty. It is also at each rank or degree—more properly stated, for each person—an efficacious love of neighbor. It corresponds in each soul to a direct participation in the charity of Christ.

As for the great themes of Christianity where they involve soteriology, the incarnation, Christ's redemptive Passion, and his "imitation" by his followers—these are by no means ignored, even if they are sometimes unduly sublimated or even distorted according to Occidental Christian views.

BENEDICT TO GREGORY THE GREAT

The history of contemplation from the sixth to the twelfth century reflects an age that is monastic in its fundamental concepts and practices. A spiritual revival is foreshadowed less by distinctive treatises than by the occasional literary deposits that accrue about the centers and leaders of contemplative retreat.

Benedict (d. 555), though he never mentions contemplation as such, receives and transmits earlier impulses to it. The common life of stability and familial dedication fosters an experience of worship and a utilization of the Fathers—Basil and Cassian, particularly—that will mature the renunciatory spirit.

---

[50] *Hiér. cél.*, IV, 1; *Œuvres*, 199, 41–42.
[51] *Hiér. cél.*, VIII, 1; *Hiér. eccl.*, I, 2; *Œuvres*, 240 B, 372 D–373 A, pp. 214, 247.
[52] *Hiér. eccl.*, I, 3–4; *Œuvres*, 376 A–B, pp. 248–49, 42.

Contemporary with Benedict, Julianus Pomerius (c. 500) had, in his *De vita contemplativa*, made clear the subordination of earthly interests necessary if the heavenly realities were to be anticipated now and realized hereafter. An active life of good works was not only tolerated by the contemplative desire but also insured by it. The third book of Julianus' *Contemplative Life*, though not given to contemplation per se, shows this sense of social responsibility that links the pilgrimage toward the eternal vision with the ministry of present need. It forever joins the service of contemplatives and scholars with administrators and actives generally (ch. 28). Julianus left a heritage to the Middle Ages at this point, as well as in his summary of four approaches to the meaning of contemplation. These included knowledge of future things, abstention from all worldly occupations, the study of sacred letters, and, finally, the vision of God proper.

Boethius (d. 526) is almost exclusively referable to mysticism at the point of intellectual speculation. This will become apparent in the Victorines. Cassiodorus (477–570) combines the monastic regimen, the study of the liberal arts as a preparation for spiritual inquiry and sacred commentary, and the meditative perusal of the Fathers and other Christian sources conducive to divine contemplation.[53]

GREGORY THE GREAT (540–604)

In the contemplative tradition, Gregory has been said to stand midway between Augustine and Bernard. That is, he is less intellectual than Augustine, less emotional than Bernard. Obviously, his place in this company is secure as one of the pre-eminent doctors of the contemplative life. He shows a real indebtedness, however indirect, to Augustine and reflects, in some small degree, the Neoplatonic influences derived via the Bishop of Hippo. His borrowing from Augustine is, however, mainly that of practical, doctrinal emphasis rather than philosophical or even theological speculation. The place of Benedict and his Rule is admittedly large in his spiritual formation, as in his pontifical administration of monastic resources.

---

[53] See DS II, 1929–33 for the foregoing treatment. On Benedict, consult Berlière *L'ascèse*, pp. 1 ff., and Schmitz, *Histoire*, Vol. I, pp. 15 ff., and Vol. II, pp. 346 ff. Julianus Pomerius, *The Contemplative Life*, The Newman Press, Westminster, Maryland, 1947, is a translation by Sister Mary Josephine Suelzer.

Suited by temperament to the contemplative persuasion, Gregory exemplified in his own life the unselfish ministrations of the active tradition as well. His whole tenure of the papal office fell in precarious times, and his active witness was given just when mystic repose would have been most welcome. With Augustine and Bernard, he symbolizes, for Dom Butler, the great triumvirate of Western mysticism at its representative best in the equipoise of contemplation and action.[54]

Briefly analyzed after the commendable interpretation of Gillet, in his introduction to the *Morals on Job*, Gregory's mysticism is characterized by its luminosity.[55] Here at the forefront Gregory considers the light without limit, i.e., the *lumen incircumscriptum*. It is impossible to know God as he is, given the fact of man's fall, the limitations of thought imposed by "images," and the characteristic vacillations of the human spirit. Man must, therefore, be raised above himself by the Divine. To this end man must prepare himself through detachment and active good works, that is, by the ascetic way. In all of this there is place, also, for the findings of a negative route, but not after the fashion of a Dionysius seeking the God of obscurity.

The act of contemplation is, as Gillet points out, truly gratuitous. Without effort on his part, man finds himself raised by an all-powerful force. Passive under the divine inspiration, save for desire and aspiration, the soul is elevated above itself. The mind is lifted by the divine breath above its wonted function of animating the body. The intelligence finds itself carried beyond its habitual modes of apprehending and knowing. The soul goes out of itself, as it were. The intelligence, being but one of the mind's aspects, also finds itself transcended. The Creator's beauty is contemplated in a knowledge of love (*per amorem agnoscimus*). For the love of the spiritual Fatherland influences man's soul, and God himself shows the way thither.[56]

Gregory's mysticism, then, may be said to anticipate, by means of an obscure vision, the clear vision of heaven. Drawn toward God and his repose, the human spirit finds itself fettered by the body, even as it is elicited by the Divine. It longs for

---

[54] This sketch of Gregory is based upon DS II, 1933–34; Butler, *Western Mysticism*, pp. 65 ff., 171 ff., and the sources there analyzed; the introduction and sources of Dom R. Gillet et Dom A. de Gaudermaris, *Grégoire le Grand: Morales sur Job, livres 1 et 2*, Paris, 1952; the *Moralia* as edited in MPL 75–76; and the treatments in Schmitz, *Histoire*, Vol. I, pp. 41 ff., and II, pp. 365 ff.; also Berlière, *L'ascèse*, pp. 64–68, 216–20, etc.
[55] Pp. 20 ff. and the references to the *Moralia* there given.
[56] Gillet, *op. cit.*, pp. 36–39; *Mor.*, Lib. X, sec. 13, MPL 75: 927–28.

deliverance from its enslavement, even at the price of death. This it seeks avidly as the only sure way of release.[57] Here below one cannot concentrate his gaze on God. Dazzled and repulsed by God's incomparable brightness and light, the soul falls back on itself, fatigued and, as it were, thunderstruck. This is, by the way, one of Gregory's most persistent figures, that of the *reverberatio*. The soul is *reverberata*, at once dazzled and driven back upon itself.[58] The soul then returns into itself, fatigued by its search for an object which it realizes to be infinitely beyond it. Seeing its own mortal involvements, it declares itself unworthy to look upon Him who knows not death. The act of contemplation is, by nature, brief; like the half hour of silence in heaven spoken of by the Revelator. Again the soul resumes its life of desire and temptation, these being all the stronger for its having been granted a higher than merely mortal experience for a season. There is now vacillation between joy and sorrow, a dialectic of fear and hope. Fear prompts perpetual tears; love gives rise to tears of joy.[59]

Here, truly, in the very hazard of temptation is its utility also. Purification by temptation and the evil one must pave the precarious way to contemplation. As for the requisites to the contemplative state, they are circumspection and self-knowledge, humility and purity of heart, fear and godly compunction.[60]

Gregory moves realistically in a barbarous civilization. He evokes living response from untutored spirits by means of spiritual concretions rather than by any attempt at speculative abstractions. He makes explicit the discretion implicit in the Benedictine Rule, thereby implanting it in contemplative psychology as in institutional moderation. How well he has ministered contemplatively in terms of Benedictine *ascesis*, Berlière and Schmitz eloquently testify.[61]

The relation of Gregory to Augustine is easily discernible. This, Butler readily notes; even though, as Gillet suggests, there is too large an emphasis in Butler upon Gregory's divergence from Augustine. Gillet parallels the writings of the two in terms of significant likenesses.[62]

For himself, Butler remarks in Gregory the threefold life,

[57] *Mor.*, VII, 18, MPL 75: 775; Gillet, *op. cit.*, p. 48.
[58] *Mor.*, V, 58; XVI, 38; XXIV, 11–12; MPL 75: 711, 1140, 76: 292–93; Gillet, *op. cit.*, pp. 50 ff.; Butler, *op. cit.*, pp. 74, 81.
[59] Butler, *op. cit.*, pp. 81, 79.
[60] Gillet, *op. cit.*, pp. 54–81; Butler, *op. cit.*, pp. 82 ff.
[61] See note 54.
[62] Butler, *op. cit.*, pp. 74–75; Gillet, *op. cit.*, pp. 29 ff., 86 ff.

ascetic training as inescapable preparation for contemplative experience, and the roles of recollection, introversion, and contemplation. These three stages are set forth in the *Homilies on Ezekiel* and in the *Morals*, XXIII, 42. The Sermon on Ezekiel, II, v, 9, is a veritable treatise on the contemplative and the active life, together with an analysis of the nature of contemplative union. The vision of God in Gregory's interpretation draws heavily on the *Morals*, also.[63]

FROM GREGORY TO BERNARD

Countless manuscripts witness Gregory's immense influence on the Middle Ages. Isidore of Seville (d. 636), borrowing from him, surmounts the active with the common life. Bede the Venerable (d. 735) reflects Augustine and Gregory consistently, especially in his commentaries. Those seeking perfection must necessarily espouse contemplative practices. The soul on the way to the Lord's mountain and its Sabbath repose is not thereby exempted from the active practice of virtues. But the contemplative life, the *speculativa*, yearns to see God's face and to enjoy the eternal vision in the company of the angelic choirs. The Lord alone grants contemplative light to those whom he chooses for such graces. Stemming from divine rather than human initiative, this heavenly boon falls to the Christian few who have elected the more perfect life. These, out of the receptiveness induced by sacred studies, by meditation on the Saviour's life, by fasts and prayers, as well as by laborious preparations in faith, receive a mystic illumination. It is brief in duration and enigmatic in character.[64]

In the monastic environment of ninth and tenth century spirituality, the Benedictine temper and the Gregorian stamp persist. But the Benedictine Rule expands and intensifies its hold through a noticeably larger emphasis on cultural interests, theological inquiry, and prayer, both private and liturgical. Monks are, moreover, becoming priests, increasingly. Benedict of Aniane's reforms reunify cenobitic life wherever possible through the imposition of the Benedictine Rule. The role of knowledge is accented, and the study of sacred letters is supplemented increasingly by access to the Fathers, Gregory in

[63] Butler, *op. cit.*, pp. 66–71, 87–92; *Hom. in Ezech.*, Lib. II, Hom. v, sec. 8–20, MPL 76: 989–996; *Mor.*, XXIII, 42, MPL 76: 277, for example.
[64] See the account in DS II, 1935 f.; Berlière, *L'ascèse*, p. 220; Schmitz, *Histoire*, Vol. II, p. 373.

particular. The necessity of understanding the faith as it conduces to love is emphasized. Prayer, reading, meditation, and
study are held favorable to contemplation. Long prayers, the
intensified use of psalmody, and cultic proliferations are
espoused in the monasteries, those isles of *oraison*. Of course
Benedict's own admonition is still held normative, inasmuch as
chapter 20 of the Rule calls for prayer that is brief and pure
unless one is strongly moved by divine graces.[65]

Rabanus Maurus (d. 856) and Paschasius Radbertus (d. 860)
alike place a premium on contemplative repose after the pattern of the celestial country. They likewise recall Gregory in
joining it with an active spiritual witness here below. John
Scotus Eriugena makes his contribution by translating and commenting upon Dionysius, who had previously been presented by
the Abbot Hilduin. But Eriugena's own doctrines have little
weight and his translation does not make Dionysius a force until
the twelfth century.[66]

Meanwhile, the Benedictine reform at Cluny registers significant contemplative advances. Saintly abbots and distinctive
usages develop to a high peak the liturgical resourcefulness of
reformed Benedictinism. A widely diversified library and the
growing use of Cassian, the early Fathers, and Gregory in the
monastic cycle of renunciatory habits are noteworthy. The writings of Odo, Majolus, Odilon, and Hugh, for instance, show
little originality. They reflect, rather, the influence of earlier
contemplatives and a measured employment of spiritually sane
customs environing new liturgical experiences.

The Cluniacs abjure high theories and subtle dialectics as
well as scholastic theology and the Dionysian discipline. Their
ascetic and mystical preoccupations are with acts of love rather
than with systematic disquisitions about that love. Cluniac piety
is fostered and channeled through the divine office. This piety
makes large place for devotion to the humanity of Christ, the
mysteries of his life, and his earthly vicissitudes. In the contemplative life of Cluny the Psalter is perhaps the most all-
comprising source.[67]

---

[65] DS II, 1936–38. On Alcuin and Benedict of Aniane, see Schmitz, *op. cit.*,
Vol. II, pp. 377–82.

[66] Schmitz, *op. cit.*, Vol. II, pp. 383–91; DS II, 1937–39. Consult also,
H. Dorries, *Zur Geschichte der Mystik: Erigena und der Neuplatonismus*,
Tübingen, 1925, and Gilson, *History*, pp. 113–28, 609–13.

[67] DS II, 1939–41; Schmitz, *op. cit.*, Vol. II, pp. 392–99; G. de Valous, *Le
monachisme clunisien des origines au 15ᵉ siècle*, Paris, 1935, Vol. I, pp. 329 ff.

Within the Benedictine orbit in Italy, Romuald (d. 1027) and Peter Damian (d. 1072) are significant for spiritual fervor and regalvanized asceticism. With Romuald new forms of contemplative enthusiasm eventuate in sublimer ecstasies. Peter Damian assumes that contemplation, for the monk, is that perfection referred to at the end of Benedict's Rule. Monks are called to intimacy with God, *domestica familiaritas*. He thinks of this higher life variously as repose, marriage, vision, solitude, liberty. In the midst of episcopal administration, he yearns in retrospect for contemplative leisure. He struggles to protect the mystic vision against the obfuscations of the encroaching world. In his doctrine of tears and in his meditations on Christ's love, he suggests Bernard. He praises the contemplative persuasions of Cluny. Reform preacher and fiery perfectionist, he is Jerome-like in his ardor, blunt in speech, indefensible in his scriptural exegesis, almost savage in his ascetic prescriptions. He meditates dolefully and penitentially upon the sufferings of the Master.[68]

John of Fécamp (d. 1078), deriving from Ravenna, was doubtless influenced by Damian. An indefatigable collector of contemplative anthologies, he was himself the deeply gifted adapter of Augustinian and Gregorian sentiments. He was immediately responsible for collections of prayers and meditations long and confidently ascribed to Augustine and Anselm. These, including meditations and prayers of his own authorship, provided the centuries with edifying source studies in contemplation that approached the later popularity of the *Imitation of Christ*. These are the more remarkable inasmuch as they were produced out of a welter of monastic administrative duties.[69]

Anselm of Canterbury (d. 1109) provided spiritual works in a double category. A varied set of treatises emphasizes speculative theology. The *Prosologion*, for example, is an essay on Christian philosophy with overtones of mystical experience. In it faith is fostered through intelligence. The mystery of God cultivated in love is also analyzed and justified by means of dialectic. His *Letters*, *Meditations*, and *Prayers* are reduced in number but accentuated in spiritual value by present-day researches. Reminiscent of the character and method, though not of the intensity, of John of Fécamp, they also serve as source booklets for contemplative exercise. In these, speculative and affective

---

[68] DS II, 1941–43; Schmitz, *op. cit.*, Vol. II, pp. 403–06.
[69] DS II, 1943–44; J. Leclercq, et J. P. Bonnes, *Un maître de la vie spirituelle au xie siècle, Jean de Fécamp*, Paris, 1946; also studies in A. Wilmart, *Auteurs spirituels et textes dévots du moyen âge latin*, Paris, 1932.

approaches are clearly joined. Speculative works unite thought and love. Doctrinal preoccupations are clearly apparent in his meditative prayers.[70]

Peter the Venerable (d. 1156), friend of Bernard and worthy abbot apologist for Cluniac uses, shows little originality of contemplative thought or action. Gregory is clearly deducible from his statements as being the spiritual inspiration of his order in his time. The *Life*, the *Homilies*, and the *Dialogues* of the great pontiff are the regular spiritual diet of the Cluniac monks. Peter de Celle (d. 1183) gives, with Peter the Venerable, an essentially similar picture of Cluniac exercises. He also accents the role of humility, divine readings, ascetic discipline, frequent confession, and daily communion in order to unite the soul with its spouse. The typical Cluniac centrality of the Eucharist is here depicted.[71]

Summarized in the most cursory fashion the contemplative life of the sixth to the twelfth century in the West permits of a few generalizations already supported by specific cases. Contemplation is regarded as the vision of God, impossible on earth, realizable only in heaven. The mystical vocation is, in a general sense, issued to all, but it finds its earthly realization on the higher levels feasible for a few only. Contemplation is impossible without asceticism, that is, the active life in its ancient meaning. Eschatologically oriented and validated, the contemplative life is embraced in faith, hope, and love. It is not primarily a matter of knowledge, specialized science, or psychic phenomena. Experienceable at different grades, the highest form is an ecstasy without images, a ravishment of soul (or *excessus*) that defies ordinary means of knowing and doing.

The role of knowledge is to invite contemplation through

---

[70] DS II, 1944; also the edition of his *Opera* by T. S. Schmitt, Vol. III, Edinburgh, 1946, and the translation from earlier texts by D. A. Castel, *Méditations et prières*, Paris, 1923; also studies in Wilmart, *op. cit.*

[71] DS II, 1944–45; J. Leclercq, *Pierre le Vénérable*, Saint-Wandrille, 1946; also *La spiritualité de Pierre de Celle*, Paris, 1946. The "divine readings," i.e., the *lectio divina* (or *sacra*) here referred to involved a distinctively monastic reading or study of Scripture, the arts, the Fathers, and Catholic tradition as these conduced, through ascetic discipline and liturgical uses, to contemplative ends. The *lectio divina* is put in Biblical and patristic focus with particular reference to the Vulgate, Jerome, Cassian, Augustine, Cassiodorus, and others by B. Smalley, *The Study of the Bible in the Middle Ages*, Philosophical Library, New York, 1952, pp. 26 ff. Compare H. H. Glunz, *History of the Vulgate in England*, Cambridge, 1933, and Denys Gorce, *La lectio divina des origines du cénobitisme à Saint Benoît et Cassiodore*, Vol. I, Paris, 1925 (vol. title: *Saint Jérôme et la lecture sacrée*).

preparatory reading and Scriptural meditation. Contemplation, proper, witnesses the capitulation of the soul to the divine mystery whereupon the function of the intelligence is to focus the adhesion of the spirit rather than the work of explication. Contemplative knowledge is knowledge by love, even as Gregory had set it forth.

The contemplative existence seeks a milieu favorable to it, as well as separation from typically worldly occupations. The monastic life, eremitic and cenobitic, especially, provides the ideal environment. Within it is a regularity of spiritual exercises. Its liturgy is the cadre of the contemplative experience.

The relation of the contemplative and the active is different, of course, for the monk and for the Christian at large. The monk's vocation is specifically contemplative. His active exercises refer mainly to the intramural ministrations of his monastic calling. For clerics, laity, and particular monks given to definite apostolate in the world, the problem is necessarily different. Their preoccupation must be to accord contemplation its due place in the midst of worldly turbulence. The contemplative experience, however distinctively fostered by the monastic fraternity, is no prerogative of this group. All Christians and clerics, especially, are encouraged to incline themselves to the mystical experience. The ideal for them is to "unite the contemplative life, by which they detach themselves from the world, to the active life which they lead in the world."

As for the contemplative tone of medieval monastic literature, the accent is on serenity. The deepest security of the soul is sought in an atmosphere of calm, peaceful repose.[72]

[72] DS II, 1946–48.

I

Bernard of Clairvaux (1090–1153)

INTRODUCTION

BERNARDINE ERA

TWELFTH CENTURY SPIRITUALITY, THE CONTEMplative age of gold, finds in Bernard of Clairvaux, William of St. Thierry, and Guarric of Igniac a nucleating interpretation of the mystical life. All find contemplative rest to be the fruit of humility and of the active labors attendant upon progression through its various degrees. Just as Bernard accents "theoretical" contemplation in contrast with "active" contemplation or "consideration," so William's contemplative fruition realizes itself on the highest rung of humility as a species of "apathy." Guarric first makes place for active labors and the works of humility that reflect the earlier espousal of Leah and the activated modesty of Martha. Like the rest, he seeks the ultimate boon in the quietude of contemplation represented by marriage with Rachel, and by Mary's better part.

For all of these, love's possession, or the experience of divine companionship, rather than the mind's comprehension of God, is paramount. Thus in Bernard, for instance, consideration seeks to think and know but contemplation longs to see, savor, and taste. Furthermore, *scientia*, that erstwhile, estimable knowledge of divine things that comes with consideration, must give way to *sapientia*, that supreme wisdom which is the fruition of the love of charity. Both William and Guarric see this wisdom as a joyous, incommunicable earnest of celestial happiness. Even for William, the most intellectualized of this group, intellectual love (*amor intellectus*) is less a matter of sheer knowledge than it is a fruitive participation in the life of God.

The contemplative mood accentuates the intimately disciplined experience of the divine society. Reverently seeking to prefigure the nuptials of the affianced soul with its divine

47

Bridegroom, these seekers after the contemplative gift long for the sacred kiss. This kiss symbolizes the yearning, not so much for knowledge and spiritual doctrine, however good, as for the privilege of contemplating the joy of one's Lord. The Bride, having received the kiss, is led into the wine room. This is, perhaps, less a realm of liquid than of light. It is more a concentration of truth than of fermented beverages. Yet, there is here a double transport of spirit and heat, light and fervor, knowledge and devotion; a veritable liquefaction of the soul lost in spiritual delights.

Ravished out of itself (*abalienatio*), the soul is unable to contain itself or to remain in its senses by reason of excessive joy. But the soul regains its calm in God's presence. The wine cellar gives place to the nuptial chamber. The sacred kiss leads to the pure embrace of the Bridegroom. The Bride has indeed a foretaste of heavenly ecstasies. Here is rapture and vital repose anticipating the very serenity of the angels themselves.

But this rest is short-lived, this ravishment a matter of brief intervals only. Here below, the divine vision is fugitive at best. This *theōria* and these "theophanies" granted as contemplative solace to the faithful on earth are advance tastes only. The divine life and revelation in Christ become, for the contemplative, the way of savoring now the eternal realities later to be fully experienced.

For such as these, the present life is given alike to the church's worship and to the world's need. Divine office and liturgical regularity are the never-exhausted source of contemplative fervor. But the dedication to the Divine there fostered is continued at the divine behest in a balancing service to the world. Action prepares the way for, and sustains, the contemplative life. A laudable versatility in handling contemplative realities and active necessities is discernible in twelfth century spirituality, to the later decades at least.

BIOGRAPHICAL NOTICE

Bernard was born at Fontaines near Dijon. He was educated at the school of St. Vorles and at twenty-one years of age served a spiritual apprenticeship at Châtillon-sur-Seine. With some thirty companions he entered the monastery of Citeaux in 1112. At Stephen Harding's instance he founded Clairvaux in 1115. His abbacy there reflected the fullest devotion to the Benedictine ideal, which he debated in its reform application with his friend, the Cluniac abbot, Peter the Venerable. He helped secure approval for the Order of Templars in 1128, established the papal claims of Innocent II (1130–1143) over those of the schismatic Anacletus II (1130–1138), and effected Abelard's condemnation at the Council of Sens in 1140. He also brought about Gilbert of Porrée's recantation in 1148 at the Council of Rheims. Reflecting his unparalleled influence in the temporal, as well as spiritual, affairs of Europe, he preached at Pope Eugenius III's request the second crusade at Vezelay in 1146. Deeply dejected over its failure in 1149 he nevertheless planned, at one time, with Suger of St. Denis for a new one. He died in 1153. Canonized in 1174, he was made a Doctor of the Church in 1830.

BIBLIOGRAPHICAL ESSAY

William and Guarric are suggestively analyzed in relation to Bernard by DS II, 1947–59. Basic texts and studies of William include *Deux traités de l'amour de Dieu: De la contemplation de Dieu & de la nature et de la dignité de l'amour*, ed. by M. M. Davy, J. Vrin, Paris, 1953; *Un traité de la vie solitaire, Epistola ad Fratres de Monte Dei*, also ed. by Davy, J. Vrin, Paris, 1940; and *Le miroir de la foi*, tr. by J. M. Dechanet, Charles Beyaert, Bruges, 1946.

A standard life is that by E. Vacandard, *Vie de Saint Bernard*, 2 vols., Paris, 1895. See, also, his article in the *Dictionnaire de théologie catholique*, Vol. II, pt. 1 (1932), cols. 746–785. Bernard's *Opera* are in MPL 182–83. The comprehensive *Bernard de Clairvaux, Commission d'histoire de l'ordre de Citeaux*, III, Paris, 1953, is indispensable. See B. S. James, *The Letters of St. Bernard of Clairvaux*, Burns Oates & Washbourne, Ltd., London, 1953. W. Williams, *Saint Bernard of Clairvaux*, University of Manchester, 1935, is basic.

Consult W. Williams, *The Mysticism of Saint Bernard of Clairvaux*, Burns Oates & Washbourne, Ltd., London, 1931, chs. IV and II, and the articles by J. Leclercq, M. Standaert, and E. Wellens on Bernard's theology, spirituality, and mysticism in *S. Bernardo: Pubblicazione commemorativa Nell' VIII Centenario Della Sua Morte*. [Pubblicazioni Dell' Università Cattolica Del S. Cuore, Nuova Serie, Vol. XLVI.], Milan, 1954, pp. 30–91. Another pertinent collaboration is *Bernhard von Clairvaux, Mönch und Mystiker:* Internationaler Bernhardkongress, Mainz, 1953, Franz Steiner Verlag, Wiesbaden, 1955. Compare Pourrat, *Christian Spirituality*, Vol. II, pp. 19 ff., 63 ff., and Schmitz,

Histoire, Vol. VI, pp. 223 ff. The progression of the theme of love in Bernard's spiritual writings is set forth in DS I, 1474 ff. *De diligendo* explains the reasons for, and degrees of, love. *On Conversion*, the *Sermons* on Ps. 90, and chapters 10–22 of the *Grades of Humility* show the transformation of carnal, self-love into the love of God. *Epistle 11* (chs. 12–15 of the *De diligendo*), the first nine chapters of the *Grades*, and Books 2–5 of *On Consideration* stress the degrees of elevation in the love of God. The commentary on the *Canticles* is essentially concerned with the description and explanation of the highest degree of love, i.e., the mystical or unitive stage, proper. É. Gilson, *La théologie mystique de Saint Bernard*, Paris, 1947, is excellent here. Nos. 8, 23, 31, 45, 52, 71, 74, 82, 83, and 85 in the *Canticles* series are preoccupied with contemplative experience. Dom Butler's *Western Mysticism* utilizes large translated portions of this series, pp. 95 ff., 191 ff. Complete translations are available in S. J. Eales, *The Life and Works*, 4 vols., London, 1889–1896, Vol. 4, and in the edition of the *Sermons on the Canticle of Canticles* by the Priest of Mount Melleray, 2 vols., Dublin, 1920. Large portions are given in M. M. Davy, *Œuvres*, 2 vols., Paris, 1945, in J. Leclercq, *St. Bernard, Mystique*, Paris, 1948, and in Beguin, *Œuvres mystiques*, Paris, 1953. The Latin text is in MPL 183. See the close references in R. Linhardt, *Die Mystik des hl. Bernard von Clairvaux*, Munich, 1926.

Synopsis

There is a sense in which Bernard may be said to have written but one treatise on spirituality, to have elucidated but one relationship of the soul with God. That treatise and that relationship center in love. His work called *De diligendo Deo* has been predominantly utilized in this source book because this treatise is, in itself, as it signifies by the title, at the heart of Bernard's contemplative thought and life. Out of the complexity of his writings and the varied circumstances of monastic leadership, as well as the European-wide considerations that prompted them, the theme of love constantly recurs. The treatise *On the Love of God* is at the heart of Bernard's mysticism of love. It is most closely associated with the series *On the Song of Songs* in which this same theme is commented at length. The combined passages of the anthology, though they might easily be exchanged for others of Bernard's works, set forth clearly the main outlines of his contemplative concern.

Bernard has left no mystical treatise as such. For him, mysticism, or mystic union, is simply the highest degree of the scale of love. All of Bernard's treatises on love conclude with an exposition of this last mystical degree. The sermons on the *Canticles* series may be thought of in their entirety as preparatory to mystical union. At the center of Bernard's mysticism is a divine operation that empowers the soul, elicits it, and raises it up in love. This mysticism is, primarily, "a perfect participation in the love which God has for himself in the unity of the Spirit." As Bernard says, "To become thus is to be deified." [1]

The chief outlines of Bernard's thought on the mystic union as a marriage, that is, on the occupations of the soul as being the relations of a Bride with her Bridegroom, or of the Soul with the Word, may be briefly stated. The cogent chapter 7 of *The Grades of Humility* reveals the course of the sacred nuptials. [2] The divine action has the initiative. Under its ministrations, the soul has been rendered spotless and without wrinkle, thanks to the workings of humility and charity. The will no longer fights against reason. Reason ceases to represent the truth falsely to the will. The Father joins himself to the soul in intimate espousal. With her reason no longer preoccupied with itself, and with her will forgetting to put even neighbor first, the happy soul is suffused with joy: "The king hath brought me into his storerooms." [3]

Sermon 23, after the introduction of the soul into the wine or store room, the *cellaria* (nos. 1–8), shows the entry of the espoused into the peace of the bridal room, the *cubiculum* (nos. 9–16). Sermon 83 highlights the resemblance of the soul with God, the actual occasion of the marriage. With such a marital conformity drawing her to the Word, the soul, like Him by nature, is impelled to resemble Him, also, in her will; thus loving Him as she is loved by Him.

Bernard, in commenting upon the mystical marriage, uses the words *raptus*, or ravishment, and *excessus*, or ecstasy. Ravishment, as the transforming action of God, is focused in ch. 10 of the *De diligendo Deo* and adverted to in ch. 11. In Sermon 71 on the *Canticles*, Bernard makes it clear what he means by this

---

1 *Sic affici, deificari est. De diligendo Deo*, X, 28. Cf. the translation by "A Religious of C.S.M.V.," New York, 1950, p. 66.
2 Cf. *Cant. serm.* 23, 83; DS I, 1479 ff.; Gilson, *La théologie*, pp. 158–62. See, especially, Pourrat, *Christian Spirituality*, Vol. II, pp. 68–75.
3 *Cant.* 1:3 (4); cf. Vacandard, *Dictionnaire de théologie catholique*, Vol. 2, pt. 1 (1932), pp. 746–85, especially, pp. 779–80.

transforming union. It is the destruction of man's *proprium,* the obliteration of his private singularity or individual possessiveness, and his metamorphosis into unity of spirit with God. The soul, adhering wholly to God, without vestige of its own self-centeredness, becomes one spirit with him. Gilson has, at this juncture, celebrated in felicitous language, this "perfect accord between the will of the human substance and that of the divine substance in a strict distinction of substances and wills." [4]

As for *excessus,* or ecstasy, Bernard never attributes to this such corporal effects as levitation, for example. The connotation of *excessus* for Bernard is, first of all, "pure love." In this, the soul loves itself still, but only because it loves all that is in God, and itself as having become a single spirit with God. *Epistle 11* (i.e., *De diligendo Deo,* 15) puts this in proper perspective. Within this condition of pure love, the single function of the espoused soul is one of loving, as Sermons 52 and 83 of the *Canticles* series describe it. Gilson's commentary on the last of these, especially, is a moving interpretation. Here the soul stands forth emancipated at last from all cupidity and fear. The *excessus* is, finally, the illumination of the Spirit. [5]

The conception of the *Verbum sponsus* reminds us that, with the exception of the remarkably early passage in *De gradibus,* 7, where the Father himself calls the soul to spiritual marriage, it is the person of the Word which Bernard presents as the Bridegroom. Significantly enough, the Word is the Spouse of the soul, with its likeness to God, precisely because the Word is the image and the splendor of the Father. The Word is, naturally, the mediator of this similitude. The transforming union is, therefore, an accomplishment of the Word. This is the fruitage of his visits and colloquies with the soul. [6]

The work of the soul, in response to the divine action is the researching of the Word. In Sermon 85 of the *Canticles,* probably written shortly before Bernard's death, a beautiful summation of mystical doctrine is subsumed. Here the soul seeks out the Word in order to accept the corrections that he will mete out to her; knowing well that she will thereby be illumined unto new truth, initiated into further virtue, conformed to his conduct,

---

[4] *La théologie,* pp. 148, 142–56.
[5] *Ibid.,* pp. 163–72; cf. *Cant. serm.* 23, nos. 15–16; 41, no. 3; 52, no. 3; *De consid.,* V, 14.
[6] DS I, 1480–81; *Cant. serm.* 82, 8, 31, 71, 45, 77; also Gilson, *op. cit.,* pp. 48 ff., 115 ff., "on dissimilarity and similarity."

joined with him unto fruitfulness, and delighted with him unto lasting happiness in his presence.

This is a fitting conclusion to the course on the *Canticles* which Bernard had opened with the text: "Let Him kiss me with the kisses of his mouth." In the *Canticles*, Sermons 3 and 4, Bernard had detailed the description of the purgative, illuminative, and unitive stages of the contemplative life under the imagery of the threefold kiss. Kissing first the feet of Christ, we prostrate ourselves in sorrowful repentance for our sins. In kissing his hand we will be lifted up by the bestowal on us of the grace of continence, fruits worthy of penance, and acts of piety; we will thereupon be made to stand upright. Only then may we lift our eyes to the countenance full of glory, not only to gaze upon it but —with fear and trembling be it said—also to kiss it. The spirit thus presented to us is Christ the Lord, "to whom being united in a holy kiss, we are by his condescension made to be one spirit with him." [7]

The kiss of his mouth signifies, then, the reception of the Spirit's inpouring with a revelation that illumines understanding and intensifies love. The Bride's modest request that she yearns to have granted her under the semblance of the Kiss is this: That the grace of the triple knowledge of the Trinity be hers so far as present mortality permits it—that the light of knowledge and the unction of true devotion both be conferred. [8]

As Butler's texts so well illustrate, the willingness in Sermon 85 to be led to highest contemplation and most active fruition is a parable on Bernard's balance between the two lives. Like Gregory, Bernard found the purely contemplative life infeasible, the mixed life actually best, the contemplative life generative of active zeal. Mary and Martha are sisters and spiritual roommates. The spiritual marriage previously discussed produces spiritual fecundity in soul-winning. There is a healthy alternation between sacred repose and necessary action. One should wisely show himself a reservoir rather than a canal. A canal spreads water abroad as it receives it. A reservoir waits until it is filled before overflowing and communicating its superabundance without loss to itself. [9]

[7] *Cant. serm.* 3, no. 5; Williams, *Mysticism*, pp. 35–40; Butler, *Western Mysticism*, p. 96.
[8] *Cant. serm.* 8, nos. 2–6; Butler, *op. cit.*, pp. 98–100; DS II, 1952–54.
[9] *Western Mysticism*, pp. 191–227; *Cant. serm.* 51, no. 2; 58, no. 1; 8, nos. 2, 3.

Bernard of Clairvaux

ON THE LOVE OF GOD [10]

THE TEXT

Chapter One

Why We Should Love God, and How We Ought to Do It

You wish me to tell you why God should be loved, and in what way or measure we should love him. I answer then: the reason for our loving God *is* God; and measure of that love there should be none.[11] Is that enough to say about the matter? For a wise man most probably it is, but I am under obligation to the foolish also; and though I may have said enough for those with understanding, I must have due regard for others too. For those less apt, then, I gladly will explain what I have said more fully, if not with greater depth.

I might have said there was a twofold reason for our loving God solely for himself. First: nothing can be loved more justly. And, second: nothing can be loved with so much profit to ourselves. The question *Why should God be loved?* includes both these, for it may mean either *What is his claim upon our love?* or *What benefit shall we derive from loving him?* My former answer stands in either case: there is no other worthy cause for loving God except himself. As to his claim upon our love, he surely merits much from us who gave himself to us, unworthy as we were: what better gift *could* he have given than himself? If, then, it is his claim we have in mind when asking, *Why should God be loved?* the first and foremost answer is, "Because he first loved us." Most plainly is he worthy of our answering love, especially if we consider who he is who thus bestows his love on us, who are the objects of it,

---

10 From the text of *De diligendo Deo*, ed. by W. W. Williams in *Select Treatises of S. Bernard of Clairvaux*, Cambridge University Press, London, 1926, pp. 8–69, translated by "A Religious of C.S.M.V.," 1950, and used by permission of A. R. Mowbray and Co., Ltd., London, and Morehouse-Gorham Co., Inc., New York.
11 *Modus, sine modo diligere.*

and how great it is. For who is he, save he whom every soul confesses, "Thou art my God, my goods are nothing unto thee"? [12] His is indeed the sovereign charity, which seeks for nothing for itself. But who are they to whom he shows this selfless love? "When we were enemies," the apostle says, "we were reconciled to God." [13] God, then, has loved us freely, while we were enemies. How much has he loved us? "*So*," says John, "God loved the world that he gave his only begotten Son." [14] "He that spared not his own Son," says Paul, "but delivered him up for us all." [15] The Son, moreover, tells us of himself, "Greater love hath no man than this, that a man lay down his life for his friends." [16] This is the claim the Just One has on sinners, the Highest on the lowest, and he who is Almighty on the weak. You say, perhaps, Yes, that is true of men, but with the angels it is otherwise. That I admit: the angels had not our human need. For the fact is that he who helped man in his misery kept them from falling into such a plight at all; and he whose love gave men the means to leave their lost estate, by a like love preserved the angels from sharing in our fall.

Chapter Seven

That Loving God Is Not Without Its Fruit and Due Reward; and that the Human Heart Cannot Be Satisfied with Earthly Things

Now let us see what benefit accrues to us from loving God. What we can understand of this is but a fraction of the mystery: and yet it is not right that we should refrain from speaking about the very little that we can take in. Just now when we were speaking of the reason and the measure of our love for God, I said the question might be taken in two ways. One, which concerns his title to our love, has been discussed already, not worthily indeed but to the best of my ability. It remains now for me to speak (again as God shall give) about the second sense: *What benefit shall we derive from loving God?*

God is not loved without reward, although he should be loved without reward in view. True charity is never left with empty hands; and yet she is no hireling,[17] out for pay, but "seeketh not her own." [18] The disposition of the will in love is not a bargain; no stipulation enters into it. It is a voluntary movement of the

---

12 Ps. 15 (16):2.   13 Rom. 5:10.   14 John 3:16.
15 Rom. 8:32.   16 John 15:13.   17 *Mercennaria.*
18 I Cor. 13:5.

affective faculty, an action of free will.[19] True love is therefore self-sufficient, self-contented; its object is itself its recompense. When you apparently love anything because of something else, what you are really loving is the end, the object of your love; the means you value only in relation to it. Paul does not preach the gospel for his daily bread; he eats his daily bread that he may preach. It is the gospel that he loves, not food.[20] True love seeks no reward; and yet it merits one. Nobody ever dreams of offering to pay for love; yet recompense is owed to him who loves, and he will get it if he perseveres. On lower levels, we hold out promise of reward to laggards; we need not so encourage willing men. Who ever thought a person ought to be rewarded for doing what he wanted of his own free will? No one gives money to a hungry man to make him eat, nor to a thirsty one to make him drink; nor does one bribe a mother to suckle her own child.[21] And you would think it just as strange to use entreaty or offer of reward to get a man to fence in his own vineyard or care for his own trees, or build a house for his own dwelling place. Much more, the soul that loves God seeks for God, and wants no other prize. Where it is otherwise, you may be sure it is some other thing, not God, that really is the object of her love.

It is natural for a rational being always to seek those things which, in his judgment, are better and more useful for his ends; and he is never satisfied until he has acquired the thing that he prefers. A man who has a pretty wife, for instance, looks round with roving eye to find a fairer woman; if he has got a costly suit of clothes, he wants one even better; however rich he is, he will be jealous of anyone who is more wealthy still. You see it happening every day: landowners still "lay field to field" and seek by all means to extend their property, however much they may possess already; and those who live in spacious palaces and royal habitations are daily joining house to house and ever in a fever building new or taking down or altering the old— rectangular for round or round for square. And men in high position too, are they not always on the climb, trying to hoist themselves to higher places still? There is no limit to such restlessness, because in all these things the absolute can never be attained. And yet why should we wonder at man's discontent with what is less and worse, since he can find his peace in nothing save only

---

[19] *Affectus est non contractus*, i.e., "a matter of affection, not a contract," as A. C. Pegis renders it in *The Wisdom of Catholicism*, Random House, Inc., New York, 1949, p. 246.
[20] Cf. I Cor. 9:14-18.   [21] Cf. Isa. 49:15.

in the highest and the best? The foolish thing, the rank, the utter madness, is to spend all this energy on trying to get things which, when acquired, can never satisfy or even take the edge off our desires! There is no peace in the possession of such things as these; whatever you have got you still want more; always you are worrying for what you lack. And so it happens that the restless heart, worn out with fruitless toil, is never satisfied however much it gluts; and ceaseless torment of desire for what it has not got kills all its pleasure in the things it has. For, after all, who can have everything? The little anybody can acquire must be won by toil and is a ceaseless terror to possess. The owner knows, moreover, that he is bound to lose it in the end, although he does not know just when that grief will come.[22] In this way the perverted will hastens to sate itself with what it deems the best; but its own vanity makes sport of it, its own iniquity deceives it in a maze of winding paths. If the satisfaction of all your desires is what you are looking for, why must you waste time on all these other things? You travel by a long road to your goal, and you may make a fool of yourself long before it brings you where you want to be.[23]

It is on this endless treadmill that the ungodly walk, who try to find their satisfaction on the natural plane and in their folly spurn the means that lead to their true end, the end in which alone they find themselves made whole and not destroyed.[24] They waste their energies in unrewarding efforts; yet they accomplish nothing, for, setting their affections on created things, they try them all in turn before they dream of trying God, from whom all things proceed. Suppose they did get everything they wanted, what would happen then? One treasure after another would fail to satisfy, and then the only object of desire left would be the Cause of all. It is our nature's law that makes a man set higher value on the things he has not got than upon those he has, so that he loathes his actual possessions for longing for the things that are not his. And this same law, when all things else in earth and heaven have failed, drives him at last to God, the Lord of all, whom hitherto alone he has not had.

[22] Cf. Eccl. 5:14.
[23] Reading *moreris*, "you may make a fool of yourself"—from *mŏror*, not from mŏror, "I delay." This is preferable to reading *morieris*, "you may die"—from *mŏrior*. Cf. Williams, *De diligendo Deo*, p. 36 and notes, also the translator, p. 49 and note.
[24] The original emphasizes "consummation," not "consumption": *fini dico non consumptioni sed consummationi.*

Once God is found, the soul has rest; for just as on this side no rest recalls, so beyond the grave no unrest ever troubles any more. So with the psalmist she cries out: "It is good for me to hold me fast by God. Whom have I in heaven but thee, and there is none upon earth that I desire in comparison of thee. God is the strength of my heart and my portion forever." 25 In this way, therefore, as I said, a soul would reach its highest Good at last if it could try in sequence first all lesser things than He.

It is, however, a practical impossibility to make such trial of all other things before we turn to God. Life is too short, our strength too limited, the number of competitors for this world's goods too great; so long a journey, such unfruitful toil would wear us out. We want to satisfy all our desires, and find we cannot get possession of all desirable things. Much wiser should we be to make the choice not by experiment but by intelligence, for this we could do easily and not without result. The rational mind is swifter in its action than the carnal sense, and vastly more discerning. Indeed, God gives us reason for that very purpose, that it may guide the senses in their choice and see to it they be not satisfied, except by that which reason has approved: hence the apostle's counsel, "Prove all things, hold fast that which is good," 26 i.e., let reason so provide for the carnal sense that it may attain its desire only as reason wills. There will be therefore no ascent to God for you, no standing in his Holy Place, the gift of reason will have been bestowed on you in vain if, like the beasts, you let yourself be guided by your senses, while reason just looks on. Isaiah speaks of those who have "no judgment in their goings." 27 They run indeed, whose steps are not controlled by reason, but not along the track; setting at nought the apostolic word, they run without a chance of winning in the race. How can they win, seeing they want the prize only when they have tried all else and failed? Theirs is an endless road, 28 a hopeless maze, who seek for goods before they seek for God.

But with the righteous it is otherwise. Hearing the blasphemy of the multitude thus marking time upon their endless round (for the broad road to death has many passengers), they choose themselves to tread the Royal Road, and turn not to the right

---

25 Ps. 72 (73):28, 25, 26.
26 I Thess. 5:21.
27 Isa. 59:8.
28 The *circuitus infinitus* amounts, actually, to standing still.

hand nor the left.[29] These are the souls of whom the prophet
speaks, "The way of the just is uprightness, a direct path is his
to walk upon." [30] They take the timely warning to avoid the
irksome and unprofitable maze; their choice is for the short
word, cut short in righteousness; [31] they do not grasp at everything they see, but rather sell what they possess and give it to the
poor. "Blessed" indeed "are the poor, for theirs is the Kingdom
of Heaven." [32] "They which run in a race run all," [33] but there
is difference between the runners. "The Lord knoweth the way
of the righteous, but the way of the ungodly shall perish." [34]
"A small thing that the righteous hath is better than great
riches of the ungodly," [35] for, as the wise man says and the fool
proves, "He that loveth money shall not be satisfied with
money," [36] but "those who hunger and thirst after righteousness, they shall be filled." [37] Righteousness is, for those who use
their reason, their spirits' natural and essential food; but money
no more satisfies the hunger of the mind than air supplies the
body's need in place of bread. Suppose you saw a starving man
inhaling great deep breaths, filling his cheeks with wind to stay
his hunger, would you not call him mad? And it is just as mad to
think that blowing yourself out with earthly goods can satisfy
your reasonable soul. They are as powerless to meet its need as
spiritual blessings are to satisfy the body. "Praise the Lord, O
my soul, who satisfieth thy mouth with good things" [38]—yes,
satisfies thy longing with the good, incites thee to its quest, is
ever first with thee in giving it, sustains thee, fills thee full. He
kindles thy desire Himself, who is Himself its Goal.

I said in the beginning: the reason for our loving God *is* God.
I spoke the truth, for he is both prime mover of our love and
final end.[39] He is himself our human love's occasion; he also
gives the power to love, and brings desire to its consummation.
He is himself the Lovable in his essential being, and gives himself to be the object of our love. He wills our love for him to issue
in our bliss, not to be void and vain. His love both opens up the
way for ours and is our love's reward. How kindly does he lead

29 Matt. 7:13; cf. the "royal road," or the "king's highway": *regiam eligit
viam*—Num. 20:17; 21:22.

30 Isa. 26:7.   31 Rom. 9:28: *verbum abbreviatum.*

32 Matt. 5:3; Luke 6:20.   33 I Cor. 9:24.

34 Ps. 1:6.   35 Ps. 36 (37):16.

36 Eccl. 5:9.   37 Matt. 5:6.

38 Ps. 102 (103):1, 5.

39 *Nam et efficiens et finalis.* Cf. the valuable notes of Williams, *De diligendo
Deo*, p. 40.

us in love's way, how generously he returns the love we give, how sweet he is to those who wait for him! He is rich unto all that call upon him, for he can give them nothing better than himself. He gave himself to be our Righteousness, and keeps himself to be our great Reward. He sets himself to the refreshment of our souls, and spends himself to free the prisoners. Thou art good, Lord, to the soul that seeks thee. What, then, art thou to the soul that finds? The marvel is, no one can seek thee who has not found already.[40] Thou willest us to find that we may seek, to seek that we may find. We can both seek and find thee, but we can never be before with thee. For though we say, "Early shall my prayer come before thee," [41] a chilly, loveless thing that prayer would be, were it not warmed by thine own breath and born of thine own Spirit.

We have now spoken of the way in which our love for God receives its consummation. We go on to consider how that same love begins.

Chapter Eight

The First Degree of Love, Which Is the Love of Self for Self [42]

Love is a natural affection, one of four,[43] as everybody knows, so that there is no need to name them here. And, because love is natural, it would indeed be just for nature to give her service first to Him from whom she takes her being; whence comes, of course, the first and great commandment, "Thou shalt love the Lord thy God." [44] For, though our nature's law directs us thus to love God first of all, our weakness and infirmity require the binding force of the commandment too; because what really takes the first place in our lives is love for self. We have indeed no feeling that is not for self. "First that which is natural and afterward that which is spiritual"—so says Paul.[45] Who ever hated his own flesh? But if this love, according to its wont, run to excess and like a flooded river burst its banks and overflow the plain, it finds its way blocked then by *this* commandment,

---

40 Augustine, *Confess.*, XI, ii, 4; cf. Pascal, *Le mystère de Jésus*, in *Pensées*, ed. L. Brunschvicg, p. 576.   41 Ps. 87:14 (88:13).
42 Compare with Letter XI, sec. 8, Eales, *Works*, Vol. I, pp. 172–73; James, *Letters*, no. 12, pp. 46–47; and *Cant. serm.* 20. See the discussion in Berlière, *L'ascèse*, pp. 101–02; Pourrat, *Christian Spirituality*, Vol. II, pp. 30–33.
43 Love, fear, joy, and sorrow, according to the Benedictine editor.
44 Matt. 22:37.   45 I Cor. 15:46.

"Thou shalt love thy neighbor as thyself." [46] Justly should he who shares our nature share our love, and all the more since love is part of the endowment our nature has from God. A man who finds it burdensome to serve his brother's interests and pleasures should discipline his own, if he would keep from sin. Let him show all consideration to himself, indeed, provided only he does not forget to show the same to others! This is the curb imposed on thee, O man, by thine own nature's law and discipline, lest thou go after thine own lusts to ruin and put the gifts, that God has given thee, at the disposal of thine enemy— that is, of wanton, unrestrained desire. It is but just and honest to give of what thou hast to thine own fellow, rather than to a foe. And if you follow the wise man's advice and curb your appetites, and if, content with food and raiment as the apostle bids, you shrink not for a while to keep your love detached, abstaining from those "fleshly lusts that war against the soul," you will, I think, have little trouble in bestowing on your fellow men what you have taken away from your soul's enemy. A love both just and balanced will be yours, if you deny not to your brother's need what you refuse to your own base desires. The love of God extended thus becomes benevolence.

But what if, by giving to our neighbor, we find ourselves in want? What should we do save go with confidence to God, "who giveth to all men liberally and upbraideth not," and openeth his hand and all things living are filled with plenteousness? Without a doubt he who gives most men more than what they need will not deny us bare necessities. Has he not told us, "Seek ye first the Kingdom of God and his righteousness, and all these things shall be added unto you"? [47] He has bound himself to give all things needful to him who disciplines himself and loves his neighbor; and you do seek his Kingdom and strive against the tyrant of sin, if you refuse to let sin reign in your mortal body and take the yoke of purity and self-control upon yourself instead. It is moreover (as I said before) but justice that we should share the blessings of this life with other men.

But for our love of others to be wholly right, God must be at its root. No one can love his neighbor perfectly, unless it is *in God* he holds him dear. And nobody can love his fellow men in God who loves not God Himself. We must begin by loving God; and then we shall be able, *in him*, to love our neighbor too. God, author of all good, is author of our love in this way too, in that, creator of our nature as he is, he makes himself to its

---

[46] Matt. 22:39.   [47] Matt. 6:33; Luke 12:31.

keeper also; for our nature is so constituted that it needs to be sustained, and he who made us is the one who meets that need. We depend on him for our subsistence, then, no less than for the fact that we exist. That we may grasp this fact and not (which God forbid!) take credit to ourselves for God's good gifts, his fathomless and loving wisdom has ordained we should be subjected to tribulations. We fail in these; and God comes to our aid. He sets us free; and we, as is most meet, give glory to his name. "Call upon me in the time of trouble; so will I hear thee and thou shalt praise me" [48]—that is what he says. In this way man, by nature animal and carnal, loving himself alone, begins to learn it is to his own profit to love God, because in him alone (as he has often proved) can he do all things which it profits him to do; he is quite powerless apart from him.

Chapter Nine

The Second Degree of Love, Which Is the Love of God for What He Gives. The Third, Which Is the Love of God for What He Is

Man begins by loving God, not for God's sake but for his own. It is, however, something that he should know his limitations and that he cannot do without God's help. And it is something too, if he knows what he can do by himself and what with God's help only, and if he can keep himself from giving God offense, who keeps him from all harm. But and if troubles come one after another, and he betake himself to God and find deliverance every time, though his heart be of stone within a breast of iron, he surely must melt down in gratitude at last. The love of God *for what God gives* will thus begin to dawn.

Recurrent troubles throw us back on God, and each occasion proves how kind he is. And this experience of his sweetness provides an urge to the pure love of God, more powerful than the impetus our trouble gave before. We say with the Samaritans, told by the woman that the Lord was there, "Now we believe, not because of thy saying, for we have heard him for ourselves and know that this is indeed the Saviour of the world." [49] We say this to our natural self, our carnal appetites. "It is not because of your demands," we tell them, "that we now love God, but because we have tasted for ourselves and know how gracious the Lord is." In this way our needs of the flesh become a kind of language, proclaiming joyfully the benefits of which they have

[48] Ps. 49 (50):15.   [49] John 4:42.

taught us the value; and, once this has been learned, we find no difficulty in obeying the command to love our neighbor. The man who loves like this loves truly; and in so doing he loves the things of God. He loves purely and without self-interest, and so will readily obey God's pure command, purifying his heart in love's obedience, as Peter says. He loves justly, and takes this just commandment to his heart. This love—true, pure, and just —he does not offer upon terms, and so it is acceptable with God. It is pure love, for it is shown in deed and truth, not merely in vain words. It is just love, because he freely gives who freely has received. Love of the quality of God's own love is this, seeking no more its own but those things which are Christ's, even as he sought ours—or rather *us*, and never sought his own. "O give thanks unto the Lord, for he is gracious"—that is what this love says, gracious and good, not only to his lovers but in his very self. It is the love of God *for* God, not merely for oneself. But he of whom the psalmist says, "He will give thanks to Thee when Thou hast done him kindness,"[50] loves God as yet but in the second degree. The third degree is that in which the love of God is purely for Himself.

Chapter Ten

The Fourth Degree of Love, Which Is the Love Even of Self Only for God's Sake [51]

Happy is he who can attain the fourth degree of love, and love *himself* only for God's sake! "Thy righteousness, O God, is as the mountains of God." A mountain is this fourth degree of love, God's own "high hill," a mountain strong, fertile, and rich. Who shall go up into this mountain of the Lord? "O that I had wings as a dove, that I might flee away and be at rest," in that dear place of peace! Woe is me that my sojourn here must be so long! When will this flesh and blood, this mortal clay, this earthly frame, arrive up there? When shall I know this kind of love, when will my soul, inebriated by his love, forget herself, yea, know herself but as a broken vessel, and go clean out to God and cleave to him, her spirit one with his?[52] When shall I make the psalmist's words my own, "My flesh and my heart faileth,

50 Ps. 48:19 (49:18).
51 On Williams' summation of the four grades see *De diligendo Deo*, pp. 46–47, and notes.
52 Cf. Augustine, *De quantitate animae*, 74; Williams, *op. cit.*, p. 47 and notes.

but God is the strength of my life and my portion forever"?[53]
Happy is he, and holy too, to whom it has been given, here in
this mortal life rarely or even once, for one brief moment only,
to taste this kind of love! It is no merely human joy to lose oneself like this, so to be emptied of oneself as though one almost
ceased to be at all; it is the bliss of heaven. And yet, if some poor
mortal do attain to swift and sudden rapture such as this, forthwith this present evil world must drag him back, the daily ills
of life must harass him, the body of this death will weigh him
down, his fleshly needs cry out for satisfaction, the weakness of
his fallen nature fails. Most violent of all, his brother's need calls
on him to return.[54] Alas, he has no choice but to come back,
back to himself and to his own affairs; and in his grief he cries,
"O Lord, I am oppressed, undertake for me," or yet again, "O
wretched man that I am, who shall deliver me from the body of
this death?"[55]

We read in Scripture that God has made all things for himself. His creatures must aim, therefore, at conforming themselves perfectly to their creator and living according to his will.
So we must fix our love on him, bit by bit aligning our own will
with his, who made all for himself, not wanting either ourselves
or anything else to be or to have been, save as it pleases him,
making his will alone, and not our pleasure, our object of desire. The sating of our own requirements, the happiness that *we*
choose for ourselves, will never bring us to the joy that comes
from finding his will done in and concerning us, even as every
day we ask in prayer, "Thy will be done, in earth as it is in
heaven."[56] O chaste and holy love, affection sweet and lovely!
O pure and clean intention of the will, the purer in that now at
last it is divested of self-will, the lovelier and the sweeter since
its perceptions at last are all divine! To become thus is to be
deified.[57] As a small drop of water, mingled in much wine, takes
on its taste and color so completely that it appears no longer to
exist apart from it; as molten, white-hot iron is so like the fire,
it seems to have renounced its natural form; as air when flooded
with the sun's pure light is so transformed as to appear not lit so

---

[53] Ps. 72 (73):26.
[54] Apropos of this inevitable balancing of the contemplative claims by the
active needs, consult Williams, *op. cit.*, pp. 48–49, 42–43, and notes. Cf.
I Peter 1:22 and Heb. 13:1.
[55] Cf. Isa. 38:14 and Rom. 7:24.
[56] Matt. 6:10.
[57] *Sic affici, deificari est.* See Williams' extended note, *De diligendo Deo*, p. 50,
on *deificare*, together with Butler, *Western Mysticism*, pp. 109 ff.

much as very light itself; so, with the saints, their human love
will then ineffably be melted out of them and all poured over,
so to speak, into the will of God. It must be so. How otherwise
could God be "all in all," if anything of man remained in man?
And yet our human substance will remain: we shall still be ourselves, but in another form, another glory and another power.
When will that be? Who will be there to see? Who will possess
it? "When shall I come to appear before the presence of God?"
O Lord my God, "my heart hath talked of thee, my face hath
sought thee: thy face, Lord, will I seek." Shall *I* see, thinkest
thou, thy holy house?[58]

I think myself that the command to love the Lord our God
with all our heart and soul and strength will not be perfectly
fulfilled until the mind no longer needs to think about the flesh,
and the soul ceases having to maintain the body's life and
powers. Only when she has been relieved of these encumbering
cares will she be fully strengthened by the power of God: she
cannot concentrate her faculties on God and fix her gaze upon
his face, while they are being both absorbed and dissipated in
caring for this weak, rebellious frame. But in the spiritual and
immortal body, the body perfected,[59] at peace and unified, the
body made in all things subject to the spirit, there she may hope
to reach the fourth degree of love—or, rather, to be taken into
it, for it is not attained by human effort but given by the power
of God to whom he will. Then she will easily attain this perfect
love, when no allurement of the flesh deters her, no bodily
vexations can distract her in her willing, eager passage to the
joy of Christ her Lord. The question here arises, What of the
holy martyrs? Did they attain this love, at any rate in part, while
still in their triumphant mortal bodies? Beyond all doubt some
mighty power of love possessed those souls who, dying thus to
outward things, could so expose their bodies to the foe and set
their pains at nought. Yet, even so, their sufferings could hardly
fail to mar their peace to some extent, although they could not
touch the root of it. But souls loosed from their bodies, we believe, will be immersed completely in that sea of endless light
and bright eternity.[60]

58 Ps. 41:3 (42:2); 26 (27):8; 26(27):4; etc.
59 *In corpore integro.* Regarding this and the concluding lines see Williams,
    De diligendo Deo, pp. 51–52 and notes.
60 *Eterni luminis, et luminose eternitatis.*

OF THE THREE WAYS IN WHICH WE LOVE GOD (SERMON XX ON THE SONG OF SONGS)

THE TEXT [61]

Let this sermon take for a beginning the words of a master in the spiritual life: *If anyone love not the Lord Jesus Christ, let him be Anathema.*[62] Without doubt he is altogether to be loved by whom I have my very existence, my life, and my reason; and I cannot be ungrateful without being unworthy of all these. He is plainly worthy of death who refuses to live for thee, O Lord Jesus; and he is, in fact, dead, as he who does not devote his reason to thy service is unreasonable, and he who cares to be anything except for thee is good for nothing, and is nothing. Indeed, what is man, except that thou hast taken knowledge of him?[63] It is for thine own self, O my God, that thou hast created all things; and he who desires to exist for himself, and not for thee, begins to be as nothing among all things that are. What is it that the wise man says: *Fear God, and keep his commandments: for this is the whole [duty of] man.*[64] If, then, this is the whole man, without this man is nothing. Incline toward thyself, O my God, what thou hast deigned to enable me to be, humble as it is; take wholly to thyself, I entreat, the brief remainder of the years which pertain to my poor life; and for all the years which I have lost, because I have occupied them in losing myself, despise not, I entreat, a humble and contrite heart. My days have declined as a shadow, they have perished without fruit. It is impossible

61 *Cantica canticorum*, Serm. xx, translated from the edition of Dom. J. Mabillon by S. J. Eales, *Life and Works*, Vol. IV, pp. 109–15. Cf. MPL 183: 867–72. This and the following sermon have been reproduced in R. C. Petry, *No Uncertain Sound*, The Westminster Press, Philadelphia, 1948, pp. 150 ff. Used with permission. A good translation is that of the Priest of Mount Melleray, *Sermons on the Canticle of Canticles*, 2 vols., Dublin, 1920, pp. 194–206.
62 I Cor. 16:22.
63 Ps. 143 (144):3.
64 Eccl. 12:13.

for me to recall them; make me, in thy goodness, at least to
meditate upon them before thee in the bitterness of my soul.
Thou seest that wisdom is the whole desire and purpose of my
heart: if there were any in me it is in thy service I would employ
it. But, O God, thou knowest my simpleness; unless it be perhaps a beginning of wisdom to recognize my ignorance; and,
indeed, this is by thy gift. Augment it in me, I pray; I shall not
be ungrateful for the least of thy gifts, but shall strive to supply
that which is lacking in me. It is, then, for these thy benefits that
I love thee with all my feeble powers.

2. But there is a fact which moves, and excites, and fires me
much more than this. Above all things, it is the cup which thou
didst drink, O Jesu, merciful and kind, the great task of our redemption undertaken by thee, which is a stronger motive than
any other for love to thee. It is this which easily draws to itself
all the love I have to give, which attracts my affection more
sweetly, which requires it more justly, which retains it by closer
ties and a more vehement force. To this end the Saviour endured
many and great things, nor in the making of the whole world
did its Creator take upon himself a task so laborious. For in that
earlier work *he spake, and it was done: he commanded, and it stood
fast.*[65] But in the later one he had to bear with men who con-
tradicted his words, met his actions with ill-natured criticism,
insulted his sufferings and even revived his death. Behold, then,
how he loved us! Add to this that he loved us thus of his free
gift, not to make return for any love which we had for him. *For
who hath first given to him, and it shall be recompensed unto him again?*[66]
And St. John Evangelist says expressly: *Not that we loved God, but
that he* [previously] *loved us.*[67] Indeed, he loved us while as yet
we did not exist; he did even more, for he loved us when we
were opposed to, and were resisting, him, as St. Paul testifies:
*When we were enemies, we were reconciled to God by the death of his
Son.*[68] In other words, if he had not loved us when enemies, he
would not now have us for friends; just as, if he had not loved
those who did not as yet exist, they would not be existing now
for him to love.

3. In the next place, his love is tender, wise, and strong. I say
that it is tender, since he has taken upon him our flesh; wise,
since he has held himself free of all sin; and strong, since it
reached to the point of enduring death. For those whom he

[65] Ps. 32 (33):9.   [66] Rom. 11:35.
[67] I John 4:10.   [68] Rom. 5:10.

visited in the flesh yet he loved not in the flesh, but in the fore-seeing wisdom of the Spirit. For the Lord Christ is a Spirit who hath made himself visible to us,[69] being moved toward us with a zeal of God, not of man, and with a love wiser assuredly than the first Adam felt for his Eve. Therefore those whom he sought out in the flesh he loved in the spirit, and redeemed in his power and courage. It is a thing full of ineffable sweetness to behold the Creator of man as a man. But while by his wisdom he separated [human] nature from sin, by his power he banished death from [that] nature. In taking flesh he condescended to me; in separating it from all stain of sin he consulted his own dignity; in submitting to death he made satisfaction to his Father, and thus showed himself at once the kindest of friends, a prudent counselor, and a powerful helper. In him with full confidence I trust, who was willing to save me, who knew the means, who had the power to carry them out. The soul whom he sought out, whom he also called by his grace, will he cast out when it comes to him? But I do not fear that any violence or fraud will have the power to pluck me out of his hand; for in vanquishing death he vanquished all enemies, and in deluding the old serpent, the seducer of the world, by an artifice more holy than that he had employed, he was at once wiser than the one and more powerful than the other. He took upon him human flesh in truth, but only the likeness of sin; in the former giving sweet consolation to weak and ailing man, and in the latter prudently concealing from the devil the snare by which he was deceived. Further-more, that he might reconcile us with his Father, he bravely underwent death and overcame it, pouring forth his blood as the price of our redemption. If, then, that sovereign Majesty had not tenderly loved me, he would not have sought for me in my prison. But to this affection he joined wisdom to circumvent our tyrant, and patience to placate the just wrath of God his Father. These are the ways of loving which I promised to give you, but I have set them before you first as shown forth in Christ, that you might hold them in greater esteem.

4. Learn, O Christian, from the example of Christ the manner in which you ought to love Christ. Learn to love him tenderly, to love him wisely, to love him with a mighty love: tenderly, that you be not enticed away from him; wisely, that you be not deceived and so drawn away; and strongly, that you be not separated from him by any force. Delight yourself in Christ, who is Wisdom, beyond all else, in order that worldly glory or

[69] Lam. 4:20.

fleshly pleasures may not withdraw you from him; and let Christ, who is the Truth, enlighten you, so that you may not be led away by the spirit of falsehood and error. That you may not be overcome by adversities, let Christ, who is the Power of God, strengthen you. Let charity render your zeal ardent, wisdom rule and direct it; let constancy make it enduring. Let it be free from lukewarmness, not timid, nor wanting in discretion. Are not those the three things prescribed to thee in the law, when God said: *Thou shalt love the Lord thy God with all thy heart, with all thy soul, and with all thy strength?* [70] It seems to me, if no other sense occurs to you better to give to that threefold distinction, that the love of the heart answers to the earnestness of affection; the love of the soul, to the purpose or judgment of the reason; and love with the strength, to the constancy and vigor of the mind. Love then the Lord thy God with the entire and full affection of the heart; love him with all the vigilance and all the foresight of the reason; love him with the full strength and vigor of the soul, so that for his love you would not fear even to die; as it is written in a later verse of this canticle: *Love is strong as death, jealousy as hard as hell.* [71] Let the Lord Jesus be to your heart sweet and pleasant, so as to destroy the false attractiveness of the carnal life; let his sweetness overcome the other, as one nail drives out another. To your understanding and your reason let him be a wise leader and a guiding light, not only to enable you to avoid the snares of heretical fraud, and to preserve the purity of your faith from their cunning devices, but also to make you cautious to avoid excessive or indiscreet vehemence in your conduct. Let your love be intrepid and constant, neither yielding to fear nor exhausted by sufferings. Finally, let us love tenderly, wisely, ardently, knowing that the love of the heart, which we call tender, is indeed sweet, but easily led astray—at least, if it be not accompanied by the love of the soul; while the latter, again, though it be rational, yet is apt to be weak, unless courage and ardor go with it to strengthen it.

5. And recognize in clear examples that what I say is true. When the disciples had heard with dismay their Master, shortly before his ascension, speaking of his departure from them, they heard from him: *If ye loved me, ye would rejoice, because I said I go unto the Father.* [72] What then? Did they not love him for whose departure they were grieving? In a certain sense they loved him, and yet they did not really love him. That is, they loved him

[70] Deut. 6:5.   [71] Cant. 8:6.   [72] John 14:28.

tenderly, but not wisely; they loved in a carnal way, not reasonably; finally, they loved with all their heart, but not with all their soul. Their love was against the interests of their salvation; wherefore he said to them also, *It is expedient for you that I go away*,[73] blaming their deficiency in wisdom, not in affection. When, again, he was speaking of his coming death, Peter, as you remember, who loved him, and desired to retain him, replied, endeavoring to hinder him; to whom he made answer, so reproving him as to show that it was his want of prudence only that he blamed. For what is the force of the words following: *Thou savorest not the things which be of God*,[74] but, Thou lovest not wisely, as following the impulse of human affection against the design of God? And he even called him Satan, inasmuch as in seeking to hinder the Saviour from dying he was an adversary of salvation, though unknowingly. And, therefore, having been thus corrected, he no longer opposed himself to the Saviour's death when the sad prophecy of it was again made by him, but declared that he would die with him. But that promise he did not fulfill, because he had not yet attained to the third degree of love, which consists in loving God with all our strength. He had learned to love [God] with all his soul, but he was still weak; he knew well what he ought to do, but was without the help which would enable him to perform it; he was not ignorant of the mystery [of salvation] but he shrank from martyrdom. That love was plainly not strong as death, which yielded to [the fear of] death; but afterward it became so, when being, according to the promise of Jesus Christ, endued with power from on high, he began to love with courage so great that, having been forbidden in the council of the Jews to preach the adorable name of Jesus, he replied firmly to those who forbade him, *We ought to obey God rather than men*.[75] Then, indeed, he loved God at length with all his power, since he did not spare his own life for that love. *For greater love hath no man than this, that a man lay down his life for his friends*; [76] and he laid down his life at that time, though he did not actually give it up. To be not drawn away by flattery, nor seduced by artifices, nor violently removed from it by injuries and outrages, that is to love God with all the mind, with all the soul, and with all the strength.

6. And notice that that love of the heart is in a manner carnal, with which the heart of man is affected toward Christ according to the flesh, and toward the actions which he did or

---

73 John 16:7.   74 Mark 8:33.
75 Acts 5:29.   76 John 15:13.

commanded while in the flesh. A person who is filled with that love is easily touched with any discourse which dwells on that subject. There is nothing he listens to more willingly, reads more attentively, recalls oftener to memory, meditates upon with greater enjoyment. His sacrifices of prayer receive from it a new perfection, and resemble, as it were, victims as fat as they are beautiful. As often as he prays, the image of the God-man arises before him, either in His birth or His infancy, either in His teaching of His death, His resurrection, or His ascension; and all these, or similar images, necessarily animate the soul to the love of holiness, drive away fleshly vices, put to flight temptations, and calm desires. I consider that a principal cause why God, who is invisible, willed to render himself visible in the flesh, and to dwell as a man among men, was to draw, in the first place, to the salutary love of his sacred flesh all the affections of carnal men who were unable to love otherwise than in a carnal manner, and so by degrees to draw them to a pure and spiritual affection. Were not those, for instance, who said to Jesus, *Behold, we have left all and followed thee,*[77] still in this [first] degree of love? They had left all things for the sole love of the bodily presence of Jesus, so that they were not able even to listen with equanimity to the announcement of his salutary Passion and death as near at hand, and even afterward it touched them with a profound sadness to look up to the glory of his ascension. For this reason it was that he said to them: *Because I have said these things unto you, sorrow hath filled your heart.*[78] Thus in the meantime he had drawn them away, and kept them, from every carnal affection by the grace of his personal presence in the flesh.

7. But he afterward pointed out to them a higher degree of love, when he said, *It is the Spirit that quickeneth, the flesh profiteth nothing.*[79] I think that he who said, *Though we have known Christ after the flesh, yet now henceforth know we him no more,*[80] and perhaps the prophet also, notwithstanding [that he lived before Christ], when he said, *The Spirit before our face was Christ the Lord,* stood upon this higher ground; for that which he adds, *Under thy shadow shall we live among the Gentiles,*[81] it seems that he speaks in the name of those who are beginning to rest at least in the shadow, since they do not feel themselves to be capable of sustaining the heat of the sun; and, being nourished with the sweetness of the flesh, are not as yet capable of perceiving the things

[77] Matt. 19:27. [78] John 16:6. [79] John 6:64 (63).
[80] II Cor. 5:16. [81] Lam. 4:20.

which are of the Spirit of God. By the shadow of Christ I suppose to be meant his flesh, with which Mary was overshadowed,[82] so that it was to her as a veil to temper the heat and light of the Spirit. Let him be consoled then with the devotion of the flesh who has not as yet the life-giving Spirit, or, at least, who has him not in the manner of those who say: *The Spirit before our face was Christ the Lord,* and, *Though we have known Christ after the flesh, yet now henceforth know we him no more.*[83] For it is assuredly not without the Spirit that Christ is loved, even in the flesh, though he be not loved in his fullness [thus]. And of this devotion the measure is this, that the sweetness of it occupies the whole heart; draws it entirely to itself from all love of the flesh or of carnal things, and frees it from their temptations; this it is to love with all the heart. Otherwise, if I prefer to the flesh of my Lord any ties of relationship, or any pleasure that I may receive—I mean in such a way as to be able to perform fewer of those good works which he has taught me by word and by example while he abode in the flesh—does it not plainly appear that I do not love him with all my heart, since it is divided, and I seem to have given a part to the love of him, and a part to the love of myself? For he himself says, *He that loveth father or mother more than me is not worthy of me; and he that loveth son or daughter more than me is not worthy of me.*[84] Therefore, to express it briefly, to love Jesus with the whole heart is to prefer the love of his most sacred flesh to all things which engage our affections or our vanity, either in our own self, or that of another; in which I equally comprehend the glory of the world also, because it is essentially carnal; and those who delight in it are, without doubt, carnally minded.

8. But yet such devotion toward the flesh of Christ is a gift of the Holy Spirit, and a great gift; yet I must call such love carnal, at least in comparison with that other affection, which has regard, not so much to the Word as flesh, as to the Word as wisdom, as righteousness, as truth, as holiness, goodness, virtue, and all other perfections of whatever kind. For Christ is all these, inasmuch as by God *he is made unto us wisdom, and righteousness, and sanctification, and redemption.*[85] Does it appear to you that two persons have equal and similar love toward Christ, of whom the one sympathizes indeed piously with his sufferings, is moved to a lively sorrow by them, and easily softened by the memory of all that he endured; who feeds upon the sweetness of that devotion, and is strengthened thereby to all salutary, honorable, and

---

[82] Luke 1:35.　　[83] II Cor. 5:16.　　[84] Matt. 10:37.　　[85] I Cor. 1:30.

pious actions; while the other, being always fired by a zeal for righteousness, having everywhere an ardent passion for truth, and earnestly desiring wisdom, prefers above all things sanctity of life, and a perfectly disciplined character; who is ashamed of ostentation, abhors detraction, knows not what it is to be envious, detests pride, and not only avoids but dislikes and despises every kind of worldly glory; who vehemently hates and perseveres in destroying in himself every impurity of the heart and of the flesh; and lastly, who rejects, as if it were naturally, all that is evil, and embraces all that is good? If you compare these two types of affection, does it not appear to you that the second is plainly the superior? and that in comparison with it the former is in a manner carnal?

9. Yet that love, by which a carnal life is shut out, and the world is contemned and overcome, is good, though it be carnal. In that type of affection it becomes *rational* as it makes progress, and it is perfected when it becomes *spiritual*. It is called *rational* when in all the sentiments cherished regarding Christ the proportion of the faith (*ratio fidei*) is so carefully observed that no deviation is made from the pure doctrine of the Church by any apparent similarity to truth, nor by any snare of heretical or diabolical deception. As also in our personal conduct this caution must be observed, that the bounds of discretion be not exceeded through the influence of superstition, or of levity, or of the zeal of an unregulated disposition. And this it is to love God with all the soul, as I have already said. If to this be added force so great, and an assistance so powerful, as that of the Holy Spirit, so that neither troubles nor sufferings, however violent, nor even the fear of death, can ever cause the desertion of righteousness, then God is loved with all the strength, and that is *spiritual* love. And I think this name peculiarly suitable to such love, because of the fullness of the Spirit which so particularly distinguishes it.[86] But I think that these observations may suffice with regard to that saying of the bride: *Therefore have the virgins loved thee beyond measure.*[87] May our Lord Jesus Christ, who is our Guardian, deign to open to us the treasures of his mercy, that we may be able to expound the words which follow, Who liveth and reigneth with the Father, in the unity of the Holy Spirit, one God forever and ever. Amen.

[86] Cf. this classification (in sec. 6 ff.) of the degrees of love as carnal, rational, and spiritual with that of *On the Love of God*, chs. 8 ff., and *Letter*, XI, 8; cf. Berlière, *L'ascèse*, pp. 101–03; Pourrat, *Christian Spirituality*, Vol. II, pp. 30–33.   [87] Cf. Cant. 1:2 (3).

THAT THE SOUL, SEEKING GOD, IS ANTICI-PATED BY HIM: AND IN WHAT CONSISTS THAT SEARCH FOR GOD IN WHICH IT IS THUS ANTICIPATED (SERMON LXXXIV ON THE SONG OF SONGS)

THE TEXT [88]

By Night on My Bed I Sought Him Whom My Soul Loveth.—
Cant. 3:1

It is a great good to seek God. I think that, among all the blessings of the soul, there is none greater than this. It is the first of the gifts of God; the last degree of the soul's progress. By no virtue is it preceded; to none does it give place. To what virtue is that added which is not preceded by any? And to which should that give way which is the consummation of all virtues? For what virtue can be ascribed to him who is not seeking God, or what limit prescribed to one who is seeking him? *Seek his face evermore*, says the psalmist; [89] nor do I think that when a soul has found him, it will cease from seeking. God is sought, not by the movement of the feet, but by the desires of the heart; and when a soul has been so happy as to find him, that sacred desire is not extinguished, but, on the contrary, is increased. Is the consummation of the joy the extinction of the desire? It is rather to it as oil poured upon a flame; for desire is, as it were, a flame. This is, indeed, the case. The joy will be fulfilled; but the fulfilment will not be the ending of the desire, nor therefore of the seeking. But think, if you can, of this earnest love of seeking God as being without any deprivation of him, and of the desire for him as without anxiety or trouble of mind. His presence excludes the one, and the abundance of his graces prevents the other.

2. But now observe why I have made these introductory remarks. It is that every soul among you that is seeking God

---

[88] Also in the translation of S. J. Eales, *Works*, Vol. IV, pp. 511–15. Cf. MPL 183: 1184–87. Cf. Petry, *No Uncertain Sound*, pp. 162–67. Cf. also the translation by the Priest of Mount Melleray, Vol. II, pp. 495–502.
[89] Ps. 104 (105):4.

should know that it has been anticipated by him, and has been sought by him before it began to seek him. For without this knowledge it might be that out of a great blessing might arise great harm, if, when it has been filled with the good gifts of the Lord, it treats those gifts as if they had not been received from him, and so does not render to God the glory of them. It is, doubtless, in this way that some who appeared very great before men, because of the graces which had been conferred upon them, were counted as the least before God, inasmuch as they did not render back to him the glory which was due on their account. But in saying this I have used inadequate terms. To spare you, I have spoken of "greatest" and of "least," but I have not thus expressed my thought in all its force. I will make clearer the distinction which I have tried to mark. I ought to have said that he who is the best of men becomes in this way the worst. For it is a thing certain and without doubt that such a person becomes as blamable as he before was praiseworthy, if he ascribe to himself the praise of that which was excellent in him. For this is one of the worst of crimes. Someone will perhaps say, "God forbid that I should be of that mind; I fully recognize that by the grace of God I am what I am; but suppose that a person should try to take for himself a little spark of glory for the grace that he has received, is he, therefore, a thief and a robber?" Let one who speaks thus listen to the words: *Out of thine own mouth will I judge thee, thou wicked servant.*[90] For what can be more wicked than the servant usurping to himself the glory which belongs to his Lord?

3. *By night on my bed I sought him whom my soul loveth.* The soul seeks the Word, but it had been previously sought by the Word. For otherwise, when it had been once driven out or cast forth from the presence of the Word, it would have returned no more to obtain the sight of the good things it had lost if it had not been sought by the Word. Our soul, if abandoned to itself, is a spirit which goes to and fro, but does not return. Listen to a fugitive and wandering soul, and learn what it complains of, and what it seeks: *I have gone astray like a lost sheep: seek thy servant.*[91] O man, dost thou desire to return? But if that depends upon thy own will, why dost thou entreat help? Why dost thou ask for from another what thou hast in abundance in thy own self? It is plain that he does desire this, and is not able to perform it; he is a spirit which goes to and fro, and returns not;

---

[90] Luke 19:22. [91] Ps. 118 (119):176.

though he who has not even the wish to return is farther removed still. Yet I would not say that the soul which longs to return, and desires to be sought, is wholly exposed and abandoned. For from whence comes this willingness which is in it? It comes, if I do not mistake, from its having been already sought and visited by the Word; nor is that visitation fruitless, since it has so worked in the soul as to produce that good will without which a return would not be possible. But it does not suffice to be sought once only, so great is the languor of the soul, and so great the difficulty of the return. What if the will of a soul is to return? The will lies inoperative if it be not supported. by the power to do so. For, *To will is present with me*, says the apostle, *but how to perform that which is good I find not.*[92] What is it, then, that the psalmist seeks in the passage that I have quoted? He plainly seeks nothing else than to be sought: which he would not seek if he had not been sought; and yet again, which he would not seek if he had been sought sufficiently. This latter grace, indeed, is what he entreats: *Seek thy servant;*[93] that is, that what it has been granted to him to desire it may be granted to him also perfectly to attain, according to the good pleasure of God.

4. Yet it does not seem to me that the present passage is capable of being applied to a soul such as this, which has not attained the second grace, and, though desiring to approach Him whom she loves, has not the ability to do so. For how can the words which follow be made to apply to such a soul; namely, that she rises and goes about the city in the streets, and in the broad ways seeks her Beloved,[94] seeing that she herself needs to be sought? Let her do this as she is able; only let her remember that, as she was first loved, so she was first sought; and to that she owes it that she herself loves and is engaged in seeking. Let us, too, pray, beloved, that those mercies may speedily anticipate us, for we are brought into extreme need of them. But I do not say this of you all; for I know that very many of you are walking in the love wherewith Christ hath loved us, and are seeking him in simplicity of heart. But there are some (I say it with sorrow) who have not yet given us any mark of this saving and preventing grace being in them, and therefore no sign of their salvation; they are men who love their own selves, not the Lord, and seek their own interests, not those of Jesus Christ.

5. *I have sought*, says the bride, *him whom my soul loveth.* It is to

---

92 Rom. 7:18.   93 Ps. 118 (119):176.   94 Cant. 3:2.

this that the goodness of Him who has anticipated you in seeking you and loving you first—it is to this that his goodness is calling and arousing you. You would not seek him at all, O soul, nor love him at all, if you had not been first sought and first loved. You have been anticipated by a twofold benediction, that of love and of seeking. The love is the cause of the seeking; the seeking is the fruit and the clear proof of the love. You have been loved, so that you might not fear that you were sought for to be punished; you were sought for, that you might not complain that you were loved to no purpose. Each of these two great and unmistakable favors has given you courage, has removed shyness and timidity, has touched your feelings, and disposed you to return. Hence arises that zeal and ardor in seeking Him whom thy soul loveth; because, just as you were not able to seek him, until you had first been sought, so now that you have been sought, you are not able to do otherwise than seek him.

6. Again, never forget whence it is that you have come hither. And that I may apply the better to myself what has been said (which is the safer course), is it not thou, O my soul, who, having left thy first Bridegroom, by whose side all had been well with thee, hast broken the faith first pledged to him, and gone after others? And now that thou hast sinned with them to the full, and art perhaps fallen into contempt with them, dost thou impudently and with effrontery desire to return to him to whom thou hast behaved with so much pride and insolence? What? when thou art fit only to hide thyself, dost thou seek the light, and though more deserving of correction than favor, dare to run unto the Bridegroom? Wonderful it will be if you do not find a judge to condemn you instead of a husband to receive you. Happy is he who shall hear his soul replying to these reproaches: I do not fear because I love, and also I am loved; nor could I have loved unless He had first loved me. Let those fear who have no love; but for the soul that loves there is nothing to be feared. How can those who have no love do otherwise than be under constant apprehension of injury? But because I love, I no more doubt that I am loved than I doubt of my own love; nor can I possibly fear his countenance whose affection for me I have assuredly felt. In what have I felt it, do you inquire? In this: that not only has he sought me, unhappy as I am, but has caused me to seek him, and to feel sure of succeeding in my search. Why should I not respond to him in his search to whom in his affection I respond? Why should he be angry at my seeking him, who, when I showed contempt for him, forgave it? He

sought me when I contemned him; why should he contemn me when I seek him? Benign and gentle is the Spirit of the Word, and gentle is his greeting to me; he makes me aware of his kindness toward me; he whispers to me and convinces me of the earnest love of the Word for me, which cannot be hidden from him. For he searches the deep things of God, and knows that the divine thoughts are thoughts of peace and not purposes of vengeance. How can I be otherwise than encouraged to seek him who have had experience of his clemency, and am persuaded of his reconciliation with me?

7. My brethren, to think seriously of these truths is to be sought by the Word; to be persuaded of them is to be found by him. But not all are capable of receiving that Word. What shall we do for the little children among us—I mean those who are still in the stage of beginners (*incipientes*), and yet are far from being without understanding (*insipientes*), since they possess already the beginning of wisdom, being subject one to the other in the fear of Christ? How, I say, shall we cause them to believe that the spiritual life of the bride is marked by such experiences as these, since they know nothing as yet of such feelings themselves? But I send them to one to whom they cannot refuse credence. Let them read in a book [of Scripture] that which they fail to discern in the heart of a fellow man, and therefore will not believe. For it is written in one of the prophets: *If a man put away his wife, and she go from him, and become another man's, shall he return unto her again? shall not that land be greatly polluted? but thou hast played the harlot with many lovers, yet return again to me, saith the Lord.*[95] They are the words of the Lord, and it is not permitted to doubt or hesitate. Let them believe what they have not experienced, that by the merit of their faith they may one day attain the fruit of experience. I think that now it has been sufficiently explained what it is to be sought by the Word, and how this is necessary, not for the Word but for the soul, so that the soul that has experienced this knows him both more fully and more happily. It remains to be treated of in the next discourse how souls that thirst for Christ seek him by whom they have been sought; or rather that we should learn that from her who is brought before us in these verses as seeking Him whom her soul loveth, him who is the Bridegroom of the soul, Jesus Christ our Lord, who is above all, God blessed forever. Amen.

95 Jer. 3:1.

II

The Victorines
Hugh (c. 1096–1141)
Richard (c. 1123–1173)
Adam (d. 1192)

INTRODUCTION
BIOGRAPHICAL NOTICES

T HE ABBEY OF ST. VICTOR, HOME OF THE AUGUS-
tinian canons regular in Paris, was founded by William
of Champeaux between 1108 and 1110. Here spiritual
fervor inclining toward total contemplation was closely knit to
intensive intellectual ardor. William, thinking to start a house
of prayer, found himself, at the behest of the Bishop of Paris,
establishing a school. This was chartered in 1113. Rapidly
attracting international attention, this refuge for the harmoni-
ous union of intellect and spirit flourished under William, the
Abbot Gilduin, and especially under Hugh.

Hugh (c. 1096–1141), possibly Flemish, probably a Saxon,
came to St. Victor at about eighteen years of age. Having
begun his training at the abbey of Hamersleben, he continued
it at St. Victor, where he was in 1133 charged with the
direction of studies. Surprisingly little is known of his life
beyond his large scholarly and spiritual productivity and
the high esteem in which he was held at the time of his death
in 1141.

Richard, born in Scotland at an undetermined date (c. 1123),
took the canon's vow at St. Victor and made his profession to
Abbot Gilduin. An appreciative disciple of Hugh, "the second
Augustine," he became known for both knowledge and disciplined piety. He was made subprior in 1159 and prior in 1162.
Serving under the undisciplined abbot the English-born Ervisius, Richard fought against spiritual relaxation and liturgical
deterioration. This is established in a new clarity by some re-
cently published works. His predominantly contemplative writings reflect an inner serenity quite removed from the outer turmoil of Ervisius' administration. There remained but a few

months of outer peace, after the abbot's ejection in 1172, until Richard's death in 1173.

Adam the Breton (d. 1192) has with some reason been denominated the "greatest poet of the Middle Ages." He came to St. Victor around 1130. His liturgical sequences imparted to mystical contemplation its highest artistic form. Not exclusively a poet, he stood in his own right as an author and as a person within the Victorine tradition of scholarship and piety. His liturgical poems, however, and not his studies on Jerome or his exegetical *Summa*, gave him immortality. One of his most beautiful series commemorated (1173) the martyrdom and canonization of Thomas à Becket, archbishop of Canterbury, who had preached at St. Victor in 1169.

BIBLIOGRAPHICAL ESSAY

On the intellectual and spiritual climate of St. Victor, see G. Dumeige, *Richard de Saint-Victor et l'idée chrétienne de l'amour*, Paris, 1952, pp. 11–35; also DS II, 1961 ff. Excellent notices and bibliographies on Hugh are to be found in J. de Ghellinck, *Le mouvement théologique du xii⁰ siècle*, 2d ed., Paris, 1948, pp. 185 ff., and in his *L'essor de la littérature latine au xii⁰ siècle*, Paris, 1946, Vol. I, pp. 50 ff. His role in medieval Bible study is intensively analyzed in B. Smalley, *The Study of the Bible in the Middle Ages*, Philosophical Library, New York, 1952, pp. 83 ff. See C. H. Buttimer, *Hugonis de Sancto Victore Didascalion, de Studio Legendi*, Washington, D.C., 1939. Note C. Spicq, *Esquisse d'une histoire de l'exégèse latine au moyen âge*, J. Vrin, Paris, 1944. A good anthology of Hugh, Richard, and Adam in German, with a helpful introduction, is *Die Viktoriner: Mystische Schriften*, edited by Paul Wolff, Vienna, 1936. There is a useful study by F. L. Battles, "Hugo of Saint-Victor as a Moral Allegorist," *Church History*, Vol. 18, no. 4 (December, 1949), pp. 220–240. Consult F. Vernet, "Hughes de Saint-Victor," *Dictionnaire de théologie catholique*, Vol. VII (1922), cols. 240–308. There are suggestive treatments by H. O. Taylor, *The Mediaeval Mind*, Harvard University Press, Cambridge, 1949, Vol. II, pp. 86 ff., 386 ff. Cf. F. Cayré, *Patrologie*, Vol. II, pp. 437 ff. Hugh's *Opera* are in MPL 175–177. Consult B. Hauréau's, *Les œuvres de Hugues de St.-Victor: essai critique*, 2d ed., Paris, 1886. Gilson, *History*, pp. 633 ff., has excellent bibliographies and notes on the Victorines.

Pourrat, *Christian Spirituality*, Vol. II, pp. 104 ff., is important. Note also M. Grabmann, *Die Geschichte der scholastischen Methode*,

Freiburg i/B, 1911, pp. 229 ff. For detailed, critical analyses of Richard's works and the most recent literature, as well as modern editions of key sources, consult Dumeige, *Richard de Saint-Victor*, above, and J. Chatillon, W. J. Tulloch, and J. Barthélemy, editors and translators, *Richard de Saint-Victor, Sermons et opuscules spirituels inédits:* I, *L'édit d'Alexandre ou les trois processions*, Paris, 1951. See Richard's *Opera omnia*, MPL 196, including the "Notice" of M. Hugonin and the account of John of Toulouse. The bulk of the *Benjamin Minor* and *Benjamin Major* is edited in the German of P. Wolff, *Die Viktoriner*. See also Ghellinck, Smalley, Spicq, above. Compare G. Fritz, in the *Dict. de théol. cath.*, Vol. 13 (1937), cols. 2676–2695. An exemplary study is that of J. Ebner, "Die Erkenntnislehre Richards von St. Viktor," *Beiträge zur Geschichte der Philosophie des Mittelalters*, Münster i/W, 1917, Vol. XIX, no. 4. Suggestive is J. A. Robilliard, "Les six genres de contemplation chez Richard de Saint-Victor et leur origine platonicienne," *Revue des sciences philosophiques et théologiques*, Vol. 28 (1939), pp. 229–233. Consult F. Cohrs, "Richard von St. Viktor," *Realenzyklopedie für protestantische Theologie*, Vol. 16, pp. 749–754. On Adam see, Wolff, *Die Viktoriner*, pp. 43–44, 308–336; MPL 196:1421 ff.

SYNOPSIS

Doctrinally in sympathy with Bernard, Hugh fostered in sane interrelationship the claims of reading or teaching, meditation, prayer, contemplation, and action. Looking to the eternal joys of divine love, one joins contemplation here below to the exercise of charity. Contemplation presupposes learning. "True learning in everything shows nothing in learning to be useless," is a basic tenet of his *Didascalion: de studio legendi* (VI, 3), his treatise on what and how to read. In this work he recalls refractory science to the Scriptural designs of Augustine's *De doctrina*. In his *De sacramentis christianae fidei*, he lays down his theological *Summa*. In these together, as in his books on *The Moral Ark of Noah* and *The Mystical Ark of Noah*, and in his commentaries on Dionysius, he shows the clear influence of Augustine, Gregory, and the Neoplatonists. Throughout his writings we sense his catholicity of intellect and spirit, his utilization of the liberal arts put at the service of the Scriptures and spiritual research. Mystic that he was, Hugh did not have recourse to artificial categories of "exceptional experience" and "revelation." From natural things he deduces allegorical significance, even as he teaches the soul how to find inner peace and unity through contemplative exercises. The world of matter suggests the world of spirit. The Scriptures unlock the correspondence of the material and the spiritual with instruction in the mystical significance to be attached to natural phenomena.

It is fitting that the present anthology emphasize Hugh's searching the Scriptures for the allegorical key to cosmic truth, for the symbolic light revealing the sacrament of the divine working. One may profitably mount with him in the way of cogitation, meditation, and contemplation. It is imperative that we accompany him in the joint pilgrimage of knowledge and love. The heart must be inquired into and the conversation of man with his soul must be reverently observed until the divine Presence rules supreme. As he points out in the prologue to the great work on *The Moral Ark of Noah*, we must trace to their source the vicissitudes arising in the heart of man and show how the human mind can be brought to stable peace therein. This is possession of, and by, God.

Hugh points the way for all the Victorines in the soul's preparation for contemplative experience. There must be a long, hard apprenticeship of moral purification from the vices and inculcation of the virtues. The soul has to discover, gradually, how to recede from sensible reality and from the realm of images that distract its inner vision. Ultimately, if slowly, the soul will learn to re-enter itself, to experience self-knowledge, and, finally, to transcend itself on the way to God, who lies beyond it. Hugh's way is that of sacramental life, of the cryptic universe unfolded, of God's love demonstrated in creation and restoration, of love's exercise prepared for by outer and inner knowledge.

From Hugh, Richard accepts the bequest of self-inquiry and self-knowledge. His work *Benjamin Minor* outlines the way to contemplation.[1] Painfully the soul seeks liberation from its passions, release from the prison house of sense images. Slowly it learns how to use its reason with discretion. Employing that reason, it finds in its "invisibles" the image and mirror of God's own. Looking admiringly at the beauty within itself, the soul feels a growing urge to discern that which is above it. It begins to know itself better and to appreciate increasingly the splendors of the Deity reflected in its hidden recesses.

Then in a flash, as it were, and in God's own time comes the

[1] The treatise is in MPL 196:1–64; also in large part in Wolff, *Die Viktoriner*, pp. 34–36, 131 ff.

purely gratuitous inrush of divine contemplation. Years having been passed in productive householding with Leah, Zilpah, and Bilhah—prolific spouses all—there comes at last the fruitful cohabitation with Rachel. She first bears Joseph, that representative of discretion by which reason discerns true good. Only then is Benjamin born. Contemplation is symbolized by the youngest son because it is the last fruit of the spirit. Elder sons who signify the disciplining in the virtues and God's preparatory gifts must precede him. This is the readying of the spirit for contemplative fruition. The soul is a mirror of godly realities. But it can reflect godly things only when it is wholly purified. Contemplation is the goal of purification. The *Benjamin Minor*, having set forth as its objective the outlining of the soul's preparation for contemplation, gives briefly the character of the mystical apogee itself. Reason, having had its respected role to this point, will, finally, be superseded by the contemplative experience. This brings a totally different kind of knowledge, one not only above, but even in opposition to, the old.[2] Contemplation, proper, is therefore the theme of the *Benjamin Major*.[3]

This work concerns itself first with the six genera of contemplation subdivided finally from three types probably suggested by Boethius.[4] Here is the ascending order of the soul's progression from the outward, inward; from the inward, upward; and beyond. According to Boethius' classification basically adopted by Richard, the human spirit contemplates the categories of Sensibles, Intelligibles, and Intellectibles. Each of these three is now expanded to include two genera, the first and lowest preoccupied with (1) visible things and (2) the reasons for such. The second, higher, group concerns (3) the qualities of invisible things seen by their likeness with visible things and (4) things of the angelic as well as the human spirit. The third and highest bracket introduces (5) the divine nature and (6) the Trinity.[5]

Richard in Book I, chapter 6, of his *Benjamin Major*, outlines his types of contemplation from bottom to top in terms of that which is (1) in the imagination according to the imagination alone; (2) that which is in the imagination according to reason; (3) that in the reason according to imagination; (4) that in the

---

2 *Benjamin Minor*, caps. 86–87; in MPL 196:61–64.
3 MPL 196:63–202; Wolff, *op. cit.*, pp. 35 ff., 197 ff.
4 See the article of Robilliard cited in the Bibliographical Essay, above.
5 The most profound analysis of Richard's thought is that of Ebner's article, above. On the six genera see Ebner, *op. cit.*, pp. 105–20. Especially pertinent are chs. 6–7 of Book I, *Benjamin Major*, MPL 196:70–73.

reason according to reason; (5) that above but not opposed to the reason; and (6) that beyond and even against reason.

In his seventh chapter of Book I, Richard revises the old Boethian categories into Sensibles, Intelligibles, and Intellectibles. With these he now associates his own interplay of imagination, reason, and intelligence, together with the sexpartite subdivision of chapter 6. The world of Sensibles is considered in relation to the imagination. The realm of invisibles calls chiefly upon the reason. The sweep of Intellectible realities, the Trinity and sacraments of the faith, that elude the grasp of reason, now summon up the intelligence. Ascending from the world of externalities, the soul is preoccupied at first with sensible things. Then it catches its first glimpse of invisible realities. Bringing reason into sharper focus, the soul plumbs its own depths and contemplates the more perfect mirror of Deity found there. Finally, going beyond itself and concentrating its attention on God, the soul, now in the realm of Intellectibles, invokes the power of the intelligence. It has attained contemplation proper, which, clinging to reason for a time, will at last slough it off in the truly intellectual regard for the divine nature and the "Trinity." Obviously, we are here in a fully Augustinian and Neoplatonic climate.[6]

The "modes" of contemplation are the main concern of the fifth and last book of the *Benjamin Major*. Far from being in opposition to the six types, they are actually capable of being co-ordinated with them. These modes are three in number. They regard: first, the dilatation or enlargement of the mind (*dilatatio mentis*); second, elevation of the mind (*sublevatio mentis*); and, third, alienation of the mind (*alienatio mentis*), also referred to as *excessus mentis*.[7]

The first mode, "dilatation," is the simplest and the most common. Meditation having conduced to a new, spiritual apperception, the soul now embraces instantaneously the objects that it considers. This is still on the purely natural plane. According to the second mode, "elevation," the intelligence is, for the one part, enlightened from on high; for the other, it attains objects that transcend purely human limits (*metas industriae humanae transcendit*). Nevertheless, the spirit still does not desert the plane of its normal functioning. Contrary to this, in the third mode, that of "alienation" or *excessus*, the soul not only breaks its normal bounds and attains realities which are above and be-

---

6 DS II, 1963.   7 In MPL 196:167 ff.

yond its reason, but it is so absorbed by its object that its faculties fail and it loses consciousness of the external world and of
itself.[8]

As to these three modes, the first is the fruit of human activity.
The third is situated outside the control of this activity and proceeds from the working of divine grace alone. The second is the
result of the simultaneous action of divine grace and human
effort.

There are, finally, the four "degrees" of contemplation. These
grow out of Richard's work *On the Four Grades of Violent Love*.[9]
The first degree is that of the love that wounds (*caritas vulnerans*).
The reference is, of course, to the wounds sustained by the lover
in Canticles (chs. 4:9; 5:7). The second is the love that binds or
unites (*caritas ligans*). The third is that of ravishment—in a word,
excessus mentis (*caritas languens*). The fourth degree (*caritas
deficiens*) is one of configuration with Christ. The soul here
despises itself utterly for the glory of God. Now, as in Bernard,
action crowns contemplation. The aspersions often cast upon
Richard fail to take account of this consummation found in the
fourth degree of "violent charity." Responsible studies have
shown irrefutably, with close documentation, the role of this
outgiving, socializing love in the thought of Richard.[10]

The contemplative raptures analyzed in the *Benjamin Major*
come in the *Four Grades* to depict that ineffable, selfless love
which the Victorine ideal holds forth and which the *Benjamin
Minor* prefigures.

---

[8] On the *alienatio* or *excessus*, see *Benjamin Major*, V, 5 ff., MPL 196:174 ff.;
Ebner, *op. cit.*, pp. 100 ff., 108 ff. See also in the *Trois processions*, above,
pp. 68–73, 80–82, 94 ff., 100 ff., and notes; DS II, 1963–64.
[9] In MPL 196:1207–24: *De quatuor gradibus violentae charitatis.*
[10] See Dumeige's excellent study, *Richard . . . et l'idée chrétienne de l'amour*,
especially pp. 110 ff., and, on the last grade, pp. 148–53. Cf. MPL
196:1214 ff., 1220–24.

The Victorines
Hugh (c. 1096-1141)
Richard (c. 1123-1173)
Adam (d. 1192)

HUGH: THE REALM AND THE ROLE OF LIGHT [11]

THE TEXT

XI. That Light Illumined Three Days; and Why It Was Made Before the Sun

Therefore, let no one say: How could there have been day before the sun was made?, because, before the sun was made, there was light: "And God saw the light that it was good, and he called the light Day, and the darkness Night" (Gen. 1:4 and 5). And the light itself made those first three days before the sun was made, and illumined the world. But what does it signify that the sun was not made immediately from the time that light must have been made, but that there was light, so to speak, before clear light? Very possibly the confusion was not worthy of full light; yet it received some light, that it might see how to proceed to order and disposition.

XII. The Sacrament of the Divine Works

I think that here a great sacrament is commended, because every soul, as long as it is in sin, is in a kind of darkness and confusion. But it can not emerge from its confusion and be disposed to the order and form of justice, unless it be first illumined to see its evils, and to distinguish light from darkness, that is, virtues from vices, so that it may dispose itself to order and conform to truth. Thus, therefore, a soul lying in confusion cannot do without light, and on this account it is necessary first that light be made, that the soul may see itself, and recognize the horror and

---

[11] Translated from the critical text of Brother Charles Henry Buttimer by Roy J. Deferrari, *Hugh of Saint Victor on the Sacraments of the Christian Faith (De sacramentis)*, Cambridge, Massachusetts, 1951, and used by permission of The Mediaeval Academy of America (Publication No. 58). The passage is pp. 16–18, drawn from Book One, Part One, chs. 11–12 (cf. MPL 176:195–97). On the mystical significance of the *De sacramentis*, see Wolff, *Die Viktoriner*, pp. 20–25, with texts on pp. 49 ff.

shamefulness of its confusion, and extricate itself, and fit itself to that rational disposition and order of truth. Now, after all relating to it has been put in order and has been disposed according to the exemplar of reason and the form of wisdom, then straightway will the sun of justice begin to shine for it, because thus it has been said in promise: "Blessed are the clean of heart: for they shall see God" (Matt. 5:8). First, therefore, light is created in that rational world of the human heart, and its confusion is illumined that it may be reduced to order. After this, when the interior of this confusion has been purified, the clear light of the sun comes and illuminates it. For it is not worthy to contemplate the light of eternity, until it has become clean and purified, having, as it were, beauty through matter and disposition through justice.

Thus the law preceded grace; the word, spirit; thus John as a precursor, Christ; light, light; a lamp, the sun; and Christ himself first showed his humanity, that he might thereafter make manifest his divinity; and everywhere light precedes light; the light which illumines sinners to justice, that light which illuminates the justified to blessedness. Therefore, light was made before the brightness of the sun was made manifest; and there was day; and there were three days when there was light, but no sun. On the fourth day the sun shone, and that day was bright, because it had true light, and there was no darkness. Thus no soul deserves to receive the light of the sun and to contemplate the brightness of the highest truth, unless these three days precede in it. Now, on the first day, light is made, and light and darkness are divided; light is called and is made day, and darkness, night. On the second day the firmament is made and is placed between the higher waters and the lower waters; and the firmament is called heaven. On the third day the waters which are under heaven are gathered into one place; and the dry land is ordered to appear and put on its dress of plants.

Now all these things represent spiritual examples. Light is first created in the heart of the sinner, when he begins to recognize himself, so that he distinguishes between light and darkness, and begins to call light day, and darkness night, and is no longer of those of whom it is said: "Woe to them that call evil good, and good evil; that put darkness for light, and light for darkness" (Isa. 5:20). After this, however, when he has begun to distinguish between light and darkness, and also to call light day, darkness night—that is, when he has begun truly to condemn his evils by the judgment of reason, and to choose the works of light, which are good and praiseworthy—there remains for the firmament to be made in him. This means that he must be strengthened in his good resolution to distinguish between the upper and lower waters, namely, the desires of the flesh and of the spirit, so that as an interposer and mediator he may not suffer two mutually hostile elements to be mingled or to be transposed, nor suffer what should be divided to be brought together, nor what should be placed below to be above, nor what should be placed above to be below. Finally, there follows in the order of disposition the work of the third day: the waters which are under the heavens are to be gathered into one place, lest the desires of the flesh should be floods, and expand beyond the bound of necessity, so that the whole man, being recalled to the status of his nature and disposed according to the order of reason, may collect into one place every desire, to the end that the flesh may be subject to the spirit and the spirit to the Creator. Whoever is so ordered is worthy of the light of the sun, so that, when the mind is directed upward and the desires fixed upon heavenly things, the light of the highest truth may beam forth upon the beholder, and no longer "through a glass in a dark manner" (I Cor. 13:12), but in itself as it is, he may recognize and know truth.

But this also, which is said, must not be passed over neglectfully: "And God saw the light, that it was good; and he divided the light from the darkness. And he called the light Day, and the darkness Night" (Gen. 1:4 and 5). For he made and saw; then he divided and called. Why did he see? He did not wish to divide before he had seen; he first saw whether it was good; and then afterward he divided light from darkness; and he called the light day, and the darkness night. For he will bring all his work into judgment; and not only the other works which he made in the light did God see that it was good, but he also saw the light itself that it was good, and he divided the light and the darkness. For the evil angel himself at times transforms himself into an angel of light, and tries to deceive the mind, as if he were the true light. But this light is not to be divided from darkness, and is not to be called day, but night, because it has indeed the appearance of light but is true darkness. Therefore, God first saw the light, whether it was good, so that we may not at once "believe every spirit, but may try the spirits if they be of God" (I John 4:1); and when we have seen the light, that it is good, then let us divide the light from the darkness, and let us call the light day, and the darkness night. Therefore, we should not only de-

sire ardently that light precede in our works, and that our works
be done in the light; but the light itself also must first be seen
and considered diligently; and thus at last when we have seen
the light, that it is good, let us divide light from darkness, and
let us call light day, and darkness night.

HUGH: THE GRADES OF KNOWLEDGE [12]

The Text

Three are the modes of cognition (*visiones*) belonging to the rational soul: cogitation, meditation, contemplation. It is cogitation when the mind is touched with the ideas of things, and the thing itself is by its image presented suddenly, either entering the mind through sense or rising from memory. Meditation is the assiduous and sagacious revision of cogitation, and strives to explain the involved, and penetrate the hidden. Contemplation is the mind's perspicacious and free attention, diffused everywhere throughout the range of whatever may be explored. There is this difference between meditation and contemplation: meditation relates always to things hidden from our intelligence; contemplation relates to things made manifest, according to either their nature or our capacity. Meditation always is occupied with some one matter to be investigated; contemplation spreads abroad for the comprehending of many things, even the universe. Thus meditation is a certain inquisitive power of the mind, sagaciously striving to look into the obscure and unravel the perplexed. Contemplation is that acumen of intelligence which, keeping all things open to view, comprehends all with clear vision. Thus contemplation has what meditation seeks.

There are two kinds of contemplation: the first is for beginners, and considers creatures; the kind that comes later, belongs

[12] The following excerpt from the first of Hugh's *Nineteen Sermons on Ecclesiastes*, based on MPL 175:115 ff., is according to the translation of H. O. Taylor, *The Mediaeval Mind*, Cambridge, Massachusetts, 4th ed., 1949, Vol. II, pp. 388–89. Used by permission of Harvard University Press. Cf. Battles, *op. cit.*, pp. 227–28. See similar passages from the *De modo dicendi et meditandi* (8–9), MPL 176: 879, on the different kinds of cogitation and contemplation. Cf. Wolff, *Die Viktoriner*, pp. 28 ff., 48, 76–81.

to the perfect, and contemplates the Creator. In The Proverbs, Solomon proceeds as through meditation. In Ecclesiastes, he ascends to the first grade of contemplation. In The Song of Songs, he transports himself to the final grade. In meditation there is a wrestling of ignorance with knowledge; and the light of truth gleams as in a fog of error. So fire is kindled with difficulty on a heap of green wood; but then, fanned with stronger breath, the flame burns higher, and we see volumes of smoke rolling up, with flame flashing through. Little by little the damp is exhausted, and the leaping fire dispels the smoke. Then *victrix flamma*, darting through the heap of crackling wood, springs from branch to branch, and with lambent grasp catches upon every twig; nor does it rest until it penetrates everywhere and draws into itself all that it finds that is not flame. At length the whole combustible material is purged of its own nature and passes into the similitude and property of fire; then the din is hushed, and the voracious fire, having subdued all and brought all into its own likeness, composes itself to a high peace and silence, finding nothing more that is alien or opposed to itself. First there was fire with flame and smoke; then fire with flame, without smoke; and at last pure fire with neither flame nor smoke.

HUGH: LOVE THE CURE OF THE SOUL'S SICKNESS [13]

THE TEXT

As I was sitting once among the brethren, and they were asking questions, and I replying, and many matters had been cited and adduced, it came about that all of us at once began to marvel vehemently at the unstableness and disquiet of the human heart; and we began to sigh. Then they pleaded with me that I would show them the cause of such whirlings of thought in the human heart; and they besought me to set forth by what art of exercise of discipline this evil might be removed. I indeed wished to satisfy my brethren, so far as God might aid me, and untie the knot of their questions, both by authority and by argument. I knew it would please them most if I should compose my matter to read to them at table.

It was my plan to show first whence arise such violent changes in man's heart, and then how the mind may be led to keep itself in stable peace. And although I had no doubt that this is the proper work of grace, rather than of human labor, nevertheless I know that God wishes us to co-operate. Besides, it is well to know the magnitude of our weakness and the mode of its repairing, since so much the deeper will be our gratitude.

The first man was so created that if he had not sinned he would always have beheld in present contemplation his Creator's face, and by always seeing him would have loved him al-

---

[13] The text of this passage from the Prologue of the *De arca Noe morali* is that of MPL 176:617–20 and the following is from Lib. I, cap. 2, MPL 176: 621. Both are translated in H. O. Taylor, *The Mediaeval Mind*, 4th ed., Cambridge, Massachusetts, 1949, Vol. II, pp. 396–97. Used by permission of the publishers, Harvard University Press. See Lib. IV, cap. 3, cap. 9, etc., of the *De arca Noe morali*, cols. 667, 677 ff., for the *opus creationis et reparationis*.

ways, and by loving would always have clung close to him, and by clinging to him who was eternal would have possessed life without end. Evidently the one true good of man was perfect knowledge of his Creator. But he was driven from the face of the Lord, since for his sin he was struck with the blindness of ignorance, and passed from that intimate light of contemplation; and he inclined his mind to earthly desires, as he began to forget the sweetness of the divine. Thus he was made a wanderer and fugitive over the earth. A wanderer indeed, because of disordered concupiscence; and a fugitive, through guilty conscience, which feels every man's hand against it. For every temptation will overcome the man who has lost God's aid.

So man's heart which had been kept secure by divine love, and one by loving One, afterward began to flow here and there through earthly desires. For the mind which knows not to love its true good is never stable and never rests. Hence restlessness, and ceaseless labor, and disquiet, until the man turns and adheres to Him. The sick heart wavers and quivers; the cause of its disease is love of the world; the remedy, the love of God.

GOD'S DWELLING IN THE SOUL THROUGH KNOWLEDGE AND LOVE [14]

In two ways God dwells in the human heart, to wit, through knowledge and through love; yet the dwelling is one, since every one who knows him loves, and no one can love without knowing. Knowledge through cognition of the faith erects the structure; love through virtue paints the edifice with color.

[14] MPL 176:621; Taylor, *op. cit.*, Vol. II, p. 397.

HUGH: THE SOUL'S DEEPEST DESIRE: [15]
DIALOGUE BETWEEN MAN AND HIS SOUL

THE TEXT

The Soul: What is that sweet thing that comes sometimes to touch me at the thought of God? It affects me with such vehemence and sweetness that I begin wholly to go out of myself and to be lifted up, whither I know not. Suddenly I am renewed and changed; it is a state of inexpressible well-being. My consciousness rejoices. I lose the memory of my former trials, my soul rejoices, my mind becomes clearer, my heart is enflamed, my desires are satisfied. I feel myself transported into a new place, I know not where. I grasp something interiorly as if with the embraces of love. I do not know what it is, and yet I strive with all my strength to hold it and not to lose it. I struggle deliciously to prevent myself leaving this thing which I desire to embrace forever, and I exult with ineffable intensity, as if I had at last found the goal of all my desires. I seek for nothing more. I wish for nothing more. All my aspiration is to continue at the point that I have reached. Is it my Beloved? Tell me, I pray thee, if this be he, that, when he return, I may conjure him not to depart, and to establish in me his permanent dwelling place?

The Man: Yes, it is truly thy Beloved who visits thee. But he comes *invisible, hidden,* incomprehensible. He comes to touch thee, not to be seen; to intimate his presence to thee, not to be understood; to make thee taste of him, not to pour himself out

---

[15] The translation of the end of the "Confessio" from the *Soliloquium de arrha animae,* made from the text of MPL 176:970, is that used in A. Poulain, *The Graces of Interior Prayer,* translated from the 6th edition by L. L. Y. Smith *et al.,* London, 1950, pp. 108–109, and used by permission of the publishers, Routledge & Kegan Paul, Ltd., London, and B. Herder Book Company, St. Louis, Missouri. Cf. Wolff, *Die Viktoriner,* pp. 113–14, as well as a complete text by K. Müller, in *Kleine Texte,* No. 123.

in his entirety; to draw thy affection, not to satisfy thy desire; to bestow the first fruits of his love, not to communicate it in its fullness. Behold in this the most certain pledge of thy future marriage: that thou art destined to see him and to possess him eternally, because he already gives himself to thee at times to taste, with what sweetness thou knowest. Therefore in the times of his absence thou shalt console thyself; and during his visits thou shalt renew thy courage, which is ever in need of heartening. We have spoken at great length, O my soul. In conclusion, I ask thee to think of none but Him, love none but him, listen to none but him, take hold of none but him, possess none but him.

The Soul: That indeed is what I desire, what I choose; that is what I long for from the depths of my heart.

RICHARD: THE WAY TO CONTEMPLATION

HERE FOLLOWETH A VERY DEVOUT
TREATISE, NAMED BENJAMIN, OF THE
MIGHTS AND VIRTUES OF MAN'S SOUL,
AND OF THE WAY TO TRUE CONTEMPLA-
TION, COMPILED BY A NOBLE AND
FAMOUS DOCTOR, A MAN OF GREAT
HOLINESS AND DEVOTION, NAMED
RICHARD OF SAINT VICTOR [16]

A TREATISE NAMED BENJAMIN [17]

The Text

The Prologue

A great clerk that men call Richard of Saint Victor, in a book that he maketh of the study of wisdom, witnesseth and saith that two mights are in a man's soul, given of the Father of Heaven of whom all good cometh. The one is reason, the other is affection; through reason we know, and through affection we feel or love.[18]

Of reason springeth right counsel and ghostly wits; [19] and of affection springeth holy desires and ordained feelings. And right

[16] E. G. Gardner has pointed out that, of Bernard, Richard of St. Victor, and Bonaventure, who were the major influences in the development of English mysticism, perhaps Richard ranks first. The text of one of the numerous manuscript adaptations of the *Benjamin Minor* current in fourteenth century England serves a double purpose in this anthology. Obviously a paraphrase-translation of the heart of the *Benjamin Minor* with certain liberties taken in free translation, omission, and expansion, this Middle English text does present the sprawling original in more concentrated form. Furthermore, it shows us one of the prevailing ways in which the Latin Richard entered our English mystical tradition in the vernacular. This 1521 printing by Henry Pepwell, published from the Harleian MS. 1002 by C. Horstman, *Richard Rolle of Hampole . . . and His Followers*, London, 1895, Vol. I, pp. 162–72, and edited with notes by E. G. Gardner in his work *The Cell of Self-knowledge*, London, 1925, pp. 3–33, is used by permission of the publishers, Chatto & Windus.

[17] The title in the original, *Benjamin Minor*, recalls the medieval attribution of contemplative uses to the Vulgate rendering of Ps. 67:28: *Ibi Beniamin adolescentulus, in mentis excessu:* "There is Benjamin, a youth, in ecstasy of mind." Here the Authorized Version reads: "Little Benjamin [with] their ruler . . ." (Ps. 68:27). Cf. Gardner, *Cell of Self-knowledge*, p. xiv; Wolff, *Die Viktoriner*, p. 129.

[18] The treatise in full, in MPL 196, is cols. 1–64, eighty-seven chapters in all. Wolff translates a large part, pp. 131–98. The first part of the Prologue here is from cap. 3 of the original.

[19] I.e., spiritual insight: *spiritualis sensus.*

as Rachel and Leah were both wives unto Jacob, right so man's soul through light of knowing in the reason and sweetness of love in the affection is spoused unto God. By Jacob is understanden God; by Rachel is understanden reason; by Leah is understanden affection. Each of these wives, Rachel and Leah, took to them a maiden: Rachel took Bilhah and Leah took Zilpah. Bilhah was a great jangler [20] and Zilpah was ever drunken and thirsty. By Bilhah is understanden imagination, the which is servant unto reason, as Bilhah was to Rachel; by Zilpah is understanden sensuality, the which is servant unto affection, as Zilpah was to Leah. And so much are these maidens needful to their ladies that without them all this world might serve them of nought. For why: without imagination reason may not know and without sensuality affection may not feel. And yet imagination cryeth so inconveniently in the ears of our heart that, for ought that reason her lady may do, yet she may not still her. And therefore it is that ofttimes when we should pray, so many divers fantasies of idle and evil thoughts cry in our hearts that on no wise we may by our own mights drive them away. And thus it is well proved that Bilhah is a foul jangler. And also the sensuality is evermore so thirsty that all that affection her lady may feel may not yet slake her thirst. The drink that she desireth is the lust of fleshly, kindly, and worldly delights, of the which the more that she drinketh the more she thirsteth; for why: for to fill the appetite of the sensuality all this world may not suffice; and therefore it is that ofttimes when we pray or think on God and ghostly things, we would fain feel sweetness of love in our affection, and yet we may not, for are we so busy to feed the concupiscence of our sensuality; for evermore it is greedily asking, and we have a fleshly compassion thereof. And thus it is well proved that Zilpah is evermore drunken and thirsty. And right as Leah conceived of Jacob and brought forth seven children, and Rachel conceived of Jacob and brought forth two children, and Bilhah conceived of Jacob and brought forth two children, and Zilpah conceived of Jacob and brought forth two children, right so the affection conceiveth through the grace of God, and bringeth forth seven virtues; and also the sensuality conceiveth through the grace of God and bringeth forth two virtues; and also the reason conceiveth through the grace of God and bringeth forth two virtues; and also the imagination conceiveth through the grace of God and bringeth forth two virtues, or two

[20] Caps. 5–6: garrulous.

7—L.M.M.

beholdings. And the names of their children and of their virtues shall be known by this figure that followeth:

Husband: Jacob temporally, God spiritually. Wives to Jacob: Leah, that is to say, Affection; Rachel, that is to say, Reason. Maid to Leah is Zilpah, that is to understand, Sensuality; and Bilhah maiden to Rachel, that is to understand, Imagination.

The sons of Jacob and Leah are these seven that followeth: Reuben signifieth dread of pain; Simeon, sorrow of sins; Levi, hope of forgiveness; Judah, love of righteousness; Issachar, joy in inward sweetness; Zebulun, hatred of sin; Dinah, ordained shame.

The sons of Jacob and Zilpah, servant of Leah, are these: Gad, Abstinence; Asher, Patience.

The sons of Jacob and of Rachel are these: Joseph, Discretion; Benjamin, Contemplation.

The sons of Jacob and Bilhah, servant to Rachel, are these: Dan, sight of pain to come; and Naphtali, sight of joy to come.

In this figure it is shewed apertly of Jacob and of his wives, and their maidens, and all their children. Here it is to shew on what manner they were gotten, and in what order:

First, it is to say of the children of Leah; for why: it is read that she first conceived. The children of Leah are nought else to understand but ordained affections or feelings in a man's soul; for why: if they were unordained, then were they not the sons of Jacob. Also the seven children of Leah are seven virtues, for virtue is nought else but an ordained and a measured feeling in a man's soul. For then is man's feeling in soul ordained when it is of that thing that it should be; then it is measured when it is so much as it should be. These things in a man's soul may be now ordained and measured, and now unordained and unmeasured; but when they are ordained and measured, then are they accounted among the sons of Jacob.[21]

Capitulum I [22]

How the Virtue of Dread Riseth in the Affection

The first child that Leah conceived of Jacob was Reuben, that is, dread; and therefore it is written in the psalm: "The beginning of wisdom is the dread of our Lord God." [23] This is the first felt virtue in a man's affection, without the which none

---

[21] The foregoing is compiled from caps. 1–7 of the original.
[22] Cap. 8.   [23] Ps. 110 (111):10.

other may be had. And, therefore, whoso desireth to have such a son, him behoveth busily and oft also behold the evil that he hath done. And he shall, on the one party, think on the greatness of his trespass, and, on another party, the power of the doomsman. Of such a consideration springeth dread, that is to say Reuben, that through right is cleped [24] "the son of Sight." For utterly is he blind that seeth not the pains that are to come, and dreadeth not to sin. And well is Reuben cleped the son of sight; for when he was born, his mother cried and said, "God hath seen my meekness." [25] And man's soul, in such a consideration of his old sins and of the power of the doomsman, beginneth then truly to see God by feeling of dread, and also to be seen of God by rewarding of pity. [26]

Capitulum II [27]

How Sorrow Riseth in the Affection

While Reuben waxeth, Simeon is born; for after dread it needeth greatly that sorrow come soon. For ever the more that a man dreadeth the pain that he hath deserved, the bitterlier he sorroweth the sins that he hath done. Leah in the birth of Simeon cried and said, "Our Lord hath heard me be had in despite." [28] And therefore is Simeon cleped "hearing"; for when a man bitterly sorroweth and despiseth his old sins, then beginneth he to be heard of God, and also for to hear the blessed sentence of God's own mouth: "Blessed be they that sorrow, for they shall be comforted." [29] For in what hour the sinner sorroweth and turneth from his sin, he shall be safe. Thus witnesseth holy Scripture. And also by Reuben he is meeked, and by Simeon he is contrite and hath compunction of tears; but, as witnesseth David in the psalm: "Heart contrite and meeked God shall not despise"; [30] and without doubt such sorrow bringeth in true comfort of heart.

Capitulum III [31]

How Hope Riseth in the Affection

But, I pray thee, what comfort may be to them that truly dread and bitterly sorrow for their old sins, ought but a true

---

[24] Called: *vocetur.*   [25] Gen. 29:32.
[26] *Per respectum pietatis*; hence, "pity" in the sense of "piety."
[27] Cap. 9.   [28] Gen. 29:33.   [29] Matt. 5:5 (4).
[30] Ps. 50:19 (51:17).   [31] Cap. 10.

hope of forgiveness? The which is the third son of Jacob, that is
Levi, the which is cleped in the story "a doing to." [32] For when
the other two children, dread and sorrow, are given of God to
a man's soul, without doubt he, this third, that is hope, shall not
be delayed, but he shall be done to; [33] as the story witnesseth of
Levi, that, when his two brethren, Reuben and Simeon, were
given to their mother Leah, he, this Levi, was done to. Take
heed of this word, that he was done to and not given. And
therefore it is said that a man shall not presume of hope of forgiveness before the time that his heart be meeked in dread and
contrite in sorrow; without these two, hope is presumption, and
where these two are, hope is done to; and thus after sorrow
cometh soon comfort, as David telleth in the psalm that "after
the muchness of my sorrow in my heart," he saith to our Lord,
"thy comforts have gladded my soul." [34] And therefore it is
that the Holy Ghost is called *Paracletus*, that is, Comforter, for
ofttimes he vouchethsafe to comfort a sorrowful soul.

Capitulum IV [35]

How Love Riseth in the Affection

From now forth beginneth a manner of homeliness [36] for to
grow between God and a man's soul; and also on a manner a
kindling of love, in so much that ofttimes he feeleth him not only
be visited of God and comforted in his coming, but ofttimes also
he feeleth him filled with an unspeakable joy. This homeliness
and this kindling of love first felt Leah, when, after that Levi
was born, she cried with a great voice and said, "Now shall my
husband be coupled to me." [37] The true spouse of our soul is
God, and then we are truly coupled unto him when we draw
near him by hope and soothfast love. And right as after hope
cometh love, so after Levi was Judah born, the fourth son of
Leah. Leah in his birth cried and said, "Now shall I shrive to
our Lord." [38] And therefore in the story is Judah cleped
"shrift." [39] Also man's soul in this degree of love offereth it
clearly to God, and saith thus, "Now shall I shrive to our Lord."
For before this feeling of love in a man's soul, all that he doth is
done more for dread than for love; but in this state a man's soul

[32] *Additus, vel additio.*   [33] Added (cf. Gen. 29:34).
[34] Ps. 93 (94):19.   [35] Caps. 11–13.
[36] A kind of intimacy: *quaedam familiaritas.*   [37] Gen. 29:34.
[38] Gen. 29:35 (Vulgate): *Modo confitebor Domino.*   [39] *Confitens.*

feeleth God so sweet, so merciful, so good, so courteous, so true, and so kind, so faithful, so lovely, and so homely, that he leaveth nothing in him—might, wit, conning,[40] or will—that he offereth not it clearly, freely, and homely unto Him. This shrift is not only of sin, but of the goodness of God. Great token of love it is when a man telleth to God that He is good. Of this shrift speaketh David full ofttimes in the Psalter, when he saith, "Make it known to God, for he is good." [41]

Lo, now have we said of four sons of Leah. And after this she left bearing of children till another time; and so man's soul weeneth that it sufficeth to it when it feeleth that it loveth the true goods. And so it is enough to salvation, but not to perfection. For it falleth to a perfect soul both to be inflamed with the fire of love in the affection, and also to be illumined with the light of knowing in the reason.

Capitulum V [42]

How the Double Sight of Pain and Joy Riseth in the Imagination

Then when Judah waxeth, that is to say, when love and desire of unseen true goods is rising and waxing in a man's affection, then coveteth Rachel for to bear some children; that is to say, then coveteth reason to know these things that affection feeleth, for as it falleth to the affection for to love, so it falleth to the reason for to know. Of affection springeth ordained and measured feelings; and of reason springeth right knowings and clear understandings. And ever the more that Judah waxeth, that is to say love, so much the more desireth Rachel bearing of children, that is to say, reason studieth after knowing. But who is he that woteth not how hard it is, and near-hand impossible to a fleshly soul, the which is yet rude in ghostly studies, for to rise in knowing of unseeable things,[43] and for to set the eye of contemplation in ghostly things? For why: a soul that is yet rude and fleshly knoweth nought but bodily things, and nothing cometh yet to the mind but only seeable things. And, nevertheless, yet it looketh inward as it may; and that that it may not see yet clearly by ghostly knowing, it thinketh by imagination.

And this is the cause why Rachel had first children of her maiden, than of herself. And so it is that, though all a man's soul may not yet get the light of ghostly knowing in the reason,

---

40 Learning.   41 Ps. 106 (107):1.   42 Caps. 13–14 ff.
43 *Invisibilium.* See the *Benjamin Major*, I, 6, 7.

yet it thinketh it sweet to hold the mind on God and ghostly things in the imagination. As by Rachel we understand reason, so by her maiden Bilhah we understand imagination.[44] And, therefore, reason sheweth that it is more profitable for to think on ghostly things, in what manner so it be—yea, if it be in kindling of our desire with some fair imagination—than it is for to think on vanities and deceivable things of this world. And, therefore, of Bilhah were born these two: Dan and Naphtali.[45] Dan is to say sight of pains to come; and Naphtali, sight of joys to come. These two children are full needful and full speedful unto a working soul, the one for to put down evil suggestions of sins and the other for to raise up our wills in working of good and in kindling of our desires. For as it falleth to Dan to put down evil suggestions of sin by sight of pains to come, so it falleth to the other brother Naphtali to raise up our wills in working of good, and in kindling of holy desires by sight of joys to come. And therefore holy men, when they are stirred to any unlawful thing, by inrising of any foul thought, as oft they set before their mind the pains that are to come; and so they slaken their temptation in the beginning, ere it rise to any foul delight in their soul. And as oft as their devotion and their liking in God and ghostly things cease and wax cold (as ofttimes it befalleth in this life, for corruption of the flesh and many other skills [46]), so oft they set before their mind the joy that is to come. And so they kindle their will with holy desires, and destroy their temptation in the beginning, ere it come to any weariness or heaviness of sloth. And for that [47] with Dan we damn unlawful thoughts, therefore he is well cleped in the story "doom." [48] And also his father Jacob said of him thus: "Dan shall deem his folk." [49] And also it is said in the story that, when Bilhah brought forth Dan, Rachel said thus: "Our Lord hath deemed me," [50] that is to say, "Our Lord hath evened me unto my sister Leah." And thus saith reason, when the imagination hath gotten the sight of pains to come, that our Lord hath evened her with her sister affection; and she saith thus, for she hath the sight of pains to come in her imagination, of the which she had dread and sorrow in her feeling. And then after came Naphtali, that is to say, the sight of joys to come. And in his birth spake Rachel and said, "I

---

[44] Caps. 14–16, etc. On the Victorine role of reason and imagination, see *Benjamin Major*, I, 7, and Ebner's commentary, *op. cit.*, pp. 29 ff., 38 ff., 60 ff., 105 ff.   [45] Caps. 18 ff.   [46] Reasons.
[47] Because, since.   [48] *Judicium*, i.e., judgment.
[49] I.e., "judge his people," Gen. 49:16.   [50] Gen. 30:6.

am made like to my sister Leah"; [51] and therefore is Naphtali cleped in the story "likeness." [52] And thus saith reason that she is made like to her sister affection. For there as she had gotten hope and love of joy to come in her feeling, she hath now gotten sight of joy to come in her imagination. Jacob said of Naphtali that he was "a hart sent out, giving speeches of fairhead." [53] So it is that, when we imagine of the joys of heaven, we say that it is fair in heaven. For wonderfully kindleth Naphtali our souls with holy desires, as oft as we imagine of the worthiness and the fairhead of the joys of heaven.

Capitulum VI [54]

How the Virtues of Abstinence and Patience Rise in the Sensuality

When Leah saw that Rachel her sister made great joy of these two bastards born of Bilhah her maiden, she called forth her maiden Zilpah, to put to her husband Jacob, that she might make joy with her sister, having other two bastards gotten of her maiden Zilpah. And thus it is seemly in man's soul for to be, that from the time that reason hath refrained the great jangling of imagination, and hath put her to be underlout[55] to God, and maketh her to bear some fruit in helping of her knowing, that right so the affection refrain the lust and the thirst of the sensuality, and make her to be underlout to God, and so to bear some fruit in helping of her feeling. But what fruit may she bear ought but that she learn to live temperately in easy things, and patiently in uneasy things? These are they, the children of Zilpah, Gad and Asher: Gad is abstinence, and Asher is patience. Gad is the sooner born child and Asher the latter; for first it needeth that we be attempered in ourself with discreet abstinence, and after that we bear outward disease [56] in strength of patience. These are the children that Zilpah brought forth in sorrow; for in abstinence and patience the sensuality is punished in the flesh; but that that is sorrow to the sensuality turneth to much comfort and bliss to the affection. And therefore it is that when Gad was born Leah cried and said, "Happily"; [57] and

---

[51] Gen. 30:8.   [52] *Comparatio vel conversio*; cap. 22.
[53] Gen. 49:21: "Naphtali is a hind let loose; he giveth goodly words." Cap. 23.   [54] Caps. 25–26.
[55] Participial form of an Old English word meaning "to stoop beneath" or "submit to." Cf. Wycliffite Bible, Gen. 37:8.   [56] Discomfort.
[57] *Dixit: feliciter* (Gen. 30:11).

therefore Gad is cleped in the story "happiness," or "seeli-
ness." [58] And so it is well said that abstinence in the sensuality is
happiness in the affection. For why: ever the less that the sensuality is delighted in her lust, the more sweetness feeleth the
affection in her love. Also after when Asher was born, Leah said,
"This shall be for my bliss"; [59] and therefore was Asher called
in the story "blessed." [60] And so it is well said that patience in
the sensuality is bliss in the affection. For why: ev∠r the more
disease that the sensuality suffereth, the more blessed is the soul
in the affection. And thus by abstinence and patience we shall
not only understand a temperance in meat and drink, and suffering of outward tribulation, but also [in] all manner of fleshly,
kindly,[61] and worldly delights, and all manner of disease, bodily
and ghostly, within or without, reasonable or unreasonable,
that by any of our five wits torment or delight the sensuality.
On this wise beareth the sensuality fruit in help of affection,
her lady. Much peace and rest is in that soul that neither
is drunken in the lust of the sensuality, nor grutcheth[62] in the
pain thereof. The first of these is gotten by Gad and the latter by
Asher. Here it is to wete that first was Rachel's maiden put to
the husband or the maiden of Leah; and this is the skill why.
For truly, but if the jangling of the imagination, that is to say,
the in-running of vain thoughts, be first refrained, without
doubt the lust of the sensuality may not be attempered. And
therefore whoso will abstain him from fleshly and worldly lusts,
him behoveth first seldom or never think any vain thoughts.
And also never in this life may a man perfectly despise the ease
of the flesh, and not dread the disease, but if he have before
busily beholden the meeds and the torments that are to come.
But here it is to wete how that, with these four sons of these two
maidens, the city of our conscience is kept wonderfully from all
temptations. For all temptation either it riseth within by
thought or else without by some of our five wits. But within
shall Dan deem and damn evil thoughts by sight of pain; and
without shall Gad put against false delights by use of abstinence.
Dan waketh [63] within and Gad without; and also their other two
brethren helpen them full much: Naphtali maketh peace within
with Dan, and Asher biddeth Gad have no dread of his enemies.
Dan feareth the heart with ugsomeness of hell, and Naphtali
cherisheth it with behighting [64] of heavenly bliss. Also Asher

[58] *Felicitas.*   [59] Gen. 30:13.   [60] *Beatus.*
[61] Natural.   [62] Murmurs, complains.   [63] Watches.
[64] Promises: *fovet promissis.*

helpeth his brother without, so that, through them both, the wall of the city is not broken. Gad holdeth out ease, and Asher pursueth disease. Asher soon deceiveth his enemy, when he bringeth to mind the patience of his father[65] and the behighting of Naphtali, and thus ofttimes ever the more enemies he hath, the more matter he hath of overcoming. And therefore it is that, when he hath overcome his enemies (that is to say, the adversities of this world), soon he turneth him to his brother Gad to help to destroy his enemies. And without fail, from that he be come, soon they turn the back, and flee. The enemies of Gad are fleshly delights; but truly, from the time that a man have patience in the pain of his abstinence, false delights find no woning stead [66] in him.

Capitulum VII [67]

How Joy of Inward Sweetness Riseth in the Affection

Thus when the enemy fleeth and the city is peased,[68] then beginneth a man to prove what the high peace of God is that passeth man's wit. And therefore it is that Leah left bearing of children unto this time that Gad and Asher were born of Zilpah, her maiden. For truly, but if it be so that a man have refrained the lust and the pain of his five wits in his sensuality by abstinence and patience, he shall never feel inward sweetness and true joy in God and ghostly things in the affection. This is that Issachar, the fifth son of Leah, the which in the story is cleped "meed." [69] [And well is this joy of inward sweetness cleped meed] for this joy is the taste of heavenly bliss, the which is the endless meed of a devout soul, beginning here. Leah, in the birth of this child, said, "God hath given me meed, for that I have given my maiden to my husband in bearing of children." [70] And so it is good that we make our sensuality bear fruit in abstaining it from all manner of fleshly, kindly, and worldly delight, and in fruitful suffering of all fleshly and worldly disease; therefore our Lord of his great mercy giveth us joy unspeakable and inward sweetness in our affection, in earnest of the sovereign joy and meed of the Kingdom of Heaven. Jacob said of Issachar

65 An odd garbling of the original, cap. 33.
66 Dwelling place.   67 Cap. 36.
68 Pacified.   69 Merces, i.e., wages, reward.
70 Gen. 30:18.

that he was "a strong ass dwelling between the terms." [71] And so it is that a man in this state, and that feeleth the earnest of everlasting joy in his affection, is as "an ass, strong and dwelling between the terms"; because that, be he never so filled in soul of ghostly gladness and joy in God, yet, for corruption of the flesh in this deadly life, him behoveth bear the charge of the deadly body, as hunger, thirst, and cold, sleep, and many other diseases; for the which he is likened to an ass as in body; but as in soul he is strong for to destroy all the passions and the lusts of the flesh by patience and abstinence in the sensuality, and by abundance of ghostly joy and sweetness in the affection. And also a soul in this state is dwelling between the terms of deadly life and undeadly life. He that dwelleth between the terms hath near-hand forsaken deadliness, but not fully, and hath near-hand gotten undeadliness, but not fully; for whiles that him needeth the goods of this world, as meat and drink and clothing, as it falleth to each man that liveth, yet his one foot is in this deadly life; and for great abundance of ghostly joy and sweetness that he feeleth in God, not seldom but oft, he hath his other foot in the undeadly life. Thus I trow that Saint Paul felt, when he said this word of great desire: "Who shall deliver me from this deadly body?" [72] And when he said thus: "I covet to be loosed and to be with Christ." [73] And thus doth the soul that feeleth Issachar in his affection, that is to say, the joy of inward sweetness, the which is understanden by Issachar. It enforceth it to forsake this wretched life, but it may not; it coveteth to enter the blessed life, but it may not; it doth that it may, and yet it dwelleth between the terms.

Capitulum VIII [74]

How Perfect Hatred of Sin Riseth in the Affection

And therefore it is that, after Issachar, Zebulun is born, that is to say, hatred of sin. And here it is to wete why that hatred of sin is never perfectly felt in a man's affection ere the time that ghostly joy of inward sweetness be felt in the affection, and this is the skill [75]: for ere this time was never the true cause of hatred felt in the affection. For the feeling of ghostly joy teacheth a man

[71] Gen. 49:14: *Issachar asinus fortis accubans inter terminos;* i.e., crouching between close boundaries, confined within narrow straits—"lying down between the borders."

[72] Rom. 7:24.   [73] Phil. 1:23.

[74] Caps. 40–44.   [75] Reason, cause.

what sin harmeth the soul. And all after that the harm in the soul is felt much or little, thereafter is the hatred measured, more or less, unto the harming. But when a soul, by the grace of God and long travail, is come to feeling of ghostly joy in God, then it feeleth that sin hath been the cause of the delaying thereof. And also when he feeleth that he may not alway last in the feeling of that ghostly joy, for the corruption of the flesh, of the which corruption sin is the cause; then he riseth with a strong feeling of hatred against all sin and all kind of sin. This feeling taught David us to have, where he saith in the psalm: "Be ye wroth and will ye not sin" [76]; that is thus to mean: Be ye wroth with the sin, but not with the kind.[77] For kind stirreth to the deed, but not to sin. And here it is to wete that this wrath and this hatred is not contrary to charity, but charity teacheth how it shall be had both in a man's self and in his even Christian [78]; for a man should [not] hate sin [so that he destroy his kind, but so that he destroy the sin and the appetite of sin] in his kind. And, as against our even Christian, we ought to hate sin in him, and to love him; and of this hatred speaketh David in the psalm, where he saith thus: "With perfect hatred I hated them." [79] And in another psalm he saith that "he had in hatred all wicked ways." [80] Thus it is well proved that ere Zebulun was born Judah and Issachar were both born. For but if a man have had charity and ghostly joy in his feeling first, he may in no wise feel this perfect hatred of sin in his affection. For Judah, that is to say, charity, teacheth us how we shall hate sin in ourself and in our brethren; and Issachar, that is to say, ghostly feeling of joy in God, teacheth us why we shall hate sin in ourself and in our brethren. Judah biddeth us hate sin and love the kind; and Issachar biddeth us destroy the sin and save the kind; and thus it falleth for to be that the kind may be made strong in God and in ghostly things by perfect hatred and destroying of sin. And therefore is Zebulun cleped in the story "a dwelling stead of strength." And Leah said in his birth, "My husband shall now dwell with me" [81]; and so it is that God, that is the true husband of our soul, is dwelling in that soul, strengthening it in the affection with ghostly joy and sweetness in his love, which travaileth busily to destroy sin in himself and in others by perfect hatred of the sin and all the kind of sin. And thus it is said how Zebulun is born.

[76] Ps. 4:5 (4).
[77] Human nature or kind.
[78] Fellow Christian.
[79] Ps. 138 (139):21.
[80] Ps. 118 (119):104.
[81] Gen. 30:20.

Capitulum IX [82]

How Ordained Shame Riseth and Groweth in the Affection

But though all that a soul through grace feel in it perfect hatred of sin, whether it may yet live without sin? Nay, sikerly; [83] and therefore let no man presume of himself, when the apostle saith thus: "If we say that we have no sin, we deceive ourself, and soothfastness is not in us." [84] And also Saint Austin saith that he dare well say that there is no man living without sin. And, I pray thee, who is he that sinneth not in ignorance? Yea, and ofttimes it falleth that God suffereth those men to fall full grievously, by the which he hath ordained other men's errors to be righted, that they may learn by their own falling how merciful they shall be in amending of others. And for that ofttimes men fall grievously in those same sins that they most hate, therefore, after hatred of sin, springeth ordained shame in a man's soul; and so it is that after Zebulun was Dinah born. As by Zebulun hatred of sin, so by Dinah is understanden ordained shame of sin. But wete thou well: he that felt never Zebulun, felt never yet Dinah. Evil men have a manner of shame, but it is not this ordained shame. For why: if they had perfect shame of sin, they should not so customably do it with will and advisement; [85] but they shame more with a foul cloth on their body than with a foul thought in their soul. But whatso thou be that weenest that thou hast gotten Dinah, think whether thee would shame as much if a foul thought were in thine heart, as thee would if thou wert made to stand naked before the king and all his royalme; and sikerly else wete it thou right well that thou hast not yet gotten ordained shame in thy feeling, if so be that thou have less shame with thy foul heart than with thy foul body, and if thou think more shame with thy foul body in the sight of men than with thy foul heart in the sight of the King of Heaven and of all his angels and holy saints in heaven.

Lo, it is now said of the seven children of Leah, by the which are understanden seven manner of affections in a man's soul, the which may be now ordained and now unordained, now measured and now unmeasured; but when they are ordained and measured, then are they virtues; and when they are unordained and unmeasured, then are they vices. Thus behoveth a man have children, that they be not only ordained but also

---

[82] Cap. 45.
[84] I John 1:8.

[83] Assuredly.
[85] Deliberate intention.

measured. Then are they ordained when they are of that thing that they should be, and then are they unordained when they are of that thing that they should not be; and then are they measured when they are as much as they should be, and then are they unmeasured when they are more than they should be. For why: overmuch dread bringeth in despair, and overmuch sorrow casteth a man in to bitterness and heaviness of kind,[86] for the which he is unable to receive ghostly comfort. And overmuch hope is presumption, and outrageous love is but flattering and faging,[87] and outrageous gladness is dissolution and wantonness, and untempered hatred of sin is woodness.[88] And on this manner, they are unordained and unmeasured, and thus are they turned into vices, and then lose they the name of virtues, and may not be accounted amongst the sons of Jacob, that is to say, God: for by Jacob is understanden God, as it is shewed in the figure before.

Capitulum X [89]

How Discretion and Contemplation Rise in the Reason

Thus it seemeth that the virtue of discretion needeth to be had, with the which all others may be governed; for without it all virtues are turned into vices. This is Joseph, that is the late born child, but yet his father loveth him more than them all. For why: without discretion may goodness neither be gotten nor kept, and therefore no wonder, though that virtue be singularly loved, without which no virtue may be had nor governed. But what wonder though this virtue be late gotten, when we may not win to the perfection of discretion without much custom and many travails of these other affections coming before? For first behoveth us to be used in each virtue by itself, and get the proof of them all serely,[90] ere we may have full knowing of them all, or else can deem sufficiently of them all. And when we use us busily in these feelings and beholdings before said, ofttimes we fall and ofttimes we rise. Then, by our oft falling, may we learn how much wariness us behoveth have in the getting and keeping of these virtues. And thus sometime, by long use, a soul is led into full discretion, and then it may joy in the birth of Joseph. And before this virtue be conceived in a man's soul, all that

---

86 Disposition.   87 Coaxing.   88 Madness.
89 Caps. 67–87, with which compare Ebner, op. cit., pp. 34 ff.
90 In particular.

these other virtues do, it is without discretion. And therefore, in as much as a man presumeth and enforceth him in any of these feelings beforesaid, over his might and out of measure, in so much the fouler he falleth and faileth of his purpose. And therefore it is that after them all and last is Dinah born; for often after a foul fall and a failing cometh soon shame. And thus after many fallings and failings, and shames following, a man learneth by the proof that there is nothing better than to be ruled after counsel, the which is the readiest getting of discretion. For why: he that doth all things with counsel, he shall never forthink it [91]; for better is a sly man than a strong man; yea, and better is list than lither strength,[92] and a sly man speaketh of victories. And here is the open skill why that neither Leah nor Zilpah nor Bilhah might bear such a child, but only Rachel; for, as it is said before, that of reason springeth right counsel, the which is very discretion, understanden by Joseph, the first son of Rachel; and then at the first bring we forth Joseph in our reason when all that we are stirred to do, we do it with counsel. This Joseph shall not only know what sins we are most stirred unto, but also he shall know the weakness of our kind, and after that either asketh, so shall he do remedy, and seek counsel at wiser than he, and do after them, or else he is not Joseph, Jacob's son born of Rachel. And also by this foresaid Joseph a man is not only learned to eschew the deceits of his enemies, but also oft a man is led by him to the perfect knowing of himself; and all after that a man knoweth himself, thereafter he profiteth in the knowing of God, of whom he is the image and the likeness. And therefore it is that after Joseph is Benjamin born. For as by Joseph discretion, so by Benjamin we understand contemplation. And both are they born of one mother, and gotten of one father. For through the grace of God lightening our reason, come we to the perfect knowing of ourself and of God—that is to say, after that it may be in this life. But long after Joseph is Benjamin born. For why: truly but if it so be that we use us busily and long in ghostly travails, with the which we are learned to know ourself, we may not be raised into the knowing and contemplation of God. He doth for nought that lifteth up his eye to the sight of God, that is not yet able to see himself. For first I would that a man learned him to know the unseeable [93] things of his own spirit, ere he presume to know the unseeable things of the spirit of God; and he that knoweth not yet himself and weeneth that

[91] Regret.   [92] Proverbially: "Better is art than evil strength."
[93] On the foregoing *Invisibilia*, see cap. 71; Ebner, *op. cit.*, pp. 65 ff., 70 ff.

he hath gotten somedeal knowing of the unseeable things of God, I doubt it not but that he is deceived; and therefore I rede that a man seek first busily for to know himself, the which is made to the image and the likeness of God as in soul. And wete thou well that he that desireth for to see God, him behoveth to cleanse his soul, the which is as a mirror in the which all things are clearly seen, when it is clean; 94 and when the mirror is foul, then mayst thou see nothing clearly therein; and right so it is of thy soul, when it is foul, thou knowest neither thyself nor God. As when the candle brenneth, thou mayst then see the self candle by the light thereof, and other things also; right so, when thy soul brenneth in the love of God, that is, when thou feelest continually thine heart desire after the love of God, then, by the light of his grace that he sendeth in thy reason, thou mayst see both thine own unworthiness and his great goodness. And therefore cleanse thy mirror and proffer thy candle to the fire; and then, when thy mirror is cleansed and thy candle brenning, and it so be that thou wittily behold thereto, then beginneth there a manner of clarity of the light of God for to shine in thy soul, and a manner of sunbeam that is ghostly to appear before thy ghostly sight, through the which the eye of thy soul is opened to behold God and godly things, heaven and heavenly things, and all manner of ghostly things. But this sight is but by times, when God will vouchsafe for to give it to a working soul, the whiles it is in the battle of this deadly life; but after this life it shall be everlasting. This light shone in the soul of David, when he said thus in the psalm: "Lord, the light of thy face is marked upon us; thou hast given gladness within mine heart." 95 The light of God's face is the shining of his grace, which reformeth in us his image which hath been disfigured with the darkness of sin; and therefore a soul that brenneth in desire of his sight, 96 if it hope for to have that that it desireth, wete it well it hath conceived Benjamin. And, therefore, what is more healful 97 than the sweetness of this sight, or what softer thing may be felt? Sikerly, none; and that woteth Rachel full well. For why: reason saith that, in comparison of this sweetness, all other sweetness is sorrow, and bitter as gall before honey. Nevertheless, yet may a man never come to such a grace by his own slight. 98 For why: it is the gift of God without desert of man. But without doubt, though it be not the desert of man, yet no man may take such grace without great study and brenning desires coming before;

94 Cap. 72.   95 Ps. 4:7 (6–7).   96 One MS. reads "light."
97 Salutary.   98 Skill.

and that woteth Rachel full well, and therefore she multiplieth her study, and whetteth her desires, seeking desire upon desire; so that at the last, in great abundance of brenning desires and sorrow of the delaying of her desire, Benjamin is born, and his mother Rachel dieth [99]; for why, in what time that a soul is ravished above itself by abundance of desires and a great multitude of love, so that it is inflamed with the light of the Godhead, sikerly then dieth all man's reason.[1]

And therefore, whatso thou be that covetest to come to contemplation of God, that is to say, to bring forth such a child that men clepen in the story Benjamin (that is to say, sight of God), then shalt thou use thee in this manner. Thou shalt call together thy thoughts and thy desires, and make thee of them a church, and learn thee therein for to love only this good word "Jesu," so that all thy desires and all thy thoughts are only set for to love Jesu, and that unceasingly as it may be here; so that thou fulfill what is said in the psalm: "Lord, I shall bless thee in churches" [2]; that is, in thoughts and desires of the love of Jesu. And then, in this church of thoughts and desires, and in this onehead of studies and of wills, look that all thy thoughts, and all thy desires, and all thy studies, and all thy wills be set only in the love and the praising of this Lord Jesu, without forgetting, as far forth as thou mayst by grace, and as thy frailty will suffer; evermore meeking thee to prayer and to counsel, patiently abiding the will of our Lord, unto the time that thy mind be ravished above itself, to be fed with the fair food of angels in the beholding of God and ghostly things: so that it be fulfilled in thee that is written in the psalm: *Ibi Benjamin adolescentulus, in mentis excessu* [3]; that is, "There is Benjamin, the young child, in ravishing of mind." The grace of Jesu keep thee evermore.[4] Amen.

[99] Gen. 35:18.
[1] On contemplative ecstasy, see the notes in the Victorine introduction, especially *Benjamin Minor*, caps. 86, 87; *Benjamin Major*, Lib. V, caps. 2 ff.; Wolff, *op. cit.*, pp. 35 ff., 192 ff.; Ebner, *op. cit.*, pp. 100 ff., 108 ff., and the references to the *Trois processions* and the studies by Dumeige.
[2] Ps. 25 (26):12.   [3] Ps. 67:28 (68:27).
[4] Though not in the original, at least in this form, this paragraph is definitely related to caps. 74–85 of the *Benjamin Minor*, as well as to the latter part of the *Quatuor gradibus* and the *Trois processions*.

ADAM: GOSPEL SYMBOLS AND THE MYSTIC GOAL

OF THE HOLY EVANGELISTS [5]

The Text

O be joyful, faithful nation!
Seed of God's own generation!
Mindful of the revelation
  In Ezekiel's prophecy:
In that witness John uniteth,
Who the Apocalypse inditeth:
"Witness true my true pen writeth
  Of what truly met mine eye!"

Round the footstool of the Godhead,
'Mongst the blessed saints included,
Stand four creatures there embodied,
  Diverse in their form to view.
One an eagle's semblance weareth,
One a lion's likeness beareth,
But as man or ox appeareth
  Each one of the other two.

As Evangelists, these creatures
Figure forth, in form and features,
Those, whose doctrines' stream, like nature's
  Rain, is on the Church outpoured;

---

[5] The selection is No. CII, "Of the Holy Evangelists," as translated from the
early text of Gautier by D. S. Wrangham, *The Liturgical Poetry of Adam of
St. Victor*, Kegan Paul, Trench & Co., London, 1881, Vol. III, pp. 162–69.
Used by permission of the publishers, now Routledge & Kegan Paul, Ltd.
See the *Œuvres poétiques d'Adam de Saint-Victor, texte critique par Léon Gautier*,
3d ed., Paris, 1894. Cf. Wolff, *Die Viktoriner*, pp. 43–44, 307 ff., for an in-
troduction to, and other examples of, the *Sequences*. Cf. MPL 196:1423 ff.
Consult, also, F. Wellner's edition, *Sämtliche Sequenzen: Lateinisch und
Deutsch*, 2d ed., Im Kösel-Verlag, Munich, 1955.

Matthew, Mark, and Luke portraying,
Him too, who his sire obeying,
By the nets no longer staying,
   Came to follow thee, O Lord!

Matthew as the man is treated,
Since 'tis he, who hath related,
How from man, by God created,
   God did, as a man, descend.
Luke the ox's semblance weareth,
Since his Gospel first declareth,
As he thence the law's veil teareth,
   Sacrifices' aim and end.

Mark, the lion, his voice upraises,
Crying out in desert places:
"Cleanse your hearts from all sin's traces;
   For our God a way prepare!"
John, the eagle's features having,
Earth on love's twain pinions leaving,
Soars aloft, God's truth perceiving
   In light's purer atmosphere.

Thus the forms of brute creation
Prophets in their revelation
Use; but in their application
   All their sacred lessons bring.
Mystic meaning underlieth
Wheels that run, or wing that flieth;
One consent the first implieth,
   Contemplation means the wing.

These four writers in portraying
Christ, his fourfold acts displaying,
Show Him—thou hast heard the saying—
   Each of them distinctively:
Man—of woman generated;
Ox—in offering dedicated;
Lion—having death defeated;
   Eagle—mounting to the sky.

These four streams, through Eden flowing,
Moisture, verdure, still bestowing,

Make the flowers and fruit there growing
   In rich plenty laugh and sing:
Christ the source, these streams forth sending;
High the source, these downward trending;
That they thus a taste transcending
   Of life's fount to saints may bring.

At their stream inebriated,
Be our love's thirst aggravated,
More completely to be sated
   At a holier love's full fount!
May the doctrine they provide us
Draw us from sin's slough beside us,
And to things divine thus guide us,
   As from earth we upward mount! Amen.

III

Francis of Assisi (1182-1226)

INTRODUCTION

BIOGRAPHICAL NOTICE

JOHN BERNARDONE, SUBSEQUENTLY CALLED FRANCIS, was born at Assisi in 1182. Abortive military participation in 1200–1205 led, around 1206, to the transmutation of his knightly ideals into the espousal of Lady Poverty. Between 1206 and 1209, he encountered the crucifix calling him to renunciatory service; he renounced his earthly father for the heavenly one; and, while participating in the Mass, he answered the summons to apostolic poverty. Innocent III gave severely qualified, verbal approval to Francis' use of a primitive gospel rule in 1210. This was not for the foundation of an order, which Francis never sought, but for the guidance of a small company of dedicated, voluntary renunciants. Clare precipitated the founding of a woman's movement in 1212, and Francis, having visited the crusaders in the East in 1219, surrendered his leadership in 1220. His followers underwent transformation into an order in 1220, received a tentative rule in 1221, and an official one in 1223. The third order came into being in 1221. Always loyal to the Church and ever conformable to the poor Christ, Francis received the stigmata in 1224. He composed the "Sun Song" in 1225, and in 1226 he died, leaving behind in his spiritual Will and "Testament" the bequest of truest poverty. He was canonized in 1228.

SYNOPSIS

Poverty for Francis meant total renunciation. This required surrendering the whole self to the embrace of divine unity. Life wholly unified in the love of God and his Son required the singleness of mind and the inflammability of the loving heart that the way of poverty most truly connoted for him. The love of Christ prompted imitation of the poor Christ. This was reminiscent of the Saviour's human renunciation as well as of the Lord's offering himself entirely unprotected in the eucharistic sacrifice.[1]

In the brief passages of this anthology, both the sacrificial dedication of the self in ardent, ecstatic love and the joyousness of spiritual liberation involved in poverty are represented. The "Lauds" are the spiritual troubadour's praises of the Divine. These are reflected in the "Sun Song," which depicts the whole world of creation gathered about the loving Creator. Included also is the "Exposition on the Pater Noster," which celebrates contemplative prayer. Noteworthy is the "Praises of the Virtues" in which poverty, chastity, obedience, humility, and simplicity are symbolically related to the whole loving, renunciatory passion to serve God and Christ.[2]

Each of these works bears the closest possible relationship to the "divine office" and to the liturgical Church.[3] Each celebrates the total community of life lived under the Divine in an apostolate among the human. "The Praises of the Virtues," with its personification of Queen Wisdom and Lady Poverty, constitutes an unbroken ring of lauds in which the renunciatory life is enshrined. Wisdom, Poverty, Charity, Simplicity, Humility, Obedience, and the rest are possessed together, if at all. They can be experienced only by one who has died to himself and who has, thereby, become alive to the Divine through the indwelling graces of God. God the Father, Mary Queen of Heaven ever Virgin, God's beloved Son, and the Holy Ghost, as well as the celestial hierarchies—all are praised.

These are the rulers of the universe, in relation with whom all created life, both man and animal, is graded in orderly submission. Francis, as the lover of Christ, of his palace, his tabernacle, and his mother, hails these and the personified virtues "who by means of grace and the illumination of the Holy Ghost are infused in the hearts of the faithful." [4]

---

[1] The main outlines of Francis' renunciation are traced out in my *Francis of Assisi: Apostle of Poverty*, Duke University Press, Durham, North Carolina, 1941. See the extended source and secondary literature, as well as ch. VII, on "Mysticism and the Divine Union."

[2] A good brief set of texts and introductions is P. Gratien's *Les opuscules de Saint François d'Assise*, Paris, 1935. It is based on the Quaracchi *Opuscula* of 1904 by P. Lemmens, and the numerous researches by P. Sabatier. See Gratien, *Les opuscules*, pp. 121 ff., for the "Laudes et prières."

[3] *Ibid.*, pp. 127 ff., 148 ff.   [4] *Ibid.*, p. 150.

Francis, and his followers through him, may have been greatly influenced by Bernard and his tender devotion to Christ, His mother, and His renunciatory suffering. Francis is less immediately indebted to these, however, than to the Gospels and the Psalms. His spirituality is, indeed, affective. As in his "Testament" and in his early gospel Rule, there is in his *Opuscula*, his Lauds, and even in the hagiographical *Fioretti*, the language of the Bible and the aura of the primitive apostolate.[5]

The ecstatic, rapturous encounter of Francis with the Divine on Mt. Alverna later set forth, for Bonaventure, the drama of inebriating, consuming affectivity.[6] The holocaust of renunciatory love that emerges in the stigmatization is celebrated also in the "Paraphrases on the Lord's Prayer." On Alverna, Francis was fused with the loving, renunciatory Christ in triumphant, suffering love. The contemplative raptures of the stigmata have their counterpart, not only in the purified suffering of the "Canticle to the Sun," but also in the ecstatic, unitive prayer of the "Our Father." "Thy Kingdom come; that thou shouldst reign within us with thy grace and let us come to thy Kingdom, where we will see thee face to face, and have perfect love, blessed company, and sempiternal joy."[7] Prayerfully celebrated are the hallowed name, the divine will to be done on earth as in heaven—among men, because these are within the divine companionship.

Here, then, is the secular knight, converted, renounced, and given to spiritual chants among men. He would elicit from them, in turn, their own responsive song to the Lord. The praises of the Father, the glorification of the Creator in the Canticle, the joyous paean to the personified virtues associated with the Lord's mother—all of these are in context with the poor man made free to love, to rejoice, and to sing praises. The divine praises were commended to Francis' followers by a "Rule" (1221), and to all the Christian faithful by a "Letter." They were integrated by Francis with his keeping of the canonical hours of prayer as with his assistance at the Mass. They were commended to the "Poor Brethren" for exhortation and, where properly authorized, for preaching to the people. The apostolate of renunciatory love is the jocund message of praises for the Creator God, the universal King, the Father of Christ, and of redeemed humanity.

---

[5] Petry, *Francis*, chs. 4–6; F. Vernet, *La spiritualité médiévale*, pp. 32 ff.
[6] Bonaventure, *The Life of St. Francis*, ed. by T. Okey, London, 1910, ch. 13.
[7] O. Karrer, *St. Francis of Assisi: the Legends and Lauds*, New York, 1947, p. 266.

In the "Sun Song," the sweet singer of God's love provides something quite other than a mere Renaissance upsurge of nature feeling. This is rather the Lord's *joculator* still celebrating His way with creatures and all creation. Light and suffering, pain and joy, fire and water, all proclaim the "Hierarchy of Heaven" and the ordered gradations of the universe held safe in the orbit of God's unchanging love. Who shall say how much of Francis' own poetry of renunciatory love, how much of his teaching of the divinely exampled poverty in Christ, how much of his passage by way of the created hierarchy to the hierarchy of heaven, is to be found in Bonaventure, in Ramon Lull, and in myriads of less famous followers?

In the "Canticle to the Sun" the renunciatory life is as regnant as in the "Rule," the "Testament," or the "Sermon to the People." Here too are the vernacular outbreathings of the little *idiota*, as Francis called himself, the free rhythms of the unprofessional *joglar*, the bursting release from temporary fears and hurts of the body, the cry of triumphant, fondly unfettered love. This is indeed a message of such joy as only the poor in spirit may know, a formula for relieving others' burdens, an occasion for celebrating, in minstrel jocularity, the call to repentance issued to the little people of all ages. The ecstasies of Alverna, the "Praises" of God and of the "Virtues," the "Song" to God in joy over his creation, all are the reminiscent celebrations of love made joyous in renunciation. They will become, moreover, the spiritual constitution for the philosopher-administrator-mystic John Fidanza, called Bonaventure, and the troubadour-missionary-mystic Lull. The hierarchy of creation, the exemplarism of divine love, the *Itinerarium* of John Fidanza, and the poverty mission of Ramon, are all here in symbol.

The "Canticle of the Sun" is veritably a triumphant chant out of suffering and approaching death—"song of praises, cry of love, of joy and of acknowledgment to the Father, infinitely good, of this boundless family which is his whole creation." [8]

[8] Gratien, *op. cit.*, p. 154.

Francis of Assisi (1182–1226)

EXPOSITION OF THE LORD'S PRAYER [9]

THE TEXT

Our Father,[10] our most blessed, most holy Creator, our Saviour and our Comforter; who art in heaven, in the angels, in the saints, enlightening them to know thee; because thou, O Lord, art the light that inflames them by thy divine love; because thou, O Lord, art the love which is in them and fills them to render them blessed; because thou, O Lord, art the highest good, and the eternal good, from which all good things come, and without which there is no good anywhere.

Hallowed be thy name: let the knowledge of thee become apparent to us, so that we may know how plentiful are thy blessings, how long thy promises, how lofty thy majesty, how profound thy judgments.[11]

Thy Kingdom come; that thou shouldst reign within us with thy grace and let us come to thy Kingdom, where we will see

---

[9] The passages that follow are taken from *St. Francis of Assisi: The Legends and Lauds*, edited, selected and annotated by Otto Karrer, and translated by N. Wydenbruck, New York, 1947. They are used by permission of the publishers, Sheed & Ward, Inc., of London and New York. The selections are, in the order of the English edition, pp. 261–62 for the "Canticle of Brother Sun," pp. 265–66 for the "Praises of the Virtues," and pp. 266–67 for the "Exposition of the Lord's Prayer." These are, in the German edition, *Franz von Assisi, Legenden und Laude*, Zürich, 1945, and in the above order, pp. 520–23; 534–37; 538–41—here in Italian-German parallels.

[10] The paraphrase of the "Pater" is, without sufficient cause, relegated to the "Dubia" by H. Boehmer and F. Wiegand, *Analekten zur Geschichte des Franciscus von Assisi*, 2d edition, Tübingen, 1930, pp. 48–49. Cf. Karrer, *Legends*, p. 260.

[11] *Longitudo promissorum tuorum, sublimitas maiestatis et profunditas iudiciorum.* Boehmer and Wiegand, *op. cit.*, p. 49.

thee face to face, and have perfect love, blessed company, and sempiternal joy.[12]

Thy will be done on earth as it is in heaven; so that we may love thee with all our heart, thinking ever of thee; with all our soul, ever desiring thee; with all our mind, directing all our intentions to thee, and seeking thy honor in all things; and with all our strength, employing all the power of our spirit and all the senses of our body in the service of thy love, and in naught else: and that we may also love our neighbors as ourselves, drawing all men, as far as it is in our power, toward thy love, rejoicing in the good things of others and grieving at their ills as at our own, and never giving offense to anyone.

Give us this day our daily bread, that is thy beloved Son, our Lord Jesus Christ, in memory of the love he bore us, and of what he said, did and suffered for us.

And forgive us our trespasses as we forgive those who trespass against us; and what we do not forgive entirely, make thou, O Lord, that we should forgive, so that for thy sake we should sincerely love our enemies, and intercede devoutly for them with thee, and never render evil for evil, and strive with thy help to be of assistance to all men.

And lead us not into temptation, hidden or manifest, sudden or protracted.

And deliver us from evil, past, present, and future.

So be it, with good will and without hope of reward.[13]

---

12 *Te visione manifesta, amore perfetto, società beata, godimento sempiterno.* Karrer, *Franz*, p. 538.

13 *E gratuitamente.* Karrer, *Franz*, p. 540.

PRAISES OF THE VIRTUES WITH WHICH THE MOST HOLY VIRGIN WAS ADORNED AND WHICH SHOULD ADORN THE HOLY SOUL

The Text

Hail, Queen Wisdom, God save thee with thy holy sister pure Simplicity.

Hail, Lady holy Poverty, God save thee with thy holy sister Humility.

Hail, Lady holy Charity, God save thee with thy sister, holy Obedience.

Hail, all you holy virtues, may God save you, he from whom you come and are derived.

There is not a man in the world who could possess even one of your number unless he first has died. He who possesses one and does not offend the others, possesses them all, but he who violates even one, possesses none at all and violates them all.

Each virtue routs vice and sin, covering them with confusion. Holy Wisdom confounds Satan and all his malice. Pure holy Simplicity confounds all the wisdom of this world and of the body. Holy Poverty confounds the cupidity, the avarice and the cares of this life.[14] Holy Humility confounds all arrogance, all the men who live for this world and likewise all things that are of the world. Holy Charity confounds all temptations of the flesh and the devil, and all fear of the flesh. Holy Obedience confounds all corporal and carnal desires and keeps a man's body mortified, so that he may obey the spirit and obey his brother, and be subject and submissive to all men in the world; and not to men alone, but also to all animals and wild beasts, so that they can do with him what they will, so far as is permitted to them by the Lord on high. Thanks be to God. Amen.

Hail, O holy Lady, most holy Queen, Mother of God, Mary,

---

14 *E le cure di questo secolo*. Karrer, *Franz*, p. 534.

thou who art everlastingly virgin, chosen by the most holy
Father in Heaven and consecrated by him with his most holy
and beloved Son and with the Holy Ghost our Comforter, thou
in whom there is and has been all fullness of grace and every
good.

Hail, palace of Christ; hail, tabernacle of Christ, hail, Mother
of Christ! [15] Hail to you, holy virtues, who by means of grace
and the illumination of the Holy Ghost are infused in the hearts
of the faithful, so that, from having been infidels, they may become members of the faith.

---

[15] *Vi saluto, palagio di Lui . . . tabernacolo . . . Madre di Lui.* Karrer, *Franz,*
p. 536; cf. Boehmer and Wiegand, *op. cit.,* p. 47.

THE CANTICLE OF BROTHER SUN [16]

The Text

Most high, omnipotent, merciful Lord,[17]
Thine is all praise, the honor and the glory and every benediction
To thee alone are they confined,
And no man is worthy to speak thy name.

Praised be thou, my Lord, with all thy creatures,
Especially for Sir Brother Sun.
Through him thou givest us the light of day,
And he is fair and radiant with great splendor,
Of thee, Most High, giving signification.[18]

Praised be thou, my Lord, for Sister Moon and the stars
Formed in the sky, clear, beautiful, and fair.
Praised be thou, my Lord, for Brother Wind,
For air, for weather cloudy and serene and every weather
By which thou to thy creatures givest sustenance.

Praised be thou, my Lord, for Sister Water,
Who is very useful and humble, precious and chaste.

Praised be thou, my Lord, for Brother Fire,
By whom thou dost illuminate the night;
Beauteous is he and jocund, robustious, and strong.[19]

[16] Karrer reminds us that this is the only text certainly known to have been conceived in the "'sweet' tongue of St. Francis's Umbria." *Legends*, p. 258. Cf. the account in the *Speculum perfectionis*, cap. 101, and see cap. 123 for the addition of the verses on death. Cf. Boehmer and Wiegand, *op. cit.*, pp. 44–45, for the full text also.

[17] *Altissimu onnipotente bon Signore.*   [18] *Porta significatione.*

[19] *Et ello è bello e jocondo
e robustoso e forte.*

Praised be thou, my Lord, for our Mother Earth,
Who sustains and rules us
And brings forth divers fruits and colored flowers and herbs.
Praised be thou, my Lord, for those who grant forgiveness
    through thy love
And suffer infirmities and tribulation.
Blessed are they who bear them with resignation,
Because by thee, Most High, they will be crowned.

Praised be thou, my Lord, for our [sister] [20] bodily Death,
From whom no living man can ever 'scape.
Woe unto those who die in mortal sin.
Blessed those who are found in thy most holy will;
To them the second death will bring no ill.
Praise and bless my Lord, render thanks to him
And serve him with great humility.

[20] The original Italian reads: *per sora nostra morte corporale*—"for our sister
    bodily Death." Karrer, *Franz*, p. 522; *Speculum perfectionis*, cap. 120;
    Boehmer and Wiegand, *op. cit.*, p. 45. Karrer, *Franz*, p. 523, reads,
    Bruder.

IV

Bonaventure (1221-1274)

INTRODUCTION

BIOGRAPHICAL NOTICE

JOHN FIDANZA WAS BORN IN TUSCANY NEAR VITERBO in 1221. Having recovered at four years of age from a malady purportedly healed by the merits and intercessions of Francis, he entered the Franciscan order between 1238 and 1243. A student of Alexander Hales at Paris, he taught there from 1248 to 1255. Together he and Thomas Aquinas fought for the rights of the Religious against the secular masters and were together made Doctors in 1257. Bonaventure became minister general of his order in 1257 and gave a balanced administration in an era of altercated interpretations of Franciscan poverty. After a visit to Mt. Alverna in 1259, he wrote his *Life of Francis,* later approved by the order in 1263. Created a cardinal in 1273 and bishop of Albano, he died at the council of Lyons in 1274. He was canonized in 1482 and declared a Doctor of the Church by Sixtus V in 1587.

SYNOPSIS

Bonaventure, with all his devotion to the academic disciplines, is a true Franciscan renunciant at heart. The *Itinerarium mentis in Deum* [1] is a genuinely revealing exposé of Francis' own postulates. The primitive Franciscan devotion is here definitely re-

---

[1] The *Itinerarium* is provocatively analyzed by P. L. Landsberg in "La philosophie d'une expérience mystique . . .," *La vie spirituelle,* Vol. 51 (1937), Supplément, pp. [71]–[85], and by P. I. Squadrani, in "S. Bonaventura christianus philosophus," *Antonianum,* Vol. 16 (1941), pp. 256–304. The text itself is in the *Opera omnia,* Quaracchi, 1891, Vol. V, pp. 295–313. See Gilson, *History of Christian Philosophy in the Middle Ages,* pp. 332 ff., on the mystical trend in Bonaventure's doctrine of "itinerary" and illuminative grades.

lated to the ecstasy of the Poverello. The prologue of this work, like Bonaventure's *Life of Francis* (ch. 13), itself, draws for its inspiration upon the spiritual Father who so feared the over-expansion of worldly wisdom. What it deduces from Francis, however, is the renounced disciple of Christ in stigmatic rapture. The Christocentrism of Bonaventure's philosophy is thus a direct heritage from Francis.

Bonaventure's philosophy may be said to be that of a mystical experience—his own as well as that of the Poverello. The plan of the *Itinerarium* was conceived by Bonaventure, thirty-three years after Francis' death, in the solitude of that same Alverna where the Little Poor Man had received the stigmata. His unique experience of love mediating the act of the spirit left its impress on the body. Both spirit and body attested to Francis' identification with the Christ, which union later became in Bonaventure's *Itinerarium* a symbolic commentary of Francis' vision on the sacred mount. Francis' experience may seem to have left all too little place for philosophical analysis. Nonetheless, Bonaventure does express that primitive *élan* in terms of a philosophical treatise with a specifically mystical consummation. The *Franciscan Vision*, as Father James translates the *Itinerarium*, is true to Francis' renunciation, even as it is true to Bonaventure's philosophical system and his mystical insight. It is "the philosophy of a mystical experience."

The treatise is built about a crucified seraph with six wings. These properly betoken the six stages of illumination by which the soul is made ready to mount from creatures Godward, and to enter the way of eternal peace. This preparation utilizes the progression of true Christian wisdom. This way is, of course, that of the burning, seraphic love of the Crucified. The six stages of illumination, then, begin with God's creatures and lead up to God. Here, again, the Franciscan orientation observed in the "Sun Song" celebrates the life experience of true Franciscanism in the universe of God's creation.

Man has three faculties. He addresses himself to three spiritual directions or outlooks (*tres aspectus principales*). The first of these employs animality or sensual perceptions (*animalitas seu sensualitas*) of the external world. The second, that of spirit (*spiritus*), permits man's entrance into himself. The third, or mind (*mens*), connotes his regard for self-transcending realities. Augustine had introduced the sense of mind (*mens*) thus inextricably oriented to the spirit's sight (*oculi mentis, acies mentis*). As re-employed by Bonaventure, mind (*mens*) indicates the inclination of the soul toward that which is beyond itself; toward spiritual things and pure truth; in a word, toward God, the Logos, and Christ, who are the very heart of Bonaventure's teaching. Doubling each of the triple aspects or directions, one gets six gradations in the soul's ascent. Thus in the range of sense perception one sees God mirrored in the external world, not only *per speculum*, i.e., as the cause of this world, but, also, *in speculo*, or as present in this outer world. Similarly, man, in gauging his interior depths, contemplates therein not only the image of the God who is his Creator and Sustainer but also the image of that One who is his intimately experienced Re-Creator and Re-Former. Finally, the soul is able to contemplate the Transcendent Being beyond him who is recognized both as the God who is the "Esse" of metaphysics and the gracious, beneficent, Trinitarian God of Christian revelation.

Following these three fundamental regards, extended as in Richard of St. Victor into six ascending stages, Bonaventure comes at last to the seventh or distinctively mystical level. At last there has been reached the intelligence-transcending, though still mentally referable, grade of ecstatic love and mystic Sabbath repose. Here, like Dionysius, he can describe better with negations of banal language than with affirmations of the ineffable.[2]

The ascent to God here marked out, then, leads along the path followed by the Christian philosopher for six steps until it attains unto the mystic rest (*requies mystica*) in the seventh chapter of the *Itinerarium*.[3] At this point, *The Triple Way* clarifies and further directs the quest.[4] For Bonaventure, with his heritage of Neoplatonic, Augustinian, and Victorine thought, theology is of three kinds: symbolical, theological (proper), and mystical. Symbolical theology teaches, in exemplarist fashion, the right employment of sensible phenomena and the way of one's being

---

[2] *Itin.*, Prolog., 3, cap. I, 4; Landsberg, *op. cit.*, pp. [77] ff.

[3] Cf. Squadrani, *op. cit.*, pp. 260 ff., 282 ff.

[4] The *De triplici via* is reprinted, together with other mystical texts from the Quaracchi *Opera*, in *Decem opuscula ad theologiam mysticam spectantia in textu correcta*, 4th ed., 1949, pp. 1–39. It is translated and interpreted in R. P. Valentin=M. Breton, *Saint Bonaventure, œuvres* . . ., Aubier, Paris, 1943, pp. 115 ff.; the *Itinerarium* is pp. 425 ff. A good commentary is R. P. Jean-Fr. Bonnefoy, *Une somme Bonaventurienne de théologie mystique: Le "De triplici via*," Paris, 1934. Cf. DS I, 1791 ff., and D. Dobbins, *Franciscan Mysticism*, New York, 1927. Consult D. Phillips, "The Way to Religious Perfection According to St. Bonaventure's De triplici via," in *Essays in Medieval Thought*, ed. by J. H. Mundy, R. W. Emery, and B. W. Nelson, Columbia University Press, New York, 1955, pp. 31–59.

raised to God by universal analogy. Theology proper, or speculative, shows the right use of intelligibles through the reason.
It renders believable things intelligible. Mystical theology en-
visages its specific goal as the following in the way that leads to
rapturous union with the Divine. It conduces to reason-tran-
scending ecstasy and to self-transcending love. Here contemplative love follows the triple, hierarchical modes of purification,
illumination, and perfection, or consummate union.[5]

The Holy Ghost effects the soul's re-creation in the image of
the Trinity. A life regularized by the operation of the virtues
knows rectified powers. Sacramental graces bring healing to the
soul's wounds. Graciously impelled and divinely elicited to the
way of perfection, the soul now takes up its final journey to contemplative heights.

Here, Francis on Mt. Alverna is its model. Divinely renewed
in its contemplative endowments and spiritually reoriented to
the life of union with Christ, the soul is prepared to traverse the
three ways of mystic ascent.[6]

For there are three ways that lead to ecstasy and perfection.
They are the perfect *trivium* subject to full exemplarist application. "The Church Militant must be conformed to the Church
Triumphant." Purification, illumination, and perfection serve
a hierarchical function. Following the law of universal analogy
and the laws of the heavenly hierarchies, they order the soul to
its proper actions and to its distinctive end.[7]

The three ways are set in clear focus. Purgation leads to
peace through the expulsion of sin. Illumination emphasizes the
truth and the imitation of Christ. Perfection and the life of
union make ready in charity the reception of the Spouse. The
first way represents withdrawal from evil. The second symbolizes perfection in good. The third marks accession to the
best and highest. In the first two ways the activity of the soul itself predominates. In the third, or the unitive, there is passivity
for the soul matched by the activity of grace.[8]

As for the purgative way, it consists in active cleansing. Mystical peace requires peace of conscience as a prime condition.
All the soul-cleansing spiritual exercises, as well as deepest
humility and the practice of the virtues, serve purificatory ends.

[5] *Itin.*, cap. 1, no. 7; Gilson, *History*, pp. 331 ff.; DS I, 1772 ff.
[6] *Itin.*, cap. 7, nos. 3–5; *Trip. via*, Prol., no. 1; cap. 1, no. 15; cap. 3, nos.
1, 13.
[7] *Trip. via*, cap. 3, no. 1; cap. 1, sec. 1; *Itin.*, cap. 4, nos. 6–7.
[8] *Trip. via*, cap. 1, nos. 3–9, 12; DS I, 1792.

These are advanced with the aid of meditation, prayer, and contemplation.[9]

The illuminative life practices the imitation of Christ according to the triple ways of meditation, prayer, and contemplation. Gifts, special exercises, devotion to the Virgin—all are placed in true perspective.[10]

The unitive way exercises and develops love to the point of mystic union. Thus a train of powder is laid for igniting the spark of wisdom. Heretofore, the activity of the soul has been paramount. Now the unitive way focuses the passivity of the spirit and the dominating action of grace. This way knows a consummate charity. Its fruit is mystic wisdom. Its proper object in love is the divine Spouse. Here is the full range of meditation. Adoration reaches its farthest limits. The eucharistic life permeates all things.[11]

Contemporary scholars observe Bonaventure's attempt at the reconstruction of human knowledge and the whole universe apropos of the unique peace of love. The ultimate end of Bonaventure's thought is, Gilson also feels, "a metaphysic of Christian mysticism." His doctrine "marks the culminating point of speculative mysticism and constitutes the most complete synthesis that it has ever achieved." [12]

"A metaphysic of Catholic mysticism," as it has been called, the doctrine of Bonaventure also reveals itself as the learned, theological expression of Francis' own religious experience. Francis' fundamental assumptions have a profound elaboration in the Bonaventurian system—a system based on the words of Christ as the way, truth, and life. The trend is that accented significantly in Bonaventure's sermon "Christ the One and Only Master." The Cross, likewise, becomes the genuine Tree of Life, *lignum vitae*. Christ, the poor man in Galilee, the Saviour on the cross, the sacrificer and sacrificed One in the Mass—he it is who, for Francis and for Bonaventure, is the heart of mystical experience as he is the epitome of renunciatory love.[13]

Many would agree that, if in *The Triple Way* we have the mystical treatise of Bonaventure, par excellence, we have in the

---

9 *Ibid.*, cap. i, nos. 3 ff.; DS I, 1793–1800.
10 *Ibid.*, cap. i, nos. 10–14.
11 *Ibid.*, cap. i, nos. 15–19, cap. 3, nos. 1–14; Dobbins, *Mysticism*, pp. 124–57; DS I, 1810–15, 1818, 1840–42; Bonnefoy, *op. cit.*, pp. 42 ff.
12 *La philosophie de Saint Bonaventure*, 3d ed., Paris, 1953, p. 396; *History*, pp. 331 ff.; DS I, 1841.
13 DS I, 1841–42; cf. the sermon in Breton, *op. cit.*, pp. 369 ff.; the *lignum vitae*, in *Decem opusc.*, pp. 155 ff.; also Breton, *op. cit.*, pp. 235 ff.

philosophical *Itinerarium* no less a clue to the contemplative consummation.

Bonaventure is the exposition via philosophy of a Franciscan primitivism that elucidates Francis' own mysticism. In Bonaventure and through him there come to expression the exemplarist directions and the Christocentric passion, as well as the hierarchical ordering, that will play so large a part in Ramon Lull's contemplative experience. With Gilson, as we read Bonaventure's works, we can almost imagine "a Saint Francis of Assisi gone philosopher and lecturing at the University of Paris." [14]

[14] *History*, p. 340.

Bonaventure (1221-1274)

THE JOURNEY OF THE MIND TO GOD [15]

THE TEXT

Chapter I

Degrees of the Soul's Ascent: God's Footprints in Creation [16]

1. "Happy the man whose help is from Thee, when he hath set pilgrimages in his heart through the Valley of Tears, to the goal he hath fixed." [17] Since happiness is nothing else but the enjoyment of the Supreme Good, and the Supreme Good is above us, no one can be happy who does not rise beyond himself. This raising up of man is to be understood, of course, of mind and heart and not of body, and since there is question of reaching above himself on the part of man, he must be helped by supernatural strength and be lifted up by a higher power that stoops to raise him. However much, then, a man's inward steps are ordered and progress made, it is of no avail unless accompanied by help from on high. But divine aid is at hand for those who seek it with a devout and humble heart, and sigh for it in this Valley of Tears; this is done by fervent prayer. Prayer is, therefore, the source and origin of every upward progress that has God for goal. Wherefore, Dionysius in his "Mystical Theology," wishing to instruct us in these transcendent workings of the soul, sets down prayer as the first condition. Let us each, therefore,

[15] Chapters 1 and 7 are here reproduced by permission of Burns, Oates and Washbourne, Ltd., from Father James's *The Franciscan Vision: Translation of St. Bonaventure's "Itinerarium mentis in Deum,"* London, 1937, pp. 13–22, and 69–74. See the original text in Vol. V of the Quaracchi *Opera omnia*, pp. 295–313.

[16] See G. Boas, tr., *Saint Bonaventura: The Mind's Road to God*, The Liberal Arts Press, New York, 1953, p. 7, note 1, on the inadequacy of translating *vestigia* as "vestiges," "footprints," or even "traces," as he himself does. Bonaventure simply means, he thinks, "that by considering the work of art one will know the artist." On the analysis of *vestigia*, see Gilson, *History*, pp. 332 ff., and Squadrani, *op. cit.*, pp. 262 ff.

[17] Ps. 83:6–7 (84:5–6).

have recourse to prayer and say to our Lord God: "Lead me, O Lord, on thy path, that I may walk in thy truth. Let my heart rejoice that it feareth thy name." [18]

2. By so praying we are led to discern the degrees of the soul's ascent to God. For, inasmuch as, in our present condition, this universe of things is a ladder whereby we may ascend to God, since among these things some are God's footprints, some God's image, some corporeal, some spiritual, some temporal, some eternal, and, hence, some outside of us, and some inside, it follows that if we are to attain to the contemplation of the First Principle and Source of all things, in himself altogether spiritual, eternal, and above us, we must begin with God's footprints which are corporeal, temporal, and outside us and so enter on the Way that leads to God. We enter in within our own souls, which are images of the eternal God, spiritual and interior to us, and this is to enter into the Truth of God. Finally, we must reach out beyond and above ourselves to the region of the eternal and supereminently spiritual and look to the First Principle of all, and that is to enjoy the knowledge of God in reverential contemplation of his majesty.

3. Here we have the three days' journey in the wilderness: "The Lord God of the Hebrews hath called us: we will go three days' journey into the wilderness, to sacrifice unto the Lord, our God." [19] Here we have also the threefold illumination of the day in Genesis when the Lord divided the light from darkness, when the first was evening as it were, the second morning, and the third was noonday. We have also that triple existence of things, first in matter, then in mind, and finally in the divine art, as it is written: "Let it be made, he accomplished, and it was made." [20] Finally, there is reference to the triple substance of Christ, who is the Way to God, that is, to the corporeal, the spiritual, and the divine.

4. In direct relation with this threefold progress of the soul to God, the human mind has three fundamental attitudes or outlooks. The first is toward corporeal things without, and in this respect it is designated as animal or simply sensual; the next is where it enters in within itself to contemplate itself, and here it ranks as spirit; the third is where its upward glance is beyond itself, and then it is designated *"mens"* or mind.[21] In all three

---

[18] Cap. 1, sec. 1; cf. cap. 7, no. 5 of the *Itin.*; cf. Ps. 85 (86):11; *Trip. via*, cap. 2.
[19] Ex. 3:18.   [20] Gen. 1:3.
[21] Cf. Landsberg, *op. cit.*, pp. [77] ff.; Squadrani, *op. cit.*, p. 260.

ways the human soul must prepare to raise itself to God so that
it may love him with the whole mind, with all its heart, and
with its whole soul,[22] for in this consists the fullness of the law
and the highest Christian wisdom.[23]

5. But since every one of the aforesaid modes is doubled,
according as we come to consider God as Alpha and as Omega,[24]
or according as we come to contemplate God in each as in and
through a mirror,[25] or because each of these modes of contemplation may be joined with another, or operative simply and
purely in itself, so it is necessary that these three primary grades
should be raised to the number six; whence, as God completed
the universal world in six days, and rested on the seventh, so the
smaller world of man is led in the most orderly way, by six successive grades of illumination, to the quiet of contemplation.
A symbol of this may be seen in the six steps that led to the
throne of Solomon;[26] in the six-winged seraphim which Isaiah
beheld in vision;[27] in the six days after which God called Moses
from the midst of darkness;[28] and in the six days after which, as
read in Matthew, Christ led his disciples up into a mountain,
and was transfigured before them.[29]

6. Corresponding to the six degrees of the soul's ascent to God
there are within the soul six kinds of faculties or powers by
which we rise from depths to the heights, from external to
things internal, from things of time to those of eternity, to wit,
sense, imagination, reason, intellect, intelligence, and the fine
point or apex of the soul.[30] These powers we have implanted in
us by nature; by sin deformed, they are reformed through
grace; and they must be purified by justice, exercised by knowledge, and made perfect by wisdom.

7. In his primitive constitution man was created by God
capable of untroubled contemplation, and for that reason was
placed by God in a "garden of delights." But, turning his back
on the true light in order to pursue the mutable good, he found
himself, through his own fault, diminished and removed from
his pristine stature. With him the whole human race, through
original sin, was afflicted in a twofold manner: the human mind

22 Mark 12:30.
23 *Trip. via*, cap. 3, no. 7; cf. Bonnefoy, *op. cit.*, pp. 66 and 54 ff.
24 Rev. 1:8.
25 As to "*per* speculum et *in* speculo," see Squadrani, *op. cit.*, pp. 260 ff., and
Landsberg, *op. cit.*, p. [78].
26 I Kings 10:19.　　　　　　　　27 Isa. 6:2.
28 Ex. 24:16.　　　　　　　　　　29 Matt. 17:1.
30 Cf. the introduction to the Victorines and notes on the six grades.

by ignorance and the human body by concupiscence. As a result man, blinded and bent down, sits in darkness and sees not the light of heaven, unless he be strengthened against concupiscence by grace with justice, and against ignorance by knowledge with wisdom. All this is done by Jesus Christ, "who of God is made unto us wisdom and justice and sanctification and redemption." [31] He, being the Power and Wisdom of God, the incarnate Word full of grace and truth, is the Author of both grace and truth. He it is who infuses the grace of charity which, when it comes "from a pure heart, and a good conscience, and an unfeigned faith," is capable of ordering the whole soul according to the threefold aspect above mentioned. He also taught the knowledge of truth according to the triple mode of theology: by symbolic theology in which he teaches us how we might rightly use sensible things, by theology properly so called wherein we learn the use of things intelligible, and by mystical theology through contact with which we may be raised aloft to things unspeakable. [32]

8. Whoso, therefore, would set out in quest of God must first leave aside such sins as deform nature, and engage in the exercise of the aforesaid powers of his soul. By prayer he may hope for grace which will readjust his powers in harmony; in a holy life he must seek for purifying justice; in meditation he will seek that knowledge which enlighteneth; in contemplation he will acquire perfecting wisdom. Therefore, just as no one comes to wisdom save through grace, justice, and knowledge, so no one comes to contemplation save by clear-sighted meditation, by a holy life and devout prayer. As grace is the foundation of an upright will, and of a clear-sighted enlightened reason, so we must first pray, then live holily, and thirdly, we must look long and attentively at the manifestations of truth; and, so attending, we must rise, step by step, until we reach the high mountain where God of gods is seen in Sion. [33]

9. Since it is imperative first to make the ascent of Jacob's ladder before we can hope to descend, let us place the first step of the ascent at the bottom, holding up this whole sensible world before us as a mirror, through which we may rise to God,

---

31 I Cor. 1:30.
32 *Scilicet symbolicae, propriae et mysticae . . . per mysticam rapiamur ad supermentales excessus, Opera omnia*, V, 298; Bonnefoy, *op. cit.*, pp. 72 ff.
33 See *Trip. via*, Prol., and its references to Dionysius, *Hiér. cél.*, III, 2, VII, 3, IX, 2, and X, etc.; *Hiér. eccl.*, I, 2; Hugh's *Didascalion*, Lib. III, cap. 11, etc. Ps. 83:8 (84:7).

the supreme Craftsman. In that way we shall be true Israelites passing forth from the land of Egypt to the land of promise, and also true Christians going forth from this world to the Father, and lovers of wisdom who answer the call which says: "Come unto me all ye that desire me, and be ye filled with mine offspring." "For from the greatness and beauty of created things, their Creator may be seen and known." [34]

10. The supreme wisdom, power, and benevolence of the Creator are reflected in all created things. This is intimated in a threefold manner by the adjustment of external and internal senses in man. The bodily senses minister to the mind, whether it be engaged in rational investigation, in docile faith, or in intellectual contemplation. In contemplation it considers the actual existence of things; in faith it examines the unfolding of events; and in reasoning it surmises their potential pre-excellence.

11. The first point of view, which is that of contemplation, considering things in themselves, discerns in them weight, number, and measure: weight which marks the point to which they tend, number whereby they are distinguished, and measure whereby they are limited. Hereby it sees in things mode, species, order, as well as substance, virtue, and action, from which the mind may arise, as from footprints, to the knowledge of the power, wisdom, and boundless goodness of the Creator.

12. The second point of view, which is that of faith, when it considers the universe, goes on to reflect upon its origin, its course, and its end. For "by faith we understand that the world was framed by the word of God." [35] By faith we know that the three epochs—of nature, of the law, and of grace—have succeeded one another in order. By faith we know that the world will terminate with a final judgment. In the first, we observe God's power; in the second, his providence; and in the third, his justice.

13. The third point of view, that of reason, when it investigates the universe recognizes that some things have only being, others being and life, and others possess not only being and life but knowledge and discernment. This gives us three levels of reality, ranging from lowest to highest. From this viewpoint, also, it is clear that some things are merely corporeal, and some partly corporeal and partly spiritual, while others, ranking highest in perfection and dignity, are purely spiritual. Likewise some things, it is seen, are mutable and corruptible, such as

terrestrial things; others are mutable and incorruptible, such as celestial bodies; whence it may be concluded that some things are both immutable and incorruptible, such as supercelestial things. From these visible things, therefore, the human mind rises up to consider the power and goodness and wisdom of God in whom reside Being and Life and Intelligence, in a purely spiritual, incorruptible, and immutable state.

14. This reflection may be amplified and rounded off by taking into account the sevenfold condition of all creatures as a witness to the power and goodness and wisdom of God. Thus we may consider apart the origin, magnitude, multitude, beauty, plenitude, action, and order of all things. For the origin of things, in respect to their creation, their distinction and splendor as seen in the work of the six days, proclaims the power of God, producing all things from nothing; the wisdom of God, clearly arranging and distinguishing all things; the goodness of God, generously adorning all things. The immensity of creation according to mass in length, breadth, and depth, and according to the excellence of power extending itself in length, breadth, and depth as is revealed in the diffusion of light, and according to the efficacy of action, intimate, continuous, and diffused as is manifested in the action of fire, brings home to us the power and wisdom and goodness of the triune God, who is uncircumscribed by space and who is present to all created things by his power, his presence, and his essence. The multitude of things created in respect to their diversity, general, special, and individual, in substance and in form or figure, and in efficacy, beyond all human estimation, manifestly insinuates and displays the immensity of the three above-mentioned conditions in God. The beauty of things, in respect of their variety of light, figure, and color, in bodies simple, mixed, and organized, as in the heavenly bodies and minerals, as in stones and metals, plants and animals, likewise proclaims these same three divine qualities. The plenitude of things, matter being full of forms by virtue of its *rationes seminales*,[36] forms being full of power, and ordained to efficacy, manifestly announces the same conclusion. See the manifold and diverse character of activity in the universe according as it is natural, artificial, or moral and realize that its very variety points to the immensity of that power, art, and goodness which indeed is to all things the cause of their being, the ground of their understanding, and the ultimate reason of their harmony. The order to be discerned in the book of

36 "Seminal reasons"; cf. Boas, *op. cit.*, p. 13.

creation, in respect to the ratio of duration, situation, and influence, namely, by first and last, superior and inferior, noble and ignoble, indicates the primacy, sublimity, and dignity of the First Principle in relation to the infinitude of power. In the book of the Scriptures the order of the divine laws, precepts, and judgments indicates the immensity of divine wisdom, and in the body of the Church the order of the divine sacraments, benefits, and retributions indicates the treasures of God's goodness. The very existence of order leads us thus by the hand to that which is first and highest, mightiest, wisest, and best.

15. Whosoever, then, misses this all-pervading splendor of things, and is not enlightened to behold it, is blind; he who is not awakened by such thunders is deaf; he who, looking on such effects, is not prompted to praise is dumb; and he who in the presence of such intimations of God does not behold the First Principle of creation must be pronounced a fool. Open, therefore, thine eyes; draw near with ears of spiritual hearing; unseal thy lips and apply thy heart, that in all created things thou mayest see, hear, praise, love, magnify, and honor God, lest perchance the universal frame of things should rise up against thee. A time will come when for this reason the whole universe will fight against the foolish [37] and on that day it will redound to the glory of the wise who can say with the prophet: "For thou gladdenest me, Lord, by thy deeds; I rejoice o'er the works of thy hands." [38] "How manifold are thy works, O Lord. All of them in wisdom thou hast made. The earth is full of thy creations." [39]

Chapter VII

The Quiet of Contemplation

1. In its progress toward the possession of God the soul has now passed through six stages. The number of these gradients in the journey of the soul is not without its own significance. Six steps led up to the throne of Solomon and to peace, where, as in some inner Jerusalem, the true man of peace reposed in peace of soul. Six wings too enveloped the seraph, thereby suggesting to us a picture of the true contemplative raised up from things of earth and enlightened by supernal wisdom. And in six days was the labor of creation completed before the rest of the Sabbath supervened. Recall these six stages of human progress toward the quiet of contemplation. In the first, the soul was led to

[37] Wis. 5:21.   [38] Ps. 91:5 (92:4).   [39] Ps. 103 (104):24.

God by going out to external things to admire in them the work
of God's creative power. Then, looking at creation, the soul beheld God's footprints upon the world's surface: the material
world became a mirror in which it beheld its God. Next, turning
its attention inward to itself, the soul began to reach God from
a consideration of itself as God's created image, and then a
further step was made when it began to behold God in the
mirror of its renovated being. Whereupon, the soul was led to
raise its gaze above and beyond itself, seeking, as it were, the
light of God's countenance and rejoicing in its own progress.
But no rest was possible until it found God in his own reflected
light, for all this progress was achieved in a degree suitable for
those who are still pilgrims on the way to God and who must
depend upon their own efforts to scale the heights of contemplation. But when the soul shall have reached the sixth step and
begun to contemplate the First and Highest Principle of all and
Jesus Christ, the Mediator of God and man, then it shall have
contact with spiritual things, so sublime that any comparison
with created things becomes impossible and so deeply mysterious that all intellectual keenness is unavailing. Then it will
be swept up, not only beyond the wonders of all creation, but
out of its very self and above it. By means of Jesus Christ, the
Way, the Door, the Ladder, shall this transition be effected, for
he is, as it were, the Seat of Mercy, placed over the ark of God,
and the Sacrament hidden from the ages.

2. With face fully turned toward this Seat of Mercy, seeing
him hanging on the cross, in faith, hope, charity, devotion, delight, exaltation, appreciation, praise, and jubilation, the soul
is ready to celebrate its Passover, that is, its transition from
things of time to the eternal, passing over, by the power of the
Cross, the Red Sea into the desert, where it will begin to taste the
hidden manna, there to rest in the tomb of Christ, to all appearance dead, yet experiencing, in so far as a pilgrim may, what
was promised on the hill of Calvary to the good thief: "This day
thou shalt be with me in paradise." [40]

3. This was the vision of Blessed Francis on the lofty mountain, where he was raised into an ecstasy of contemplation [41]
and upon which I thought out the things here written. To him
appeared a six-winged seraph fastened to a cross. From the
companion who was with him when these things happened and
when he was taken up by God in ecstasy, I and many others

[40] Luke 23:43.
[41] *Cum in excessu contemplationis in monte excelso.* . . .

have gathered this account. In this, Blessed Francis, another Jacob become Israel, is for us a perfect model of the contemplative life, just as hitherto he had proved himself outstanding in the life of action, so that more by the force of his example than by word, God invited the truly spiritual to seek after such quiet of contemplation and ecstasy of soul as was experienced by him on Mount Alvernia.[42]

4. If this transition, however, is to be genuine and perfect, then must all labor on the part of the soul's reasoning faculty cease and the soul's deep affection be centered in God and transformed, as it were, into him. So mysterious and sublime is this experience that none save he to whom it has been given knows anything of it, that nobody receives except he who desires it, and this desire comes to him only whose being is inflamed by the fire of the Holy Spirit sent by Christ upon the earth. Hence it is that the "hidden things" of God were revealed, as the apostle says, by the Holy Ghost.[43]

5. Since, therefore, to arrive at this rapturous state of soul nature is of no avail and human industry of comparatively little value, little heed must be paid to inquiry but much to unction, little account must be taken of human language but much of internal experience of joy, attention must be weaned away from words and writing so as to concentrate on God's gift to man, his Holy Spirit. In a word, the human soul must turn away its eyes from all created essences to fix them on the uncreated Essence of the Father, the Son, and the Holy Ghost; the words of Dionysius must well up within it and address themselves to the triune God: "O supereminent and transcendent Holy Trinity, inspiration of all Christian philosophy, direct our steps to the unknown, sublime, and resplendent heights of mystic utterances. On these heights are to be found the new, the absolutely unquestionable and unchanging, mysteries of theology, hidden away, as it were, in the obscurity of excessively lightsome darkness and illuminating silence. Here on these heights, so resplendent in their excessive light, men are enlightened and spiritual souls are filled with the splendors of the true good." These things we address to God. But to the friend to whom this writing is directed we also speak and say: Do thou, O friend, push on boldly to the mystic vision, abandon the work of the senses and

---

[42] *Life of Francis*, ch. 13; *Trip. via*, cap. 1, nos. 15–17; cap. 3, nos. 1, 8, 11–14; cf. Gen. 35:10.
[43] I Cor. 2:10. Cf. Dionysius, *Mystical Theology*, cap. 3, and *Divine Names*, cap. 7, no. 3.

the operations of the reasoning faculty, leave aside all things visible and invisible, being and nonbeing, and cleave as far as possible, and imperceptibly, to the unity of Him who transcends all essences and all knowledge. In this immeasurable and absolute elevation of soul,[44] forgetting all created things and liberated from them, thou shalt rise above thyself and beyond all creation to find thyself within the shaft of light that flashes out from the divine, mysterious darkness.[45]

6. But if thou wouldst know how such things are accomplished, then ask grace, not learning; desire, not understanding; the groanings of prayer, not industry in study; the Spouse, not the master; God, not man; obscurity, not clarity. Seek not so much light as fire which inflames one totally, filling the soul with unction and ardent desires, and raising it out of its very self aloft to God. This fire is indeed God, whose "furnace is in Jerusalem." [46] It was kindled on earth by the Man Jesus, in the fervor of his most ardent passion. In this fervor he participates who can say: "My soul hath chosen strangling and my bones death." [47] He shall see God who chooses such a death, for it is undoubtedly true that "man shall not see me and live." [48] Let us die, therefore, and by the door of death enter into this darkness. Let us impose silence on our anxieties, our concupiscences, and upon the working of our imagination. Let us, with Christ crucified, pass from this world to the Father, that when he shall be revealed to us we may say with Philip, "It is enough for us."[49] Let us listen with St. Paul to the words: "My grace is sufficient for thee." [50] Let us cry out exultingly with David: "My flesh and my heart faileth, but God is the strength of my heart and my portion for ever." [51] "Blessed be the Lord for evermore; and let all the people say: Amen and Amen." [52]

---

44 *Etenim te ipso et omnibus immensurabili et absoluto purae mentis excessu.* . . .
45 See the *Mystical Theology*, cap. 1, no. 1, and our introduction to Dionysius. Note the relation of the *Trip. via*, cap. 3, no. 13, to the negative and affirmative ways of Dionysius as well as the *Mystical Theology*, caps. 1–5, and the *Hiér. cél.*, cap. 2, no. 3. See the notes, 1–3, to the *Itin.*, cap. 7, no. 5, in the *Opera omnia*, Vol. V, p. 313. Cf. Dionysius the Carthusian, *De contemplatione*, Lib. III, art. 8, on Dionysius the Areopagite, *Opera omnia*, Tournai, 1912, Vol. XLI, pp. 263–64, and the *divina caligo*. Cf. Bonnefoy, *op. cit.*, pp. 69 ff., on this light flashing out "from the divine mysterious darkness." Cf. Squadrani, *op. cit.*, pp. 284–86 and notes. Note that Bonaventure employs the edition of Scotus Eriugena (MPL 122) for Dionysius.
46 Isa. 31:9.   47 Job 7:15.   48 Ex. 33:20.
49 John 14:8.   50 II Cor. 12:9.
51 Ps. 72 (73):26.   52 Ps. 88:53 (89:52).

V

Ramon Lull (c. 1232-1315)

INTRODUCTION

BIOGRAPHICAL NOTICE

RAMON LULL WAS BORN IN 1232, OR PERHAPS 1235, of noble Catalan parents at Palma in Mallorca. About 1246 he entered the service of King Don Jaimie II. In 1257, after a period of courtly amours, he married. He was converted sometime between 1263 and 1265. The years 1265 to 1274 were given over to study and writing, with *The Great Book of Contemplation* being produced between 1272 and 1277. In all his literary productivity and traveling, the missionary aims of his life were paramount. These were the motivation for his lecturing, establishing language schools such as the Mallorcan college of Miramar founded in 1276, and his visiting temporal and spiritual princes as well as Church councils. He may have entered the religious life as early as 1275, with initial affinities for the Dominicans and possible membership in the Franciscan Third Order in 1292 or 1295. From 1277 to 1282 he traveled widely. He first attended the Dominican Chapter general in 1283, the year of his beginning *The Blanquerna*. This was redolent of Franciscan ideals though he did not visit the Minors' Chapter general until 1287. He carried on various missionary enterprises in Asia (1279), Armenia (1302), Africa (1280, 1292 or 1293, 1306, 1314–1315). He wrote over three hundred works in Catalan and Latin, of which the *Grand Art* was one of the most famous. In spite of his lacking a degree, he lectured at Paris with varying degrees of approval in 1287–1289, 1297–1299, and 1309–1311. He attended the council of Vienne in 1311 to press for language teaching preparatory to effective Christian missions. His last missionary journey was in North Africa, where he was stoned by a mob of Arabs at Bugia in Tunis. According to legend he expired thereupon, June 29,

1315, but he may have returned to Palma to die of his wounds as late as 1316.

BIBLIOGRAPHICAL ESSAY

The best biography in English is A. E. Peers, *Ramon Lull*, S.P.C.K., London, 1929. See the anonymous *Vida coetània*, ed., F. D. Moll, Palma de Mallora, 1935. Compare the Latin *Vita*, edited by J. B. Sollier, in the *Acta sanctorum*, re-edited by J. Carnandet, Paris and Rome, 1867, June, Vol. 7, pp. 606–618; also the Mayence edition of the *Opera*, Vol. I, pp. 1–12, below. See L. Wadding, *Annales minorum*, Quaracchi, 1931–1935, Vols. 4–6. Source literature is fully given in Peers and with specialized details in Petry, "Social Responsibility and the Late Medieval Mystics," *Church History*, Vol. 21, no. 1 (March, 1952), pp. 5–7, 16–17. The works are available in the *Opera omnia*, ed., Y. Salzinger *et al.*, 8 vols., 1–6, 9–10, Mayence, 1721–1742, and in the *Obres*, 14 vols., Palma de Mallorca, 1906–1928. An invaluable study is C. Ottaviano, *L'ars compendiosa de R. Lull*, J. Vrin, Paris, 1930, with chronological orientation of Lull's works. P. Golubovich, *Biblioteca Bio-Bibliografica della Terra Santa*, Quaracchi, 1906, Vol. I, pp. 361–392 gives a useful *vita*, chronology, and literature. Helpful résumés are supplied by M. P. E. Littré and B. Hauréau, in the *Histoire littéraire de la France*, Vol. 29 (Paris, 1885), pp. 1–386; by E. Longpré in *Dict. théol. cath.*, Vol. 9, no. 1 (Paris, 1926), pp. 1072–1141; and by P. O. Keicher, "Raymundus Lullus und seine Stellung zur arabischen Philosophie," *Beiträge*, Vol. 7, pts. 4-5 (Münster i/W, 1909), pp. 1–223. An excellent study with a newly edited text of the Catalan *Art of Contemplation*, is J. H. Probst, "La mystique de Ramon Lull et l'art de contemplació" in the *Beiträge*, Vol. 13, pts. 2–3 (Münster i/W, 1914), pp. 1–126. See Peers, *op. cit.*, pp. 170, 415 ff., for Lull's Franciscanism.

SYNOPSIS

Ramon Lull was a true son of Francis. His earliest spiritual associations upon leaving family, wealth, and the world seem, perhaps, more specifically oriented to the Preaching Order than to the Friars Minor. Yet these orders appear for him, from the very first, to have played mutually reinforcing roles.

As frequently observed, Lull follows closely the path of Bonaventure's *Itinerarium*. Here is the hierarchical ordering in which one makes the meditational ascent from creatures through man on the way to God and his attributes.[1] This is the route described in the little Catalan work, the *Art de contemplació*.[2]

The *Liber contemplationis*, or *The Great Book of Contemplation*,[3] distinguishes three main steps in this ascent to God, of which the first two are the sensible and the intellectual and the third an experience of mystic union that is accomplished by an ecstatic encounter of the human "Lover" and the divine "Beloved." It may be added that this encounter is at once affective and intellectual; that "it is neither pantheist, nor Freudian, nor abnormal." [4]

Ramon Lull, so often and so exclusively identified with the involved ratiocinations of the *Grand Art*, is certainly as much the protagonist of medieval Catholicism against Averroism and non-Christian faiths as he has been pictured. He is, however, something more. He is the mystic and poet as well. Thus the Lull who so consistently resorts to logic and geometric schematizations in the *Grand Art* must also be represented, in quite a different guise, as the clear, simple Franciscan. Having accepted with Bonaventure the necessity of philosophizing the truths of Christianity, Lull, in keeping with Bonaventure as well, strives to reincarnate thereby the direct, heart-moving Poverello. Even more than Bonaventure, however, Lull succeeds in throwing off the philosopher's mantle on occasion in order to wear, like Francis himself, the unassuming garb of the vernacular poet. In so doing Lull is, indeed, the Franciscan realist and exemplarist; at one and the same time, the contemplative and the man of action that both Francis and John Fidanza had been.[5]

Granted that Lull was a psychologist, he was much more. His mystical writings clearly portray the practicing troubadour of the renounced spirit. *The Blanquerna*, for instance, from which the diverse passages of this anthology are drawn, has the character of a spiritual confession. The chief characters, whether the Court fool, the Lover, or Blanquerna himself, suggest Lull personified. The Lull who argues for the faith in the ponderous tomes of the Latin treatises is not here repudiated. But, whereas

---

[1] DS II, 1991; Probst, *op. cit.*, pp. 2, 7–12.
[2] See the Probst edition, pp. 58–104, of the brief Catalan *Art de contemplació* (cf. *Obres*, Vol. 9) and the Mallorcan text of the extended *Libre de contemplació en Deu* in Vols. 2–8 of the *Obres*.
[3] The Latin text, also entitled *Liber magnus contemplationum in Deum*, is Vol. 9 (1740) and Vol. 10 (1742) in the Mayence edition of the *Opera omnia*. Compare the Catalan text in the *Obres*, Vols. 2–8, cited in note 2. See Peers, *Ramon Lull*, ch. 3.   [4] DS II, 1991; cf. Probst, *op. cit.*, pp. 1–2.
[5] Peers, *op. cit.*, pp. 401 ff., 415 ff.

in the former he celebrates the hierarchies by way of geometric demonstrations and learned dialectics, in the latter effusions of the vernacular *Contemplation*, for example, he is the burning Franciscan joculator of poverty and love. The incontestably authentic Catalan works, such as the *Lover and the Beloved* and *The Art of Contemplation*, are now incorporated in the spiritual romance, *The Blanquerna*. These depict the Franciscan poet and mystic singing the same faith so weightily set forth elsewhere. The exemplarist realism, at once Augustinian and Franciscan, that has been remarked in the Latin treatises is here subsumed as basically sound and continuously operative. Now, however, in the poetic appeal of the vernacular works, the inner reserves of the philosopher-dialectician are broken down. Never one to accent rapturous states unduly, Lull is here, nonetheless, a willing revealer of his inner inquiries, yearnings, and devotions. And the poet-mystic who emerges is a far cry from the wooden artificer of the *Grand Art*, or the half-deranged eccentric of popular misconception. His is an inspiringly balanced unity of mind and heart speaking by way of prose-poetry, in vernacular power, to the heart of the Christian ages.[6]

It has been well said that, for Lull, mysticism is not cold, dead knowledge, but something mobile, varied, and as impassioned as life itself. This is the language of love, the effusion of passionate affection for the Creator, who is the highest Good, the most absolute Beauty. However reticent about ecstatic claims, the Lord's chevalier, like Francis also, shares his actual joys in rhythmic cadences of disciplined ardor. And, even as for Francis, so for Ramon, trees, lights, fountains, water, air, and all animate beings elicit his praises of the divine Spirit, who made and rules the entire universe beneficently. The poet, the painter of inner experiences, the dreamer of celestial visions shimmering in the lights and shadows of a divine-human world, here emerges in the unified sentiment of renunciatory love.

Not all of Lull's vernacular writing is sheer affectivity any more than his entire corpus is poetry. The *Book of the Lover and the Beloved* has its foundation of metaphysics and systematic theology, even as the little *Art of Contemplation* has its lambent, prayerful poesy. We may rightfully insist on an ambivalence of the intellectual and the affective in these as in all other works of Lull. True, there is gradation in the mystical life, explicating a diversity of expressions and experiences, whether primarily

6 Probst, *op. cit.*, pp. 1–7. See the Catalan text of *The Blanquerna* in the *Obres*, Vol. 9, pp. 3–490.

affective or intellectual. At the apex, of course, is ecstasy, a rare, fleeting union with the beloved object, an ineffable familiarity with God. Below this is a semiecstatic state of union wherein the soul is preoccupied with the divine objects and not distracted by other thoughts. It is characterized by a very exalted love inexpressible except by way of affective metaphors. Lower still is a state of quietude, where the divine action on the contemplative's heart is still more or less hindered by intellectual abstraction. Here the ordinary, day-by-day, mental life is not obliterated or wholly replaced by the affective.

But whatever the gradatory of contemplative or active life, there is always apparent Lull's consistent love imagery, his encounter, at whatever level, of the Lover with his Beloved. It is a commonplace that, before his conversion, Lull moved at will in a world of sensuous love such as Francis had once envisioned afar. The life of the jongleur, of troubadours, and of beautiful ladies had been for him much more than an imaginative foray. He was no knight of fancy but rather one of all too evident fleshliness. However theoretical any speculation may be as to what effect a less concupiscent background might have had on his later spiritual amours, one thing is certain: The later, mystical loves of the Lover seeking his Beloved have all the overtones of actual chivalric existence transmuted into heavenly commerce. Like Francis, Ramon is the troubadour of the spirit, the poet of inner gallantry, the Franciscan renunciant following with courtly force the gentle, yet brutal, realism of the crucified Poverello.[7]

Ramon Lull is, then, a meditative renunciant who also reveals to his readers his own personal experiences within the hierarchy of worlds, i.e., the divine, human, and natural. His mystical writings mix didactic moralism, ascetic admonitions, and mystical confessions. In hierarchical benediction, the lower world serves for the understanding of the higher; it permits the passage from finite to infinite. Reflecting upon the profound implications of nature and life, Lull progresses to the comprehension of the soul and of human destiny, from which he mounts to the knowledge of God and his majestic intent for the universe. Not only in the *Grand Art* and in *The Great Book of Contemplation*, but also in *The Blanquerna* and in other mystical works, Ramon conveys his exemplarist assumptions. More and more, the divine Lord, the One passionately beloved of the human lover, is encountered in the ascent from the world of creatures,

7 Probst, *op. cit.*, p. 7.

through the world of the human soul, to the world of the divine consummation. Everywhere divine love shows the way, even as human love thereby learns to follow in the way.

And the way outlined is that of the Poor Man of Galilee; the renounced Lord who comes down into the hands of priests in the Mass; the teaching, preaching, loving Master of all life who calls upon his followers for a sacrificial, missionary evangelism among the infidels. In *The Blanquerna* as we have it today, then, the whole story is unfolded. The little *Art of Contemplation* now attached to *The Blanquerna* is the most typical expression of Lullian mysticism after the *Book of the Lover and the Beloved*, which it completes and explains. *The Art of Contemplation* contains the epitome of Ramon's ascetic and mystical principles without the redundancies and reduplications of the larger treatises. The *Book of the Lover and the Beloved* exalts the divine majesty even while it pays tribute to the Augustinian, Franciscan psychology of memory, understanding, and will. Nature is heavily levied upon as a stage in the contemplation of the Creator. Properly employing the fittingly disciplined imagination, one may, in contemplating creatures, discover divine participations in corporal things. Exalting these divine workings as seen in spiritual objects, to which one applies his understanding, one goes on by an act of will to adore these divine participations in the created universe. A similar hierarchical concern is spelled out in the little *Art of Contemplation*.

All the chapters of the *Art* are prayers to God or meditations on his magisterial grandeur. They are systematic reflections on the sacraments, on the divinely approved virtues, even as they are aspersions against the disapproved actions, the vices. Here, above all, is the spiritual reporting of a spirit capable of reflecting, and of leading others to meditate, upon nature, the inner world of man, and God, in order that all may come into the realm transcendent.

In résumé, one finds in Ramon Lull, generally, and in *The Blanquerna*, especially, the drama of Franciscan renunciation. Lull is the follower of the Poor Christ; the court fool for human kings; the court troubadour and sweet singer of God's praises in the heavenly mansions. He is the preacher and teacher of the gospel; the disputer and proclaimer of Catholic truth; the missionary for the heavenly gentry and the Queen of Heaven among the world's unbelievers; the knight of the poor Lord and the gracious Lady. Above all, he is the practicer of *The Art of Contemplation*, the reader and teacher out of the *Book of the Lover and the Beloved.* He capitalizes the mind, the university, the monastery, the pontificate, for Christian instruction and evangelization via the learned disciplines and the world's languages. He lays hold upon the heart for the visions, the inner movements of the spirit, the propulsive affections of the soul that lead to divine union.[8]

[8] *Ibid.*, pp. 7–30.

Ramon Lull (c. 1232-1315)

THE BLANQUERNA [9]: THE LULLIAN IDEAL

THE TEXT

Chapter LXXX

Gloria in Excelsis Deo

The Pope Blanquerna went into the consistory with the cardinals to the end that through their good works glory might be given to God in the heavens; [10] and the pope said to the cardinals that he prayed them that they would assist him to use his office to the glory of God, in such wise that they might be able to bring men back to the first intent of the offices and the sciences, namely, that glory might be given to God; for the world has come to such a sinful state that there is scarce any man who has his intent directed toward that thing for the which he was created, nor for the which he holds the office which is his. While the pope spake thus with the cardinals, a Saracen messenger came before him and the cardinals, and presented to him a letter from the soldan of Babylon. In that letter were written many things, and among them the soldan said to the pope that he marveled greatly concerning him, and concerning all the kings and princes of the Christians, that in conquering the Holy Land beyond the seas they acted according to the manner of the prophet Mahomet, who held by force of arms the lands which he conquered. He marveled that the pope and the Christians worked not after the manner of Jesus Christ and of the apostles, who through preaching and through martyrdom converted the world, and that they followed not the manner of those who preceded them in conquering other countries; for this cause, he

---

[9] The English text here utilized is that of *Blanquerna: A Thirteenth Century Romance*, translated from the Catalan of Ramon Lull by E. Allison Peers, London, 1925, pp. 322–31, 411 ff., 485–88, 492–96. Used by permission of Jarrolds Publishers. The Catalan text is Vol. 9 of the *Obres*, Commissio Editora Lulliana, Palma de Mallorca, 1914.

[10] *En los cels.*

said, God willed not that they should possess the Holy Land beyond the seas.[11] These letters the Saracen brought to the holy Apostolic Father, and like letters brought he to the kings and princes of the Christians. Deeply thought the pope and the cardinals upon the words which the soldan had written to them; and Ramón the Fool [12] spake these words: "Faith sent Hope to Contrition, that she might send her Devotion and Pardon, to the end that they might honor her in those places wherein her Beloved is dishonored." The Jester of Valor said that Valor is brought to great dishonor in those places wherein the Son of God and the apostles did her more grace and honor than in any place that is in the world. After these words there entered the court a messenger bringing the news that two unbelievers had been suborned to slay a Christian king, and that they had now themselves been delivered up to a cruel death. When he had spoken these words, the Jester of Valor said: "Of what avail are the humility and charity of Jesus Christ which he had himself toward his people, when he willed to suffer passion of them, if unbelievers, who are in error, have greater devotion in dying for their master than have Christians in honoring their superior?" The Fool saw two cardinals speaking, and he supposed that they spake of his Beloved, but they spake of the election of two bishops who had been elected after a contest; wherefore the Fool said to the cardinals that the most pleasant words are those that are between the Lover and the Beloved.

2. The pope was marvelously moved to ordain how that example might be given of the faith of Holy Church and how the devotion to the honor of God which aforetime existed might return; so he sent messengers throughout divers lands to the superiors of religious houses and to the Masters of the Temple and of the Hospital that they should come to speak with him concerning the making of ordinances whereby glory should be given to God. When all these had come, and were before the pope and the cardinals, Ramón the Fool spake thus: "The Lover and the Beloved met, and kept silence with their tongues; and their eyes, wherewith they made signs of love, were in tears; and the love of the one spake with the love of the other." "This story," said the Jester of Valor, "has relation to that which has been reported to the Holy Father and the cardinals concerning the soldan and the assassins; and if naught that is useful follows

---

11 We may recall Roger Bacon's like concern for preaching missions.
12 Note Ramon's dual role in representing Blanquerna's ideals and his own
—actually two projections of the same renunciatory theme.

therefrom, great wrong is done to Valor, and the most honorable of creatures, who die for love, are not loved; albeit it is of greater valor that lovers should speak the one to the other than that mouths should eat." The Fool said: "A certain man wrote, and in a book he wrote the names of lovers and loved, and a man that was a lover inquired of him if in that book he had written the name of his beloved; and he that wrote said to him: 'Hast thou eaten food that was cooked with the fire of love? And hast thou washed thine hands with the tears of thine eyes? And art thou inebriated and become as a fool through the love which thou hast drunk? Hast thou ever been in peril that thou mightest honor thy beloved? Hast thou the materials of love wherewith a man may make ink for thy beloved to write? If all these things be not so, then is thy beloved not worthy to be written of in this book.'"

3. After these words, the pope and the cardinals and the Religious, to honor the glory of God, ordained that to all monks that had learning there should be assigned friars to teach divers languages, and that throughout the world there should be builded divers houses, which for their needs should be sufficiently provided and endowed, according to the manner of the monastery of Miramar, which is in the island of Majorca.[13] Right good seemed this ordinance to the pope and to all the rest, and the pope sent messengers through all the lands of the unbelievers to bring back certain of them to learn their language and that they at Rome might learn the tongues of these unbelievers, and that certain men should return with them to preach to the others in these lands, and that of those unbelievers that learned Latin, and gained a knowledge of the holy Catholic faith, should be given money and garments and palfreys, that they might praise the Christians, who when they had returned to their own lands would continue to assist and maintain them.

4. Of the whole world the pope made twelve parts, and appointed to represent him twelve men, who should go each one throughout his part and learn of its estate, to the end that the pope might know the estate of the whole world. It came to pass that those who went to the unbelievers brought from Alexandria and from Georgia and from India and Greece Christians

13 A continuing preoccupation with Lull, culminating in his only partly successful plea to the council of Vienne in 1311. Cf. Petry, "Social Responsibility," *Church History*, Vol. 21, no. 1, pp. 6–7, and note 19, pp. 16–17, for the sources; cf. H. J. Schroeder, *Disciplinary Decrees of the General Councils*, St. Louis, 1937, pp. 395–96, 615–16.

who were monks, that they might dwell among us, and that their will might be united with the will of our monks, and that during this union and relationship they might be instructed in divers manners concerning certain errors against the faith, and should then go and instruct those that were in their country. Wherefore the pope sent also some of our monks to the monks aforesaid, and ordered that each year they should send to him a certain number of their friars, that they might dwell with us, and, while they dwelt among us, learn our language.

5. "Beloved sons!" said the pope to the monks: "Jews and Saracens are among us who believe in error, and disbelieve and despise the holy faith whereby we are bound to honor the glory of God. I desire and ask that to these Jews and Saracens who are in the lands of the Christians there be assigned certain persons to teach them Latin and to expound the Scriptures, and that within a certain time they shall learn these, and if they have not done so, that there shall follow punishment; and while they learn let them be provided for from the possessions of Holy Church; and after they have learned let them be made free men and honored above all others, and then will they convert their fellows and be the better fitted to understand the truth and to convert these others."

6. When the pope had spoken these words, the chamberlain said that, if the pope made this establishment, the Jews and the Saracens that are among the Christians would take flight to other lands and the income of Holy Church would be diminished. But Ramón the Fool said to the chamberlain: "Once on a time a man loved a woman, and said to her that he loved her more than any woman beside, and the woman enquired of him wherefore he loved her more than any other woman, and he replied that it was because she was fairer than any. The woman made sign with her hand in a certain direction, saying that in that direction there was a woman that was fairer; and when the man turned and looked in that direction the woman said that if there were another woman that was fairer, he would love her more, and this signified that his love to her was not perfect." The Jester of Valor said that if there were another thing better than God the chamberlain would love it more than God; so there was question among them which thing was the more contrary to the glory of God and to Valor, whether the diminution of the income of Holy Church or the dishonor which the Jews and the Saracens show to the glory of God and to Valor.

7. As the pope desired, even so was it ordained. After this the

pope enquired of the Masters of the Temple and of the Hospital what part they would take in honoring the glory of God, and both these Masters answered and said that they were already in the Holy Land beyond the seas to defend that land and to give example of the Catholic faith. The Jester enquired of Ramón the Fool if the love which he had to his Beloved was growing in proportion as his Beloved gave him greater pleasures. The Fool answered: "If I could love him more, it would follow that I should love him less if he diminished the pleasures which he gives me." And he said likewise that, since he could not do other than love his Beloved, neither could he increase the love which he bore to him; but the trials which he suffered grew daily, and the greater they were, the more were the joys increased which he had in loving his Beloved." The holy Apostolic Father said to the two Masters that from that which was signified by the aforesaid words, it followed that to honor the glory of God both the Masters should make ordinance whereby an Order should be created, that the Jester of Valor should not cry out upon the dishonor which is done to Valor by disputes concerning that wherein there would be agreement if they made an Order. He said furthermore that they should use their houses and masterships to make schools and places of study wherein their knights should learn certain brief arguments, by means of the *Brief Art of Finding Truth*; that they might prove the articles of the holy faith and give counsel to Masters, princes, and prelates through the art aforesaid; and that they might learn divers languages, and go to kings and princes of the unbelievers that one knight might challenge another to maintain, by feats of arms or by learning, the honor and truth which beseem the valor that is in the holy Catholic faith.[14] The ordinance afore-mentioned was granted to the pope by the two Masters and by all the friars of their Order, and Ramón the Fool spake these words: "Humility conquered Pride, and the Lover said to his Beloved, 'If thou, Beloved, wert to die, I should go to weep upon thy tomb.' And the Beloved answered, 'Weep before the Cross, which is my monument.' The Lover wept bitterly, and said that through

---

[14] Regarding the combination of chivalric and clerical virtues, see the *Libre del Orde de Cavalleria* in its Catalan original and ancient French translation in the *Obres*, Vol. 1, pp. 203–94, and the *Libre de Clerecia (Liber clericorum)*, including Latin text and French translation in Vol. 1 of the *Obres*, pp. 295–386. Compare the *Libre de contemplació en Deu (The Great Book of Contemplation)*, Vol. 2, cap. 110, *Obres*, Vol. 4, pp. 45–50 for the clergy, and cap. 112, *Obres*, Vol. 4, pp. 57–63 for chevaliers of the wrong and right kind in relation to crusades and missions.

overmuch weeping the sight of his eyes was blinded and knowledge became clear to the eyes of his understanding. Wherefore the Order did all that it could to honor the glory of God."

8. According to the manner aforesaid, the holy Apostolic Father made ordinance concerning the ordinance of the glory of God, and he appointed officers and ministers, and representatives to see that this order was carried out; and he endeavored daily with all his power to bring it to pass that benefit might come from the ordinance afore-mentioned. It came to pass one day that Ramón the Fool and the Jester of Valor brought ink and paper before the pope, and said that they desired to send in writing the afore-mentioned ordinance to the soldan and the caliph of Bagdad, that they might see if they had subjects as noble as those of the pope, or could make as fair an ordinance as the pope had made to do honor to the glory of God in the Heavens and cause Valor to return to the world.

9. It came to pass one day that the cardinal of Domine Deus sent to a certain country to spy out the government of the bishop and all the princes of that country. While this spy was in that land, commandment came from the pope to the bishop that he should provide yearly for fifty Tartars and ten friars whom the pope sent to that diocese, that the Tartars might teach their language to the friars and the friars teach theirs to the Tartars, according as it was ordained in the court; and that the bishop should found a monastery without the city where they should live, and that endowment should be given to it in perpetuity. Greatly was the bishop displeased at the commandment which the pope had given him, bewailing the expense thereof; and he spake ill of the pope and of the cardinals in the presence of the prince of that country. But the prince rebuked the bishop sternly, and said that never before had he heard of any pope or any cardinals who had to such extent and to the best of their power made ordinances whereby the glory of God was so greatly honored, and that he himself, to honor the glory of God, and to follow the good example which the pope and the cardinals gave him, desired to have a share in the expenses which the students would incur, and to bear the moiety of the cost of the monastery. The king praised the ordinance of the pope and of the cardinals greatly, and said that it seemed to him that the time had come wherein God desired that his servants should do him great honor, and that those that had strayed should be converted.

10. So soon as the spy had heard the words which the prince

and the bishop had uttered, he reported in writing to his lord the cardinal those very words that he had heard, and he wrote likewise that, according to the knowledge which he had gained, the bishop had bought a castle for a nephew of his for twenty thousand pounds. These letters were read in the consistory before the pope and the cardinals, and the cardinal to whom the letter had come wrote down the name of the king, to the end that, if an expedition were set on foot, or an occasion occurred wherein the Church might show any favor to a king, it should be shown to that king. The pope sent his messenger to the king, and gave him thanks, and commanded that the castle should be his, and that he should give ten thousand pounds for the building of the monastery; and he sent to the chapter of that diocese commanding that, if the bishop desired not to hold his office and contribute that which he commanded him to give, they should elect another in his place, and that the bishop who had spoken ill of him should have only the income of a canon. The Fool said to the Beloved, "Pay me and give me my recompense for the time that I have served thee." The Beloved increased in his Lover his love for Him and the grief which he had suffered for the sake of love, and he said to him: "Behold the pope and the cardinals who honor the glory of their Lord." And the Jester sent letters by Devotion to comfort Valor, who wept for the dishonor which for long her enemies had done to her Lord.

11. Throughout all the world went forth the fame of the holy life of the pope and the great good which he did, and daily was valor increased and dishonor diminished. The good which came from the ordinance which the pope had established illumined the whole world, and brought devotion to them that heard the ordinance recounted; and throughout all the world was sent in writing an account of the process of the making thereof. It chanced one day that the pope had sent to a Saracen king a knight who was also a priest, and of the Order of Science and Chivalry. This knight by force of arms vanquished ten knights, one after the other, on different days, and after this he vanquished all the wise men of that land by his arguments, and proved to all that the holy Catholic faith was true. By messengers of such singular talent, and by many more, did the ordinance afore-mentioned, which was established by the holy Apostolic Father, illumine the world.

12. It came to pass that of the fifty Tartars who learned our language and gained understanding of our faith, thirty were converted, and the pope sent them with five friars to the court

of the khan. These thirty, together with the five friars who had learned the language of the Tartars, came before the great khan and preached the faith of the Christians, and converted many people in his court, and they turned the great khan from the error wherein he lived and made him to doubt it; and after a time, by process of this doubt, he came to everlasting life.

13. In a certain land there were studying ten Jews and ten Saracens together with ten friars of religion; and when they had learned our holy law and our letters, the half of them were converted to our law, and they preached our law to other Jews, and to Saracens our holy Christian faith, in the presence of many that had not yet been converted, and thus did they daily and continually. And because the papal court did all that was in its power, and through the continuance of the disputation, and because truth has power over falsehood, God gave grace to all the Jews and Saracens of that country so that they were converted and baptized, and preached to others the holy faith. Wherefore the good and the honor which, through the Pope Blanquerna, was done to the Christian faith, can in no wise be recounted.[15]

[15] This final paragraph is a wistful hope for the support Lull anticipated, but never received, for his projects from papacy, temporal rulers, and scholarly Christians. See Petry, *op. cit.*, p. 7, and notes 19–20, pp. 16–17.

THE BLANQUERNA: OF THE BOOK OF THE LOVER AND THE BELOVED

The Text

Prologue

Blanquerna was in prayer, and considered the manner wherein to contemplate God and his virtues, and when he had ended his prayer, he wrote down the manner wherein he had contemplated God; and this he did daily, and brought new arguments to his prayer, to the end that after many and divers manners he should compose the *Book of the Lover and the Beloved*, and that these manners should be brief, and that in a short space of time the soul should learn to reflect in many ways. And, with the blessing of God, Blanquerna began the book, the which book he divided into as many verses as there are days in the year; and each verse suffices for the contemplation of God in one day according to *The Art of the Book of Contemplation*.

1. The Lover asked his Beloved if there remained in Him anything still to be loved. And the Beloved answered that he had still to love that by which his own love could be increased.

2. Long and perilous are the paths whereby the Lover seeks his Beloved. They are peopled by considerations, sighs, and tears. They are lit up by love.

3. Many lovers came together to love One only, their Beloved, who made them all to abound in love. And each one had the Beloved for his possession, and his thoughts of Him were very pleasant, making him to suffer pain which brought delight.

4. The Lover wept and said: "How long shall it be till the darkness of the world is past, that the paths to hell may be no more? When comes the hour wherein water, that flows downward, shall change its nature and mount upward? When shall the innocent be more in number than the guilty?"

5. "Ah! When shall the Lover with joy lay down his life for

the Beloved? And when shall the Beloved see the Lover grow faint for love of Him?"

6. Said the Lover to the Beloved, "Thou that fillest the sun with splendor, fill my heart with love." And the Beloved answered: "Hadst thou not fullness of love, thine eyes had not shed those tears, neither hadst thou come to this place to see Him that loves thee."

7. The Beloved made trial of his Lover to see if his love for him were perfect, and he asked him how the presence of the Beloved differed from his absence. The Lover answered, "As knowledge and remembrance differ from ignorance and oblivion."

8. The Beloved asked the Lover, "Hast thou remembrance of aught wherewith I have rewarded thee, that thou wouldst love me thus?" "Yea," replied the Lover, "for I distinguish not between the trials that thou sendest me and the joys."

9. "Say, O Lover!" asked the Beloved. "If I double thy trials, wilt thou still be patient?" "Yea," answered the Lover, "so that thou double also my love."

10. Said the Beloved to the Lover, "Knowest thou yet what love meaneth?" The Lover answered, "If I knew not the meaning of love, I should know the meaning of trial, grief, and sorrow."

13. "Say, Fool of Love! Which can be the better seen, the Beloved in the Lover, or the Lover in the Beloved?" The Lover answered, and said: "By love can the Beloved be seen, and the Lover by sighs and tears, by trials and by grief."

22. The Lover came to drink of the fountain which gives love to him that has none, and his griefs redoubled. And the Beloved came to drink of that fountain, that the love of one whose griefs were doubled might be doubled also.

23. The Lover was sick and thought on the Beloved, who fed him on his merits, quenched his thirst with love, made him to rest in patience, clothed him with humility, and as medicine gave him truth.

24. They asked the Lover where his Beloved was. And he answered: "See Him for yourselves in a nobler house than all the nobility of creation; but see him too in my love, my griefs, and my tears."

29. The Lover and the Beloved met, and the Beloved said to the Lover, "Thou needest not to speak to me. Sign to me only with thine eyes, for they are words to my heart—that I may give thee that which thou dost ask."

31. The Beloved filled his Lover with love, and grieved not for

his tribulations, for they would but make him love the more deeply; and the greater were the Lover's tribulations, the greater was his delight and joy.

42. The keys of the doors of love are gilded with meditations, sighs, and tears; the cord that binds them is woven of conscience, contrition, devotion, and satisfaction; the door is kept by justice and mercy.

46. The Lover longed for solitude,[16] and went away to live alone, that he might have the companionship of his Beloved, for amid many people he was lonely.

47. The Lover was all alone, in the shade of a fair tree. Men passed by that place, and asked him why he was alone. And the Lover answered, "I am alone, now that I have seen you and heard you; until now I was in the company of my Beloved."

54. As one that was a fool went the Lover through a city, singing of his Beloved; and men asked him if he had lost his wits. "My Beloved," he answered, "has taken my will and I myself have yielded up to him my understanding; so that there is left in me naught but memory, wherewith I remember my Beloved."

57. They asked the Lover, "Wherein is all thy wealth?" He answered, "In the poverty which I bear for my Beloved." "And wherein thy repose?" "In the afflictions of love." "Who is thy physician?" "The trust that I have in my Beloved." "And who is thy master?" "The signs which in all creatures I see of my Beloved."

61. They asked the Lover where his love first began. He answered, "It began in the glories of my Beloved; and from that beginning I was led to love my neighbor even as myself, and to cease to love [17] deception and falsehood."

62. "Say, Fool of Love! If thy Beloved no longer cared for thee, what wouldst thou do?" "I should love him still," he replied. "Else must I die; seeing that to cease to love is death and love is life."

65. They asked the Lover what he meant by happiness. "It is sorrow," he replied, "borne for love."

68. Said the Lover to his Beloved: "Thou art all, and through all, and in all, and with all. I would give thee all of myself that I may have all of thee, and thou all of me." The Beloved answered: "Thou canst not have me wholly unless thou art

16 *Solitat*, according to MS. "D" instead of *soliditat* in other versions. Cf. Peers, *Blanquerna*, p. 418, note, and preface, p. 13.
17 *Desamar;* Peers, *op. cit.*, p. 420, note.

wholly mine." And the Lover said: "Let me be wholly thine and be thou wholly mine." The Beloved answered: "What, then, will thy son have, and thy brother and thy father?" The Lover replied: "Thou, O my Beloved! art so great a whole, that thou canst abound, and be wholly of each one who gives himself wholly to thee."

70. The paths of love are both long and short. For love is clear, bright, and pure, subtle yet simple, strong, diligent, brilliant, and abounding both in fresh thoughts and in old memories.

79. "Say, O Fool! When came love first to thee?" "In that time," he replied, "when my heart was enriched and filled with thoughts and desires, sighs and griefs, and my eyes abounded in weeping and in tears." "And what did love bring thee?" "The wondrous ways of my Beloved, his honors and his exceeding worth." [18] "How came these things?" "Through memory and understanding." "Wherewith didst thou receive them?" "With charity and hope." "Wherewith dost thou guard them?" "With justice, prudence, fortitude, and temperance."

80. The Beloved sang, and said: "Little knows the Lover of love if he be ashamed to praise his Beloved, or if he fear to do him honor in those places wherein he is most grievously dishonored; and little knows he of love who is impatient of tribulations; and he who loses trust in his Beloved makes no agreement between love and hope."

97. They asked the Lover, "Whence art thou?" He answered, "From love." "To whom dost thou belong?" "I belong to love." "Who gave thee birth?" "Love." "Where wast thou born?" "In love." "Who brought thee up?" "Love." "How dost thou live?" "By love." "What is thy name?" "Love." "Whence comest thou?" "From love." "Whither goest thou?" "To love." "Where dwellest thou?" "In love." "Hast thou aught but love?" "Yea," he answered, "I have faults; and I have sins against my Beloved." "Is there pardon in thy Beloved?" "Yea," answered the Lover, "in my Beloved there is mercy and justice, and therefore am I lodged between fear and hope."

142. The Lover was glad, and rejoiced in the greatness of his Beloved. But afterward the Lover was sad because of overmuch thought and reflection. And he knew not which he felt the more deeply—whether the joys or the sorrows.

143. The Lover was sent by his Beloved as a messenger to

[18] *Valors;* Peers, *op. cit.,* p. 423, and note, p. 175.

Christian princes and to unbelievers, to teach them an *Art* and *Elements*,[19] whereby to know and love the Beloved.

168. Imprisoned was the Lover in the prison of love. Thoughts, desires, and memories held and enchained him lest he should flee to his Beloved. Griefs tormented him; patience and hope consoled him. And the Lover would have died, but the Beloved revealed to him his presence and the Lover revived.

173. Said the Lover, "O ye that love, if ye will have fire, come light your lanterns at my heart; if water, come to my eyes, whence flow the tears in streams; if thoughts of love, come gather them from my meditations."

179. "Say, O Fool! Which of these knows the more of love—he that has joys thereof or he that has trials and griefs?" He answered: "There can be no knowledge of love without both the one and the other."

204. Sins and merits were striving among themselves in the conscience and the will of the Lover. Justice and remembrance increased his remorse, but mercy and hope increased the assurance of pardon in the will of the Beloved; wherefore in the penitence of the Lover merits conquered sins and wrongs.

218. The Lover met his Beloved, and saw him to be very noble and powerful and worthy of all honor. And he cried, "How strange a thing it is that so few among men know and love and honor thee as thou deservest!" And the Beloved answered him and said: "Greatly has man grieved me; for I created him to know me, love me, and honor me, and yet, of every thousand, but a hundred fear and love me; and ninety of these hundred fear me lest I should condemn them to hell, and ten love me that I may grant them glory; hardly is there one who loves me for my goodness and nobility." When the Lover heard these words, he wept bitterly for the dishonor paid to his Beloved; and he said: "Ah, Beloved, how much hast thou given to man and how greatly hast thou honored him! Why, then, has man thus forgotten Thee?"

233. The marks of the love which the Lover has to his Beloved are, in the beginning, tears; in the continuance, tribulations; and, in the end, death. And with these marks does the Lover preach before the lovers of his Beloved.

234. The Lover went into solitude; and his heart was accompanied by thoughts, his eyes by tears, and his body by

---

[19] Two of Lull's own works; Peers, *op. cit.*, p. 432.

afflictions and fasts. But when the Lover returned to the companionship of men, these things afore-mentioned forsook him, and the Lover remained quite alone in the company of many people.

235. Love is an ocean; its waves are troubled by the winds; it has no port or shore. The Lover perished in this ocean, and with him perished his torments, and the work of his fulfillment began.

246. "Say, O Fool! What is solitude?" He answered, "It is solace and companionship between Lover and Beloved." "And what are solace and companionship?" "Solitude in the heart of the Lover when he remembers naught save only his Beloved."

258. Far above love is the Beloved; far beneath it is the Lover; and love, which lies between these two, makes the Beloved to descend to the Lover, and the Lover to rise toward the Beloved. And this ascending and descending are the beginning and the life of that love whereby the Lover suffers and the Beloved is served.

281. "Preach, thou, O Fool, and speak concerning thy Beloved; weep and fast." So the Lover renounced the world, and went forth with love to seek his Beloved, and praised him in those places wherein he was dishonored.

288. "Say, O Fool! Wherein is the beginning of wisdom?" He answered, "In faith and devotion, which are a ladder whereby understanding may rise to a comprehension of the secrets of my Beloved." "And wherein have faith and devotion their beginning?" He answered, "In my Beloved, who illumines faith and kindles devotion."

292. "Say, O Fool! Hast thou seen one without his reason?" He answered, "I have seen a bishop who had many cups on his table, and many plates and knives of silver, and in his chamber had many garments and a great bed, and in his coffers great wealth—and at the gates of his palace but few poor."

316. "Thou hast placed me, O Beloved, between my evil and thy good. On thy part may there be pity, mercy, patience, humility, pardon, restoration, and help; on mine let there be contrition, perseverance, and remembrance, with sighs and weeping and tears for thy sacred Passion."

366. "Say, O Fool! What is this world?" He answered, "It is the prison house of them that love and serve my Beloved." "And who is he that imprisons them?" He answered: "Conscience, love, fear, renunciation, and contrition, and the com-

panionship of willful men; and the labor that knows no reward, wherein lies punishment."

Because Blanquerna had to compose the book of *The Art of Contemplation*, therefore desired he to end the *Book of the Lover and the Beloved*, the which is now ended, to the glory and praise of our Lord God.

THE BLANQUERNA: THE ART OF CONTEMPLATION[20]

THE TEXT

Chapter IV

Of Unity

Blanquerna turned his thoughts and considerations with his love to the contemplation of the Unity of God, and he said these words: "Sovereign Good! Alone is thy Goodness in infinite greatness and in eternity and in power, for there is none other goodness such as can be infinite, eternal, and of infinite power; wherefore, O Sovereign Good, I adore thee alone in one God who is Sovereign in all perfections. Thou art one only Good, whence all other good descends and springs. Thy Good of Itself alone sustains all good beside. Thy Good alone is the source of my good, wherefore all my good gives and subjects itself to the honor, praise and service of Thy Good alone."

2. "O loving Lord! Greatness that art without beginning and end in thy Essence full of virtue and complete in all perfection, thou dost accord with one God alone and not with many, because eternity that is without beginning or end in its abidingness accords well with greatness which in essence and virtue has neither beginning nor end, but is itself both beginning and end in all its fullness. And were it not so, O Lord, it would follow that justice and perfection were contrary things in eternity, if eternity, which has neither beginning nor end in duration, accorded also with greatness in essence, which has finite and determined quantity. And since thou, my God, art One with thy justice and perfection, thereby is it signified to my understanding that thou art One God eternal and alone."

3. The memory of Blanquerna remembered the goodness, greatness, eternity, wisdom, will, and power of God. By His

[20] A variant Catalan text of the *Art de contemplació* here imbedded in *The Blanquerna* is that of Probst in the *Beiträge*, Vol. XIII, pts. 2–3, pp. 58–104, heretofore referred to.

goodness he understood a power with more of goodness than any other; by His greatness, a power that was greater; by eternity, a power more abiding; by wisdom, a power more wise; by will, a power more gracious than any other power soever. Wherefore, when the understanding had comprehended Divine power, the memory thought upon one power alone, above all others Sovereign, and therefore the understanding comprehended that God was One and One only, for, were there many gods, it were a thing impossible that the understanding could comprehend a greater and nobler power than all beside.

4. Blanquerna considered the virtue that is in the plants and in things which Nature orders to one end, and his understanding comprehended that everything that is in nature has one virtue which is lord over all other virtues that are in that body; and therefore Nature in each elemental body has natural appetite rather to one end than to another, since one end—that is, one perfection—has below it all perfections beside. While Blanquerna considered this, his memory bore his understanding to the comprehension of the end for which all men are made and created, and of how beasts, birds, plants, metals, elements, heavens, stars have one end only, namely, to serve man; and thereby is signified, according to the perfection of power, justice, wisdom, and will, that all men are to honor and serve one God alone; for were there many gods, each god, according to his perfection and justice and power, knowledge and will, would have made and created men and creatures for many ends. As Blanquerna contemplated the Unity of God according to the manner aforesaid, he felt himself to be uplifted exceedingly in his memory and understanding and will.

5. To man is given will, whereby he wills to possess for himself alone his castle or his city or his kingdom, or his possessions or his wife or his son, or his memory or his understanding or his will, and so of other things. And when to his hurt he finds his peer in these things, he is moved to passion thereby, which is contrary to glory and dominion. When Blanquerna had remembered all this, he remembered the glory and the dominion of God, and comprehended that if there were many gods and lords of the world, their glory and dominion could not be so great as is that of one God alone. And since there must needs be postulated of God the highest glory and dominion, there was demonstrated therefore to the understanding of Blanquerna that God is One and One only. And, that his understanding might rise to greater heights of comprehension, his will was greatly

exalted in fervor to the contemplation of his Beloved, the Spouse of his Will. And he said these words:

6. "True is it, O Lord God, that there is no other God save thyself alone. To thee alone I offer and present myself, that I may serve thee. From thee alone I hope for pardon, for there is none other liberality to give nor mercy to forgive, save thine only. Humble am I indeed if I humble myself to thee. Lord am I, if I am thine alone. Victory have I above mine enemies if I can only suffer for thee. Wheresoever I may be, with all that I am, I give myself to thee alone, and thine alone I am, a guilty sinner. Of thee alone I beg forgiveness, in thee I trust, and for thee I incur perils. Whatsoever may become of me, let it be all to one end, to wit, thy praise, honor, and glory. Thee alone do I fear, from thee alone is my strength, for thee I weep, for thee I burn with love, and none other Lord will I have, save thee only." [21]

Chapter VI [22]

Of Incarnation

Blanquerna remembered the holy Trinity of our Lord and God, that his understanding might comprehend how through the influence of the great goodness of eternity, power, wisdom, and will of the glorious Trinity, God should perform a work in the creature which should be of great benignity, abidingness, power, wisdom, and charity; and for this cause his understanding comprehended that according to the operation which is in the Divine Persons, it was fitting that God should take our human nature, in which and through which might be shown forth his Divine virtues and his works which he has in his Divine Persons; and that thus the wills of Blanquerna and all men beside might love God and his works. Wherefore Blanquerna spake these words:

2. "Divine Virtue," said Blanquerna, "thou art infinite in goodness, greatness, eternity, power, wisdom, love and all perfection; wherefore if there were aught else infinite in greatness, eternity, and patience, thou couldst infinitely work therein through greatness, eternity, action, and the like, since thou hast the power to work, as that thing would have power to receive.

---

[21] In the Catalan of the Probst text (cap. III, p. 74): "*De Vos tot sol e temor, de Vos sol e vigor, per Vos plor e m enamor, e no vull altre Senyor.*"
[22] Cap. V, pp. 77–81 in the Probst text.

But inasmuch as all virtue is finite, save thine, therefore neither in eternity nor in infinite greatness is anything sufficient to receive the impress of thy work, without beginning of time or quantity. Now to show forth all these things thy wisdom willed to create a creature greater in goodness and virtue than all other creatures and virtues created, and the Son of God willed to be one Person with that creature, to show that thy goodness had been able to give him greater virtue than all creatures else, even as he could make him greater than the creature and than all other creatures."

3. "Thy human nature, O Lord, has a glory greater than all other glories created, and this because its perfection surpasses all other perfection; and since thy justice, O Lord, has greater goodness, power, wisdom, and love than any other, therefore it was fain to give greater glory and perfection to thy humanity than to any other nature created. Whence, since this is so, it is most meet that all the angels, and all the souls of the saints, yea, and all the bodies of the just when the resurrection is past, should have glory in thy human nature, and thereby rise to have greater glory in thy Divine Nature."

4. When Blanquerna had considered for a great space of time the things set down above, he felt his memory, understanding, and will to be greatly uplifted in contemplation. Yet even so his heart gave no tears to his eyes that they might be bathed in weeping, and therefore did Blanquerna prepare to uplift the powers of his soul still higher that they might multiply devotion the more in his heart, and fill his eyes with weeping and with tears; for high contemplation goes ill save with weeping. Wherefore Blanquerna caused his memory to descend, and to think upon the vileness and the misery of this world, and the sins that are therein, and the great wickedness committed by our father Adam against his Creator, in disobeying him, and the great mercy, liberality, humility, and patience of God, when it pleased him to take human flesh and when he willed to give his Body to poverty, scorn, torments, trials, and to vile and grievous death; although he had no guilt nor sin such as are ours. While the remembrance of Blanquerna called these things to mind, his understanding was lifted up to comprehend and follow his remembrance, and together they contemplated the lofty and Divine virtues, to wit, goodness, infinity, eternity, and the rest. And therefore the will had so much devotion from the nobility of the virtues and the Passion and Death of the Nature of Jesus Christ that it gave to the heart sighs and griefs, and the heart

gave to the eyes weeping and tears, and to the mouth confession and praise of God.

5. For a great space of time did Blanquerna weep as he contemplated the Incarnation of the Son of God after the manner aforesaid; but as he wept the imagination strove to represent the fashion wherein the Son of God conformed himself to human nature; and since he might not imagine it, the understanding had no longer knowledge and Blanquerna fell to doubting, and his tears and sighs ceased, by reason of his doubt, which destroyed his devotion and made it to vanish. When Blanquerna felt to what state his thoughts had descended, he lifted up once more his memory and understanding to the greatness of the goodness, power, wisdom, and perfection of God, and in the greatness of these virtues his understanding comprehended that God may conform to himself human nature, though the imagination know it not neither may imagine it. For greater is God in goodness, power, wisdom, and will than is the imagination in its imagining; and in remembering and understanding thus Blanquerna destroyed the doubt which he had had concerning the Incarnation; and devotion and contrition returned to his heart, and weeping and tears to his eyes, and his contemplation was loftier and more fervent than at the beginning.

6. Long did Blanquerna contemplate the Incarnation of the Son of God after the manner aforesaid. And when he felt that his mind was wearied by one matter he took another, that through the renewing of the matter his mind might regain strength and virtue for contemplation. So Blanquerna remembered how the holy Incarnation and Passion of the Son of God are honored in the goodness, greatness, eternity, power, etc., of God, and how in this world he has honored with his grace many men who render him not the honor which they might. After this he remembered how many men there are in this world who are unbelievers and honor not the human nature of Jesus Christ which God in himself has so greatly honored, but believe not, and blaspheme that same nature, and hold that sacred land wherein he took that nature, and wherein, to honor us and restore us to the Sovereign dominion which we had lost, he suffered Passion and Death. Then, after Blanquerna had fixed the powers of his mind upon that matter, his devotions, sighs, tears, and griefs were renewed within him, and his mind soared higher and yet higher in contemplating the sacred Incarnation of the Son of God. And therefore he said these words: "Oh Lord God, who hast so highly honored and exalted our nature in thy Divine

virtues! When comes that time wherein thou wilt greatly honor
our remembrance, understanding, and will, in thy holy Incarnation and Passion?"

7. So lofty was the contemplation of Blanquerna that the
powers of his soul discoursed with one another within his mind.
Memory said that great goodness performed a great work, and
great power worked great might. Understanding answered that
great mercy, humility, liberality, and love conformed lesser virtues to greater. And Will said that above all creatures he must
needs love his Lord Jesus Christ. But at one thing he marveled
—to wit, how that Jesus Christ so greatly loved his people, and
willed to suffer for them so great Passion, and how God willed
so greatly to humble himself, and how in the world there are so
many men, unbelievers, idolaters, and ignorant of his honor.
Understanding answered and said that that thing was matter
for the will, how that it should have such devotion as to make a
man desire martyrdom that the Incarnation should be honored;
and that it was matter for the memory, how that it should have
remembrance so lofty of the virtues of God that he might be
exalted in such necessary demonstrations as should show forth
to unbelievers the sacred Incarnation and Passion of the Lord
Jesus Christ.

8. By the Divine Light the spirit of Blanquerna was illumined
and inflamed, and he spake these words: "O Incarnation, O
greatest truth of all truths, uncreated and created! Wherefore
are greater in number the men that scorn thee, and know thee
not, neither believe thee, than they who honor and believe thee?
What wilt thou do? Wilt thou punish so great and mortal failings? O mercy wherein is so great benignity, love, patience, and
humility! Wilt thou pardon them?" So Blanquerna wept, and
between fear and hope he sorrowed and joyed, as he contemplated the sacred Incarnation of the Son of God.

VI

Meister Eckhart (c. 1260–1328)

INTRODUCTION

BIOGRAPHICAL NOTICE

JOHN, LATER CALLED "MEISTER" OR "MASTER," ECK-hart was born at Hochheim near Gotha around 1260. He became a Dominican at Erfurt and attended the Order's studium at Cologne. He was made prior at Erfurt and then provincial vicar of Thuringia. His *Treatise on Distinctions* or *Talks of Instruction* stemmed from this early period. Here the way of *Abgeschiedenheit*, or true, spiritual disinterestedness and self-denial, already appeared. Having become a master at Paris in 1302 or 1303, he rose in turn to be provincial-general of Saxony (in 1303), vicar-general of Bohemia (1307), and superior-general of the order for all Germany (in 1312). A second Parisian period, possibly from 1311–1314, saw the production of his *Opus tripartitum*. In his chief capacity as a friar-preacher he was at Strassburg from 1313 or 1314 to 1320. Returning to teach at Cologne from 1321 to his death, he became embroiled in charges of heresy and during the last years of his life underwent investigations of his teachings. By the time of his death in 1327 or 1328, he had defended himself against numerous aspersions on his doctrinal soundness. In 1329, Pope John XXII condemned twenty-eight propositions from his writings, pronouncing seventeen of these heretical and the eleven others "rash." "Rash" or even "dangerous" he may have been on occasion. "Disloyal" he never was to the Church for which he gave so much.

BIBLIOGRAPHICAL ESSAY

The texts of the *Quaestiones Parisienses*, the *Opus tripartitum prologi*, and others are in the Leipzig edition of the *Opera omnia*, Vols. 13, 2, etc. See, also, further works in the Latin sections of *Meister Eckhart: die deutschen und lateinischen Werke*, edited by K.

Weiss, J. Koch, and J. Quint, W. Kohlhammer, Stuttgart-Berlin, 1936 —. A full bibliography of texts and secondary treatments is provided in J. M. Clark's *The Great German Mystics: Eckhart ,Tauler and Suso*, Basil Blackwell, Oxford, 1949. In addition to the pioneer collection of F. Pfeiffer, *Meister Eckhart*, 1857, 4th ed., Göttingen, 1924, the early work of F. Jostes, *Meister Eckhart und seine Jünger: ungedruckte Texte zur Geschichte der deutschen Mystik*, Freiburg (Schweiz), 1895, and the useful anthology of O. Karrer, *Meister Eckhart . . . Textbuch aus den gedruckten und ungedruckten Quellen . . .* Jos. Müller, Munich, 1926, there are numerous editions of basic parts of Eckhart's writings. A useful modernized version of selected sermons is H. Büttner, *Schriften und Predigten*, Jena, 1923. M. de Gandillac, *Maître Eckhart: traités et sermons*, Aubier, Paris, 1942, is helpful. A basic translation from the text of Pfeiffer is that of C. de B. Evans, *Meister Eckhart*, 2 vols., John M. Watkins, London, 1924, 1931. R. B. Blakney, *Meister Eckhart, a Modern Translation*, Harper & Brothers, New York and London, 1941, is must readable. A convenient edition of *Die Reden der Unterscheidung* is by E. Diedrichs, Bonn, 1913. Compare that of J. Bernhart, Munich, 1922. An excellent critical edition of *Meister Eckharts Buch der Göttlichen Tröstung und von dem Edlen Menschen (Liber "Benedictus")* is that of J. Quint, Walter De Gruyter & Co., Berlin, 1952. Valuable texts are in A. Daniels, "Eine lateinische Rechtfertigungsschrift des Meister Eckhart," *Beiträge*, Vol. 23, pt. 5 (1923), and in G. Théry, "Édition critique des pièces relatives au procès d' Eckhart . . .," *Archives d'histoire doctrinale et littéraire du moyen âge*, Vol. 1 (1926), pp. 129–268. E. Gilson, *History of Christian Philosophy in the Middle Ages*, 755 ff., appraises critical editions and literature. Literature is also summarized in F. W. Wentzlaff-Eggebert, *Deutsche Mystik zwischen Mittelalter und Neuzeit*, Berlin, 1944, pp. 301–307. The following discussion leans heavily on Gilson's *History* and its preceding French editions as on Gandillac's estimable "Tradition et développement de la mystique rhénane: Eckhart-Tauler-Seuse," in *Mélanges de science religieuse*, Vol. 3 (1946), pp. 37–82. See his *Traités* also. Brief key texts with extended commentaries on the relation of being, intellection, and unity are found in H. Hof, *Scintilla animae*, Lund, 1952, pp. 17 ff., 196–216 and in G. Della Volpe, *Eckhart O della filosofia mistica*, Rome, 1952, pp. 101–107.

SYNOPSIS

Meister Eckhart, well acquainted with the Christian, as well as the pre-Christian, tradition, posits in the Paris lectures of 1313–1314 his most distinctive contentions. However much there may seem to be a preoccupation later with the problem of being, the priority ascribed to intellection as over against being at the outset will persist. Far from knowing because he is, God is because he knows. In so far as it is seen as an attribute of creatures, being is not in God. God is wholly pure of it, as he must be who is the cause of all being. The great "I am" is entirely anterior to being. He is identifiable with intellection even as the Johannine saying, "In the beginning was the Word," establishes intellection as the corner stone of being. Any variation in emphasis from the key identification of God with the act of intellection will serve chiefly to lift the priority from intellect to unity. God is One. Unity is his attribute. Unity thus being the prerogative of the intellect means that pure intellect alone can qualify as pure unity. Saying that God is wholly intellect is therefore tantamount to saying that God is One.[1]

Though the apex of Eckhart's ontology must be sought in the Christian Trinity, the summit of his mystical philosophy is to be found in that rootage of divine being which is its priority or unity rather than its essence. The central peak is that immobile unity, rest, and solitude which is "the very desert of the Deity." This is the Unity, "pure of all being," to which God-Intellect as discovered by the Scriptures actually leads. Deity thus understood transcends the Trinity of Christian revelation.[2]

God may be said to possess being because of his oneness. Nothing else has either of these in the fullest sense. Viewed thus, being is not attributable to beings. Man, always in the process of being produced and created, "never truly is." Since of itself it is not, the creature to this extent is a pure nothingness. Creatureliness in itself is nullity (*nulleitas*). Only in so far as it is a manifestation of divine fecundity, and to the degree that it shares in the nature of the intellect and of the intellectual, can it be said to have being. Man gets back to the One through intellectual knowledge much after the fashion of Plotinus.[3]

---

[1] Gilson, *History*, pp. 438–40.

[2] *Ibid.*, p. 440; Gandillac, "La mystique rhénane," *Mélanges*, Vol. 3, pp. 47–48; Serm.: *Expedit vobis*, Pfeiffer, no. 76 (2), pp. 248–49; Blakney, *Meister Eckhart*, pp. 200 ff.

[3] Gilson, *History*, pp. 440–41. On the nullity of the creature, see, for example, Predigt 4: *Omne datum* (Pfeiffer, no. 40, pp. 134–37), Quint, *Meister Eckharts Predigten, Deutsche Werke*, Vol. I, pt. 1, pp. 70 ff.; Blakney, *Meister Eckhart*, pp. 185 ff.

Meister Eckhart of course regards the soul as a spiritual substance. The God-created faculties of memory, intellect, and will are associated in it with a more hidden and distinctively divine element still. This is identifiable on occasion as "the citadel of the soul," "the little castle," or "the tabernacle." Again, it is called "the spark," or the "*Fünklein*" of the soul, the "*Grund*," or "core" of it. This spark of the divine intellect is, according to one of Eckhart's censured propositions (1329)—one that he refuses to own in its most unqualified form—a something in the soul that is uncreatable as well as uncreated, namely, its intellect. To find union with God, one has merely to incarcerate himself in this fortress of the soul. Here he is no longer distinguished from God as something apart. For a truly mystical union to come about, man must detach himself completely from all that is not God. This is the true entering into the tabernacle which, in its utter simplicity and unity, is like to that of the divine intellect. In this entry into its *cubiculum*, the soul knows the purity and freedom that Deity alone possesses. This is the soul's clinging "by its innermost depths to the Deity." It can never be outside God. But it can be self-orienting and so recede from him or it can research its own depths and thus find union with him.[4] This, of course, means finding God beyond

---

[4] Predigt 2: *Intravit Iesus in quoddam castellum* (Pfeiffer, no. 8, pp. 42–47): Quint, *Deutsche Werke*, Vol. I, pp. 24 ff., especially 39 ff.; cf. Blakney, *Meister Eckhart*, pp. 210–11; Evans, *Meister Eckhart*, Vol. I, pp. 35 ff. Cf. Pfeiffer, no. 21: *Qui odit*, p. 89; Evans, *op. cit.*, Vol. I, p. 67; Karrer, *op. cit.*, p. 90. *Castellum* when used in medieval texts of such passages as Luke 10:38 carried the literal sense of town or village. Eckhart, like many others of his own and previous times, adapted it to serve figurative ends. The fortified castle played an expanding role in feudal society from the twelfth century onward. Religious imagery made increasing use of such Latin and vernacular terms as *castrum*, *castellum*, *bürgelín*, *château*, *bourgade*, castle, and fortress. These were applied to the spiritualized consideration of the body, heart, and soul, especially in connection with the Virgin Mary. Robert Grosseteste saw in her a *château*, "a castle of love and grace." Al-Ghazzali, by no means unknown to the West, stressed the necessity of defending "the fortress of the heart" against the devilish wiles of the tempter, Shaitán. That the "castle" theme was not foreign to Eckhart's contemporaries is evidenced by such researches as those of J. Murray, *Le château d'amour de Robert Grosseteste*, Paris, 1918, and of R. D. Cornelius, *The Figurative Castle*, Bryn Mawr, Pennsylvania, 1930. See D. M. Donaldson, *Studies in Muslim Ethics*, S.P.C.K., London, 1953, pp. 150 ff., on the "fortress of the heart" as treated in the *Ihyâ 'al-Ulúm al-Dín* (*Revivification of the Religious Sciences*, pt. III, pp. 23–27, 35–38). On the condemned propositions, see Gilson, *History*, p. 757, etc. See also G. Théry, *op. cit.* For the *Defense*, see Blakney, *op. cit.*, pp. 269, 289, 298–301, and Daniels, *op. cit.*

creaturely nothingness. Only the noblest creature of all, the soul itself, can lead directly to God. Self-abnegating love for God means self-discovery. Abandonment of self and the release of the soul toward the attainment of its pure essence is the highest end of the soul. True poverty alone brings this about. Its fullest practice removes man, once and for all, from the arena in which he can know, do, and own anything by himself. Traditional exercises of preparatory character fall into desuetude as the new birth of God is wrought in the soul, and as God and the soul reveal the blessedness of a common unity. All things, the sacraments and even God, can now be renounced. Man need not yearn further for that which is already his.[5]

To stress such renunciatory unity with God is, at the same time, to differentiate sharply between God and the Deity, between *Gott* and *Gottheit*. God differs from Godhead as much as heaven differs from earth. "God acts. The Godhead does not." The true "Nobleman," the spiritual "Aristocrat," is thus lured beyond the usual province of being, oneness, or even God himself. It is in this sense that the Meister invites the "noble" soul to exceed God and to go toward the abysm of pure Deity.[6] This is no mere conceit of theological language. It is, rather, the recourse, as in the Pseudo-Dionysius, to a mystical way in which affirmative thrusts at the divine mystery are surrendered for the more rewarding disciplines of negative theology. Here the route of detachment and self-abnegating poverty leads beyond the realm of distinctions in divine persons, beyond nominal attributes and hypostases, into an indefinable and unanalyzable, but still fully committed, alignment with the One in ineffable union.[7]

---

[5] Gilson, *History*, p. 442 and note 27, p. 757; Gandillac, "La mystique rhénane," *Mélanges*, Vol. 3, pp. 54–56; Serm.: *Beati pauperes*, Pfeiffer, no. 87, pp. 280 ff.; Evans, *op. cit.*, Vol. I, pp. 217 ff. Predigt 12: *Qui audit me* (Pfeiffer, no. 96, pp. 309–12), Quint, *Deutsche Werke*, Vol. I, pt. 3, pp. 192 ff.; Blakney, *op. cit.*, pp. 203 ff. Serm.: *Expedit vobis*, Pfeiffer, no. 76, pp. 238–43; Blakney, *op. cit.*, pp. 197–202.

[6] DS II, 1993. Gandillac, *Mélanges*, Vol. 3, pp. 47–48; Serm.: *Nolite timere eos*, Pfeiffer, no. 56, pp. 179 ff.; Evans, *op. cit.*, Vol. I, pp. 142 ff.; Blakney, *op. cit.*, pp. 224 ff., especially 225–26; Predigt 12: *Qui audit me*, Quint, *Deutsche Werke*, Vol. I, pt. 3, pp. 192–93; Blakney, *op. cit.*, pp. 203 ff.; Quint, ed., *Von dem Edeln Menschen*, pp. 67–80 and notes; *The Aristocrat*, in Blakney, *op. cit.*, pp. 74–81. Cf. *Expedit nobis*, Pfeiffer, no. 76, pp. 241–42; Blakney, *op. cit.*, pp. 200–02.

[7] Gandillac, in *Mélanges*, Vol. 3, p. 48. See *Nolite timere*, Pfeiffer, no. 56, p. 181, Evans, *op. cit.*, p. 143, on God as working and active; and the Godhead as not working, but inactive. "Got wirket, diu gotheit wirket niht. . . ."

It has been quite properly insisted that with Eckhart, during the birth of God in the soul, the Christian mystic surpasses sheerly Platonist metaphysics and every analogy with "fakir" resignation. The creature, fashioned out of God's love, responds to that love. It voluntarily accepts the call to perfection. All that self-sufficiency which, alone, spells pure nothingness for the creature and separation from its Creator, is firmly abjured. The first conditions of divine perfection are granted. "Simplicity without means" and the poverty inculcated by the Beatitudes are enthroned. The soul begins the total emptying of self. Detachment from all extraneousness is made operative. A perfect identity between the human and the divine will is sought.[8]

The professional Religious, for example, finds his cloistered vocation by no means a sufficient, or even valid, guarantee of perfection. Amid the grossly discernible challenges of the outer world, a truly spiritual soul may progress in full awareness of its dangers, while an avowed perfectionist may as easily fall before the subtle perils of the monastic calm. Gratification over good works, the sensible joys of sacramental-liturgical experience, and the ascetic's well-laid siege of the Kingdom may, together, impose their peculiar handicaps. These can be the means of defeating the soul's discovery of God through the higher way. This transcends the way of overt search and all specialized modes of spiritual operation. Eschewing every way, it attains its goal by all ways and by every mode. All the works accomplished outside the soul's royal fortress being dead, all those achieved within it now become living.[9]

Eckhart does not disparage all works. He rejects those only that are prompted by Pharisaic research for external virtue, and the undisciplined solicitation for the comfort of "special blessings."[10] So, likewise, he calls to prayer and the eucharistic life that goes beyond merest participation to fullest communication. Keeping this in mind, one may quite justifiably abandon the most rapturous contemplation to give a little soup to a sick man; one may encounter and accompany God in the street as well as in the church.[11]

For fellow-concern and Christian love do play a large role in Eckhart's mysticism, however empyrean it may sometimes

[8] Gandillac, *Mélanges*, Vol. 3, pp. 50–54.
[9] *Ibid.*, p. 55; *Talks of Instruction*, nos. 6, 22; *Beati pauperes*, Blakney, *op. cit.*, pp. 227–32.
[10] *Talks of Instruction*, no. 19.
[11] *Ibid.*, no. 10.

appear.[12] The Meister, it is true, makes short shrift of self-advertised humanitarianism. Creaturely convivialism, moreover, is scarcely a desired end. Consideration of the divine Persons themselves may seem lost in the unreserved surrender to fathomless Deity. Christians must certainly not be respecters of human persons. Even the humanity of the God-made-man tends to provide an obstacle, an obscuring image. Jesus, Eckhart reminds us, felt called upon to plead the expediency of his "going away." [13]

Is this, then, to becloud the role of God in history and of Christ incarnated in time? How can the abysmic, denuded Deity care for and sustain creatures? Is not Eckhart's refined mysticism cold comfort at best for men in need of divine-human intimacy?

Meister Eckhart, in his preaching, at least, avoids discussion of such theoretical issues. This penchant for empty speculation is, he thinks, the "cross of great clerks." *Abgeschiedenheit*, union-producing detachment and disinterested withdrawal from all that is not God, is the one necessary emphasis for him.[14] God and the soul may know an intimacy surpassing all analysis. Whatever others may hold deducible from Eckhart's premises, he himself never actually sacrifices loving service of creatures. Such love is always deduced from the love of God. However transcendent, philosophically, Deity may be, nothing is closer to the contemplative soul than its God. The selections of this anthology evidence clearly the emphasis held needful by Eckhart, through precept and example, for balancing the contemplative and the active life.[15]

---

12 On love, spiritual disinterest (*Abgeschiedenheit*), and true contemplative inwardness that socializes, see *Talks of Instruction*, no. 10, Blakney, *op. cit.*, p. 14. See *About Disinterest*, in Blakney, *op. cit.*, pp. 82 ff.; *Et cum factus*, Blakney, *op. cit.*, p. 123, on God lying in wait for man with love; also *In hoc apparuit caritas Dei in nobis*, Blakney, *op. cit.*, pp. 125 ff.

13 Gandillac, *Mélanges*, Vol. 3, pp. 56–58. Serm.: *Expedit vobis*, Pfeiffer, no. 76 (1), pp. 238–43; Blakney, *op. cit.*, pp. 197–202. Cf. John 16:7.

14 Gandillac, *Mélanges*, Vol. 3, pp. 57–60. Cf. *About Disinterest*, in Blakney, *op. cit.*, pp. 82 ff.

15 Clark, *German Mystics*, pp. 20 ff.; Petry, "Social Responsibility," *Church History*, Vol. 21, pt. 1, pp. 7–9 and notes.

Meister Eckhart (c. 1260–1328)

SERMON ON THE ETERNAL BIRTH [16]

The Text

THIS TOO IS MEISTER ECKHART WHO ALWAYS TAUGHT THE TRUTH

IN HIS, QUAE PATRIS MEI SUNT, OPORTET ME ESSE. (Luke 2:49)

"I must be about my Father's business!" This text is quite convenient to the discussion in which I shall now engage, dealing with the eternal birth, which occurred at one point of time, and which occurs every day in the innermost recess of the soul— a recess to which there is no avenue of approach. To know this birth at the core of the soul it is necessary above all that one should be about his Father's business.

What are the attributes of the Father? More power is attributed to him than to the other Persons [of the Trinity]. Accordingly, no one can be sure of the experience of this birth, or even approach it, except by the expenditure of a great deal of energy. It is impossible without a complete withdrawal of the senses from the [world of] things and great force is required to repress all the agents of the soul and cause them to cease functioning. It takes much strength to gather them all in, and without that strength it cannot be done. So Christ said, "The kingdom of heaven suffereth violence, and the violent take it by force."

Now it may be asked about this birth: does it occur constantly or intermittently—only when one applies himself with all his might to forgetting the [world of] things while yet knowing that he does so?

There are certain distinctions to be made. Man has an active intellect, a passive intellect, and a potential intellect. The presence of the active intellect is indicated by [the mind] at work, either on God or creature, to the divine honor and glory. It is

[16] This sermon, which is no. 3, pp. 18–24 in Pfeiffer, is translated by R. B. Blakney, *Meister Eckhart, A Modern Translation*, New York and London, 1941, pp. 109–17. Used by permission of Harper & Brothers.

characterized chiefly by its drive and energy and therefore is called "active." But when the action at hand is undertaken by God, the mind must remain passive. On the other hand, potential intellect is related to both. It signifies the mind's potentialities, what it has the capacity to do, what God can do. In one case, the mind is at work on its own initiative; in the other, the mind is passive, so that God may undertake the work at hand, and then the mind must hold still and let God do it, but before the mind can begin and God can finish, the mind must have a prevision of what is to be done, a potential knowledge of what may be. This is the meaning of "potential intellect," but it is much neglected and therefore nothing comes of it. But when the mind goes to work in real earnest, then God is enlisted and he is both seen and felt. Still, the vision and experience of God is too much of a burden to the soul while it is in the body and so God withdraws intermittently, which is what [Christ] meant by saying: "A little while, and ye shall not see me: and again, a little while, and ye shall see me."

When our Lord took three disciples up the mountain and showed them the transfiguration of his body, made possible by his union with the Godhead—which shall come to us also in the resurrection of the body—St. Peter at once, when he saw it, wanted to stay there with it forever. In fact, to the extent that one finds anything good, he never wants to part with it. What one grows to know and comes to love and remember, his soul follows after. Knowing this, our Lord hides himself from time to time, for the soul is an elemental form of the body, so that what once gains its attention holds it. If the soul were to know the goodness of God, as it is and without interruption, it would never turn away and therefore would never direct the body.

Thus it was with Paul. If he had remained a hundred years at that point where he first knew God's goodness, even then he would not have wanted to return to his body and would have forgotten it altogether. Since, then, the divine goodness is alien to this life and incompatible with it, faithful God veils it or reveals it when he will, or when he knows it will be most useful and best for you that he do so. He is like a trustworthy physician. The withdrawal does not depend on you but upon him whose act it is. He reveals himself or not as he thinks best for you. It is up to him to show himself to you or not, according as he knows you are ready for him, for God is not a destroyer of nature but rather one who fulfills it, and he does this more and more as you are prepared.

You may, however, say: Alas, good man, if, to be prepared for God, one needs a heart freed from ideas and activities which are natural to the agents of the soul, how about those deeds of love which are wholly external, such as teaching and comforting those who are in need? Are these to be denied? Are we to forgo the deeds that occupied the disciples of our Lord so incessantly, the work that occupied St. Paul on behalf of the people, so much that he was like a father to them? Shall we be denied the [divine] goodness because we do virtuous deeds?

Let us see how this question is to be answered. The one [contemplation] is good. The other [deeds of virtue] is necessary. Mary was praised for having chosen the better part but Martha's life was useful, for she waited on Christ and his disciples.[17] St. Thomas [Aquinas] says that the active life is better than the contemplative, for in it one pours out the love he has received in contemplation.[18] Yet it is all one; for what we plant in the soil of contemplation we shall reap in the harvest of action and thus the purpose of contemplation is achieved. There is a transition from one to the other, but it is all a single process with one end in view—that God is—after which it returns to what it was before. If I go from one end of this house to the other, it is true, I shall be moving and yet it will be all one motion. In all he does, man has only his one vision of God. One is based on the other and fulfills it. In the unity [one beholds] in contemplation, God foreshadows [variety of] the harvest of action. In contemplation, you serve only yourself. In good works, you serve many people.

The whole life of Christ instructs us in this matter, and the lives of his saints as well, all of whom he sent out into the world to teach the many the one truth. St. Paul said to Timothy, "Beloved, preach the word!" Did he mean the audible word that beats the air? Certainly not! He referred to the inborn, secret word that lies hidden in the soul. It was this that he preached, so that it might instruct the faculties of people and nourish them, and so that the behavior of men might proclaim it and so that one might be fully prepared to serve the need of his neighbor. It should be in the thoughts, the mind, and the will. It should shine through your deeds. As Christ said, "Let

---

17 Cf. the sermon in this anthology, *Mary and Martha*; also *Fragment*, 14.
18 *Summa Theol.*, 2a, 2ae, Q. 182, art. 1, Q. 188, art. 6; Butler, *Western Mysticism*, p. 209. Consult I. Mennessier, "Vie contemplative et vie active comparées," *La vie spirituelle*, Vol. 47 (1936), Supplément, pp. [129]–[145].

your light so shine before men!" He was thinking of people who care only for the contemplative life and not for the practice of virtue, who say that they have no need for this, for they have got beyond it. Christ did not include such people when he said, "Some seed fell in good ground, and brought forth fruit an hundredfold." But he did refer to them when he spoke of "the tree that does not bear fruit and which shall be hewn down."

Now some of you may say: "But, sir, what about the silence of which you have said so much?" Plenty of ideas intrude into that. Each deed follows the pattern of its own idea, whether spiritual or external, whether it be teaching, or giving comfort, or what not. Where, then, is the stillness? If the mind goes on thinking and imagining, and the will keeps on functioning, and the memory: does not this all involve ideation? Let us see.

We have already mentioned the passive and active intellects. The active intellect abstracts ideas from external things and strips them of all that is material or accidental and passes them on to the passive intellect, thus begetting their spiritual counterparts there. So the passive intellect is made pregnant by the active and it knows and cherishes these things. Nevertheless, it cannot continue to know them without the active intellect's continuing, renewing enlightenment. But notice this: all the active intellect does for the natural man, God does and much more too for the solitary person. He removes the active intellect and puts himself in its place and takes over its complete function.

Now, if a person is quite unoccupied, and his mind is stilled, God undertakes its work, and becomes controller of [the mind's] agents and is himself begotten in the passive intellect. Let us see how this is. The active intellect cannot pass on what it has not received, nor can it entertain two ideas at once. It must take first one and then the other. Even if many forms and colors are shown up by light and air at the same time, you can perceive them only one after the other. It is the same with the active intellect when it acts—but when God acts in lieu of it, he begets many ideas or images at one point. When, therefore, God moves you to a good deed, your [soul's] agents organize at once for good and your heart is set on goodness. All your resources for good take shape and gather at the same instant to the same point. This shows clearly and beyond doubt that it is not your own mind that is working, because it has neither the authority nor the resources required for that. Rather, it is the work which is begotten of Him who comprehends all ideas within himself simultaneously. St. Paul says: "I can do all things through Him that strengtheneth me and in him; I am not divided." Thus you may know that the ideas back of good deeds are not your own but are from the Superintendent of nature, from whom both the deed and the idea proceed. Do not claim as your own what is his and not yours. It is given you for a little while, but it was born of God, beyond time, in the eternity that is above all ideas or images.

You may, however, ask: "What is to become of my mind, once it has been robbed of its natural function and has neither ideas nor anything else to work on? It must always consist of something and the soul's agents are bound to connect with something on which they will go to work, whether the memory, the reason, or the will."

Here is the answer. The object and existence of the mind are essential and not contingent. The mind has a pure, unadulterated being of its own. When it comes across truth or essence, at once it is attracted and settles down to utter its oracle—for it now has a point of reference. If, however, the intellect does not discover any essential truth or touch some bedrock, so that it can say, "This is this and therefore not something else"; if it has to continue searching and expecting, arrested or attracted by nothing, it can only work on until the end, when it passes out, still searching and still expecting.

Sometimes a year or more is spent in working over a point about nature to discover what it is, and then an equal period has to be spent whittling off what it is not. Having no reference point, the mind can make no statement all this time, for it has no real knowledge of the core of truth. That is why the mind can never rest during this lifetime. For let God reveal himself here ever so much, it is nothing to what he really is. There is Truth at the core of the soul but it is covered up and hidden from the mind, and as long as that is so, there is nothing the mind can do to come to rest, as it might if it had an unchanging point of reference.

The mind never rests but must go on expecting and preparing for what is yet to be known and what is still concealed. Meanwhile, man cannot know what God is, even though he be ever so well aware of what God is not; and an intelligent person will reject that. As long as it has no reference point, the mind can only wait as matter waits for form. And matter can never find rest except in form; so, too, the mind can never rest except in the

essential truth which is locked up in it—the truth about everything. Essence alone satisfies and God keeps on withdrawing,
farther and farther away, to arouse the mind's zeal and lure it
on to follow and finally grasp the true good that has no cause.
Thus, contented with nothing, the mind clamors for the highest
good of all.

Now you may say: "But, sir, you have often told us that the
agents should all be still and yet here you have everything setting up a clamor and covetousness in the mind where quiet
should be: there is a great hubbub and outcry for what the mind
has not. Whether it be desire, or purpose, or praise, or thanks,
or whatever is imagined or engendered in the soul, it cannot be
the pure peace or complete quiet, of which you have spoken.
Rather, the mind is despoiled of its peace."

This requires an answer. When you get rid of selfishness, together with things and what pertains to them, and have trans-
ferred all to God, and united with him, and abandoned all for
him in complete trust and love, then whatever your lot, whatever touches you, for better or worse, sour or sweet, none of it is
yours but it is all God's, to whom you have left it.

Tell me: Whose is the Word that is spoken? Is it his who
speaks or his who hears it? Even though it come to him who
hears it, it still is his who speaks or conceives it. Take an illus-
tration. The sun radiates its light into the air and the air receives it and transmits it to the earth, and, receiving it, we can
distinguish one color from another. Now, although light seems
to be everywhere in the air, it is really in the sun. The rays are
really emitted by the sun and come from it—not from the air.
They are only received by the air and passed on to anything
that can be lighted up.

It is like this with the soul. God begets his Son or the Word in
the soul and, receiving it, the soul passes it on in many forms,
through its agents, now as desire, now in good intentions, now
in loving deeds, now in gratitude or whatever concerns it.
These are all his and not yours at all. Credit God with all he
does and take none for yourself, as it is written: "The Holy
Spirit maketh intercession for us with groanings which cannot
be uttered." It is he that prays in us and not we ourselves. St.
Paul says that "no man can say that Jesus is the Lord, but by the
Holy Ghost."

Above all, claim nothing for yourself. Relax and let God
operate you and do what he will with you. The deed is his; the
word is his; this birth is his; and all you are is his, for you have

surrendered self to him, with all your soul's agents and their functions and even your personal nature. Then at once, God comes into your being and faculties, for you are like a desert, despoiled of all that was peculiarly your own. The Scripture speaks of "the voice of one crying in the wilderness." Let this voice cry in you at will. Be like a desert as far as self and the things of this world are concerned.[19]

Perhaps, however, you object: "What should one do to be as empty as a desert as far as self and things go? Should one just wait and do nothing? Or should he sometimes pray, read, or do such virtuous things as listening to a sermon or studying the Bible—of course, not taking these things as if from outside himself, but inwardly, as from God? And if one does not do these things, isn't he missing something?"

This is the answer. External acts of virtue were instituted and ordained so that the outer man might be directed to God and set apart for spiritual life and all good things, and not diverted from them by incompatible pursuits. They were instituted to restrain man from things impertinent to his high calling, so that when God wants to use him, he will be found ready, not needing to be brought back from things coarse and irrelevant. The more pleasure one takes in externalities the harder it is to turn away from them. The stronger the love the greater the pain of parting.

See! Praying, reading, singing, watching, fasting, and doing penance—all these virtuous practices were contrived to catch us and keep us away from strange, ungodly things. Thus, if one feels that the spirit of God is not at work in him, that he has departed inwardly from God, he will all the more feel the need to do virtuous deeds—especially those he finds most pertinent or useful—not for his own personal ends but rather to honor the truth—he will not wish to be drawn or led away by obvious things. Rather, he will want to cleave to God, so that God will find him quickly and not have to look far afield for him when, once more, he wants to act through him.

But when a person has a true spiritual experience, he may boldly drop external disciplines, even those to which he is bound by vows, from which even a bishop may not release him. No man may release another from vows he has made to God—for such vows are contracts between man and God. And also, if a

---

19 *Expedit vobis,* Blakney, *op. cit.,* pp. 200–02; *Qui audit,* Blakney, *op. cit.,* pp. 203 ff.

person who has vowed many things, such as prayer, fasting, or pilgrimages, should enter an Order, he is then free from the vow, for once in the Order, his bond is to all virtue and to God himself.

I want to emphasize that. However much a person may have vowed himself to many things, when he enters upon a true spiritual experience he is released from them all. As long as that experience lasts, whether a week, or a month, or a year, none of this time will be lost to the monk or nun, for God, whose prisoners they are, will account for it all. When he returns to his usual nature, however, let him fulfill the vows appropriate to each passing moment as it comes, but let him not think for a moment of making up for the times he seemed to neglect, for God will make up for whatever time he caused you to be idle. Nor should you think it could be made up by any number of creature-deeds, for the least deed of God is more than all human deeds together. This is said for learned and enlightened people who have been illumined by God and the Scriptures.

But what shall be said of the simple fellow who neither knows nor understands [the meaning of] bodily disciplines, when he has vowed or promised something such as a prayer or anything else? This I say for him: If he finds that his vow hinders him and that if he were loosed from it he could draw nearer to God, let him boldly quit the vow; for any act that brings one nearer to God is best. That is what Paul meant when he said: "When that which is perfect is come, then that which is in part shall be done away."

Vows taken at the hands of a priest are very different. They are as binding as those vowed directly to God. To take a vow with the good intention of binding oneself to God is the best one can do at any time. If, however, a man knows a better way, one that experience has taught him is better, then the first way is at once superseded.

This is easy to prove, for we must look to the fruits, the inward truth, rather than to outward works. As St. Paul says, "The letter killeth (that is, all formal practices), but the spirit maketh alive (that is, inner experience of the truth)." Realize this clearly, that whatever leads you closest to this inner truth you are to follow in all you do. Let your spirit be uplifted and not downcast, burning and yet pure, silent and quiet. You need not say to God what you need or desire, for he knows it all beforehand. Christ said to his disciples, "When ye pray, use not

vain repetitions, as the heathen do: for they think that they shall
be heard for their much speaking."

That we may follow this peace and inward silence, that the
eternal Word may be spoken in us and understood, and that we
may be one with Him, may the Father help us, and the Word,
and the Spirit of both. Amen.

ANOTHER SERMON ON THE ETERNAL BIRTH [20]

The Text

ET CUM FACTUS ESSET JESUS ANNORUM DUODECIM, ETC. (Luke 2:42)

We read in the Gospel that when our Lord was twelve years old he went to the Temple at Jerusalem with Mary and Joseph, and that, when they left, Jesus stayed behind in the Temple without their knowledge. When they got home and missed him, they looked for him among acquaintances and strangers and relatives. They looked for him in the crowds and still they could not find him. Furthermore, they had lost him among the [Temple] crowds and had to go back to where they came from. When they got back to their starting point, they found him.

Thus it is true that, if you are to experience this noble birth, you must depart from all crowds and go back to the starting point, the core [of the soul] out of which you came. The crowds are the agents of the soul and their activities: memory, understanding, and will, in all their diversifications. You must leave them all: sense perception, imagination, and all that you discover in self or intend to do. After that, you may experience this birth—but otherwise not—believe me! He was not found among friends, nor relatives, nor among acquaintances. No. He is lost among these altogether.

Thence we have a question to ask: Is it possible for man to experience this birth through certain things which, although they are divine, yet they come into the man through the senses from without? I refer to certain ideas of God, such as, for example, that God is good, wise, merciful, or whatever—ideas that are creatures of the reason, and yet divine. Can a man have the experience [of the divine birth] by means of these? No! Truly no.

20 This sermon, which is no. 4 in Pfeiffer, pp. 24–30, is translated by Blakney, *Meister Eckhart*, pp. 118–24. Used by permission of Harper & Brothers. Cf. Evans, *op. cit.*, Vol. I, pp. 20 ff.

Even though [these ideas] are all good and divine, still he gets them all through his senses from without. If the divine birth is to shine with reality and purity, it must come flooding up and out of man from God within him, while all man's own efforts are suspended and all the soul's agents are at God's disposal.

This work [birth], when it is perfect, will be due solely to God's action while you have been passive. If you really forsake your own knowledge and will, then surely and gladly God will enter with his knowledge shining clearly. Where God achieves self-consciousness, your own knowledge is of no use, nor has it standing. Do not imagine that your own intelligence may rise to it, so that you may know God. Indeed, when God divinely enlightens you, no natural light is required to bring that about. This [natural light] must in fact be completely extinguished before God will shine in with his light, bringing back with him all that you have forsaken and a thousand times more, together with a new form to contain it all.

We have a parable for this in the gospel. When our Lord had held friendly conversation with the heathen woman at the well, she left her jug and ran to the city to tell the people that the true Messiah had come. The people, not believing her report, went out to see for themselves. Then they said to her: "Now we believe, not because of thy saying: for we have seen him ourselves." Thus it is true that you cannot know God by means of any creature science nor by means of your own wisdom. If you are to know God divinely, your own knowledge must become as pure ignorance, in which you forget yourself and every other creature.[21]

But perhaps you will say: "Alas, sir, what is the point of my mind existing if it is to be quite empty and without function? Is it best for me to screw up my courage to this unknown knowledge which cannot really be anything at all? For if I know anything in any way, I shall not be ignorant, nor would I be either empty or innocent. Is it my place to be in darkness?"

Yes, truly. You could do no better than to go where it is dark, that is, unconsciousness.

"But, sir, must everything go and is there no turning back?"

Certainly not. By rights, there is no return.

"Then what is the darkness? What do you mean by it? What is its name?"

It has no name other than "potential sensitivity" and it

---

21 Cf. the *Aristocrat*, in Blakney, *op. cit.*, p. 77; Serm.: *Qui audit*, Blakney, *op. cit.*, pp. 200–01.

neither lacks being nor does it want to be. It is that possible [degree of] sensitivity through which you may be made perfect. That is why there is no way back out of it. And yet, if you do return, it will not be for the sake of truth but rather on account of the world, the flesh, and the devil. If you persist in abandoning it, you necessarily fall [a victim to spiritual] malady and you may even persist so long that for you the fall will be eternal. Thus there can be no turning back but only pressing on to the attainment and achievement of this potentiality. There is no rest [in the process] short of complete fulfillment of being. Just as matter can never rest until it is made complete by form, which represents its potential being, so there is no rest for the mind until it has attained all that is possible to it.

On this point, a heathen master says: "Nature has nothing swifter than the heavens, which outrun everything else in their course." But surely the mind of man, in its course, outstrips them all. Provided it retains its active powers and keeps itself free from defilement and the disintegration of lesser and cruder things, it can outstrip high heaven and never slow down until it has reached the highest peak, and is fed and lodged by the highest good, which is God.

Therefore, how profitable it is to pursue this potentiality until, empty and innocent, a man is alone in that darkness of unself-consciousness, tracking and tracing [every clue] and never retracing his steps! Thus you may win that [something] which is everything, and the more you make yourself like a desert, unconscious of everything, the nearer you come to that estate.[22] Of this desert, Hosea writes: "I will allure her, and bring her into the wilderness, and speak to her heart." The genuine word of eternity is spoken only in that eternity of the man who is himself a wilderness, alienated from self and all multiplicity. The prophet longed for this desolated alienation from self, for he said: "Oh that I had wings like a dove! for then would I fly away, and be at rest." Where may one find peace and rest? Really only where he rejects all creatures, being alienated from them and desolate. So David said: "I would choose rather to sit at the threshold of the house of my God than to dwell with great honor and wealth in the tents of wickedness."

But you may say: "Alas, sir, does a man have to be alienated from creatures and always desolate, inwardly as well as outwardly, the soul's agents together with their functions—must all

---

[22] Serm.: *Beati pauperes*, Blakney, *op. cit.*, pp. 227 ff.; also note 21.

be done away? That would put one in a hard position—if then God should leave him without his support, and add to his misery, taking away his light and neither speaking to him nor acting in him, as you now seem to mean. If a person is to be in such a state of pure nothingness, would it not be better for him to be doing something to make the darkness and alienation supportable? Should he not pray, or read, or hear a sermon, or do something else that is good to help himself through it?"

No! You may be sure that perfect quiet and idleness is the best you can do. For, see, you cannot turn from this condition to do anything, without harming it. This is certain: You would like in part to prepare yourself and in part to be prepared by God, but it cannot be so, for however quickly you desire or think of preparing, God gets there first. But suppose that the preparation could be shared between you and God for the [divine] work of ingress—which is impossible—then you should know that God must act and pour in as soon as he finds that you are ready. Do not imagine that God is like a carpenter who works or not, just as he pleases, suiting his own convenience. It is not so with God, for when he finds you ready he must act, and pour into you, just as when the air is clear and pure the sun must pour into it and may not hold back. Surely, it would be a very great defect in God if he did not do a great work, and anoint you with great good, once he found you empty and innocent.

The authorities, writing to the same point, assert that when the matter of which a child is made is ready in the mother's body, God at once pours in the living spirit which is the soul— the body's form. Readiness and the giving of form occur simultaneously. When nature reaches its highest point, God gives grace. When the [human] spirit is ready, God enters it without hesitation or waiting. It is written in the Revelation that our Lord told people: "I stand at the door, and knock and wait. If any man let me in, I will sup with him." You need not look either here or there. He is no farther away than the door of the heart. He stands there, lingering, waiting for us to be ready and open the door and let him in. You need not call to him as if he were far away, for he waits more urgently than you for the door to be opened. You are a thousand times more necessary to him than he is to you. The opening [of the door] and his entry are simultaneous.

Still you may ask: "How can that be? I do not sense his presence." But look! To sense his presence is not within your power, but his. When it suits him, he shows himself; and he conceals himself when he wants to. This is what Christ meant when he said to Nicodemus: "The wind [Spirit] bloweth where it listeth, and thou hearest the sound thereof but canst not tell whence it cometh, and whither it goeth." There is an [apparent] contradiction in what he says: "You hear and yet do not know." When one hears, he knows. Christ meant: by hearing a man takes in or absorbs [the Spirit of God]. It was as if he wanted to say: You receive it without knowing it. But you should remember that God may not leave anything empty or void. That is not God's nature. He could not bear it. Therefore, however much it may seem that you do not sense his presence or that you are quite innocent of it, this is not the case. For if there were any void under heaven whatever, great or small, either the sky would have to draw it up to itself or bend down to fill it. God, the master of nature, will not tolerate any empty place. Therefore be quiet and do not waver lest, turning away from God for an hour, you never return to him.

Still you may say: "Alas, sir, you assume that this birth is going to happen and that the Son [of God] will be born in me. But by what sign shall I know that it has happened?"

Yes! Certainly! There may well be three trustworthy signs, but let me tell about one of them. I am often asked if it is possible, within time, that a person should not be hindered either by multiplicity or by matter. Indeed, it is. When this birth really happens, no creature in all the world will stand in your way and, what is more, they will all point you to God and to this birth. Take the analogy of the thunderbolt. When it strikes to kill, whether it is a tree or an animal or a person, at the coming of the blow, they all turn toward it and if a person's back were turned, he would instantly turn to face it. All the thousands of leaves of a tree at once turn the required sides to the stroke. And so it is with all who experience this birth. They, together with all around them, earthy as you please, are quickly turned toward it. Indeed, what was formerly a hindrance becomes now a help. Your face is turned so squarely toward it that, whatever you see or hear, you only get this birth out of it. Everything stands for God and you see only God in all the world. It is just as when one looks straight at the sun for a while: afterward, everything he looks at has the image of the sun in it. If this is lacking, if you are not looking for God and expecting him everywhere, and in everything, you lack the birth.

Still you might ask: "While in this state, should one do penances? Isn't he missing something if he doesn't?"

The whole of a life of penitence is only one among a number of things, such as fasting, watching, praying, kneeling, being disciplined, wearing hair shirts, lying on hard surfaces, and so on. These were all devised because of the constant opposition of the body and flesh to the spirit. The body is too strong for the spirit and so there is always a struggle between them—an eternal conflict. The body is bold and brave here, for it is at home and the world helps it. This earth is its fatherland and all its kindred are on its side: food, drink, and comforts are all against the spirit. Here the spirit is alien. Its race and kin are all in heaven. It has many friends there. To assist the spirit in its distress, to weaken the flesh for its part in this struggle so that it cannot conquer the spirit, penances are put upon the flesh, like a bridle, to curb it, so that the spirit may control it. This is done to bring it to subjection, but if you wish to make it a thousand times more subject, put the bridle of love on it. With love you may overcome it most quickly and load it most heavily.

That is why God lies in wait for us with nothing so much as love. Love is like a fisherman's hook. Without the hook he could never catch a fish, but once the hook is taken the fisherman is sure of the fish. Even though the fish twists hither and yon, still the fisherman is sure of him. And so, too, I speak of love: he who is caught by it is held by the strongest of bonds and yet the stress is pleasant. He who takes this sweet burden on himself gets farther, and comes nearer to what he aims at, than he would by means of any harsh ordinance ever devised by man. Moreover, he can sweetly bear all that happens to him; all that God inflicts he can take cheerfully. Nothing makes you God's own, or God yours, as much as this sweet bond. When one has found this way, he looks for no other. To hang on this hook is to be so [completely] captured that feet and hands, and mouth and eyes, the heart, and all a man is and has, become God's own.

Therefore there is no better way to overcome the enemy, so that he may never hurt you, than by means of love. Thus it is written: "Love is as strong as death and harder than hell." Death separates the soul from the body but love separates everything from the soul. It cannot endure anything anywhere that is not God or God's. Whatever he does who is caught in this net, or turned in this direction, love does it, and love alone; and whether the man does it or not, makes no difference.[23]

The most trivial deed or function in such a person is more

[23] On God and his love, see *The Book of Divine Comfort*, in Blakney, *op. cit.*, pp. 54–56, 60 ff.

profitable and fruitful to himself and all men, and pleases God better, than all other human practices put together, which, though done without deadly sin, are characterized by a minimum of love. His rest is more profitable than another's work.

Therefore wait only for this hook and you will be caught up into blessing, and the more you are caught the more you will be set free. That we all may be so caught and set free, may He help us who is love itself. Amen.

A SERMON ON THE CONTEMPLATIVE
AND THE ACTIVE LIFE [24]

MARY AND MARTHA

THE TEXT

St. Luke relates in his Gospel that our Lord Jesus Christ entered into a certain village where he was received by a woman named Martha, and she had a sister called Mary who sat at the feet of our Lord and listened to his words, but Martha moved about, waiting upon our Lord.

Three things made Mary sit at Christ's feet. One was the goodness of God possessing her soul. The second was deep, unspeakable longing: she desired she knew not why and wanted she knew not what. The third was sweet solace and joy in the eternal words proceeding from the mouth of Christ.

With Martha too there were three things which made her move about waiting upon our Lord. She was in her prime and had good grounds for thinking that no one else could do the work as well as she herself. Next, she was sensible enough to arrange her outward work as considerately as possible. The third thing was the great honor due to her dear guest.

Doctors declare that God is ready to satisfy the highest aspirations, rational and sensible, of every man. For God to give us satisfaction rationally speaking and also sensibly are two very different things to the friends of God. Sensible satisfaction means that God grants us comfort, joy, contentment; and much indulgence in these things is not good for the friends of God, for their interior life. But rational satisfaction is of a spiritual nature. As to rational satisfaction I hold that not by any inclination can the summit of the soul be brought so low as to be drowned in

[24] The translation is by C. de B. Evans, *The Works of Meister Eckhart: Doctor ecstaticus*, Vol. II, pp. 90–98. Used by permission of John M. Watkins, London, 1931, 1952. Cf. Pfeiffer, no. 9, pp. 47–53; Büttner, *op. cit.*, Vol. II, no. 4, pp. 98–108.

pleasures; rather it rebels vigorously against them. Man enjoys rational satisfaction only when creature weal and woe are powerless to affect the summit of the soul. By creature I mean anything we see or are aware of under God.

Martha says, "Lord, tell her to help me." This was not said in anger, it was affection that constrained her. It was said half in jest and half in earnest. How so?—Well, she saw Mary possessed with a longing for soul satisfaction. Martha knew Mary better than Mary knew Martha, for she had lived long and well, and life gives the best understanding. Life gauges light and delight better than anything else under God that man can have in this body and in some ways more surely than the eternal light can. Eternal light makes known oneself and God, not oneself apart from God. Where self is seen by itself, it is easier to tell what is like or unlike. Paul makes this plain and so do the heathen philosophers. Paul saw in his ecstasy God and himself, in spirit, in God, but he was not in him properly, with an intimate knowledge of the virtues, because he had not practiced them. By practicing the virtues the masters gained profound discernment, a truer knowledge of the several virtues than had Paul or any saint in his first rapture.

So with Martha. Hence her words, "Lord, tell her to help me." As though to say: "My sister thinks she can do as she likes, sitting comfortably at thy feet. Let her see if it be so. Bid her get up and go." The latter part was kindly meant, albeit she spoke her mind. Mary was filled with longing: longing she knew not why and wanting she knew not what. We have her suspected, dear Mary, of sitting there for her own pleasure rather than for spiritual profit. "Bid her rise," Martha says, fearful lest by dallying with pleasure a stop should be put to all progress. Christ answered and said, "Martha, Martha, thou art careful, art troubled, with many things: one thing is needful. Mary has chosen the best part, which shall never be taken away from her." This Christ said to Martha, not rebuking but answering her, soothing her, telling her Mary would become as she desired. Why did Christ say, "Martha, Martha," naming her twice? Isidorus says there is no doubt that prior to the time when God was man he never called anyone by name lest any should be lost whom he did not name and about whom it was doubtful. Christ's calling I take to mean his eternal knowing: changeless, eternal subsistence, before the creation of creatures, in the Book of Light: Father, Son, and Holy Ghost. Of those named therein and whose names Christ uttered in words, of

those not one was ever lost. Moses, for instance, who was told by
God himself, "I have known thee by name," and Nathanael
unto whom Christ said, "When thou wast lying under the leaves
of the fig tree I knew thee." The fig tree being God, in whom his
name was inscribed eternally. Thus it may be shown that there
never was nor ever shall be lost a single soul whom Christ has
ever named by human mouth in the eternal Word.

Why did he name Martha twice? He meant that every good
thing, temporal and eternal, destined for creature, that all this
was Martha's. The first "Martha" stood for perfection in temporal works; the second one for her eternal weal: in all things
pertaining to this her lacking nothing. He says, "Thou art careful (troubled with many things): thou art among things, but
they have no hold in thee." The careful are those who let nothing hinder them in their work. Those who let nothing hinder
them in their work are the ones who follow the lead of the eternal light. These are with things not in things. It is almost as
though they were up yonder, on the circle (confines) of eternity
and they are enjoying no less. Almost, I say, because creatures
are all of them means. Means are twofold. One, without which
I cannot get into God, is work, vocation, or calling in time,
which interferes not one whit with eternal salvation. (The other
means is selflessness.) Work is the outward practice of good
works, but calling implies the uses of discrimination. We are
brought forth into time in order that our sensible worldly occupations may lead us nearer and make us liker to God. St.
Paul had this in mind when he spoke of "redeeming the time"
and of "the days being evil." "Redeeming the time," that means
the continual ascent of the mind to God, not in imagination but
a real intellectual adventure. And, "the days are evil" may be
explained as follows. Day presupposes night. If there were no
night we should not speak of day. It would be all one light. This
was Paul's idea: one life under the sun is all too short, subject
as it is to spells of darkness which cloud and obscure the soul's
eternal home. Hence, too, Christ's exhortation, "Work while ye
have the light." He who works in the light rises straight up to
God without let or hindrance: his light is his calling, and his
calling is his light. This was the case with Martha. Accordingly
he says to her, "One thing is needful, not two." What time we
are encompassed by the eternal light thou and I are one: we
two are one. Standing over all things and under God on the
circle of eternity the fiery spirit is two, for it sees God not without means. Its knowing and being, or knowing and object of

knowledge, will never be one till it sees God (with nothing between). Then spirit is seen to be God, free from all
forms.

Now mark what the circle of eternity means. The soul has
three ways into God. One is, to seek God in all creatures, ardently longing and busily working in various ways. King David
says, "In all things have I sought rest." The second way is a
wayless way, free and yet bound, raised, rapt away well-nigh
past self and all things, will-less, formless; there seems nothing
left but sheer being. Christ makes reference to this when he says,
"Blessed art thou, Peter: flesh and blood have not enlightened
thee, but being wrought up into thy higher mind, in Him thou
dost call me God; my Heavenly Father hath revealed it to thee."
St. Peter saw God, but not face to face. True, he was caught up
in the Heavenly Father's power past all created knowledge to
the circle of eternity. Grasped by the Heavenly Father—a dear
embrace—in his tempestuous might he was carried up unknowing in an aspiration transcending all the things of sense.
Then Peter heard within him sweet tones coming down from
above, not conveyed by any mortal means, in simple truth
(direct perception of) God's and man's at-one-ment in the Person of the Heavenly Father-Son. I make bold to say, if Peter had
seen God unveiled, in his own nature, as he did later on, like
Paul when he was caught up into the third heaven, the most
exalted angel's voice would have seemed harsh to him. He said
many loving words which Jesus did not need who sees into the
heart and ground of the soul where man stands face to face with
God in the freedom of actual presence. St. Paul alludes to this
when he tells how he was caught up into God and heard ineffable things not lawful for man to utter. From this I gather
that St. Peter was standing on the circle of eternity and was not
in unity beholding God in his his-ness.

The third way is called way, but is really-home: seeing God
face to face in his his-ness. Christ says, "I am the way, the truth,
and the life": Christ Person, Christ Father, Christ Spirit, three
—way, truth, and life—the one Christ, all in him. Out of this
way creatures keep helplessly circling round. Into God, in this
way, led by the light of his Word and compassed about by the
love of them both, that beggars description. Hear and marvel!
To be out and in, be conceived and conceive, see and be seen,
save and be saved—that is the end: the spirit at rest in the one
eternal nature.

But to return to our argument. Martha, and with her all the

friends of God, are careful or troubled—not, in trouble—a state in which temporal work is as good as any communing with God, for it joins us as straitly to God as the best that can happen to us barring the vision of God in his naked nature. "Thou art troubled," he says, meaning to say she was troubled, cumbered, with her lower powers, for she was not given to indulge in spiritual sweetness: she was not pleasure-seeking.

We need three things in our work: to be orderly, honest, and wise. To do the next thing, that I call orderly. By honest, I mean doing one's best at the moment. To feel true and lively pleasure in good works, that I call wise. Where these three things are found they are just as good and unite us as closely to God as all Mary Magdalene's idle longings.

Christ says, "Thou art troubled about many things, not about one." When, perfectly simple and wholly unoccupied, she is transported to the circle of eternity, then the soul will be troubled if anything should intervene to spoil her joy in being up there. She will be anxious and distressed. But Martha, being firmly established in virtue, open-minded, not hindered by things, wanted her sister to be like her, for she realized her insecurity. She had the highest motives, wishing her all that pertains to eternal felicity. Christ says, "One thing is needful." What is this one? It is God. That is the need of all creatures. If God took back what is his, all creatures would perish. Were God to withdraw from the soul at the point where her spirit is merged in the eternal Persons, then Christ would be left merely creature. The one, truly, is needful. Martha feared that her sister would stay dallying with pleasure and sweetness, so Christ says in effect: All is well, Martha, she has chosen the best part; this will pass. The best that can befall creature lies in store for her: she shall be blessed like thee.

Here let us examine the doctrine of virtue. Good life is in three ways a matter of will, and primarily of resigning the will to God, for it is imperative to live up to one's lights, be it in taking or leaving. There are three kinds of will. The first is sensible will, the second is rational will, the third is eternal will. The sensible will needs guidance, proper teaching. The second is rational will: following in the footsteps of Christ Jesus and the saints, words, deeds, and way of life all directed toward the highest end. Given this much, God will give something more in the ground of the soul, to wit, eternal will and the amiable counsels of the Holy Ghost. Says the soul, "Lord, tell me, what is thy eternal will?" and then if she has satisfied the above conditions, and if God so please, the Father will speak his eternal Word into the soul.

Now according to our good people we have got to be so perfect that no joy can move us; we must be indifferent to weal and woe. They are wrong. I say, never was there saint so great but he could be moved. But on the other hand I hold that it is possible with a holy man even in this body that nothing can move him to turn aside from God. Do you think that as long as words can move to joy and sorrow you are imperfect? No. Christ was not. He proves it when he cries, "My soul is sorrowful even unto death." Words wounded Christ sorely. The collective woe of creatures falling upon one creature would not be so profound as Christ's woe was, owing to his exalted nature, to the blessed union of divine and human nature. By the same token I declare that no saint ever lived nor ever shall [whom] pain could not pain nor pleasure please. Now and then it happens in friendship and in love or by a miracle—on being called a heretic, for instance, or anything you will—that a person is suffused with grace and indifferent to praise or blame. And with Religious (as I said just now), it may well come about that nothing whatever from outside can induce them to depart from God. Though the heart be wrung or all discomfited, the will alone continues to abide in God, saying, "Lord, I am thine and thou art mine." Nothing that enters therein can lessen eternal well-being so long as it does not invade the summit of the mind up yonder where it is at one with the will of God.

Christ says, "Thou art troubled with many things." Martha was Martha really. Her occupation was no hindrance to her: work and calling, both, she turned to her eternal profit. She had drawbacks, it is true, but always there remained nobility of nature and unflagging industry besides her other virtues. Mary was Martha before she was Mary.[25] She was not yet Mary while she sat at the feet of our Lord. She was so in name, not in nature. She was filled with joy and longing, for the first time at school learning life. Martha was so, really, and that is why she urged, "Lord, bid her get up," meaning to say, "Lord, I do not like her

---

25 Pfeiffer reads: *Mariâ was ê Marthâ, ê si Mariâ wurde* (p. 53). Büttner's reconstructed text is clearer: *Auch Maria musste erst noch eine Martha werden, ehe sie wirklich eine Maria wurde* (p. 106). The sense of the passage seems to be this: Martha is already herself in full integrity. She knows that Mary must first be a Martha before she can become a Mary. Martha realizes that Mary has a further discipline to undergo. She asks the Lord's help in bringing Mary to her real self.

sitting there just for the pleasure of it. I want her to learn life and really possess it. Tell her to rise and really be Mary." She was not really Mary while she was sitting at Christ's feet. Mary I call a well-disciplined body obedient to wise counsels, and by obedient I mean: what discrimination dictates, will abides by. Now our good people fondly think they can reach a point where sensible things are nonexistent to the senses. They never will: that a disagreeable noise should be as grateful to the ear as the sweet tones of a lyre is a thing I shall never attain to. But this much we have a right to expect: when discrimination observes that with rational, formal will rests decision, and orders the will to be free, that the will should answer, "I will." Then, lo and behold, strife changes to peace, for what a man wins by hard work turns to heart's joy and then it is fruitful.

Again, some people hope to reach a point at which they are excused from works. I say this is impossible.[26] Not till after the disciples had received the Holy Ghost did they begin to do good works. While Mary sat at the feet of our Lord and listened to his words, she was learning. She had just gone to school to learn life. But later on, when she had learned her lesson and received the Holy Ghost, she began to serve. She journeyed overseas preaching and teaching and acting as servant and washerwoman to the disciples. Only when the saints are saints, and not till then, do they do meritorious works. Then they gather treasure of eternal life. What is done before is by way of reparation and repentance. Where do we find evidence for this? In Christ. From the very beginning when he was made man he was working for our eternal happiness, and he went on to the end, to his death upon the cross; not a member of his body but played its own particular part. May we follow him faithfully in the path of true virtue. So help us God. Amen.

[26] Cf. *Fragment*, 14, Blakney, *op. cit.*, p. 238 (Pfeiffer, no. 33, pp. 607–08); *Talks*, 6, 10; cf. the first sermon in this anthology.

ON SOLITUDE AND THE ATTAINMENT OF GOD [27]

THE TEXT

I was asked this question: "Some people withdraw from society and prefer to be alone; their peace of mind depends on it; wouldn't it be better for them to be in the church?" I replied, No! And you shall see why.

Those who do well do well wherever they are, and in whatever company, and those who do badly do badly wherever they are, and in whatever company. But if a man does well, God is really in him, and with him everywhere, on the streets and among people just as much as in church, or a desert place, or a cell. If he really has God, and only God, then nothing disturbs him. Why?

Because he has *only* God and thinks only God and everything is nothing but God to him. He discloses God in every act, in every place. The whole business of his person adds up to God. His actions are due only to Him who is the author of them and not to himself, since he is merely the agent. If we mean God and only God, then it is He who does what we do and nothing can disturb him—neither company nor place. Thus, neither can any person disturb him, for he thinks of nothing, is looking for nothing, and relishes nothing but God, who is one with him by perfect devotion. Furthermore, since God cannot be distracted

---

[27] This translation of the *Talks of Instruction*, no. 6, is that of Blakney, *Meister Eckhart*, New York and London, 1941, pp. 7–10, used by permission of the publishers, Harper & Brothers. The word translated "solitude" is actually *Abgeschiedenheit*. See Joseph Bernhart, *Meister Eckhart: Reden der Unterweisung*, Munich, 1922, p. 28; Pfeiffer, *op. cit.*, pp. 547–52. Cf. Blakney's translation of the treatise *Von Abgeschiedenheit*, pp. 82 ff. Cf. his notes, pp. x and 315; also Pfeiffer, *op. cit.*, pp. 483 ff. Cf. Serm.: *Beati pauperes*, Blakney, *op. cit.*, no. 28, pp. 227–32; Pfeiffer, no. 87, pp. 280 ff.

by the numbers of things, neither can the person, for he is one in One, in which all divided things are gathered up to unity and there undifferentiated.

One ought to keep hold of God in everything and accustom his mind to retain God always among his feelings, thoughts, and loves. Take care how you think of God. As you think of him in church or closet, think of him everywhere. Take him with you among the crowds and turmoil of the alien world. As I have said so often, speaking of uniformity, we do not mean that one should regard all deeds, places, and people as interchangeable. That would be a great mistake; for it is better to pray than to spin and the church ranks above the street. You should, however, maintain the same mind, the same trust, and the same earnestness toward God in all your doings. Believe me, if you keep this kind of evenness, nothing can separate you from God-consciousness.

On the other hand, the person who is not conscious of God's presence, but who must always be going out to get him from this and that, who has to seek him by special methods, as by means of some activity, person, or place—such people have not attained God. It can easily happen that they are disturbed, for they have not God and they do not seek, think, and love only him, and therefore, not only will evil company be to them a stumbling block, but good company as well—not only the street, but the church; not only bad deeds and words, but good ones as well. The difficulty lies within the man, for whom God has not yet become everything. If God were everything, the man would get along well wherever he went and among whatever people, for he would possess God and no one could rob him or disturb his work.

Of what does this true possession of God consist, when one really has him? It depends on the heart and an inner, intellectual return to God and not on steady contemplation by a given method. It is impossible to keep such a method in mind, or at least difficult, and even then it is not best. We ought not to have or let ourselves be satisfied with the god we have thought of, for when the thought slips the mind, that god slips with it. What we want is rather the reality of God, exalted far above any human thought or creature. Then God will not vanish unless one turns away from him of his own accord.

When one takes God as he is divine, having the reality of God within him, God sheds light on everything. Everything will taste like God and reflect him. God will shine in him all the time. He will have the disinterest, renunciation, and spiritual vision of his beloved, ever-present Lord. He will be like one athirst with a real thirst; he cannot help drinking even though he thinks of other things. Wherever he is, with whomsoever he may be, whatever his purpose or thoughts or occupation—the idea of the Drink will not depart as long as the thirst endures; and the greater the thirst the more lively, deep-seated, present, and steady the idea of the Drink will be. Or suppose one loves something with all that is in him, so that nothing else can move him or give pleasure, and he cares for that alone, looking for nothing more; then wherever he is or with whomsoever he may be, whatever he tries or does, that Something he loves will not be extinguished from his mind. He will see it everywhere, and the stronger his love grows for it the more vivid it will be. A person like this never thinks of resting because he is never tired.

The more he regards everything as divine—more divine than it is of itself—the more God will be pleased with him. To be sure, this requires effort and love, a careful cultivation of the spiritual life, and a watchful, honest, active oversight of all one's mental attitudes toward things and people. It is not to be learned by world-flight, running away from things, turning solitary and going apart from the world. Rather, one must learn an inner solitude, wherever or with whomsoever he may be. He must learn to penetrate things and find God there, to get a strong impression of God firmly fixed in his mind.

It is like learning to write. To acquire this art, one must practice much, however disagreeable or difficult it may be, however impossible it may seem. Practicing earnestly and often, one learns to write, acquires the art. To be sure, each letter must first be considered separately and accurately, reproduced over and over again; but once having acquired skill, one need not pay any attention to the reproduction [of the letters] or even think of them. He will write fluently and freely whether it be penmanship or some bold work, in which his art appears. It is sufficient for the writer to know that he is using his skill and since he does not always have to think of it, he does his work by means of it.

So a man should shine with the divine Presence without having to work at it. He should get the essence out of things and let the things themselves alone. That requires at first attentiveness and exact impressions, as with the student and his art. So one must be permeated with divine Presence, informed with the forms of beloved God who is within him, so that he may radiate that Presence without working at it.

ABOUT THE BODY OF OUR LORD, HOW OFTEN ONE SHOULD PARTAKE OF IT, WITH WHAT DEVOTION AND IN WHAT MANNER [28]

THE TEXT

Those who would like to partake of the body of our Lord should not wait until they feel an upsurge of emotion or devotion, but let them rather consider their attitude or disposition [toward it]. Attach significance, not to what you feel like, but rather to what you are to receive and to your thoughts about it.

The person who wants to go to our Lord and go with a free heart, must first make sure that his conscience is without reproach. In the second place, his will must point only to God and he must so concentrate on God that he can take pleasure in nothing but God, and so that he will be displeased by all that is not leading to God. This is the test by which one may prove how far away from God he is—or how near—according as he is less or more this way. The third rule is that his affection of our Lord shall grow with each repeated Communion and that his reverence for the sacrament does not diminish with familiarity.

It is often true that what is life to one is death to another. Therefore, be careful that your love for God grows and your reverence does not die out. Then, granted that, the oftener you take the sacrament the better off you will be and the more salutary and beneficial you will find it. Thus, do not let any speech or sermon persuade you away from your God, for the more you go the better, and the dearer God will be to you.

For our Lord takes pleasure by living in men and with them. But perhaps you say: "Yes, sir, but I feel so bare and cold and dull that I dare not go to the Lord!" To which I reply:

So much the more your need to go to God! Being joined to

28 The translation of *The Talks of Instruction*, no. 20, is that of Blakney, *Meister Eckhart*, pp. 27–30. Used by permission of Harper & Brothers. See Petry, "Social Responsibility," *Church History*, Vol. 21, pt. 1, pp. 8–9.

him, made one with him, you will be justified: for the grace you
shall find in the sacrament will nowhere else be so evident.
There, your physical powers will be assembled and focused by
the superlative power of the presence of our Lord's body, the
scattered senses brought together into unison, and several of
them, being aimed too low, will be lifted up so that they, too,
point, like true offerings, to God.

Then the loving God conditions them to spiritual ways, weans
them from the obstruction of temporal things, makes them
adroit in matters divine, strengthens and renews them by his
body. For we are to be changed into him and sometime made
one with him, so that what is his shall be ours and what is ours,
his: our hearts and his are to be one heart; our body and his, one
body. So, too, it shall be with our senses, wills, thoughts, faculties, and members: they are all to be transported into him, so
that we feel with him and are made aware of him in every part
of the body and soul.

Perhaps you say: "But, sir, I am not aware that I have anything to offer more impressive than poverty; how then can I go
to him?"

My goodness! If you want to exchange your poverty, why not
go straight to that treasury of inestimable value and get rich?
For you ought to know that, as far as you are concerned, his is
the only treasure with which you will be contented or satisfied.
Therefore say to him: "I am coming to you so that your wealth
may supply my poverty, so that the unsearchable You may fill
my emptiness and your unlimited Godhead, more than man
may conceive, shall fulfill my base, spoiled humanity."

"But, sir, I have sinned too much; I shall never be able to
atone!"

For that reason, go to him; he has richly atoned for your
guilt. It is your free opportunity to make the best of all offerings
for your guilt to the Heavenly Father through him.

"But, sir, I should like to be able to thank God; but I cannot!"

Still go to him, for our Lord alone is agreeable to the divine
goodness and a perfect, unquestionable, and true measure of
gratitude to God. In brief, if you want to be relieved of all your
defects and be clad in garments of virtue and grace, and to be
led with joy again to the Source of your being, plan to partake
worthily and often of the sacrament and so be joined to our
Lord, ennobled by his body.

Indeed, the soul too may be led so near to God by the body of our Lord that all the angels, not excepting the cherubim and seraphim, shall not see any difference. For where they touch God they touch the soul, and where they touch the soul they touch God. There never was another such union [as between the soul and God], for the soul is nearer to God than it is to the body which makes us human.[29] It is more intimate with him than a drop of water put into a vat of wine, for that would still be water and wine; but here one is changed into the other so that no creature could ever again detect a difference between them.

Still you may say: "How can this be? There is nothing in my experience to correspond to it!"

What difference does that make? The less you experience and yet believe such things the more praiseworthy your faith will be, and the more distinctive and worth-while; for perfect faith is much more than human illusion. Through our Lord we get certain knowledge. The truth is that we lack nothing but perfect faith. That it seems to us that one thing is better than another is due merely to our physical limitations, for one thing is not more than another. If you have the same faith in everything, you will get as much, and have as much, out of one thing as another.

You might also say, "How may I believe such great things, while I am still so defective and given to so many other matters?"

See! You must observe two things about yourself that our Lord also had to deal with. He too had higher and lower powers, each having its own function. By his higher powers, he possessed and enjoyed the bliss of eternity while, at the same time, by his lower powers, he went through much suffering and struggle here on earth, and still this did not inhibit the function of the higher powers. So it should be with you. Your higher faculties should be trained on God, offered up to him and consecrated to him at all times.

Moreover, we should assign suffering solely to the body, the lower faculties, and the senses, and with all our strength freely plunge the spirit into God. The spirit will not be tempted by suffering, the senses, and [concerns of] the lower faculties. The increasing struggle, becoming ever more fierce, only magnifies the victory and emphasizes the glory of it. The stronger the temptation, the more insistent the impulse to vice, the more

29 Bernhart, *Reden*, p. 68: *Denn die Seele ist viel enger mit Gott vereint, als Leib und Seele. . . .* Cf. Karrer, *Eckhart*, p. 88, for references on the proximity of God and the soul.

genuine man's virtue will be and the dearer to God, once he has overcome it. Therefore, if you wish to receive God worthily, take care that your higher powers are directed toward God, that your will is seeking his; be careful also what you think about him and to fix your faith in him.

One does not receive the true body of our Lord, having this attitude, without receiving a special measure of grace and the more often it is so the better. Indeed, it is possible to receive the body of the Lord with such devotion and consideration, one's life being otherwise well-ordered, that he is received up into the lowest choir of angels. Again, it may so be received that one is raised up into the second choir. Indeed, you may so receive it as to be worthy of the eighth or ninth choir.

Thus, if two persons lived alike and one received the body of the Lord worthily, one more than the other, he would be to that other person like a blinding sun and would have a special unity with God.

This partaking of the blessed body of our Lord and the enjoyment of it consists not only of the visible enjoyment involved, but also of the spiritual partaking of divine unison and devotion by a hungry heart. One may eat of this [inner food] until he becomes richer in grace than any other person on earth. He may eat it a thousand times a day and oftener wherever he wishes, whether sick or well. He may prepare for it as for the sacrament, by means of a well-ordered life and great desire for it. If, however, one is not orderly and has not the desire, he should compel himself to it, and keep at it, until in time he does become holy and in eternity, blessed. May the Lord grant us the truth, the requisite love of purity and life eternal.[30] Amen.

[30] Cf. the Serm.: *Expedit vobis*, Blakney, *op. cit.*, pp. 198 ff., on excessive concern with outward observances.

LOVE CANNOT BE LAZY: A FRAGMENT [31]
(Pfeiffer, 33)

THE TEXT

Meister Eckhart said that no person in his life may reach the point at which he can be excused from outward service. Even if he is given to a life of contemplation, still he cannot refrain from going out and taking an active part in life. Even as a person who has nothing at all may still be generous for his will to give, another may have great wealth and not be generous because he gives nothing; so no man may have virtues without using them as time and occasion require. Thus, those who are given to the life of contemplation and avoid activities deceive themselves and are on the wrong track. I say that the contemplative person should indeed avoid even the thought of deeds to be done during the period of his contemplation, but afterward he should get busy, for no one can or should engage in contemplation all the time, for active life is to be a respite from contemplation.[32]

[31] This fragment is translated by Blakney, *Meister Eckhart*, as no. 14, p. 238. Used by permission of Harper & Brothers. It is no. 33, pp. 607–08 in Pfeiffer, *Meister Eckhart*.
[32] Cf. the sermon on *Mary and Martha* in the anthology, as also *Talks of Instruction*, nos. 6 and 10.

VII

Richard Rolle: Hermit of Hampole (c. 1300–1349)

INTRODUCTION

BIOGRAPHICAL NOTICE

RICHARD ROLLE WAS BORN NEAR PICKERING IN Yorkshire around 1300. His education at Oxford was probably underwritten by some interested Yorkshireman. The Oxford undergraduate underwent a profound conversion. He left the university and adopted a kind of hermit life. This was presumably for a time under the patronage of John de Dalton, Esquire. A later estrangement from Dalton was possibly succeeded by a period of study at the Sorbonne. Perhaps during this time he underwent his final initiation into mystical delights which he describes in the *Fire of Love* and other like works. During a stay near Richmond, he profited from spiritual association with an anchoress, Margaret Kirkeby, and later came to be a director of a convent of Cistercian nuns at Hampole. He died in 1349, probably of the Black Death.

BIBLIOGRAPHICAL ESSAY

See DS II, 1995. For a perceptive treatment consult R. Jones, *The Flowering of Mysticism*, The Macmillan Company, New York, 1939, pp. 211 ff. A classic attempt at editing Rolle's works was that of C. Horstman, *Yorkshire Writers: Richard Rolle of Hampole and His Followers*, 2 vols., London and New York, 1895–1896. The authoritative establishment of his corpus is by H. E. Allen, *Writings Ascribed to Richard Rolle, Hermit of Hampole, and Materials for His Biography* (Modern Language Association of America; Monograph Series, III), New York and London, 1927. Her basic volume of selections, *English Writings of Richard Rolle, Hermit of Hampole*, Oxford University Press, London, 1931, has a splendid introduction as well. Also quite useful is a modernized rendering of *Selected Works of Richard Rolle, Hermit,* including *The Form of Perfect Living,* transcribed by G. C. Heseltine, Longmans, Green & Co., London, 1930. The *Incendium amoris* has been ably edited by M. Deanesly, London, 1915. Richard Misyn's translation of the *Incendium,* i.e., *Fire of Love or Melody of Love,* and *The Mending of Life or Rule of Living* has been edited and introduced by F. M. M. Comper and E. Underhill, London, 1914. G. Hodgson has editions of *The Psalms* and *Our Daily Work,* London, 1928, 1929.

SYNOPSIS

There is truth in the assertion that the English school of spirituality is, with the exception of Walter Hilton, a nonsystematic one. Its end is practical, that is, the description and the application of spirituality.

Richard Rolle inaugurates this school. Among his chief works are the *Fire of Love (Incendium amoris)* and *The Mending of Life,* both translated by Richard Misyn in 1434–1435, and *The Form of Perfect Living.* The more refined subtleties of speculative spirituality and pure abstractions of thought are here at a minimum. Contemplation in Rolle employs an intellectual approach, but this mystical state has as its end the loving union of the soul with its God. Faithful dedication to the Trinity and the life of the Divine Persons is thereby ingrained.[1] The unitive life itself surpasses the role of sheer knowledge. But God and the love of Christ are uppermost in contemplative exercise.[2] Rolle seems so far inclined to shun all distractions from heavenly communication as, at times, to proscribe even charitable activities. Allowing for misunderstandings at this point, Rolle's emphasis on "contemplation" versus "action" is a far cry from Hilton's praise of the "medeled" or "mixed" life following Gregory and Bernard. Rolle never tires of stressing the logical incompatibility between full contemplative concentration and the constant demands of social service. But, having inexorably put contemplation above any and all social claims, he manifests charitable concern for others to no mean extent.[3] Certainly, works of charity are never wholly lacking in him, although he never permits anything but the most secondary role to be ascribed to the active life. As will be noted, however, there is every evidence

[1] *Form,* 12.　　[2] *Fire,* II, 8; *Form,* 12; *Mending,* 1, 2, 8, 11.
[3] *Fire,* I, 13, 21 ff.; *Mending,* 12.

that Rolle finds the contemplative experience itself a freshly beautiful one when accentuated by the company of other seekers after unrestricted union.[4]

Rolle himself claims to have had the experience of love he so exalts in his writings. He compares the experience to fire, heat, or *calor* and to spiritual music, or chant, i.e., *canor*, equal to that of the angels.[5] He likens it also to ravishment, *raptus*, and to sweetness, *dulcor*, which accompanies it. Rolle, be it noted, distinguishes ravishment involving abstention from the bodily senses and rapture without abstention from the senses. The second is more perfect than the first. This last consists in "the lifting of the mind into God by contemplation."[6] In spite of learned pleas to the contrary, one does well to discard any thesis reducing Rolle's mysticism to that of sensible phenomena alone. Nor are *calor*, *canor*, and *dulcor* to be regarded as merely three phases often intermixed in the contemplative life.[7]

The *Incendium amoris* analyzes the nature of this sweetness, heat, and song. There are, Rolle says, two kinds of rapture. One consists of being rapt *in* the bodily senses "by love *in* the feeling of the flesh." For the other, one is rapt *from* the senses to some vision, terrifying or pleasing, "*from* bodily feeling to a joyful or dreadful sight." He prefers the rapture of Love; that is, the kind involving rapture *in* not *from* the senses. Even some sinners have known that rapture which carries the soul out of the senses. But that rapture in which the mind is raised to God through contemplation is reserved for those only who love God. Still, this is as properly called rapture as the other, for, as the term *raptus* suggests, it does come to pass by violence, and, seemingly against nature.[8] Here Allen notes that Rolle apparently claims to experience a mystic ecstasy that historians of a puristically interpreted mysticism would deny him. Even Underhill, for instance, would severely edit the ecstatic claims of Rolle.[9]

This rapture of love in the bodily senses, Rolle holds to excel all the actions of the present life. It is to him "'a kind of fore-

---

4 *Fire*, II, 5; note that the *Epistle on Mixed Life* wrongly attributed to Rolle by G. G. Perry, *English Prose Treatises*, EETS 20, London, 1866, was properly ascribed to Walter Hilton by Horstman, *op. cit.*, Vol. I, pp. 264 ff. See Petry, "Social Responsibility," *Church History*, Vol. 21, pt. 1, pp. 10–11 and notes. Cf. Comper, *Fire of Love*, p. x.

5 *Incendium*, 14, 15; *Fire*, I, 14–15; Allen, *English Writings*, pp. xxv–xxix; *Form*, 8; *Mending*, 12, 11.

6 *Incendium*, 37; *Fire*, II, 7.   7 DS II, 1996–97.

8 Cap. 37, Deanesly ed., pp. 253–57; *Fire*, II, 7; Allen, *English Writings*, pp. xxviii–xxix.   9 *English Writings*, p. xxix, note 1; DS II, 1996.

taste of eternal sweetness.'"[10] Allen declares that in this experience resides the core of Rolle's mysticism. It is the preoccupation of his writings and is emotionally rooted. It finds its expression in sense terms but entails a purity in keeping with that of the immortal body acclimated to heaven.[11]

The obscure, oft recounted, details of Rolle's early experience cannot here be retold. Somehow, following his early schooling preparatory to and at Oxford, he had an experience of conversion which he describes in the *Fire of Love* and in the *Encomium on the Name of Jesus*, among others. In the midst of this profound experience he fled the university and took up the hermit's life. The details are recounted in a generally credible fashion in the *Office* later prepared, but never used, for Rolle.[12]

Rolle perhaps took up the eremitic life as a kind of contemporary alternative to the Franciscan mode of Poverty. Clearly enough, the example of Francis was in his mind then, as afterward.[13] From several of Rolle's writings, Allen pieces together the story of his probable itinerary of the spirit. This traces his initial months or years under the patronage of John de Dalton and his difficulty, ecclesiastical in part, over the irregular methods of his somewhat arbitrary well-wisher. Apparently, Rolle did not limit himself strictly to hermit life. He seems to have served, in some restricted function at least, as a pastor of souls during perhaps this, and certainly at a later, period of his life.[14] A portion of this preparatory period may indeed have been at the Sorbonne, where Rolle probably had a part of his eighteen months' readying for the mystic life. One of his early spiritual crises carried with it the deliverance from a peculiarly stringent temptation of the flesh through the efficacy of the name of Jesus, upon whom he called in his extremity. That name had for him, ever afterward, a unique place of honor in his spiritual journey.[15] A second great crisis came perhaps soon

10 *Incendium,* cap. 37, Deanesly ed., p. 256.
11 *English Writings,* p. xxix; cf. Rolle, Ps. 83:6; *Mending,* 11.
12 Cf. Jones, *Flowering,* p. 212; *English Writings,* pp. xiv ff.; *Dict. théol. cath.,* Vol. 13, pt. 2, cols. 2844–46; *Fire,* II, 7. The *Encomium* is in Heseltine (*Of the Virtues of the Holy Name of Jesus*), *Selected Works,* pp. 81–85. The *Office* is in F. M. M. Comper, *The Life and Lyrics of Richard Rolle,* J. M. Dent & Sons, Ltd., London, and E. P. Dutton & Co., Inc., New York, 1928, Appendix I, and in Comper, *Fire,* pp. xlv ff.
13 Jones, *Flowering,* p. 213; *Mending,* 2–3; Allen, *English Writings,* p. xlv.
14 *English Writings,* xviii, xxi–xxiv; cf. the *Office;* the *Encomium,* etc.
15 Cf. the *Encomium* and numerous apostrophies to Jesus' name and his Passion in the *Lyrics,* etc. Cf. in Heseltine, *Selected Works,* the *Ego dormio, Meditations on the Passion, The Bee,* etc. Cf. also *Mending,* 11 and 12.

after his leaving the Daltons' patronage. Earlier, there had been a first opening of the heavenly door. Now he entered on the second stage of initiation into the mystical joys described in the famous chapter 15 of the *Incendium amoris* (i.e., the *Fire of Love* I, 15). This was his entrance into the triple endowment of "heat, sweetness and song."[16]

It has already been noted that Rolle prefers the rapture of Love, *in* the bodily senses, to the rapture *from* the bodily senses to some vision.[17] Rolle apparently believes that his early experiences partake already in some degree of heavenly things. In his *English Psalter*, ch. 16:7, he recalls how softly, but powerfully, heaven draws upon his soul. In the *Psalter*, ch. 35:9, he notes that God's lovers are inebriated in contemplative sweetness "'and greatly delighted in the ardent access of Christ's love.'" Allen thinks that here he has pushed to its logical conclusion the doctrine of bodily immortality. He evidently holds that it is the part of virtue "to purify the senses and the affections," not to demolish them. From first to last he insists that his mystical joy will not change in kind even when he attains to celestial bliss and the angelic society. The memory of the name of Jesus has never left him, nor the emotions evoked by it.[18]

As for the harsh judgments on Rolle by some of his contemporaries and his own aspersions against some of the spiritual institutions of his day, little need be said here. His main animadversions are against contemporary priests and monks, especially, rather than against the mendicants. For the Franciscans he continues to have a large element of sympathy. This may be connected with his stay at Hampole, whose confessors were Minors. His joy has in it the Franciscan ring. He, too, is something of a troubadour. No one can read his poetic effusions on Jesus the Christ without thinking of the Poverello. His love for Poverty set forth in the *Form*, *The Mending of Life*, the *English Psalter*, chs. 9:31–32; 46:9, etc., is extreme in its Franciscan demand. He may even have undergone influence by the Spirituals while at Paris. His criticism of the clergy carries no insinuation of schism on his part. He thinks of himself as quite orthodox. The faults he condemns in the clergy are, in the Regulars, especially, the defections from any distinctively spiritual witness.[19]

---

16 *English Writings*, pp. xxiv–xxviii; cf. the *Office*; *Mending*, 11 and 12.
17 *Incendium*, 37; *Fire*, II, 7.
18 *English Writings*, pp. xxx–xxxi.
19 *Ibid.*, pp. xvi, xliii–xlvii; *Mending*, 3; *Form*, 3. Miss Allen devotes some suggestive pages to Rolle's possible sojourns at Paris on perhaps two occa-

Surely, Rolle will have been deeply misread by any who purport to find in him a misanthrope unconcerned with daily life. As already indicated, Rolle does not disparage the social obligations of men. He definitely makes a place for this in his writings. He does as definitely eschew social busyness for the one given to the highest contemplative work. Still, even here, he is no antisocial being. "Love cannot be lazy." And in the amazing chapters 34–35 of the *Incendium* (*Fire* II, 4–5), he longs poignantly for a friend who may help him to express the *canor*, the highest ecstasy of his joyous contemplative song. In the later years at Hampole, perhaps, he finds a measure of the equilibrium that contemplation must always seek to establish with action.[20]

sions. She considers the evidence for his having undergone literary influences there, and/or at Oxford, emanating from stricter Franciscans, and Spirituals such as Angelo da Clareno and Jacopone da Todi. These speculations can have little more conclusiveness than our own queries as to his having sustained contacts, however indirect, with Marsilius of Padua, William of Ockham, and Michael de Cesena. See *English Writings*, pp. 28–33; *Writings Ascribed to Richard Rolle*, pp. 332–35; 490–500.

20 *Ibid.*, p. liii; Comper, *Fire*, p. x; *Fire*, I, 13, 21.

THE MENDING OF LIFE OR RULE OF LIVING, AS TRANSLATED BY RICHARD MISYN IN 1434 FROM "DE EMENDATIONE VITAE" BY RICHARD ROLLE OF HAMPOLE: AND NOW DONE INTO MODERN ENGLISH [21]

THIS BOOK IS OF THE MENDING OF LIFE, OR ELSE OF THE RULE OF LIVING, DISTINCT IN XII CHAPTERS:

THE FIRST: OF CONVERSION OR HOLY TURNING
THE SECOND: OF THE DESPISING OF THE WORLD
THE THIRD: OF POVERTY
THE FOURTH: OF THE SETTING OF MAN'S LIFE
THE FIFTH: OF TRIBULATION
THE SIXTH: OF PATIENCE
THE SEVENTH: OF PRAYER
THE EIGHTH: OF MEDITATION
THE NINTH: OF READING
THE TENTH: OF CLEANNESS OF MIND
THE ELEVENTH: OF THE LOVE OF GOD
THE TWELFTH: OF THE CONTEMPLATION OF GOD

Of these, as God will grant, we shall pursue.

[21] Edited by F. M. M. Comper with an introduction by E. Underhill in the *Fire of Love or Melody of Love* and *The Mending of Life or Rule of Living*, London, 1914. Used by permission of Methuen & Co., Ltd.

Richard Rolle: Hermit of Hampole (c. 1300–1349)

THE MENDING OF LIFE

THE TEXT

Chapter I

Of Conversion

Tarry thou not to our Lord to be turned, nor put it off from day to day; for ofttimes the cruelty of death ravishes the wretched, and bitterness of pains suddenly devours them that now irk to be turned. It may not be numbered by us how many of the worldly wicked presumption has beguiled.

Truly it is a great sin to trust in God's mercy and not cease from sin, trowing God's mercy be so mickle that he will not give righteous pain to sinners. "Work ye therefore whiles it is day, the night truly comes in which no man may work."[22] "Light or day" he calls this life, in which we ought never to cease from good working, knowing that death to us is sicker,[23] the hour of death truly unsicker. "The night" he calls death, in the which our members are bound, and wits put by, and we may not now work any healthful thing, but shall receive joy or tormentry according to our works. In a point we live, yea, less than a point; for if we would liken all our life to the life everlasting, it is nought.

Therefore how waste we our life in love of vanity, not without grievous damnation; and all day negligent, without repenting, we stand idle. Lord, therefore turn us and we shall be turned; heal us and we shall be healed.[24] Many truly are not healed, but their wounds rot and fester; for to-day turned to God, to-morrow [are turned][25] from Him; to-day doing penance, to-morrow turning to their ill. [Of such it is said,] "we have cured

---

[22] John 9:4.
[23] Certain; "unsicker," uncertain.
[24] Jer. 17:14.
[25] All square-bracketed words are added from Douce MS. 322; Comper, *Mending*, p. 198 and note lxxv.

Babylon and it is not healed," for to Christ it is not truly turned.[26]

What is turning to God but turning from the world and from sin; from the fiend and from the flesh? What is turning from God but turning from unchangeable good to changeable good; to the liking beauty of creatures; to the works of the fiend; to lust of the flesh and the world? Not with going of feet are we turned to God, but with the change of our desires and manners.

Turning to God is also done whiles we direct the sharpness of our minds to him, and evermore think of his counsel and his commandments, that they may be fulfilled by us, and, wherever we be, sitting or standing, the dread of God pass not from our hearts. I speak not of dread that has pain, but that is in charity,[27] with which we give reverence to the presence of so great a Majesty, and alway we dread that we offend not in any little thing. Soothly, thus disposed, to God we are truly turned [because we are turned] from the world.

To be turned from the world is nought else but to put aback all lust, and to suffer the bitterness of this world gladly for God; and to forget all idle occupations and worldly errands, in so mickle[28] that our soul, wholly turned to God, dies pithily[29] to all things loved or sought in the world. Therefore being given to heavenly desires they have God evermore before their eyes, as if they should unwearily behold Him, as the holy prophet bears witness: *Providebam Dominum in conspectu meo semper*,[30] that is to say "In my sight I saw our Lord evermore before me." Not only the space of an hour; as do they that set all fair or lovely earthly things before the eyes of their hearts, which they behold and in which they delight and desire for love to rest. And after the prophet says: *Oculi mei semper ad Dominum; quoniam ipse evellet de laqueo pedes meos*,[31] that is: "Mine eyes evermore are to our Lord, for he shall deliver my feet from the snare." By this is shewed that except our inward eyes to Christ unwearily be raised we may not escape the snares of temptation. And there are many lettings[32] so that the eyes of our heart may not be fixed on God; of which we put some: abundance of riches; flattering of women; the fairness and beauty of youth. This is the threefold rope that scarcely may be broken;[33] and yet it behoves to be broken and despised that Christ may be loved.

Truly he that desires to love Christ truly, not only without

26 Jer. 51:9.   27 I John 4:18.   28 Much.
29 I.e., to the core.   30 Ps. 15 (16):8.   31 Ps. 24 (25):15.
32 Hindrances.   33 Eccl. 4:12.

heaviness but with a joy unmeasured—he casts away all things that may let him. And in this case he spares neither father nor mother; nor himself; he receives no man's cheer; he does violence to all his letters;[34] and he breaks through all obstacles. Whatever he can do seems little to him so that he may love God. He flees from vices as a brainless man and looks not to worldly solace, but certainly and wholly directed to God, he has nearly forgotten his sensuality. He is gathered all inward and all lifted up into Christ, so that when he seems to men as if heavy, he is wonderfully glad.

But there are many that say they will turn to God, but they cannot yet, they say, for they are holden back by this occupation or other; whose cold mind sorrowingly we reprove. For withouten doubt and they were touched with the least spark of Christ's love, anon with all busyness they would seek which way they might come to God's service, and in seeking they would not cease until they had found.

Ofttimes they feign excuses, which the rather accuses them more. Riches forsooth withdraws many, and the flattering of women beguiles them; and they that have long done well sometimes are drowned, by them, in the worst dikes. For fairness is soon loved; and when it feels itself loved, it is lightly cherished;[35] and the chosen one is cast down, and after turning or conversion, he is made worse than he was before. Then his name is blackened, and he that before was worthy now is despised of all men and hated of all.

I saw a man truly of whom they said that he chastised his body with marvelous sharpness for fifteen years, and afterward he lapsed into sin with his servant's wife, nor might he be parted from her until his death. In his dying truly they said that he cursed the priests that came to him, and refused to receive the sacraments.

Therefore the newly turned ought for to flee the occasion of sinning; and with their will avoid words, deeds, and sights stirring to ill. The more unlawful a thing is, the more it is to be forsaken.

The fiend also strongly upbraids against them which he sees turned from him and turned to God, and ceases not to kindle fleshly and worldly desires. He brings to mind lusts done before, and the desolation of the contrite; and unprofitable desires that were slaked before stir themselves. Among these it behoves the

34 Hinderers.   35 Readily encouraged.

penitent manfully to use himself, and to take ghostly armor to gainstand the devil and all his suggestions; and to slake fleshly desires and ever to desire God's love; and to go not from him, despising the world: of the which now we shall speak.

Chapter II

Of the Despising of the World

To despise this world is to pass through this life without the love of all temporal and passing things; to seek nothing in this world but God; for all vainglory and solace not to care; scarcely to take thy necessaries, and if they sometimes want, to bear it goodly. This is the despising of this world. Have this in mind if thou wilt not be slain [through love of it]. Thus is the world despised and not loved.

All, soothly, that we love we worship; it is also foul to worship dirt, that is, to love earthly things. Therefore these rich niggards[36] bind themselves thrall in most foul filth and stink, and joy to be called lords of men, [though they be servants of sin]. If a man be lord of men, that is not of nature but of fortune. That man is subject to vice is from a froward will. Put away therefore thy wicked will, and thou shalt be free from the fiend and from sin and made the servant of righteousness which teaches thee not to love earthly things.

Covetousness of the world and the love of God truly are contrary, and rest not together in one soul. The place is so strait that one falls out. The more soothly[37] thou castest out covetousness the more thou tastest God's love. The more covetousness, the less charity.

O wretched soul, what seekest thou in this world where thou seest that all things are deceitful and passing? They soonest beguile thee that most flatter thee. Why busiest thou thyself for mortal things? Why yearnest thou with great desire for the things that shall perish? Seest thou not that they perish sooner than they are gotten? "But I wot where thou dwellest, where Satan's seat is,"[38] that has blinded thine eyes and by his falsehoods has scorned thee: so that thou shouldest desire fleeting things and love hateful things, and despise abiding things and be drawn to things vanishing. And so thou settest thyself on a false ground,[39] and when thou weenest to stand thou fallest into the fire.

36 Misers.   37 Surely.   38 Rev. 2:13.   39 Foundation.

The dwellers in temporal plenty are beguiled by five things that they love: by riches; by dignity; by will; by power; and by honors. These bind them in sin, and constrain them in defaults; with these lusts they are overcome, and never are loosed but by death; but their loosing is too late when there is no more save endless pain. This lets them from despising the world; from God's love; from knowledge of themselves; from the desire for the Heavenly Kingdom. No man may be saved unless he cease to love the world with all that is therein. Cease therefore whiles heat is in the body and the fair age of youth yet abides.

What things shall delight him that disposes himself to love Christ? He will despise youth and will keep his strength for God; riches he counts for nought; he will take heed that this fairness is vain, and grace deceitful. Whereto shall I run on one by one? He shall perfectly despise all things that in this world pass as a shadow.[40]

O lover of the flesh, what findest thou in thy flesh wherefore thou so delightest in it? Does the form or shape please thee, or hast thou now thy joy in a skin? Why takest thou not heed what is hid under the skin? Or knowest thou not that fleshly fairness is the covering of filth, and the dregs of corruption, and oft the cause of damnation? Therefore be it enough for thee, all other things being despised, to love God; to praise God; with God to be; in God to joy; and from him not to part, but to cleave to Him with unslakened desire.

The world itself compels us to despise the world that is so full of wretchedness; in which is abiding malice, destroying persecution, swelling wrath, fretting[41] lust, false blaming for sin, and bitterness of slander; where all things are confused and withouten order; where neither righteousness is loved nor truth approved; where faithfulness is unfaithful, and friendship cruel, that stands in prosperity and falls in adversity.

There are yet other things that should move us to the despising of the world: the changeableness of time; shortness of this life; death sicker; the chance[42] of death unsicker; the stableness of everlastingness and the vanity of things present; the truth of the joys to come.

Choose what thou wilt. If thou love the world, with it thou shalt perish; if thou love Christ, with him thou shalt reign.

---

40 Eccl. 7:1 (6:12).
41 Consuming.
42 How it befalls or comes about.

Chapter III

Of Poverty

If thou wilt be perfect, go, sell all that thou hast, and give it to the poor, and come and follow Christ.[43] In the forsaking of worldly things and in the following of Christly things, it is shown there is perfection. Forsooth, all that have forsaken their goods follow not Christ, for many are worse after the forsaking of their goods than they were before. Then certain they serve backbiting, and they dread not to withdraw the good fame of their neighbors. Then they swell with envy; they gnash with malice; they set themselves before all others; they praise their state, all others they either dispraise or condemn. Trowest thou how that the fiend has beguiled such, that have neither the world nor God, whom by divers wiles he leads to endless tormentry.

Thou that understandest what I have said, take thy poverty another way. When He says, "Go and sell," he marks the changing of thy desire and of thy thought, as thus: he that was proud now be lowly; that was wrathful now be meek; he that was envious now be charitable; before covetous, now generous and discreet. And if he were unclean, now let him abstain not only from all ill but from all likeness of ill. And if before he exceeded in meat or drink, now by fasting let him amend. He, soothly, that loved the world too mickle, now let him gather himself altogether in Christ's love; and fasten all the waverings of his heart in one desire for things everlasting. And so no marvel that willful poverty shall be fruitful to him, and the noy that he suffers for God be a glorious crown. *Beati pauperes spiritu, quoniam ipsorum est regnum caelorum.*[44] That is to say: "Blessed be they that are poor in spirit, for theirs is the Kingdom of Heaven."

What is poverty of spirit but meekness of mind, by the which a man knows his own infirmity? Seeing that he may not come to perfect stableness but by the grace of God, all things that might let him from that grace he forsakes, and he sets his desire only in the joy of his Maker. And as of one root spring many branches, so of willful poverty, taken in this wise, proceed virtues and marvelousness untrowed. Not as some that change their clothes and not their souls; soothly it seems they forsake riches; yet they cease not to gather innumerable vices.

What is worse than a proud poor man? What more cursed

---

[43] Matt. 19:21.   [44] Matt. 5:3.

than an envious beggar? If thou truly forsake all things for God, see more what thou despisest than what thou forsakest. Take heed busily how thou followest Christ in manners. *Discite, inquit, a me quia mitis sum, et humilis corde.*[45] "Learn of me," he says, "for I am meek and lowly of heart." He says not, "Learn of me for I am poor." Truly by itself poverty is no virtue but rather wretchedness; nor for itself praised, but because it is the instrument of virtue and helps to get blessedness, and makes many eschew many occasions of sinning. And therefore it is to be praised and desired. It lets a man from being honored, although he be virtuous; but rather it makes him despised and overled,[46] and cast out among lovers of the world. To suffer all which for Christ is highly needful.

Therefore Christ to our example led a poor life in this way,[47] for he knew that for them that abound in riches and liking[48] it is hard to enter into heaven.[49]

Therefore so that men should desire poverty more greedily he has behested[50] high honor and the power of justice to them that forsake all things for him, saying: *Vos qui reliquistis omnia et secuti estis me, sedebitis super sedes duodecim, judicantes duodecim tribus Israel,*[51] that is to say: "Ye that have forsaken all things and followed me, shall sit on twelve seats, deeming the twelve tribes of Israel."

They, soothly, that have willful poverty and want in the meekness and lowliness that Christ teaches are more wretched than they that have plenty of all riches, nor shall they take the apostles' place of worthiness in the day of doom; but they shall be clad with the doublet of confusion, that is, damnation of body and soul.[52] They, soothly, that shine in meekness and lowliness, though they have mickle riches, yet shall they be set on the right hand of Christ when he deems.

Some men soothly say, We cannot leave all, we are sick; it behoves us to keep our necessaries that we may live; and that is lawful. But they are the less worthy, for they dare not suffer anguish, poverty, and neediness for God. Yet by the grace of God they may come to the height of virtue, and lift themselves to the contemplation of heavenly things, if they forsake secular occupations and errands, and unwearily rise to meditate and pray; and hold not the goods they have with full love, but having them, forsake them.

[45] Matt. 11:29.   [46] Oppressed.   [47] World.
[48] Pleasure.   [49] Matt. 19:23.   [50] Promised.
[51] Matt. 19:28.   [52] Ps. 108 (109):18.

Take heed also: to seek more than enough is foul covetousness; to keep back necessaries is frailty; but to forsake all things is perfectness. Therefore whiles they see high things that they cannot reach, they empride not nor presume because of the small things that they have, so that they may mannerly[53] ascend to the ordering of man's life: of which now follows.

Chapter IV

Of the Setting of Man's Life

So that a man may be righteously dressed[54] to the worship of God and to his own profit and the profit of his neighbor, four things are to be said:

First: What is it that defiles a man?[55] There are three sins, or three kinds of sin; that is to say, of thought, of mouth, and of work. A man sins in *thought* when he thinks aught against God; if he occupies his heart not with the praise and loving of God; but suffers it [to be abstracted or stirred] with divers thoughts, and to go void in the world. In *mouth* he sins when he lies; when he forswears; when he curses; when he backbites; when he defends a wrong; when he uses fond speech, or foul speech; or brings forth vain things or idle. In *deed* he sins manywise: by lechery; touching sinfully, or kissing; defiling himself willfully; or, without great cause, procuring or sustaining occasions by which he trows he might be defiled; in robbing; stealing; beguiling; smiting; and other such.

Secondly: Which are they that cleanse a man? And they are three, against the three aforesaid, that is to say: *Contrition of thought* and pulling out of desires that belong not to the praise or worship of God and love of him. *Confession of mouth*, that ought to be timely, bare,[56] and whole. *Satisfaction of deed*, that has three parts, that is to say: *Fasting* because he has sinned against himself; *prayer* because he has sinned against God; *alms* because he has sinned against his neighbor. Yet I say not he should do alms of other men's goods, but he should restore; for sin is not forgiven unless that that is withdrawn be restored.

Third: Which things keep *cleanness of heart*? And they are three: quick[57] thought of God, that there be no time in which thou thinkest not of God except in sleep that is common to all;

---

[53] Properly, i.e., in order.　　　　　　　[54] Directed.
[55] See *The Form of Perfect Living*, ch. 6, for the following treatment.
[56] Entire.　　　　　　　[57] Lively.

busy keeping of thine outward wits that, tasting, savoring, hearing, and seeing, they may wisely be restrained under the bridle of governance. [The third is honest occupation, as reading of Holy Writ, speaking of God, writing, or some other good deed doing.]

There are three things also that save[58] *cleanness of mouth*: avisedness of speech; to eschew mickle speech; and to hate lying.

Also three things keep *cleanness of working*: moderation in meat; fleeing ill company; and oft to mind of death.

The fourth: Which things are they that allure us to *conform us to God's will?* And there are three. First, the example of creatures, that is had by consideration; the goodliness of God, that is gotten by meditation and prayer; and mirth of the Heavenly Kingdom, that is felt in a manner by contemplation.

The man of God set to live in this wise shall be as a tree that is set by running waters[59]—that is the flowing of grace—so that he shall always be green in virtue and never be dry by sin; and shall give fruit in time; that is, he shall give good works as an example, and good words to the worship of God, and these he shall not sell for vainglory. He says "in time" against them that give example of fasting in time of eating, and the reverse way also; and against covetous men that give their fruit when it is rotten; or else they give not until they die.

Therefore he prays wisely who says: *Bonitatem et disciplinam et scientiam doce me,*[60] that is to say: "Goodliness,[61] discipline, and knowledge teach me." What is discipline but the setting of, or correcting of, manners? First therefore we are taught righteousness, and corrected of ill, by discipline; and after that we know what we should do, or what we should eschew. At the last we savor not fleshly things, but everlasting, heavenly, and godly.[62]

And when a man with all busyness has dressed himself to the will of his Maker and grown in virtue, and has passed another that peradventure went before in steadfastness of living and desire of Christ, he ought not thereof to joy, nor give praise to himself, nor trow himself better than others—although they be low—but rather hold himself as the foulest and most wretched. He shall deem no man but himself, and all others set before himself; he shall not desire to be called holy of men, but worthy to be despised. When he comes amongst men, he should procure to be last in number and least in opinion; for the greater thou art the more shouldest thou meek thyself in all things [and then

---

58 Preserve.   59 Ps. 1:3.   60 Ps. 118 (119):66.
61 Goodness or kindness.   62 Col. 3:2.

thou shalt find grace before God to be made high].[63] For the might of God is great, and honored by the meek; therefore it is despised by the proud, for they seek their own joy, not God's worship.

Truly, if thou takest with gladness the favor of the people and [the honor of men that is done to thee for thy holiness and good] fame in this life, know it well thou hast received thy meed. And if thou seemest marvelous in penance and chastity whiles thou joyest more in man's joy than in angel's, in the time to come nought but tormentry shall be for thee. Therefore thou oughtest perfectly to despise thyself, and entirely to forsake all joy of this world, and to think nor do nothing but in the sight of God's love, that all thy life, inward and outward, may cry the praise of God.

In meat and drink be thou scarce and wise. Whiles thou eatest or drinkest let not the memory of thy God that feeds thee pass from thy mind; but praise, bless, and glorify him in ilka morsel, so that thy heart be more in God's praising than in thy meat, that thy soul be not parted from God at any hour. Thus doing, before Christ Jesu thou shalt be worthy a crown, and the temptations of the fiend, that in meat and drink awaits most men and beguiles them, thou shalt eschew. Either, soothly, by unmannerly[64] taking of food they are cast down from the height of virtue or by too mickle abstinence they break down that virtue.

Many, truly, there are that always fluctuate in eating, so that overlittle or overmickle they always take; and the form of living they never keep whiles they trow that now this, now that, be better. The unwise and untaught, which have never felt the sweetness of Christ's love, trow that unwise abstinence be holiness; and they trow they cannot be worthy of great meed anent God unless they be known as singular of all men by scarceness and unrighteous abstinence.

But, truly, abstinence by itself is not holiness, but if it be discreet it helps us to be holy. If it be indiscreet it lets holiness, because it destroys discipline, without which virtues are turned to vice. If a man would be singular in abstinence he ought to eschew the sight of men and their praising, that he be not proud for nought and so lose all: for men truly ween they be holiest that they see most abstinent, when in truth ofttimes they are the worst.

He certain that has truly tasted the sweetness of endless love

---

[63] Cf. Prov. 25:6–7.   [64] Immoderately.

shall never deem himself to pass any man in abstinence, but the lower he supposes himself in abstinence anent himself, the more he shall be held marvelous anent men. The best thing, and as I suppose pleasing to God, is to conform thyself in meat and drink to the time and place and estate of them with whom thou art; so that thou seem not to be willful nor a feigner of religion.

Know it truly, without doubt, if one or two think well of him, yet others will call him an hypocrite or a feigner. But there are some covetous of vainglory that in no wise will be holden as common men; for either they eat so little that they always draw the speech of men to them, or they procure other manner of meats to be seen diverse from others: whose madness and obstinacy be far from me.

Truly, it is wholesome counsel that they that fast little give preference to them of greater abstinence, and since they may not do so great abstinence be sorry in mind. And they that are of great abstinence should trow others higher in virtue; whose virtue, in which they surpass, is hidden to men, whiles *their* virtue, that is to say abstinence, is praised of many. But unless it be dight with meekness and charity before Christ, it is nought.

Truly, the virtue of others is the more in that it is not seen of men. Who may know how much love a man has anent God, how great compassion anent his neighbor? And doubtless the virtue of charity surpasses without comparison all fasting or abstinence, and all other works that may be seen; and oft it happens that he that before men is seen least to fast, within, before Christ, is most fervent in love.

It behoves him truly to be strong that will manfully use the love of God. The flesh being enfeebled with great disease, ofttimes a man cannot pray, and then mickle more he cannot lift himself to high things with hot desire. I would rather therefore that a man failed for the greatness of love than for too mickle fasting; as the spouse said of herself: *Nunciate dilecto quia amore langueo*;[65] that is: "Show thyself to my love, for I long for love."

Be thou therefore steadfast in all thy ways and dress thy life after the rule shown to thee, and if thou may not get that thou desirest in the beginning mistrust not, but abide; for by long use and time thou shalt come to perfection.

If thou be a pilgrim and rest by the way, whatever thou dost in this life, to God ever have an eye. Let not thy thought go from him; think that time lost in which thou thinkest not of God. In

[65] Cant. 5:8.

the night praise him and desire his love, that sleep may not find thee in any other wise occupied than praying or thinking of God. See that thou flow not with vain thoughts, nor give thyself to many charges, but study to get and hold this steadfastness of mind so that thou dread not the wretchedness of this world nor desire the goods thereof unmannerly. He that dreads to suffer adversity knows not yet how it behoves us to despise the world; and he that joys in earthly things is far from everlasting things.

To the virtue of strength truly belong all adversities and prosperities; and also to despise death for endless life. And charity is to desire only heavenly things. A perfect lover, forsooth, joys to die, and suffers life meekly. To which perfection if thou ascend by the gift of Christ, yet shalt thou not be without tribulation and temptation: to show which our words shall turn.

Chapter V

Of Tribulation

When the fiend sees one man out of thousands perfectly turned to God; following the steps of Christ; despising this present world; loving and seeking only the things unseen; taking perfect penance; and purging himself from all filth of mind and body, he reparels[66] a thousand beguilings of annoyance and a thousand crafts of fighting to cast him from the love of God to the love of the world, and to fill him again with the filth of sin, so that at the least with lecherous thoughts he should be made hateful to God. He raises against him persecution, tribulation, slander, false blame for sins, and all kinds of hatred; so that pain may slay and break him that prosperity could not beguile.

Now sharpness, now cherishing, he puts before him, and he brings to mind images of bodily things; he gathers together fantasies of sin; he gaincalls old shrewdness and delights of past love; he inflames heart and flesh with lecherous fire. He begins with the least but he comes to the greatest flame of wickedness. And with as great busyness he studies to blow against us all kinds of temptation, tormentry, and tribulation, as he sorrows that we, by the mercy of God, have escaped from his cheeks.

He gets[67] nothing but that he might depart us from the unbodily embrace, sweetest and most chaste, of everlasting love, and eft[68] defile us in the pit of wretchedness. That were more wretched for us than I can tell.

---

66 Contrives or devises.   67 Seeks.   68 Afterward.

Who can think his madness that from the delicacies of kings would come down to swine's meat? And yet is he more mad that forsakes the delicious meat of unwrought wisdom and puts himself under the filth of the flesh. Is not gluttony and lechery swinish filth, and they that do such, feed they not fiends?

Therefore how we must do against the tribulation and temptations of our enemies, and how to gainstand, shall patience teach us; of which now we will speak.

Chapter VI

Of Patience

The children of God disdain to come down to the meat of unreasonable beasts, but truly they despise all unlawful lusts and worldly solace for the love of Christ. He, truly, that is fed with the bread that comes from heaven[69] inclines not his desire to those things that are moved by the devil. When temptations arise or tribulation, ghostly armor is to be taken and it is time to go to battle.

Temptations truly are overcome with steadfastness of faith and love; tribulation truly with patience. What is patience but goodly and willful suffering of adversity? He therefore that is patient murmurs in no grief, but rather at all times with the prophet praises God.[70] The more patient a man is in his noys the more glorious shall he be in heaven.

Gladly therefore are tribulations to be suffered in adversity, noys, and bitterness, pains and sickness and thirst; for by these and such other our sins are cleansed and meeds increased. Truly, it either behoves us in this life [to be burned with the fire of God's love and of tribulation, or else after this life] with the fire of purgatory or hell to be most bitterly crucified and punished. Choose therefore; we shall not escape the one. Here, truly, with little pain—yea, with joy if we cleave to God—we may eschew all pain to come.

Therefore tribulations are sent to us to call us from the love of the world, that we be not punished more grievously in the other life. With sorrow truly it behoves us to be cleansed of that ill we did in lust. If sinners build upon our backs,[71] they noy us not, if we suffer it patiently, but themselves; for if they put us to a little pain, for us they work a crown, but for themselves tormentry.

[69] John 6:53–58.   [70] Ps. 34 (35):28.   [71] Ps. 128 (129):3.

The sinful, truly, are suffered to pass this life withouten great tribulations; for in the time to come no joy is kept for them. Therefore holy men love tribulations, for they wot by them to win to endless life. Contrarily, the rejected always murmur in adversity, and flee all that they can; for whiles they are given too mickle to seen things, they are deprived of the hope of things everlasting. In outward things only they find solace, because they have fully lost the savor of heavenly.

There is no reasonable soul here abiding but she loves either creatures or the Maker of creatures. If she loves creatures, she loses God and goes, with the good loved, to death. Truly, such love in the beginning is labor and fondness; in the middle languor and wretchedness; and in the end hatred and pain.

He, soothly, that loves his Maker forsakes *omnia quae* that is in the world, and he thinks it full sweet of Him and with Him to speak; his refreshment is to think on Him. He spars[72] his outward wits that death ascend not by the windows[73]; and that he be not unprofitably occupied in vanity. And sometimes despisings, reproofs, scorns, and slanders are raised against him, and therefore it is needful to take the shield of patience and be readier to forget wrongs than to know them. He shall pray for their turning that hate him and cast him down, and shall care not to please man, but dread to offend God.

If thou be tempted in the flesh, make it subject, that the spirit be not overcome. Temptation, truly, that we consent not to is a matter for using[74] virtue. For no man wots whether he be weak or strong until the time he be assayed. Likewise in peace no man is called patient but when he is pulled with wrong; then he should see if he have patience. Many seem patient when they are not pricked, but when a soft blast—I say not of wrong but of correction—touches them, anon their mind turns to bitterness and wrath; and if they hear one word against their will, they give again two more ungodly: into whose counsel my soul comes not.

Therefore the darts of our enemy are to be slakened with the meekness and sweetness of Christ's love; nor is stead[75] to be given to temptation, although it be grievous. For the greater battle the worthier victory and higher crown, as says the psalm: *Beatus vir qui suffert tentationem, quoniam cum probatus fuerit accipiet coronam vitae,*[76] *etc.*; that is to say: "Blest be the man that suffers

---

72 Bolts, fastens.   73 Cf. Jer. 9:21.   74 Exercising.
75 Place.   76 James 1:12.

temptation, for when he is proved, a crown of life he shall receive that God behested to his lovers."

Doubt not that thou art in the perfect life if despising be to thee as praising, poverty as riches, hunger as meat; so that thou sufferest them with even soul, and if thou fall in nought from height of mind. Flee and hate as mickle as thou canst the praise of man; for it is most praiseworthy to be worthy of praising and not to be praised of men. The tongues of flatterers beguile many, and also the tongues of backbiters destroy many. Despise thou therefore favor, worship, and all vainglory; suffer meekly wraths, hatreds, and detractions; and so by slander and good fame, by tribulations and anger,[77] cease not to make haste to the Heavenly Kingdoms.

Ofttimes we fall so that, taught by many chances, we should stand more strongly. The strong dread not, nor are the patient heavy, in adversity, as it is written: *Non tristabit justum quicquid ei acciderit*,[78] "Whatever happens to the righteous man it shall not heavy him." Thus disposed, no marvel thou shalt overcome all temptation and slake all malice; thou shalt see thy noyers more wretched than thee, and with all thy mind thou shalt cleave to Christ.

Chapter VII

Of Prayer

If thou be set in temptation or tribulation, to prayer anon run. Truly, if thou prayest clearly, thou shalt have help.[79] Distractions sometimes come and waverings of heart, and thoughts of divers things ravish the heart and suffer it not to stand in the praising of God. Then peradventure it were good a while to think of holiness, until the mind is more stabled, and so thy prayers are fulfilled.

Truly, if any have left all wordly occupations for the love of God, and always are given to holy prayer and holy meditation, I trow that by God's grace within a short space they shall find their heart is stabled to love and pray. They should not waver now to this and now to that, but rather abide in rest and endless peace. Full mickle it comforts[80] to get stableness of heart to be busy in frequent prayers, and devoutly to sing psalms. With busy prayers truly we overcome fiends, and we loosen their waitings and stirrings. They are enfeebled and as it were

[77] More probably "flattery," according to the better readings.
[78] Prov. 12:21.   [79] James 5:15.   [80] Strengthens.

without strength, whiles we, strong and not overcome, bide in prayer.

Truly those men that have it in custom with long exercise to pray, sometimes find more sweetness and more fervent desire of prayer. Therefore whiles that sweetness and heat last it is good not to cease from prayers. When they cease—that often happens because of the corruptible flesh—they may turn to read Holy Scripture, or do some other profitable thing, that they suffer not their thought to waver from God, so that when they rise to pray again they may be quicker than they were before.

Truly, then, we pray well when we think of no other thing, but all our mind is dressed to heaven and our soul is enflamed with the fire of the Holy Ghost. Thus truly a marvelous plenteousness of God's goodness is found in us; for from the innermost marrow of our hearts shall the love of God rise, and all our prayer shall be with desire and effect; so that we overrun not the words, but nearly every syllable with a great cry and desire we shall offer to our Lord. Our heart being kindled with hot fire, our prayer is also kindled, and in the savor of sweetness is offered by our mouth in the sight of God, so that it is great joy to pray. For whiles in prayer a marvelous sweetness is given to the one praying, the prayer is changed to song.

Here some are reproved that rather take heed to meditation than to prayer, not knowing that God's speech is fired; and with it the filth of sin is cleansed, and the minds of prayers are enflamed with love. They say that they will first meditate and so stable their hearts; but they are stabled the later in that they are not comforted by prayer.

Although we cannot gather our hearts together as we would, yet may we not leave off, but little by little we should study to grow in prayer, that at the last Jesu Christ may stable us. To which meditation helps if it pass not measure and manner.

Chapter VIII

Of Meditation

The meditation of Christ's Passion and his death is good; and oft to recall what pain and wretchedness he freely took for our health in going about and preaching, in hunger, thirst, cold, heat, reproaches, cursings, and sufferings; so that it be not grievous to an unprofitable servant to follow his Lord and Emperor.

He truly that says he dwells in Christ ought to walk as He did.[81] Christ says truly by Jeremy: "Have mind of my poverty and of my passage, of wormwood and gall"[82]; that is to say, of sorrow and bitterness, by which I went from the world to the Father.

Truly this mindfulness or meditation overcomes the fiend and destroys his gins[83]; it slakes fleshly temptation and kindles the soul to Christ's love; it raises and cleanses, and also purges the mind. I trow this meditation is most profitable of all others to them that are newly turned to Christ. For there truly is shown the manhood[84] of Jesu Christ, in the which man should be repeatedly glad; in which he has matter for joy and also mourning. Joy for the sickerness of our gainbuying; heaviness for the filth of our sinning, on account of which it is to be grieved for that so worthy an offering is offered. For the boisterous and fleshly soul is not ravished into the contemplation of the Godhead unless all fleshly lettings be wasted away by ghostly [meditation and contemplation of the manhood].

Truly when a man begins to have a clean heart, and no image of bodily things can beguile him, then sickerly he is admitted to high things, that in love of [the Godhead] he may be wonderfully made glad. Some think truly on the joy of the blessed angels and holy souls joying with Christ; and this thought belongs to contemplation. Some think on the wretchedness of man's condition and his filth, and they dispute in their thoughts about man's folly that for the vanities of this life forgets the joys unseen. Others thus dispose their thoughts: that they will nothing but the praise and desire of their Maker, so that they love him as much as is possible for men in this life. To this meditation no man comes but he that is mickle used in these things before rehearsed. For truly it is a more excellent manner than others and makes a man most contemplative.

Therefore as the works and uses of saints are divers, so are their meditations divers. Yet all, because they come of one spring, go to one end, and they come or lead to one bliss; but by divers ways, through the one charity, that is more in one than another. Therefore the psalm says: *Deduxit me super semitas justitiae*;[85] that is, "He has led me upon the paths of righteousness"; as if to say, there is one righteousness and many paths by which we are led to the joy of the life everlasting; because whiles all are one in being, they are of divers needs, and in one righteousness

81 I John 2:6. 82 Lam. 3:19. 83 Crafts.
84 One MS. reads *humilitas*, another, *humanitas*. 85 Ps. 22 (23):3.

they are led to God by divers paths. Some go by a low path, some by a mean,[86] and some by a high. The higher path is given to him that is ordained from eternity to love Christ more, not because he works more than others, or gives more or suffers more, but because he loves more. Which love is heat and sweetness, and it seeks rest in all men.

No man may set himself in any of these paths; but he takes to that which God chose him. Sometimes they that seem in the higher are in the lower, and the reverse; for that is only inward in soul before God, not in anything that may be done outward of man. According to the disposition and desire of their meditation they are dressed to this path or to that. By outward works no man may be known who is more or who less before God. Therefore it is folly to deem of the chosen and say: he passes him; or, his merits are far below the meeds of this one, when plainly they know not their minds; the which if they knew they might lawfully deem.

Therefore truly God wills it to be secret from all creatures, that they despise not some too mickle, or honor some too mickle. For doubtless if they saw men's hearts, many that they honor they would despise as stinking and foul, and others that they set not by, nor yet desire to see, they would honor as most lovely, and as the holy angels.

Good thoughts also and meditations of the elect [be of God], and such by his grace he sheds forth to each one as best accords to their state and condition. Therefore I can tell thee my meditations, but which is most effectual for *thee* I cannot opine, for I see not thy inward desires. I trow truly that those meditations in thee most please God and most profit thee that God by his mercy sheds in thee.

Nevertheless in the beginning thou mayest have the words of other men; that I know well by myself. Truly if thou despise the teachings of doctors and trow that thyself mayest find something better than they teach thee in their writings, know forsooth that thou shalt not taste Christ's love. For truly it is a fond saying: "God taught them; why, therefore, shall he not teach me?" I answer thee: Because thou art not such as they were. Thou art proud and sturdy, and they were lowly and meek; and they asked nothing of God presuming but, meeking themselves under all, took knowledge from the saints. He taught them therefore so that we should be taught in their books.

[86] Middle.

If truly thou now desirest the love of Christ in thy meditations, or to resound his praises—as meseems—thou art well disposed. But the thoughts in which thou feelest more sweetness in
God profit thee more. To meditate well without sweetness profits
thee little, except in that case when the need for sweetness is not
felt.

Chapter IX

Of Reading

If thou desire to come to the love of God, and be kindled in
thy desire for heavenly joys, and be brought to the despising of
earthly things, be not negligent in meditating and reading Holy
Scripture; and most in those places where it teaches manners,
and to eschew the deceits of the fiend, and where it speaks
of God's love, and of contemplative life. Hard sayings may be
left to disputers and to wise men used for a long time in holy
doctrine.

It helps us truly mickle to profit in good. By this we know our
defaults and good deeds; in which things we sin, and in which
not; what we should do, and what forbear; and the most subtle
deceits of our enemies are opened to us. They kindle to love, and
prick to weeping. If we have delight in them as it were in all
riches, they prepare us a table of delights. [87]

But let not covetousness of the honor or favor or praise of men
kindle us to knowledge of Scripture, but only the intent to
please God; that we may know how we should love him, and
teach our neighbor the same. We ought not to be holden wise
anent the people but rather hide our knowledge than show it so
as to be praised, as it is said: *In corde meo abscondi eloquia tua, ut non
peccem tibi*,[88] that is: "In my heart I hid thy words, that I sin not
toward thee," in void or vain showing.

Therefore the cause of our speaking should be only the praise
of God and the edification of our neighbor, that it may be fulfilled in us: *Semper laus ejus in ore meo*.[89] "Alway his praise be in
my mouth," and that is, when we seek not our own honor and
we speak not against his praise.

Chapter X

Of Cleanness of Mind

By these nine degrees before touched upon man comes to

[87] Cf. Ps. 22 (23):5.   [88] Ps. 118 (119):11.   [89] Ps. 33:2 (34:1).

cleanness of mind, where God is seen. Cleanness, I say, that may be had in this life. How may perfect cleanness be gotten here where so oft man, with venial sins at least, is defiled? The feet of saints are to be washed for they draw the dust of the earth.

Who may truly say, "I am clean from sin"? Truly none in this life; for as Job says: *Si lotus fuero aquis nivis, et effulserint velut munditiae manus meae, tamen sordibus intinges me, et abominabuntur me vestimenta mea;*[90] that is to say: "If I be washed with snow water," that means true penance, "and if my hands shine with cleanness," because of works of innocence, "yet shalt thou touch me with filth," because of venial sins that can not be eschewed; "and my clothes shall abhor me," that is to say, my flesh makes me abhor myself; and sensuality that is so frail, slippery, and ready to love the liking beauty of this world, ofttimes makes me sin. Therefore the apostle says: *Non regnet peccatum in nostro mortali corpore.*[91] "Sin reigns not in our mortal body," as who should say: Sin may un-reign in us, but it may not un-be.

What cleanness therefore can man have in this life? Truly worthy and great if he rightly use himself in the study of reading, prayer, and meditation, as it is before noted. Truly, although he sometimes sin venially, yet forthwith, because his whole mind is dressed to God, it is destroyed. The heat truly of charity wastes in him all rust of sin, as it were a drop of water put into a great fire.

The virtue therefore of a cleansed soul is to have the mind busy to God, for in this degree all the thought is dressed to Christ; all the mind, although he *seems* to speak to others, is spread unto him. Truly in a clean conscience nothing is bitter, sharp, or hard, but all is sweet and lovely. Out of cleanness of heart rises a song of joy, sweet ditty and joyful mirth. Then full oft a wonderful joy of God is given, and heavenly song is inshed. In this state a man may know that he is in charity that he shall never lose; he lives not without great dread—not lest he should suffer tormentry, but that he offend not his Lover.

I spare to say more here for I seem to myself a full great wretch. For oft my flesh is noyed and assayed. Although forsooth the love of God and contemplative life is contained in these things beforesaid, yet somewhat of them is more specially to be said to your need and profit.

---

[90] Job 9:30–31.   [91] Rom. 6:12.

Chapter XI

Of the Love of God

O sweet and delectable light that is my Maker unmade; enlighten the face and sharpness of my inward eye with clearness unmade, that my mind, pithily cleansed from uncleanness and made marvelous with gifts, may swiftly flee into the high mirth of love; and kindled with thy savor I may sit and rest, joying in thee, Jesu.[92] And going as it were ravished in heavenly sweetness, and made stable in the beholding of things unseen, never, save by godly things, shall I be gladdened.

O Love everlasting, enflame my soul to love God, so that nothing may burn in me but his halsings.[93] O good Jesu, who shall grant me to feel thee that now may neither be felt nor seen? Shed thyself into the entrails of my soul. Come into my heart and fill it with thy clearest sweetness. Moisten my mind with the hot wine of thy sweet love, that forgetful of all ills and all scornful visions and imaginations, and only having thee, I may be glad and joy in Jesu my God. Henceforward, sweetest Lord, go not from me, continually biding with me in thy sweetness; for thy presence only is solace to me, and thy absence only leaves me heavy.

O Holy Ghost that givest grace where thou wilt, come into me and ravish me to thee; change the nature that thou hast made with thy honeyed gifts, that my soul, fulfilled with thy liking joy, may despise and cast away all things in this world. Ghostly gifts she may take of thee, the Giver, and going by songful joy into undescried[94] light she may be all melted in holy love. Burn my reins and my heart with thy fire that on thine altar shall endlessly burn.

O sweet and true Joy, I pray thee come! Come, O sweet and most desired! Come my Love, that art all my comfort! Glide down into a soul longing for thee and after thee with sweet heat. Kindle with thy heat the wholeness of my heart. With thy light enlighten my inmost parts. Feed me with honeyed songs of love, as far I may receive them by my powers of body and soul.

In these, and such other meditations be glad, that so thou mayest come to the pith of love. Love truly suffers not a loving soul to bide in itself, but ravishes it out to the Lover; so that the

---

[92] Cf. *Of the Virtues of the Holy Name of Jesus*, in Heseltine, *Selected Works*, pp. 81 ff.; also *Of Delight in God and Ghostly Gladness*, in Heseltine, *op. cit.*, pp. 104–06.

[93] Embraces.   [94] MS. Bg.: *incircumscriptum.*

soul is more there where it loves than where the body is that by it lives and feels.

There are soothly three degrees of Christ's love, by one or another of which he that is chosen to love profits. The first is called, unable to be overcome; the second, unable to be parted; the third is called singular.[95]

Then truly is love *unovercomable* when it cannot be overcome by any other desire. When it casts away lettings, and slakes all temptations and fleshly desires; and when it patiently suffers all griefs for Christ, and is overcome by no flattery nor delight. All labor is light to a lover, nor can a man better overcome labor than by love.

Love truly is *undeparted* when the mind is kindled with great love, and cleaves to Christ with undeparted thought. Forsooth it suffers Him not to pass from the mind a minute, but as if he were bound in heart to Him it thinks and sighs after Him, and it cries to be holden with His love that He may loose him from the fetters of mortality, and may lead him to Him whom only he desires to see. And most this name "Jesu" he in so mickle worships and loves that it continually rests in his mind.

When, therefore, the love of Christ is set so mickle in the heart of God's lover and the world's despiser that it may not be overcome by other desire of love, it is called *high*. But when he holds undepartedly to Christ, ever thinking of Christ, by no occasion forgetting him, it is called *everlasting* and *undeparted*. And if this be high and everlasting, what love can be higher or more?

Yet there is the third degree which is called *singular*. It is one thing to be high, and another to be alone; as it is one thing to be ever presiding,[96] and another to have no fellow. Truly, we may have many fellows and yet have a place before all.

Truly, if thou seekest or receivest any comfort other than of thy God, and if peradventure thou lovest the highest, yet it is not singular. Thou seest therefore to what the greatness of worthiness must increase, that when thou art high thou mayest be alone. Therefore love ascends to the singular degree when it excludes all comfort but the one that is in Jesu; when nothing but Jesu may suffice it.

The soul set in this degree loves Him alone; she yearns only for Christ, and Christ desires; only in his desire she abides, and after him she sighs; in him she burns; she rests in his warmth.

---

[95] See the *Form*, ch. 8, where the classification is "Insuperable," "Inseparable," and "Singular."
[96] MS. C: to be present.

Nothing is sweet to her, nothing she savors, except it be made sweet in Jesu; whose memory is as a song of music in a feast of wine. Whatever the self offers to her (besides) it or comes into mind, is straightway cast back and suddenly despised if it serve not his desire or accord not with his will. She suppresses all customs that she sees serve not to the love of Christ. Whatever she does seems unprofitable and intolerable unless it runs and leads to Christ, the End of her desire. When she can love Christ she trows she has all things that she wills to have, and withouten him all things are abhorrent to her and wax foul. But because she trows to love him endlessly she steadfastly abides, and wearies not in body nor heart but loves perseveringly and suffers all things gladly. And the more she thus lives in him the more she is kindled in love, and the liker she is to him.

No marvel loneliness accords with such a one that grants no fellow among men. For the more he is ravished inwardly by joys, the less is he occupied in outward things; nor is he let by heaviness or the cares of this life. And now it seems as if the soul were unable to suffer pain, so that not being let by anguish, she ever joys in God.

O my soul, cease from the love of this world and melt in Christ's love, that always it may be sweet to thee to speak, read, write, and think of him; to pray to him and ever to praise him. O God, my soul, to thee devoted, desires to see thee! She cries to thee from afar. She burns in thee and languishes in thy love. O Love that fails not, thou hast overcome me! O everlasting Sweetness and Fairness, thou hast wounded my heart, and now overcome and wounded I fall. For joy scarcely I live, and nearly I die; for I may not suffer the sweetness of so great a Majesty in this flesh that shall rot.

All my heart truly, fastened in desire for Jesu, is turned into heat of love, and it is swallowed into another joy and another form. Therefore, O good Jesu, have mercy upon a wretch. Show thyself to me that longs; give medicine to my hurt. I feel myself not sick, but languishing in thy love. He that loves thee not altogether loses all; he that follows thee not is mad. Meanwhile therefore be thou my Joy, my Love, and Desire, until I may see thee, O God of Gods, in Syon.

Charity truly is the noblest of virtues, the most excellent and sweetest, that joins the Beloved to the lover, and everlastingly couples Christ with the chosen soul. It re-forms in us the image of the high Trinity, and makes the creature most like to the Maker.

O gift of love, what is it worth before all other things, that challenges[97] the highest degree with the angels! Truly the more of love a man receives in this life, the greater and higher in heaven shall he be. O singular joy of everlasting love that ravishes all His to the heavens above all worldly things, binding them with the bands of virtue!

O dear charity, he is not wrought on earth that—whatever else he may have—has not thee. He truly that is busy to joy in thee is forthwith lift above earthly things. Thou enterest boldly the bedchamber of the Everlasting King. Thou only art not ashamed to receive Christ. He it is that thou hast sought and loved. Christ is thine: hold him, for he cannot but receive thee, whom only thou desirest to obey. For withouten thee plainly no work pleases him. Thou makest all things savory. Thou art a heavenly seat; angels' fellowship; a marvelous holiness; a blissful sight; and life that lasts endlessly.

O holy charity, how sweet thou art and comfortable; that remakest that that was broken! The fallen thou restorest; the bond thou deliverest; man thou makest even with angels. Thou raisest up those sitting and resting, and the raised thou makest sweet.

In this degree or state of love is love chaste, holy, and willful:[98] loving what is loved for the self, not for goods, and fastening itself altogether on that that is loved. Seeking nothing outward, pleased[99] with itself: ardent, sweet-smelling, heartily binding love to itself in a marvelously surpassing manner. In the loved one joying [all other things despising and forgetting]; thinking without forgetfulness; ascending in desire; falling in his love; going on in halsing; overcome by kissing; altogether molten in the fire of love.

Thus truly Christ's lover keeps no order in his loving nor covets no degree,[1] because however fervent and joyful he be in the love of God in this life, yet he thinks to love God more and more. Yea, though he might live here evermore yet he should not trow at any time to stand still and not progress in love, but rather the longer he shall live the more he should burn in love.

God truly is of infinite greatness, better than we can think; of unreckoned sweetness; inconceivable of all natures wrought; and can never be comprehended by us as he is in himself in eternity. But now, when the mind begins to burn in the desire for its Maker, she is made able to receive the unwrought light, and so inspired and fulfilled by the gifts of the Holy Ghost—as

[97] Claims.   [98] Voluntary.   [99] Content.   [1] Rank.

far as is lawful to mortals—she has heavenly joy. [Then she overpasseth] all things seen, and is raised up in height of mind to the sweetness of everlasting life. And whiles the soul is spread with the sweetness of the Godhead and the warmness of Creating Light, she is offered in sacrifice to the everlasting King, and being accepted is all burned up.

O merry love, strong, ravishing, burning, willful, stalwart, unslakened, that brings all my soul to thy service, and suffers it to think of nothing but thee! Thou challengest for thyself all that we live; all that we savor; all that we are.[2]

Thus therefore let Christ be the beginning of our love, whom we love for himself. And so we love whatever is to be loved ordinately for him that is the Well of love, and in whose hands we put all that we love and are loved by. Here soothly is perfect love shown: when all the intent of the mind, all the privy working of the heart, is lift up into God's love; so that the might and mirth of true love be so mickle that no worldly joy, nor fleshly merchandise, be lawful nor liking.

O love undeparted! O love singular! Although there were no torments for the wicked, nor no meed in heaven should be trowed [for chosen souls], yet shouldst thou never the sooner loose thee from thy Love. More tolerable it were to thee to suffer an untrowed grief than once to sin deadly. Therefore truly thou lovest God for himself and for no other thing, nor thyself except for God; and thereof it follows that nothing but God is loved in thee. How else should God be all in ilk thing, if there be any love of man in a man?

O clear charity, come into me and take me into thee and so present me before my Maker! Thou art savor well tasting; sweetness well smelling, and pleasant odor; a cleansing heat and a comfort endlessly lasting. Thou makest men contemplative; heaven's gate thou openest; the mouths of accusers thou sparrest; thou makest God be seen and thou hidest a multitude of sins. We praise thee, we preach thee, by the which we overcome the world; by whom we joy and ascend the heavenly ladder. In thy sweetness glide into me: and I commend me and mine unto thee withouten end.

Chapter XII

Of Contemplation

Contemplative life or contemplation has three parts: reading,

2 Cf. Rom. 14:8.

prayer, and meditation. In *reading* God speaks to us; in *prayer* we speak to God. In *meditation* angels come down to us and teach us that we err not; in *prayer* they go up and offer our prayers to God, joying in our profit; that are messengers betwixt God and us.

Prayer certain is a meek desire of the mind dressed in God, with which, when it comes to him, he is pleased. Meditation on God and godly things, in which is the halsing of Rachel, is to be taken after prayer and reading.

To reading belongs reason or the inquisition of truth, that is as a goodly light marked upon us. To prayer belongs praise, song, surpassing in beholding, and marvel; and thus contemplative life or contemplation stands in prayer. To meditation belongs the inspiration of God, understanding wisdom, and sighing.

If it be asked what is contemplation, it is hard to define. Some say that contemplative life is nought else but knowledge of things to come and hidden; or to be void of all worldly occupation; or the study of God's letters. Others say that contemplation is the free sight into the visioned truths of wisdom, lift up with full high marvel. Others say that contemplation is a free and wise insight of the soul all spread about to behold His might. Others say, and say well, that contemplation is joy in heavenly things. Others say, and say best, that contemplation is the death of fleshly desires through the joy of the mind upraised.

To me it seems that contemplation is the joyful song of God's love taken into the mind, with the sweetness of angels' praise. This is the jubilation that is the end of perfect prayer and high devotion in this life. This is the ghostly mirth had in mind for the Everlasting Lover, with great voice outbreaking. This is the last and most perfect deed of all deeds in this life. Therefore the psalmist says: *Beatus vir qui scit jubilationem*,[3] that is to say, "Blest be the man that knows jubilation," in contemplation of God. Truly none alien to God can joy in Jesu, nor taste the sweetness of his love. But if he desire to be ever kindled with the fire of everlasting love, in patience, meekness, and [gentle] manner, and to be made fair with all cleanness of body and soul and dight with ghostly ointments, he is lift up into contemplation. Let him unceasingly seek healthful virtues, by which in this life we are cleansed from the wretchedness of sins, and in another life, free from all pain, we joy endlessly in the blessed life; yet in

[3] Ps. 88:16 (89:15).

this exile he thus shall be worthy to feel the joyful mirth of God's love.

Therefore be not slow to chastise thyself with prayer and waking, and use holy meditations; for doubtless with these ghostly labors, and with heaviness and weeping from inward repenting, the love of Christ is kindled in thee, and all virtue and gifts of the Holy Ghost are shed into thy heart. Begin, therefore, by willful poverty, so that whiles thou desirest nought in this world, before God and man thou livest soberly, chastely, and meekly. To have nothing is sometime of need, but to will that you may have nought is of great virtue. We may have mickle desires [and yet will to have right nought, when we hold that we have to our need and not to our lust. Right as he sometime that hath nought coveteth to have many things; right so he that seemeth to have many things hath right nought, for that that he hath he loveth it not, save only for his bodily need].

Truly it behoves the most perfect to take necessaries, else were he not perfect if he refused to take that whereof he should live.

This is the manner for perfect men to keep: all worldly goods for God to despise, and yet to take of the same meat and clothing; and if this want at any time, not to murmur but to praise God; and as much as they may to refuse superfluities. The warmer a man waxes with the heat of everlasting light, the meeker shall he be in all adversities. He that is truly and not feignedly meek holds himself worthy of being despised, and neither by harm nor reproof is provoked to wrath. Wherefore lowing himself to continual meditation, it is given him to rise to the contemplation of heavenly things, and the sharpness of his mind being cleansed as the sickness of the flesh suffers, it is given him to sing sweetly and burningly with inward joys. And truly when he goes to seek any outward thing, he goes not with a proud foot, but only joying in high delights anon with the sweetness of God's love is as it were ravished in trance, and being ravished is marvelously made glad.

Such, forsooth, is contemplative life if it be taken in due manner. By long use in ghostly works we come to contemplation of things everlasting. The mind's sight is truly taken up to behold heavenly things, yet by shadowly sight and in a mirror, not clearly and openly: whiles we go by faith we see as it were by a mirror and shadow. Truly if our ghostly eye be busy to that spiritual light, it may not see that light in itself as it is, and yet it feels that it is there whiles it holds within the savor and heat of that light unknown. Whereof in the psalm it is said, *Sicut tenebrae ejus, ita et lumen ejus*,[4] that is, "And as the darkness thereof, so the light thereof."

Although truly the darkness of sin be gone from a holy soul, and murk things and unclean be passed, and the mind be purged and enlightened, yet whiles it bides in this mortal flesh that wonderful joy is not perfectly seen. Forsooth, holy and contemplative men with a clear face behold God.[5] That is, either their wits are opened [for to understand holy writ; or else the door of heaven is opened unto them]: that is more. As one might say, all lettings betwixt their mind and God are put back, their hearts are purged, and they behold the citizens of heaven. Some truly have received both these.

As we, standing in darkness, see nothing, so in contemplation that invisibly lightens the soul, no seen light we see. Christ also makes darkness his resting place,[6] and yet speaks to us in a pillar of a cloud. But that that is felt is full delectable. And in this truly is love perfect when man, going in the flesh, cannot be glad but in God, and wills or desires nothing but God or for God. Hereby it is shown that holiness is not in crying of the heart, or tears, or outward works, but in the sweetness of perfect charity and heavenly contemplation. Many truly are molten in tears, and afterward have turned them to evil; but no man defiles himself with worldly business after he has truly joyed in everlasting love. To greet and to sorrow belong to the new-converted, beginners, and profiters[7]; but to sing joyfully and to go forth in contemplation belongs but to the perfect.

He therefore that has done penance for a long time, whiles he feels his conscience pricking for default, knows without doubt that he has not yet done perfect penance. Therefore, in the meantime tears shall be as bread to him day and night;[8] for unless he first punish himself with weeping and sighing, he cannot come to the sweetness of contemplation.

Contemplative sweetness is not gotten but with full great labor; and with joy untold it is possessed. Forsooth, it is not of man's merit but God's gift. And yet from the beginning to this day a man might never be ravished in contemplation of everlasting love unless he before had perfectly forsaken all the vanity

---

4 Ps. 138 (139):12.
5 I.e., "'beholden the ioye of God through revelation,'" according to MS. D. See Comper, *Mending*, p. 266, note xci.
6 Cf. Ps. 17:12 (18:11).
7 I.e., those advancing.   8 Ps. 41:4 (42:3).

of the world. Moreover, he ought to be used in healthful meditation and devout prayer before he come truly to the contemplation of heavenly joys.

Contemplation is sweet and desirable labor. It gladdens the laborer, and hurts not. No man has this but in joying: not when it comes, but when it goes, he is weary. O good labor to which mortal men dress them! O noble and marvelous working that those sitting do most perfectly! It behoves that he take great rest of body and mind whom the fire of the Holy Ghost truly enflames.

Many truly know not how to rest in mind, nor yet to put out void and unprofitable thoughts, and cannot fulfill what is hidden in the psalm: *Vacate, et videte quoniam ego sum Deus*;[9] that is to say: "Be void from worldly vanity and see, for I am God." Truly the void in body and wavering in heart are not worthy to taste and see how sweet our Lord is—how sweet the height of contemplation.

Truly ilk man contemplative[10] loves solitariness so that the more fervently and oftener, in that he is letted of no man, he may be exercised in his affections.

Then, therefore, it is known that contemplative life is worthier and fuller of meed than active life.[11] And all contemplatives by the moving of God love solitary life, and because of the sweetness of contemplation are especially fervent in love. It seems that solitary men raised by the gift of contemplation are high and touch the highest perfection. Unless it happen there be some in such state that they have come even with the height of the contemplative life, and yet they cease not to fulfill the office of the preacher. *They* pass these other solitaries—highest in contemplation and only given to godly things, not to the needs of their neighbors—their degrees being like, and for their preaching they are worthy a crown [that is cleped *aureola*].[12]

Truly, a very contemplative man is set toward the light unseen with so great desire that ofttimes he is deemed by man as a fool or unwise; and that is because his mind is enflamed from its seat with Christ's love. It utterly changes his bodily bearing,

---

9 Ps. 45:11 (46:10).

10 I.e., "Truly each man who is a contemplative. . . ."

11 Cf. Petry, "Social Responsibility," *Church History*, Vol. 21, no. 1, pp. 10–11 and notes.

12 "The *aureol* is generally taken by mystical writers to be the reward of those who have taken the vow of celibacy." Comper, *Mending*, p. 267, note xciii.

and his body departing also from all earthly works, it makes God's child as a man out of his mind.

Thus, truly, whiles the soul gathers all the self into endless mirth of love, withholding herself inwardly she flows not forth to seek bodily delights. And because she is fed inwardly with liking pleasure, it is no marvel though she say sighing: "Who shall give thee me, my brother, that I may find thee without, and kiss thee?"[13] That is to say: Loosed from the flesh I may be worthy to find thee, and, seeing thee face to face, be joined with thee withouten end. "And now man despises me."[14]

A devout soul given to contemplative life and fulfilled with love everlasting despises all vainglory of this world, and, joying only in Jesu, covets to be loosed. For why she is despised by these that savor and love this world, not heaven, and grievously languishes in love, and greatly desires with the lovely company of the angels to be given to the joys that worldly adversity cannot noy.[15]

Nothing is more profitable, nothing merrier, than the grace of contemplation that lifts us from these low things and offers us to God. What is this grace but the beginning of joy? And what is the perfection of joy but grace confirmed? In which is kept for us a joyful happiness and happy joy, a glorious endlessness and everlasting joy, to live with the saints and dwell with angels. And that which is above all things: truly to know God; to love him perfectly; and in the shining of his majesty to see him and, with a wonderful song of joy and melody, to praise him endlessly.

To whom be worship and joy, with deeds of thankfulness, in the world of worlds. Amen.

---

13 Cant. 8:1.
14 Actually, the R.V. says: "Yea, and none would despise me." Vulgate: *et jam me nemo despiciat.* [?] Comper, *Mending*, p. 242, note 3.
15 Annoy or hurt.

VIII

Henry Suso (c. 1295-1366)

INTRODUCTION

BIOGRAPHICAL NOTICE

SUSO WAS NOBLY BORN IN CONSTANCE ABOUT 1295 OR 1300. He became a Dominican novice at thirteen. Experiencing an ecstatic conversion at eighteen years, he underwent a decade of strict ascetic self-discipline. Following preliminary theological studies, he entered the *studium generale* at Cologne between 1324 and 1328. Whether or not he actually studied under Eckhart, he knew the Meister's teachings well and defended them ably. Returning to teach in the friary school at Constance, he was, after some years as lector, made prior, while the community was in exile, probably in 1343 or 1344. His service thus began midway in the banishment (1339–1349) of all but four of the Dominicans from Constance for supporting a papal interdict. The friars opposed the attempted enforcement by the city council, in 1339, of an imperial edict restoring services.

From about 1335 or 1340 onward, Suso in a crisis experience abandoned his ascetic seclusion for a higher school of perfect *Gelassenheit*, i.e., "resignation," "abandon," or "joyful endurance and patience in the face of adversity." For isolated teaching and writing he henceforth substituted a life of preaching and pastoral ministry. This was in widely itinerated services, not only to Dominicans, but also to Beguine communities and in association with the Friends of God. Elsbeth Stagel, daughter of a Zürich councilor, and a nun at Toss, recorded anecdotes of Suso's career that have made up the kernel of his autobiography, *The Life of the Servant*.

Often misunderstood and misjudged in a period of truly renounced service to the larger world, Suso was frequently the victim of scandalmongering. This probably led to his deposition as prior in 1348 and his being sent to Ulm. Tardily found innocent by a chapter general in 1354, he lived on at Ulm in increasingly restored good graces and under the favor of the provincial general until his death in 1366.

Bibliographical Essay

A good discussion of Suso and of the literature is to be found in J. M. Clark, *The Great German Mystics*, Basil Blackwell, Oxford, 1949. See also the introduction and notes of Clark's translation of Suso's *Little Book of Eternal Wisdom* and *Little Book of Truth*, Faber and Faber, Ltd., London, 1953. The basic edition of his works is K. Bihlmeyer, *Heinrich Seuse, deutsche Schriften*, Stuttgart, 1907. Other useful bodies of texts are H. S. Denifle, *Deutsche Schriften des sel. Heinrich Seuse*, Munich, 1876; A. Gabele, *Deutsche Schriften von Heinrich Seuse*, Leipzig, 1924; *L'œuvre mystique de Henri Suso*, with good introduction and translation by R. P. Benoit Lavaud, 5 vols., Egloff et L. U. F., Paris, 1946; and *Le Bienheureux Henri Suso: Œuvres*, tr. by Jeanne Ancelet-Hustache, Aubier, Paris, 1943. The text of Suso's Latin version of *The Little Book of Eternal Wisdom*, is by J. Strange, ed., *Henrici Susonis seu fratris Amandi Horologium Sapientiae*, Cologne, 1861. Consult M. de Gandillac, in *Mélanges*, Vol. 3 (1946), pp. 72–82, on Suso in relation to Tauler, pp. 60 ff. An excellent study of the "wisdom" motif in relation to "bride" and "bridegroom" mysticism is J. Bühlmann, *Christuslehre und Christusmystik des Heinrich Seuse*, J. Stocker, Lucerne, 1942. Note Wentzlaff-Eggebert, *Deutsche Mystik*, pp. 118 ff., and the literature, pp. 309–311. The relations of Suso to scholastic thought and to *Gelassenheit* are helpfully considered in J. A. Bizet, *Henri Suso et le déclin de la scholastique*, Aubier, Paris, 1946, and in X. de Hornstein, *Les grands mystiques allemands du xive siècle: Eckhart, Tauler, Suso*, Fribourg en Suisse, 1922.

Synopsis

Suso may well be called "the chevalier of wisdom." Dominican though he was, he reminds us frequently of the spiritual knighthood of Francis. Having undergone a spiritual crisis in his late teens, Suso had also found a gracious lady, Dame Wisdom.[1] Following the rules of the minnesinger, he gave rigorous

---

[1] This introduction follows closely the main outlines of Gandillac, in *Mélanges*, Vol. 3, pp. 72 ff.

proofs of his knightly affection.[2] He set the test in stern austerities. At the *studium generale* of Cologne, he made Tauler's[3] acquaintance. He came somewhere under the strong influence of Eckhart. He was moved by the Meister's scorn for posers of renunciation who avoid the hard school of the Master of Galilee.

Obvious in his first work, *The Little Book of Truth*, 1327, is his awareness of controverted issues raised by the Eckhart affair. Suso distinguishes carefully the role of genuine despoilment from that of the Beghard libertines. He knows the humiliations of the flesh weakened by illness. He is forced to reduce his ascetic ardors. He is even accused of seducing his spiritual advisees. Between his transfer to Ulm in 1348—for whatever reasons of discipline or protection against his foes—and his death in 1366, a world of transformation took place. The raw recruit of Lady Wisdom, the defeated knight of the early jousts, somehow graduated from the school of true renunciation. Preaching, discharging faithfully the duties of the mixed life, he gave himself in the Rhineland to a harder life than the one of sheer ascetic rigor. He found in the school of the Master—Eckhart's and his own—the veritable encounter with wisdom and glorious self-abandon. Suffering the more as he accepted more of others' woes, he finally knew the joy of entering the way of his Lord.

The *Horologium sapientiae* and its vernacular version, *The Little Book of Eternal Wisdom*, when coupled with *The Life of the Servant*, provide a rich tapestry of self-inquiry and self-detachment. They depict true *Gelassenheit*.[4] Suso's autobiography reflects clearly the mounting awareness that he, like Francis, must do more than assume the guise of the spirit if he would follow Christ. Out of the anguish of the world's repudiation and his own self-indictment, he must find in Christ's school the genuinely joyous way of spiritual selflessness. His works give us a true picture of a genuinely renounced spirit. The *Life* and *The Little Book of Eternal Wisdom* are of paramount importance in delineating his spiritual pilgrimage. The rarer *Sermons* and the *Booklets* on his active ministry confirm this story.

2 On "wisdom" in its Biblical setting and in relation to the minnesinger, see Bühlmann, *op. cit.*, pp. 30 ff., 42. For the large role of "wisdom" in the Middle Ages, consult F. W. Oediger, *Über die Bildung der Geistlichen im späten Mittelalter*, E. J. Brill, Cologne, 1953, pp. 1 ff.

3 See literature on Tauler in Petry, "Social Responsibility," *Church History*, Vol. 21, pt. 1, pp. 9–10, 18. Cf. A. L. Corin, *Sermons de Tauler*, 3 vols., Paris, 1927.

4 See the discussions by index in Bühlmann, and Bizet, *op. cit.* See especially ch. 19 of the *Life*, chs. 4 and 7 of *The Little Book of Truth*, etc.

Eckhart and Tauler, for all their preaching and teaching overtness, reserve their inmost self-revelations, their most personal experiences. They tend to ignore, when they do not positively deride, the visions and ravishments so frequently associated with the mystic union. Suso is less guarded. Purified in his own modest self-analysis, he does grow in the grace of what, in Christ, he has become beyond his own early strengths and weaknesses. He gives his testimony to this in poetic vision even as Francis does in his Praises and Lauds of the Crucified. The historic Christ, the figure of the abused, crucified Lord, is fundamental in all of Suso's meditation. The soul given to the throes of abandon sustains the vision of Calvary as being at once the occasion of the keenest sorrow and the instance for the truest consolation.

The Little Book of Truth is, of course, a series of colloquies between the "Disciple" and "Truth."[5] Here the fullest paradox of Suso's life of anguished joy and happy sorrow becomes evident. If it be asked how man can be a creature and yet not one, the answer is forthcoming. In human phrase man cannot be both a creature and God. Still, man can, in some sense and measure, provided "he is rapt into God," "be one in losing himself," while at the same time he is enjoying, contemplating, and the like. Analogically stated, the eye engaged in the process of seeing really loses itself, for, by the very act of vision, it attains oneness with the object while at the same time remaining itself.[6]

Suso, without compromising his own spiritual independence, reasserts the principal "Rhenish" themes. There is the emphasis on the transcending of "images" and "concepts."[7] One finds the rejection, at least momentarily, of reflective thought. What, above all, is the objective of the true renunciant? Self-detachment. Where is the minor difficulty? Thought! The major one? The domination of self-will! Likewise, there is the definition of *Grund* as pure simplicity and as "interior fortress."[8] Quite familiar is the stress on the transformation of man in the Deity, the pouring out of man and the pouring in of God into the self-abandoned man. Following more the Pauline figure, however,

---

[5] The shifting of gender for the principals in Suso's dialogues can usually be corrected by context, even though the change occurs sometimes in the same sequence.

[6] See ch. 5, p. 194, in J. M. Clark's translation of Henry Suso, *The Little Book of Truth.*

[7] *Ibid.*, chs. 5, 7, etc.

[8] Gandillac, in *Mélanges*, Vol. 3, p. 76; Lavaud, *Œuvre*, Vol. I, pp. 347–48, nos. 71–72, also pp. 338–39, no. 13 and note 1; p. 350, no. 85.

the accent falls on the "new man" in Christ.[9] Chapter IV of
The Little Book of Truth is on the significant "return" or "break-
through" which a self-abandoned man should make via the
only-begotten Son. This man turns "with a look that sinks away
toward the nothingness of his own self."[10] Hence the self that
is truly thus surrendered becomes "Christlike." Just the same,
this man's own being remains; albeit in a form, glory, and power
that is truly different.[11]

There is, further, the significant emphasis on the double
nothingness of the creature and of the divine abyss. Dionysius
had referred to God as non-Being or Nothing, an eternal Nothing, as it were.[12] Suso's Prologue[13] deals with the transcendence of the divine Being "and the nothingness of all other
things." Men habitually call this Nothing, "God." In so doing
man is conscious of his being one with this same Nothing. Suso
is obviously deducing the fundamental emphasis of Eckhart via
Dionysius while hoping to skirt the heterodoxies so easily
ascribable to such negativist thought. Weighty considerations of
God and the Godhead are found in the second and fifth chapters
of the *Truth*. "Godhead and God are all one," Suso insists, as if
correcting Eckhart's frequent distinction between Deity and the
God of revelation. But he quickly asserts, following Eckhart,
that the Godhead, that is Deity, neither acts nor begets as does
God. Basically, Suso says, God and Godhead "are one."[14]

These are obviously ticklish matters. In the wake of Eckhart's
condemnation, Suso is understandably cautious. He insists on
the abiding difference between created and uncreated substance. This emerges clearly in chapter six of the *Truth*. The
discussion of the "savage" or "wild man" recalls the whole
acerbated issue raised by the Beghards and Beguines, and by
the Brethren of the Free Spirit.[15]

Suso avoids the equivocation of the Taulerian discussion

---

[9] *The Little Book of Truth*, ch. 4, especially pp. 184–85 in Clark.
[10] *Ibid.*, p. 184. The whole of ch. 4 is on the *Durchbruch*.
[11] *Ibid.*, pp. 184–85. On *Durchbruch* in relation to *Gelassenheit*, seen in its
    double aspect of union with God and as the renunciatory means to that
    end, cf. Bühlmann, *op. cit.*, pp. 127–28, and Bizet, *op. cit.*, pp. 230 ff.; also,
    Gandillac, in *Mélanges*, Vol. 3, pp. 77–78.
[12] *Truth*, ch. 1, p. 176, and references to Dionysius' works.
[13] Pp. 173–75.
[14] Ch. 5, pp. 191, 199; ch. 2, p. 179.
[15] Pp. 201–05; cf. E. W. McDonnell, *The Beguines and Beghards in Medieval
    Culture with Special Emphasis on the Belgian Scene*, Rutgers University Press,
    1954.

regarding *Bild*, i.e., "picture," or "image." Suso specifies that
Christ is the sole, proper image of the Father and that man has
not been created *imago*, but only *ad imaginem*. Christ, therefore,
is the engendered Son. This we are not. He is the veritable
image of the Father. We are formed in the image of the Holy
Trinity.[16]

Suso further warns his disciples against the Beghard audacity
of committing sins in order to set the stage for true renunciation.
As to the Eckhartian paradox of placing charity above the
"rapture" of Paul, thus risking the depersonalization of love,
Suso emphasizes much more than Tauler, for instance, the singular relation of the "I" and the "you."[17]

In *The Little Book of Eternal Wisdom*, Chapter VII, there is a
beautiful passage on "How Lovable God Is." Eternal Wisdom,
the Divine, declares himself to be, in himself, the incomprehensible Good, always and forever being, but never expressible in
words. In an act of supreme renunciation, however, Eternal
Wisdom reveals both the heart of self-giving and the spiritual
meaning of all this self-abnegating love, in human words. He
will "wind the sun's radiance in a cloth. . . ."[18]

Wisdom pictures the "dear ones" enfolded in his sweet love
"swept into the only One," in a love where images and spoken
words have no place; "they are swept away into the Good, from
whom they emanated." To this the Servant replies with a revelation of his own craving from Wisdom for a "particular love
and affection" for himself. He would have the "divine eyes" of
Wisdom take a "particular pleasure" in him. Divine Wisdom's
reply is reassuring. His love is not subject to the compression of
unity or the dissipation of numbers. The Servant is always
cherished in Wisdom's innermost concern. Wisdom gives himself in endearment and preoccupation with the Servant as if
there were no other claimants of love.[19]

It appears, finally, that the suffering humanity of Christ
marks out the only sure way to his divinity. No one, as Suso so
well realizes, can scale the divine heights or come to the strange
sweetness of contemplation except by the drawing example of
Christ's human bitterness.[20] In the opening chapters, Suso apos-
trophizes the way of Christ's own poverty. In the *Life*,[21] he
learns what it really means to go to school with Christ. However

---

[16] *Truth*, ch. 6, pp. 203–04; Gandillac, *Mélanges*, Vol. 3, p. 77.
[17] Gandillac, *op. cit.*, Vol. 3, p. 78.   [18] Pp. 71–73.
[19] P. 74.   [20] *Eternal Wisdom*, ch. 2, pp. 51 ff.
[21] Ch. 19.

much revered Suso's name came finally to be, his career was mainly the anguished joy of one who knows the bitter sweetness of Christ's companionship. In leaving his disciples, in order to ascend to the Father, Christ gives, according to his Servitor, the symbol of renunciation from all creatures. One who wishes to receive the noble quest worthily must exemplify "pure detachment from all creatures." [22]

[22] *Eternal Wisdom*, ch. 6, pp. 65–66.

Henry Suso (c. 1295–1366)

THE LITTLE BOOK OF ETERNAL WISDOM [23]

The Text

Chapter One

How Some Men Are Drawn to God, Unknown to Them

Hanc amavi et exqui sivi a iuventute mea, et quae sivi mihi sponsam assumere. [24]

These words are written in the Book of Wisdom and are spoken by the fair, lovely Eternal Wisdom, and the meaning is: "I have loved her and sought her from my youth, and have chosen her as my bride."

In his early youth, an impetuous soul strayed into the paths of error. Then, in spiritual imaginings, Eternal Wisdom met him, and led him through rough and smooth ways till she brought him to the right path of divine truth. And when he recalled the wonderful guidance he had received, he spoke to God thus: "Beloved, gentle Lord, since the days of my childhood, my heart has sought for something with an ardent thirst. Lord, what that is I cannot yet fully understand. Lord, I have pursued it for many a year eagerly, and I have never yet succeeded, because I do not rightly know what it is, and yet it is something that draws my heart and soul toward itself, and without which I can never find true peace. Lord, in the first days of my youth I tried to find it in the creatures, as I saw others do; but the more I sought, the less I found it, and the nearer I went to it, the farther off it was. For of every image that appeared to me, before I had fully tested it, or abandoned myself to peace in it, an inner voice said to me: 'This is not what thou seekest.' And I have always had this revulsion from things. Lord, my heart now

---

23 Based on Bihlmeyer's text the translation is that of J. M. Clark, *Henry Suso: The Little Book of Eternal Wisdom* and *The Little Book of Eternal Truth*, London, 1953, pp. 47–56. Used by permission of Faber & Faber Ltd., London, and of Harper & Brothers, New York.
24 Wis. 8:2.

yearns for it, for it would gladly possess it, and it[25] has often experienced what it is not; but what it is, my heart has not discovered. Alas, beloved Lord of heaven, what is it, or of what nature is it, that it should so mysteriously make itself felt within me?"

Reply of ETERNAL WISDOM: Dost thou not recognize it? Has she not lovingly embraced thee, and often helped thee on thy way, until she has now won thee for herself?

THE SERVANT: Lord, I have never perceived nor heard of it; I know not what it is.

Reply of ETERNAL WISDOM: That is not surprising, for thy familiarity with the creatures and her strangeness[26] have caused that. But now open thy eyes and see who I am. It is I, Eternal Wisdom, who have chosen thee for herself from all eternity with the embrace of my eternal providence. I have supported thee so often on the way; thou wouldst have been separated from me so many times if I had forsaken thee. Thou foundest always in every creature something that repelled, and that is the truest sign of my elect, that I wish to have them for myself.

THE SERVANT: Gentle, lovely Eternal Wisdom, and art thou that which I have for so very long sought after? Art thou the one for whom my soul ever strove? Alas, my God, why didst thou not show thyself to me for this long time? How very long thou hast postponed it! How many toilsome ways I have struggled through!

Reply of ETERNAL WISDOM: Had I done so then, thou wouldst not have recognized my goodness so clearly as thou hast done now.

THE SERVANT: Ah, immeasurable Goodness, how sweetly thou hast now revealed thy loving-kindness in me! When I did not exist, thou gavest me my being. When I had departed from thee, thou wouldst not leave me. When I wished to escape thee, thou didst so sweetly hold me captive! Ah, Eternal Wisdom, if now my heart could break into a thousand pieces, and embrace thee, the joy of my heart, and spend all my days with thee in steadfast love and perfect praise, that would be my heart's desire! For truly that man is blessed whose desires thou dost so affectionately anticipate, by never allowing him true rest until he seeks his rest in thee alone![27]

25 His heart.
26 "She is a stranger to thee." Clark, *Eternal Wisdom*, p. 48, note 2.
27 Augustine, *Confessions*, Book I, ch. 1, sec. 1.

Ah, rare, lovely Wisdom, since I now have found in thee the one whom my soul loves, despise not thy poor creature. See how completely my heart is silent toward all this world in joy and sorrow! Lord, must my heart be forever silent toward thee? Grant, O grant, beloved Lord, that my wretched soul may speak a word to thee, for my full heart can bear it no longer alone. In this wide world it has no one in whom it can confide, save thee, gentle, rare, beloved Lord and Brother! Lord, thou alone seest and knowest the nature of a loving heart, and knowest that no one can love what he can in no wise understand. Therefore, since I must now love thee alone, grant that I may know thee better, that I may love thee entirely.

Reply of ETERNAL WISDOM: According to the natural order, we take the highest emanation of all beings from their first origin through the noblest beings down to the lowest. But the return to the origin takes place through the lowest to the highest. Therefore, if thou wouldst see me in my uncreated divinity, thou shouldst learn to know me in my suffering humanity,[28] for that is the swiftest way to eternal bliss.

THE SERVANT: Then, Lord, I will remind thee today of the boundless love through which thou didst descend from thy high throne, from the royal seat of the Father's heart, down to thirty-three years of exile and contempt, and of the love that thou hadst for me and for all men, which thou didst reveal most of all in the most bitter pangs of thy terrible death. Lord, remember that thou didst reveal thyself to my soul in spiritual fashion in the most lovable form to which thy boundless love has ever brought thee.

Reply of ETERNAL WISDOM: The more I am worn out, and the nearer to death from love, the more lovely am I to a properly ordered mind. My boundless love reveals itself in the whole bitterness of my sufferings, as the sun in its beams, as the fair rose in its fragrance, and as the strong fire in its burning heat. Therefore, hear with devotion how profoundly I suffered for thy sake.

Chapter Two

What Happened Before the Crucifixion

After the Last Supper, when in the anguish of my gentle heart, and in the pain of my whole body, I resigned myself on the mountain to the pangs of bitter death, finding that it was near at hand, I was covered with bloody sweat. I was captured

---

28 Augustine, *Tract. 13 in Joannem*, note 4.

by my foes, harshly bound, wretchedly led away. In the night I was shamefully ill-treated; I was scourged, was spat upon, and my eyes were blindfolded. Early in the morning I was brought before Caiaphas, accused, found guilty, and delivered to death. Ineffable grief was seen in my pure mother, from the first glance with which she saw me in anguish, until I was hanged on the cross. I was shamefully brought before Pilate, falsely accused, condemned to death. They stood opposite me, with terrible eyes, like cruel giants, and I stood before them meekly, like a lamb. I, Eternal Wisdom, was mocked as a fool before Pilate in white clothing. My fair body was painfully disfigured and bruised by the cruel lashes of the scourge. My gentle head was pierced, and my loving face was covered with spittle and blood. Thus, after being condemned, I was wretchedly and shamefully led with my cross to my death. They cried out at me very fiercely, so that their cries resounded in the air: "Hang him, hang the criminal!"

THE SERVANT: Ah, Lord, the beginning is so very painful, how can it end? If I saw a wild animal thus ill-treated in my presence, I could scarcely bear it; how, then, would thy sufferings pierce my heart and soul, and rightly so!

But, Lord, there is a great wonder in my heart. Beloved Lord, I seek thy divinity everywhere, but thou dost only reveal thy humanity. I seek thy sweetness, thou dost put forward thy bitterness. I wished to suck at thy breast, thou dost teach me to fight. Ah, Lord, what meanest thou by this?

Reply of ETERNAL WISDOM: No one can attain to divine heights or to unusual sweetness unless he be first drawn through the example of my human bitterness. The higher one climbs without passing through my humanity, the deeper one falls. My humanity is the way by which one must go, my sufferings are the gate through which one must pass, if one would attain what thou seekest. Therefore, put away the timidity of thy heart, and enter the lists of knightly courage, where I am, for weakness befits not the knight in the place where his lord stands in valiant courage. I will clothe thee with my armor, for all my sufferings must be experienced by thee, according to thy strength.

First make thyself bold, for thy heart must often die within thee before thou canst overcome thy weakness, and sweat the bloody sweat of many a painful ordeal, in which I will prepare thyself for me; for I will dung thy garden of spices[29] with red

29 The soul.

blossom.[30] Contrary to old custom, thou must be taken prisoner and bound; thou wilt often be slandered secretly by thy enemies, and publicly shamed; many a false judgment of the people will be passed on thee. Thou shalt diligently bear in thy heart my Passion with maternal hearty love.[31] Thou shalt have many a harsh judge of thy godly life, and thy godly manner of life will often be scornfully mocked by the human manner. Thy unpracticed body will be scourged with a hard, severe life. Thou wilt be scornfully crowned with the persecution of thy saintly life. Afterward thou wilt be led out with me on the sorrowful way of the cross when thou dost surrender thine own will and forsake thyself, and be as free with regard to all creatures in those matters that may cause thee to stray from thy eternal salvation, as is a dying man, when he goes hence and has nothing more to do with this world.

THE SERVANT: Alas, Lord, that is a toilsome undertaking for me! My whole nature is afraid at these words: Lord, how could I ever suffer all this? Gentle Lord, I must say one thing: couldst thou in thy eternal wisdom find no other way to save me, and to reveal thy love to me, by which thou couldst relieve thyself of thy great sufferings and me of my bitter compassion? How very strange thy judgments seem![32]

Reply of ETERNAL WISDOM: No one should enter the fathomless abyss of my mystery, wherein I ordain all things according to my eternal providence, for none can understand them. And yet there is therein a power to do this, and many other things, which is never exercised. Yet know that in the order of created things no more pleasing manner could be used. The Lord of nature does not consider what he is able to do in nature; he considers what is most fitting for every creature, and he acts accordingly.[33] How could man know better the divine mystery than in his assumption of humanity? If a man had lost joy from inordinate pleasure, how could he discover true eternal joy? How could the unpracticed way of a hard, despised life be carried on unless it was led by God himself? If thou didst lie in the judgment of death, if then someone else received the death-blow instead of thee, how could he show more loyalty and love to thee, or, on the other hand, how could he better incite thee to love him? If there be anyone whom my boundless love, my inexpressible mercy, my glorious divinity, my most gracious humanity, my most comforting friendship, move not to deep

---

[30] Of suffering.   [31] With love of motherlike tenderness.
[32] Rom. 11:33.   [33] Thomas Aquinas, *Summa theologica*, pt. I, q. 3, art. 2.

love, what then could soften his stony heart? Ask the fair order of all creatures whether there was any more beautiful way of maintaining my justice, demonstrating my boundless mercy, ennobling human nature, pouring forth my goodness, reconciling heaven and earth, than that of my bitter death?

THE SERVANT: Lord, truly, I begin to perceive indeed that it is so, and all those who are not blinded by folly, and all who consider what is just, must agree with thee, and praise thy fair, loving action above all others. But to imitate thee is painful for an indolent body.

Reply of ETERNAL WISDOM: Be not afraid of imitating my sufferings. For if God is so fully within a man that suffering becomes easy for him, then he has no cause for complaint. No one enjoys my presence more in unusual sweetness than those who share with me the hardest bitterness. No one complains more about the bitterness of the husk than he who knows not the sweetness of the kernel. If we have a good comrade, half the battle is won.

THE SERVANT: Lord, thy words of comfort have made me so valiant that methinks I can do and suffer all things in thee.[34] Therefore, I ask thee to open up fully the treasure house of thy sufferings and tell me still more of them.

Chapter Three

How He Felt on the Cross as Regards the Inner Man

ETERNAL WISDOM: When I was suspended on the high branch of the cross with boundless love, for the sake of thee and of all men, my whole form was most wretchedly disfigured; my clear eyes were dimmed and lost their luster; my divine ears were filled with mockery and insult; my noble sense of smell was assailed by an evil stench; my sweet mouth with a bitter draught; my gentle sense of touch with hard blows. Then I could not find a place of rest in the whole world, for my divine head was bowed down by pain and torment; my joyful throat was rudely bruised; my pure countenance was defiled with spittle; the clear color of my cheeks turned wan and pallid. Look, my fair form was then disfigured, as though I were a leper, and had never been fair Wisdom.[35]

THE SERVANT: O thou most charming Mirror of all grace, on whom the heavenly spirits feast their eyes, as on the beauty

---

34 Phil. 4:13.   35 Cf. Isa. 53:2, 4.

17—L.M.M.

of the spring, would that I might have seen thy beloved countenance in thy dying hour, until I had covered it with my heart-
felt tears, and gazed my fill on thy fair eyes and thy bright
cheeks, so that I might relieve my heart's grief with profound
lamentation.

Ah, beloved Lord, thy sufferings affect some persons deeply,
they can lament feelingly, and weep for thee sincerely. Ah,
Lord, would that I could lament as the spokesman of all loving
hearts, that I could shed the bright tears of all eyes, and utter
the lamentations of ail tongues: then I would show thee today
how deeply the anguish of thy Passion affects me!

Reply of ETERNAL WISDOM: None can better show how
much my Passion affects them than those who share it with me
by the testimony of their works. I would rather have a free heart,
untroubled by ephemeral love, which with steadfast diligence
follows that which is highest, imitating the example of my life,
than that thou shouldst forever lament for me, and shed as many
tears weeping over my martyrdom as ever drops of rain fell from
the sky. For I suffered the pangs of death in order that I might
be imitated, however lovable are the tears, and however acceptable to me.

THE SERVANT: Alas, gentle Lord, inasmuch as a beautiful
imitation of thy gentle life and of thy loving Passion is so very
dear to thee, I will in future strive rather after a loving imitation than a tearful lamentation, although according to thy
words, I should do both. And therefore teach me how to resemble thee in this suffering.

Reply of ETERNAL WISDOM: Break thy pleasure in frivo-
lous seeing and idle hearing; let love taste good to thee, and
take pleasure in what has been distasteful to thee; give up for
my sake all bodily luxury. Thou shalt seek all thy rest in me,
love bodily discomfort, suffer evil willingly, desire contempt,
renounce thy desires, and die to all thy lusts. That is the beginning of the school of Wisdom, which is to be read in the open
and wounded book of my crucified body. And look, even if man
does all that is in his power, can anyone in the whole world do
for me what I have done for him?[36]

---

[36] See, in relation to this paragraph, Suso's ch. 7, in *The Little Book of Truth*,
Clark ed., pp. 206 ff., which deals at length with *Gelassenheit*. Cf. Clark,
The Great German Mystics, p. 62, and the treatments of Bühlmann and
Bizet, *op. cit.*

THE LIFE OF THE SERVANT:
THE HIGHER SCHOOL OF *GELASSENHEIT* [37]

THE TEXT

Chapter XIX

How He Was Led to the Spiritual School and Instructed in the Knowledge of True Self-surrender

Once after matins, the Servant sat in his chair, and as he meditated he fell into a trance. It seemed to his inner eye that a noble youth came down toward him, and stood before him saying: "Thou hast been long enough in the lower school and hast exercised thyself long enough in it; thou hast become mature. Come with me now! I will take thee to the highest school that exists in the world. There thou shalt learn diligently the highest knowledge, which will lead thee to divine peace and bring thy holy beginning to a blessed fulfillment." Thereat he was glad and he arose. The youth took him by the hand and led him, as it seemed to him, to a spiritual land. There was an extremely beautiful house there and it looked as if it was the residence of monks. Those who lived there were concerned with the higher knowledge. When he entered he was kindly received and affectionately welcomed by them. They hastened to their master and told him that someone had come who also wished to be his disciple, and to learn their knowledge. He said, "First I will see him with my own eyes, to see if he pleases me." On seeing him, he smiled at him very kindly and said, "Know from me that this guest is quite capable of becoming a worthy master of our high learning, if he will only patiently submit to living in the narrow cage in which he must be confined."

The Servant turned to the youth who had brought him there and asked, "Ah, my dear friend, tell me, what is this highest school and what is this learning thou hast spoken of?" The youth replied: "The high school and the knowledge which is taught

---

[37] Chapters 19 and 22 of the *Life* are here used in Clark's translation (from the Bihlmeyer text): *The Life of the Servant*, London, 1952, pp. 55–57, 65–67. Used by permission of James Clarke & Co., Ltd.

here is nothing but the complete, entire abandonment of one's self,[38] that is to say, that a man must persist in self-abnegation, however God acts toward him, by Himself or by His creatures. He is to strive at all times, in joy and in sorrow, to remain constant in giving up what is his own, as far as human frailty permits, considering only God's praise and honor, just as the dear Christ did to his Heavenly Father."

When the Servant had heard all this, he was well pleased, and he thought he would learn this knowledge, and that nothing could be so hard that he would fail to achieve it. He wanted to live there and find active occupation there. The youth forbade this, however, saying, "This learning demands unbroken leisure; the less one does here, the more one has done in reality." He meant that kind of activity with which a man hinders himself, and does not strive purely for God's praise.

After these words the Servant suddenly came to himself, and sat still as he was. He began to think over the words deeply and noticed that they were the pure truths that Christ himself taught. He then fell into an inner discussion with himself, saying: "Look carefully into thyself and thou wilt find that thou art still the slave of thyself, and thou wilt observe that in spite of all thy external actions, which indeed thou dost only carry out for thy own reasons, thou art not sufficiently composed to withstand the tribulations that confront thee from without. Thou art still like a timid hare that lies hidden in a bush and starts at every leaf that falls. Thus it is with thee: thou art afraid all thy days of imaginary sufferings that may befall thee. Thou dost turn pale at the very sight of thy adversary. When thou shouldst face them, thou dost flee; when thou shouldst surrender unarmed, thou dost conceal thyself. Then, when praised thou dost smile, when blamed thou dost grieve. It may well be true that thou dost need a higher school."

---

[38] *Volkommenen Gelassenheit des Ich.* See *The Book of Truth,* chs. 7 and 4.

THE LIFE OF THE SERVANT: THE WAY OF SUFFERING AND OF THE CROSS

THE TEXT

Chapter XXII

How He Set Out to Bring Wholesome Help to His Neighbors

After he had devoted himself for many years to his own religious life, he was impelled by God through manifold revelations to promote the spiritual welfare of his neighbors. There was no end to the number of sufferings that befell him as a result of these good works, though many souls were helped in this way.[39]

God once revealed this to a chosen friend of God. Her name was Anna, and she was his spiritual daughter. Once in her devotions, she went into an ecstasy, and she saw the Servant saying Mass on a high mountain. She saw an immense host of persons living in him and attached to him. But all were not in the same position: the more each had of God in him, the more they lived in the Servant also; and the more closely they were united to him, the more God had turned to them. She saw how fervently he prayed for them to the eternal God, whom he held in his priestly hands; and she asked God to explain to her what this vision meant. Thereupon God answered her thus: "The vast number of these children who cling to him are all the people who are taught by him, who listen to him, confess to him, or are devoted to him in any other way with special affection. He drew them to me in such a way that I will bring their lives to a good end, and see that they are never to be separated from my joyous countenance. But whatever sufferings may befall him as a consequence of this, he shall be well rewarded by me."

---

[39] Apropos this 22d chapter of the *Life* and the balancing of the active and the contemplative life *à la* Gregory see the "Briefbuchlein," Brief 9, in Bihlmeyer, *Heinrich Seuse, deutsche Schriften*, pp. 388–89 and notes, and "Grosses Briefbuch," Brief 21, in Bihlmeyer, *op. cit.*, pp. 468–69 and notes. Cf. Gregory, *Moral.* VI, 18, 57; XXXI, 12.

Before the above-mentioned noble maiden knew the Servant of Eternal Wisdom, God gave her the inner impulse to see him. It happened once that she was in an ecstasy, and she was told in a vision to go to the place where the Servant was, and see him. She said, "I do not recognize him in the crowd of the friars." Then she was told: "He is easy to recognize among the others: he has a green crown on his head which is adorned round and round with red and white roses interspersed, like a child's chaplet of roses. And the white roses mean his purity, and the red roses his patience in the manifold sufferings which he must endure.

"Just as the round halo that it is customary to paint round the heads of saints denotes the eternal bliss which they enjoy in God, similarly the rosy ring denotes the manifold sufferings that the dear friends of God have to bear, as long as they serve God as his liege knights in this world." Then, in her vision, the angel conducted her to the place where he was, and she recognized him at once by the rosy ring that he had round his head.

During this time of suffering, his greatest support from within was the diligent aid of the heavenly angels. Once, when he had lost the power of his outer senses, it seemed to him in a vision that he was led to a place where there was a large host of angels. One of them, who was nearest to him, said, "Stretch forth thy hand and see!" He put his hand out, and, looking, he beheld that from the middle of his palm there sprang a beautiful red rose with green leaves. The rose grew so large that it covered his hands up to his fingers; it was so fair and bright that it gave his eyes great joy. He turned round his hand, this way and that, and there was a lovely sight on both sides of it. He said with great wonder in his heart, "Ah, dear friend, what does this vision signify?" The youth said: "It signifies sufferings and sufferings again, and more and more sufferings to follow, which God will give thee. Those are the four roses on both hands and feet." The Servant sighed and said, "Ah, gentle Lord, it is a wondrous dispensation of thy providence that suffering should cause men such pain, and yet adorn them so beautifully, in a spiritual sense."

IX

Catherine of Siena (1347-1380)

INTRODUCTION

BIOGRAPHICAL NOTICE

C ATHERINE WAS BORN IN SIENA OF A DYER'S FAMILY
in 1347. At five or six years of age she began to sustain
contemplative visitations accompanied by variously reported physical phenomena and ecstasies. During adolescence,
while her people planned a suitable marriage for her, she clung
stubbornly to early vows of virginity and to harsh austerities.
Rigidly secluded in family quarters for some years with reluctant
paternal consent, she came gradually to accept a dedicated life
in the world; all the while fostering a religious vocation in an
inner cell of the heart. Following a meeting in vision with
Dominic, she was permitted the habit of the Dominican Third
Order of Penance. Granted ever more familiar colloquies with
Christ and increasingly rapturous associations with his redemptive sufferings, she entered mystical marriage with her Lord on
the last day of Carnival, 1367. Her subsequent raptures, mystical death, and stigmata evidenced alike her heightened concern for souls and for the church, patently in need of reformation, through whom, alone, they could be saved. The more
mystical her experience became, the more active her apostolate
grew. Following 1370 she vigorously prosecuted the cause of a
Christian crusade. In correspondence with popes and Christians
of many callings, and on trips to Florence, Pisa, Avignon, and
Rome, she pressed for the end of the Babylonian Captivity and
the girding of church, clergy, and laity in Christ's cause. The
Avignon exile ended, technically, with Gregory XI's return to
Rome. Catherine's dictation in 1378 of her *Dialogue*, which has
reached us in editorialized form, virtually coincides with the
inception of the Great Western Schism and with her own labors
in support of Urban VI. Having adopted frequent Communion

in 1372 and having accepted the spiritual direction of Raymond of Capua in 1373, Catherine gave rise to popularly reported miracles which, like her ministering virtues, were cherished in a mounting crescendo of public regard. She died in 1380. Canonization followed in 1461.

BIBLIOGRAPHICAL ESSAY

A useful study is Th. Deman's "La théologie dans la vie de Sainte Catherine de Sienne," *La vie spirituelle*, Vol. 42 (1935), Supplément, pp. [1]–[24]. Compare R. Garrigou-Lagrange, "La foi selon Sainte Catherine de Sienne," *ibid.*, Vol. 45 (1935), pp. 236–249; also DS II, 327–48. The first modern vernacular edition of Catherine's works is G. Gigli, *L'opere della serafica santa Caterina da Siena*, 4 vols., Siena, 1707. The *Dialogo* is Vol. 4. Other editions and translations of the *Dialogo* are those of M. Fiorilli, Bari, 1912; I. Taurisano, Rome, 1947; *Le dialogue*, by R. P. J. Hurtaud, 2 vols., Paris, 1913; and the *Dialogue* by A. Thorold, London, 1896 and 1925. *Le lettere di S. Caterina da Siena* based on the edition of Niccolò Tommasèo were reissued in revised form with additions by Piero Misciattelli, in 6 vols., Florence, 1940. The first volume of a critical text, *Epistolario di Santa Caterina da Siena*, ed. by Eugenio Dupré Theseider, appeared at Rome in 1940. Useful sources are *Fontes vitae s. Catharinae Senensis historici*, ed., H. Laurent and F. Valli, beginning with I. *Documenti*, in Siena, 1936. Critical studies and reinterpretations of source texts include R. Fawtier's invaluable *Sainte Catherine de Sienne: Essai de critique des sources*: I. *Les sources hagiographiques*, Paris, 1921, and II. *Les œuvres de Sainte Catherine de Sienne*, Paris, 1930. Quite useful is his later work "L'expérience humaine," pp. 15–236, bound together with L. Canet's "L'expérience spirituelle," pp. 237–268 in *La double expérience de Catherine Benincasa (Sainte Catherine de Sienne)*, Gallimard, Paris, 1948. Still serviceable is *Saint Catherine of Siena as Seen in Her Letters*, translated by Vida D. Scudder, London and New York, 1905—. Thirteen letters are translated by Louis-Paul Guigues as *Ste. Catherine de Sienne: La sang, la croix, la vérité*, Gallimard, Paris, 1940. A. Grion's *Santa Caterina da Siena: Dottrine e Fonti*, Cremona, 1953, is convenient. Authoritative interpretations, largely source-based, are A. T. Drane, *The History of St. Catherine of Siena and Her Companions*, London, 1880, E. G. Gardner, *Saint Catherine of Siena*, London, 1907, and J. Jorgensen, *Saint Catherine of Siena*, tr. by I. Lund, Longmans, Green & Co.,

Inc., London and New York, 1938. A brief provocative work is
M. De La Bedoyere, *Catherine Saint of Siena*, Hollis & Carter,
London, 1947.

SYNOPSIS

Catherine displays a fiery spirit and a commanding will
linked inextricably with uncompromising theological premises.
What is the clue to her mystical integrity and her spiritual
creativity? Perhaps faith best supplies the answer. It is the
animating idea of Catherine's doctrine as it is of her life.

Key texts in the *Dialogue* seem to bear out this premise. In the
light of faith she claims to have found her strength and constancy. It is in the light of faith that she hopes. She knows that
it will not desert her on her pilgrimage. This light shows her the
way. Without it she would be plunged into the shadows. The
knowledge of God in faith aids in the knowledge of oneself. This
light of faith shines throughout the entire *Dialogue* even as it
prevails in this last chapter.[1]

Sin is, for Catherine, above all else, a blindness of the soul.
Maintaining itself in the sweet retreat of self-knowledge and of
God's goodness, the soul comes humbly to see itself for what it
is. It exists, not for itself but for God, and the fire of its love grows
with the realization that it holds from God its very being and
all the graces added thereto. The soul then conceives a holy
hatred of sin and sensuality. It unites itself, by means of God's
love, that force supreme, to the true solid virtues. Faith is the
soul of the entire apostolate, where one seeks to enfold the world
in self-giving love. It is like a water jar filled at the fountain.
Taken from its source for drinking, it is soon emptied. Held
plunged in the water, it remains ever full, to be drawn on
always. So it is in the love of neighbor.[2]

It is obvious from the *Dialogue*, chapter 64, for example, that
Catherine's is a missionary mysticism, a mysticism of apostolate.[3] The false incompatibility of the active and the contemplative life is certainly no postulate of hers. On the contrary,
"the cell of self-knowledge" goes with one on journey throughout the active pilgrimage in the world. Her religious state is,
like that of Gregory and Bernard, the mixed vocation, even as

---

[1] See the *Dialogo* (*Dial.*), ch. 167. Cf. also *Le lettere* (*Let.*), T. 272 (G.
90) = Tommaseo and Gigli nos.
[2] *Dial.*, caps. 4, 7, 8, 45–46, 51, 63–66 (especially 64, on the fountain), 72–
74. Cf. *Let.*, T. 304, G. 345.
[3] See J. Leclercq, *Sainte Catherine de Sienne*, Paris, 1947.

it is that of Thomas Aquinas, so many of whose doctrines she reflects.

Catherine is indeed a remarkable ensemble of scholastic postulates, with all their overtones of abstraction and dialectic, joined to ardent sentiments phrased in well-nigh romantic language. Faith, for her, is at once an intellectually oriented *dynamis* and a moving, empowering verity.

The *Dialogue* explains that faith is a light received in Baptism, thus showing the way to eternal life.[4] Faith is the pupil of the eye of intelligence. Its light makes possible our discerning and following the way and the teaching of the truth which is the incarnate Word. Without this pupil which is faith the soul would be blind. It would be like a man who, indeed, had eyes, the seeing pupils of which, however, were covered as with a veil. Intelligence is, then, the soul's eye. The pupil of this eye is faith.[5]

According to Catherine, the distinctive property of man is reason. Grace gives an inner vitalizing impulse to that reason which, raised to supernatural levels, finds outlet in all the virtues, as in the life of faith, hope, and charity.

God himself delcares that without the light of reason none may find the way of truth. This light of reason is held directly from him who is the True Light. This reason is in men by virtue of the intelligence and by the brightness of the faith communicated to them in holy Baptism; unless, God forbid, they have been deprived of it by their transgressions. The church's sacraments appropriated in faith, are, therefore, the soul's path of light. In Baptism, by virtue of the blood of God's Son, man receives the form of faith. This faith, once invested, eventuates in acts consonant with the light of reason. Reason and faith are obviously unopposable.

Reason, clarified by faith's light, gives life and direction in the way of truth. By means of this light humanity is enabled to reach the True Light. Without it there is nought but darkness. Two illuminations, irradiated from this light, are immediately necessary. The first enables one to sense the fragility of evanescent, worldly things. The soul is powerless to comprehend the meaning of life aside from its cognizance, first of all, of its own frailty and the inclination, by a perverse law within it, to revolt against its Creator.[6]

---

[4] *Dial.*, cap. 29.
[5] *Dial.*, caps. 45, 51; *Let.*, T. 272, G. 90; cf. Garrigou-Lagrange, *op. cit.*
[6] For the foregoing see *Dial.*, cap. 98, especially through 101, also cap. 51,

The soul, exercising its faith and reason in disciplined, renunciatory love, will have the gracious addition to its natural light of a supernatural illumination. Catherine stresses the necessity of exciting the natural light for the despising of the world and for the embracing of virtue; for the seeking out, by means of that light, of the good where it is. Such research will lead to God whence the good comes. One must, in the course of such seeking, perceive the unspeakable love shown by God in the gift of his Son, who gave so much of love for mankind's redemption. Accompanying this first, imperfect, natural light will be the acquisition of a perfect, supernatural light. This will be diffused by grace in the soul, attaching it to the operation of the virtue within. Thus the soul will be fortified everywhere, and at all times, in conformity with the divine will, which seeks always our human sanctification. Hereby, the first light, if properly developed, prepares the way for the second. This, in turn, unites us to the life of virtue.[7]

Self-knowledge, therefore, conduces to that state in which the supernatural comes to associate itself with the natural. This knowing oneself is, however, not some naïve recourse to Socratic principles, however intriguing. Knowledge does not guarantee virtue. Socrates had not allowed sufficiently for original sin and human egotism. The lien with human sin once broken, however, the light is invited to accomplish in the soul its work of cleansing and amelioration.

Far from assuming, as most do, that man naturally inclines toward evil, Catherine is convinced that, at the base of his moral life, man wishes good. What, then, deflects him from it? Self-love, of course. Catherine insists that because of this we seek the good where it is not. We are not, thereby, inclined to evil. Take away the obstacle and nature will go its proper way. Misled, however, by the erroneous calculations of self-love, the soul gropes about in self-imposed darkness. With its true light obscured, the soul fails to seek the good where it actually resides. Miraculously recalled from its abortive search to the real good, the soul is oriented anew by the blood of the loving Christ. The soul finds itself answering the divine love with a reborn, rediscovered love of its own.[8]

and the series of letters "A Misser Ristoro di Pietro Canigiani in Firenze," G. 228–32; T. 258, 266, 279, 299, and 301, especially the last. Also T. 272, G. 90.   [7] *Let.*, T. 301; *Dial.*, caps. 99–101; DS II, 342–43.
[8] *Let.*, T. 301, 304; Deman, *op. cit.*, pp. [8]–[11]; *Dial.*, caps. 1, 7, 43, 51, 63–66, 73–74, 98, 115–18, 162, 166.

Catherine resumes this theme in a letter to Peter Cardinal de Luna, later Benedict XIII.[9] Clearly, it is by the Redeemer's blood that we are able to know the truth of the light inhering in the holy faith, which brightens the eye of the intelligence. In the love of this truth the soul finds its nourishment. Because of that love for the truth, it would rather suffer death than be recreant to the truth. The soul does not balk at telling the truth when the proper time comes. Worldly men do not intimidate its witness. No fears for its life prompt the soul's action. Fearing God alone, it stands ready to lay down its life for the love of the truth. Confident that truth has justice alone for her companion, the soul does not reserve its bald indictment of evil. It reproves boldly, knowing that this precious pearl that is justice ought to be clearly evident in every rational creature; certainly in prelates of the church. Truth knows when to hold its tongue, also. Its very silence is a witness of patience and a protest. It is not ignorant, but discerningly aware, of where God's honor and the good of souls is most surely found. Catherine, in conclusion, pleads with the cardinal to enlist himself passionately for the truth, so that he may be a column in the mystical body of holy church, wherein it is necessary to spread the truth. For the truth, being in the church, yearns to be administered by those who should be most properly impassioned and brightened by it, not by the ignorant who are separated from the truth.

In the doctrine of love's development, Catherine reveals no scholastic didactic. It has its own logical integrity, however, in that it is a surely destined growth. Perhaps Catherine comes, finally, to mime theology with the force of life itself. More adequate than the preacher's gestures, the attitude of her body becomes, during her life, that of the mystery of Jesus—until the stigmata are there imprinted. Such mimicry is not one of puerile or hysterical aberration. This symbolism is the appropriate implementation of a theological predicate. Catherine lives her teaching in a sanely nurtured interiority, also in an apostolate of loving dedication out of love for Christ, for the whole world of people.

Her mysticism is, truly, one of apostolate. For her the love of Christ and neighbor is inseparable from the love of God. She bases the spiritual life on faith. Faith leads, in turn, to a better knowledge of God and oneself, hence to a better apostolate. Still in the knowledge of faith, and, more generally, throughout

9 *Let.*, T. 284, G. 25.

the whole spiritual career, the real primacy must remain with love. Here the example of Christ is pre-eminent. This love will lead, for Catherine, to frequent ecstasy and to stigmatization.[10]

[10] DS II, 1995–96; *Dial.*, caps. 7, 34, 64; *Let.*, T. 242, 272, 301, 304.

Catherine of Siena (1347–1380)

A TREATISE OF DIVINE PROVIDENCE [11]

THE TEXT

1. How a Soul, Elevated by Desire of the Honor of God, and of the Salvation of Her Neighbors, Exercising Herself in Humble Prayer, After She Had Seen the Union of the Soul, Through Love, with God, Asked of God Four Requests

The soul, who is lifted by a very great and yearning desire for the honor of God and the salvation of souls, begins by exercising herself, for a certain space of time, in the ordinary virtues, remaining in the cell of self-knowledge,[12] in order to know better the goodness of God toward her. This she does because knowledge must precede love, and only when she has attained love can she strive to follow and to clothe herself with the truth. But, in no way does the creature receive such a taste of the truth, or so brilliant a light therefrom, as by means of humble and continuous prayer, founded on knowledge of herself and of God; because prayer, exercising her in the above way, unites with God the soul that follows the footprints of Christ Crucified and thus, by desire and affection, and union of love, makes her another Himself.[13] Christ would seem to have meant this when he said: *To him who will love me and will observe my commandment, will I manifest myself; and he shall be one thing with me and I with him.*[14] In several places we find similar words, by which we can see that it is, indeed, through the effect of love that the soul becomes another Himself. That this may be seen more clearly, I will mention what I remember having heard from a handmaid of God, namely, that, when she was lifted up in prayer, with great elevation of mind, God was not wont to

---

11 This so-called "Treatise" is, in its traditional arrangement, the first part of the *Dialogo*. This translation, based on the Gigli edition, is that of Algar Thorold, *The Dialogue of the Seraphic Virgin Catherine of Siena . . .*, a new and abridged [from the 1896, London] edition, Westminster, Maryland, 1944, pp. 26–49. Used by permission of The Newman Press.
12 *Nella cella del cognoscimento di sè.*
13 *Un altro sè.*   14 John 14:21.

conceal, from the eye of her intellect, the love which he had for his servants, but rather to manifest it; and, that among other things, he used to say: "Open the eye of thy intellect,[15] and gaze into me, and thou shalt see the beauty of my rational creature. And look at those creatures who, among the beauties which I have given to the soul, creating her in my image and similitude, are clothed with the nuptial garment (that is, the garment of love), adorned with many virtues, by which they are united with me through love. And yet I tell thee, if thou shouldest ask me who these are, I should reply" (said the sweet and amorous word of God) "they are another Myself, inasmuch as they have lost and denied their own will, and are clothed with mine, are united to mine, are conformed to mine." It is therefore true, indeed, that the soul unites herself with God by the affection of love.

So, that soul, wishing to know and follow the truth more manfully, and lifting her desires first for herself—for she considered that a soul could not be of use, whether in doctrine, example, or prayer, to her neighbor, if she did not first profit herself, that is, if she did not acquire virtue in herself—addressed four requests to the Supreme and Eternal Father. The first was for herself; the second, for the reformation of the holy church; the third, a general prayer for the whole world, and in particular for the peace of Christians who rebel, with much lewdness and persecution, against the holy church; in the fourth and last, she besought the divine Providence to provide for things in general, and in particular for a certain case with which she was concerned.[16]

2. How the Desire of This Soul Grew When God Showed Her the Neediness of the World

This desire was great and continuous, but grew much more, when the First Truth showed her the neediness of the world, and in what a tempest of offense against God it lay. And she had understood this the better from a letter which she had received from the spiritual Father of her soul, in which he explained to

---

15 *Apri l'occhio dell'Intelleto;* cf. *Dial.*, 45, 51; *Let.*, G. 90, T. 272; and Jorgensen, *op. cit.*, pp. 311-20.
16 See the return to the four requests in *Dial.*, cap. 166. Compare with this, *Let.*, G. 90, T. 272; the "Relatione d'una dottrina" = "Documento spirituale" (Gigli, *op. cit.*, Vol. I, pp. 374-76; Gardner, *op. cit.*, pp. 17-19), and others correlated in the Appendix of Grion, *op. cit.*, pp. 357 ff.

her the penalties and intolerable dolor caused by offenses against God, and the loss of souls, and the persecutions of holy church.

All this lighted the fire of her holy desire with grief for the offenses, and with the joy of the lively hope with which she waited for God to provide against such great evils. And, since the soul seems, in such communion, sweetly to bind herself fast within herself and with God, and knows better his truth, inasmuch as the soul is then in God and God in the soul, as the fish is in the sea and the sea in the fish, she desired the arrival of the morning (for the morrow was a feast of Mary) in order to hear Mass. And, when the morning came, and the hour of the Mass, she sought with anxious desire her accustomed place; and, with a great knowledge of herself, being ashamed of her own imperfection, appearing to herself to be the cause of all the evil that was happening throughout the world, conceiving a hatred and displeasure against herself, and a feeling of holy justice, with which knowledge, hatred, and justice she purified the stains which seemed to her to cover her guilty soul, she said: "O Eternal Father, I accuse myself before thee, in order that thou mayest punish me for my sins in this finite life, and, inasmuch as my sins are the cause of the sufferings which my neighbor must endure, I implore thee, in thy kindness, to punish them in my person."[17]

3. How Finite Works Are Not Sufficient for Punishment or Recompense Without the Perpetual Affection of Love

Then the Eternal Truth seized and drew more strongly to himself her desire, doing as he did in the Old Testament, for when the sacrifice was offered to God, a fire descended and drew to him the sacrifice that was acceptable to him; so did the sweet Truth to that soul, in sending down the fire of the clemency of the Holy Spirit, seizing the sacrifice of desire that she made of herself, saying: "Dost thou not know, dear daughter, that all the sufferings which the soul endures, or can endure, in this life are insufficient to punish one smallest fault, because the offense, being done to me, who am the Infinite Good, calls for an infinite satisfaction? However, I wish that thou shouldest know that not all the pains that are given to men in this life are given as punishments but as corrections, in order to chastise a

[17] Observe the relation of this to neighbor, the *lagrime*, bad priests, the reform of the church, etc. (*Dial.*, caps. 87–134).

son when he offends; though it is true that both the guilt and the penalty can be expiated by the desire of the soul, that is, by true contrition,[18] not through the finite pain endured, but through the infinite desire; because God, who is infinite, wishes for infinite love and infinite grief. Infinite grief I wish from my creature in two ways: in one way, through her sorrow for her own sins, which she has committed against me her Creator; in the other way, through her sorrow for the sins which she sees her neighbors commit against me. Of such as these, inasmuch as they have infinite desire, that is, are joined to me by an affection of love, and therefore grieve when they offend me, or see me offended, their every pain, whether spiritual or corporeal, from wherever it may come, receives infinite merit, and satisfies for a guilt which deserved an infinite penalty, although their works are finite and done in finite time; but, inasmuch as they possess the virtue of desire, and sustain their suffering with desire, and contrition, and infinite displeasure against their guilt, their pain is held worthy. Paul explained this when he said: *If I had the tongues of angels, and if I knew the things of the future and gave my body to be burned, and have not love, it would be worth nothing to me.*[19] The glorious apostle thus shows that finite works are not valid, either as punishment or recompense, without the condiment of the affection of love."

4. How Desire and Contrition of Heart Satisfies, Both for the Guilt and the Penalty in Oneself and in Others; and How Sometimes It Satisfies for the Guilt Only, and Not the Penalty

"I have shown thee, dearest daughter, that the guilt is not punished in this finite time by any pain which is sustained purely as such. And I say that the guilt is punished by the pain which is endured through the desire, love, and contrition of the heart; not by virtue of the pain, but by virtue of the desire of the soul; inasmuch as desire and every virtue is of value, and has life in itself, through Christ crucified, my only-begotten Son, in so far as the soul has drawn her love from him, and virtuously follows his virtues, that is, his footprints. In this way, and in no other, are virtues of value, and in this way pains satisfy for the fault, by the sweet and intimate love acquired in the knowledge of my goodness, and in the bitterness and contrition of heart acquired

18 *La vera contritione satisfà alla Colpa, & alla Pena* (Fiorilli, *op. cit.*, p. 6: *La vera contrizione satisfa a la colpa ed a la pena*).
19 Cf. I Cor. 13:1–3.
18—L.M.M.

by knowledge of one's self and one's own thoughts. And this knowledge generates a hatred and displeasure against sin, and against the soul's own sensuality, through which she deems herself worthy of pains and unworthy of reward."

The sweet Truth continued: "See how, by contrition of the heart, together with love, with true patience, and with true humility, deeming themselves worthy of pain and unworthy of reward, such souls endure the patient humility in which consists the above-mentioned satisfaction. Thou askest me, then, for pains, so that I may receive satisfaction for the offenses which are done against me by my creatures, and thou further askest the will to know and love me, who am the Supreme Truth. Wherefore I reply that this is the way, if thou wilt arrive at a perfect knowledge and enjoyment of me, the Eternal Truth, that thou shouldest never go outside the knowledge of thyself,[20] and, by humbling thyself in the valley of humility, thou wilt know me and thyself, from which knowledge thou wilt draw all that is necessary. No virtue, my daughter, can have life in itself except through charity, and humility, which is the foster mother and nurse of charity. In self-knowledge, then, thou wilt humble thyself, seeing that, in thyself, thou dost not even exist;[21] for thy very being, as thou wilt learn, is derived from me, since I have loved both thee and others before you were in existence; and that, through the ineffable love which I had for you, wishing to re-create you to grace, I have washed you, and re-created you in the blood of my only-begotten Son, spilt with so great a fire of love.[22] This blood teaches the truth to him who, by self-knowledge, dissipates the cloud of self-love,[23] and in no other way can he learn. Then the soul will inflame herself in his knowledge of me with an ineffable love, through which love she continues in constant pain; not, however, a pain which afflicts or dries up the soul, but one which rather fattens her; for since she has known my truth, and her own faults, and the ingratitude of men,[24] she endures intolerable suffering, grieving because she loves me; for, if she did not love me, she would not be obliged to do so; whence it follows immediately that it is right for thee, and my other servants who have learned my truth in this way, to sustain, even unto death, many tribulations and

---

[20] *Che tu non esca mai del cognoscimento di te.*
[21] *Vedendo te per te non essere.*
[22] *Sparto con tanto fuoco d'Amore.*
[23] *Che s'à levata la nuvola dell'Amore proprio, per lo cognoscimento di sè.*
[24] *E la Ingratitudine, e ciechità del Prossimo. . . .*

injuries and insults in word and deed, for the glory and praise of my name; thus wilt thou endure and suffer pains. Do thou, therefore, and my other servants, carry yourselves with true patience, with grief for your sins, and with love of virtue for the glory and praise of my name. If thou actest thus, I will satisfy for thy sins, and for those of my other servants, inasmuch as the pains which thou wilt endure will be sufficient, through the virtue of love, for satisfaction and reward, both in thee and in others. In thyself thou wilt receive the fruit of life, when the stains of thy ignorance are effaced, and I shall not remember that thou ever didst offend me. In others I will satisfy through the love and affection which thou hast to me, and I will give to them according to the disposition with which they will receive my gifts. In particular, to those who dispose themselves, humbly and with reverence, to receive the doctrine of my servants, will I remit both guilt and penalty, since they will thus come to true knowledge and contrition for their sins. So that, by means of prayer, and their desire of serving me, they receive the fruit of grace, receiving it humbly in greater or less degree, according to the extent of their exercise of virtue and grace in general. I say, then, that through thy desires they will receive remission for their sins. See, however, the condition, namely, that their obstinacy should not be so great in their despair as to condemn them through contempt of the blood, which, with such sweetness, has restored them.

"What fruit do they receive?

"The fruit which I destine for them, constrained by the prayers of my servants, is that I give them light, and that I wake up in them the hound of conscience,[25] and make them smell the odor of virtue, and take delight in the conversation of my servants.

"Sometimes I allow the world to show them what it is, so that, feeling its diverse and various passions, they may know how little stability it has, and may come to lift their desire beyond it, and seek their native country, which is the eternal life. And so I draw them by these, and by many other ways, for the eye cannot see, nor the tongue relate, nor the heart think, how many are the roads and ways which I use, through love alone, to lead them back to grace, so that my truth may be fulfilled in them. I am constrained to do so by that inestimable love of mine, by which I created them, and by the love, desire, and grief of my servants, since I am no despiser of their tears, and

25 *I Cane della Coscientia.*

sweat, and humble prayers; rather I accept them, inasmuch as I am he who giveth them this love for the good of souls and grief for their loss. But I do not, in general, grant to these others for whom they pray satisfaction for the penalty due to them but only for their guilt, since they are not disposed, on their side, to receive with perfect love my love, and that of my servants. They do not receive their grief with bitterness, and perfect contrition for the sins they have committed, but with imperfect love and contrition, wherefore they have not, as others, remission of the penalty, but only of the guilt; because such complete satisfaction requires proper dispositions on both sides, both in him that gives and him that receives. Wherefore, since they are imperfect, they receive imperfectly the perfection of the desires of those who offer them to me, for their sakes, with suffering; and, inasmuch as I told thee that they do receive remission, this is indeed the truth, that, by that way which I have told thee, that is, by the light of conscience, and by other things, satisfaction is made for their guilt; for, beginning to learn, they vomit forth the corruption of their sins, and so receive the gift of grace.

"These are they who are in a state of ordinary charity, wherefore, if they have trouble, they receive it in the guise of correction, and do not resist overmuch the clemency of the Holy Spirit, but, coming out of their sin, they receive the life of grace. But if, like fools, they are ungrateful, and ignore me and the labors of my servants done for them, that which was given them, through mercy, turns to their own ruin and judgment, not through defect of mercy, nor through defect of him who implored the mercy for the ingrate, but solely through the man's own wretchedness and hardness, with which with the hands of his free will, he has covered his heart, as it were, with a diamond, which, if it be not broken by the blood, can in no way be broken.[26] And yet, I say to thee, that, in spite of his hardness of heart, he can use his free will while he has time, praying for the blood of my Son, and let him with his own hand apply it to the diamond over his heart and shiver it, and he will receive the imprint of the blood which has been paid for him. But if he delays until the time be past, he has no remedy, because he has not used the dowry which I gave him: giving him memory so as to remember my benefits; intellect, so as to see and know the truth; affection, so that he should love me, the Eternal Truth, whom he would have known through the use of his intellect.

26 *Del diamante, che se non si rompe col Sangue, non si può rompere.*

This is the dowry which I have given you all, and which ought to render fruit to me, the Father; but, if a man barters and sells it to the devil, the devil, if he choose, has a right to seize on everything that he has acquired in this life. And, filling his memory with the delights of sin, and with the recollection of shameful pride, avarice, self-love, hatred, and unkindness to his neighbors (being also a persecutor of my servants), with these miseries he has obscured his intellect by his disordinate will. Let such as these receive the eternal pains, with their horrible stench, inasmuch as they have not satisfied for their sins with contrition and displeasure of their guilt. Now, therefore, thou hast understood how suffering satisfies for guilt by perfect contrition, not through the finite pain; and such as have this contrition in perfection satisfy not only for the guilt, but also for the penalty which follows the guilt, as I have already said when speaking in general; and if they satisfy for the guilt alone, that is, if, having abandoned mortal sin, they receive grace, and have not sufficient contrition and love to satisfy for the penalty also, they go to the pains of purgatory, passing through the second and last means of satisfaction.

"So thou seest that satisfaction is made, through the desire of the soul united to me, who am the Infinite Good, in greater or less degree, according to the measure of love, obtained by the desire and prayer of the recipient. Wherefore, with that very same measure with which a man measures to me dost he receive in himself the measure of my goodness. Labor, therefore, to increase the fire of thy desire, and let not a moment pass without crying to me with humble voice, or without continual prayers before me for thy neighbors. I say this to thee and to the father of thy soul, whom I have given thee on earth. Bear yourselves with manful courage, and make yourselves dead to all your own sensuality."[27]

5. How Very Pleasing to God Is the Willing Desire to Suffer for Him

"Very pleasing to me, dearest daughter, is the willing desire to bear every pain and fatigue, even unto death, for the salvation of souls, for the more the soul endures, the more she shows that she loves me; loving me, she comes to know more of my truth, and the more she knows, the more pain and intolerable grief she feels at the offenses committed against me. Thou didst

27 *Che virilmente portiate, e morta sia ogni propria Sensualità.*

ask me to sustain thee, and to punish the faults of others in thee, and thou didst not remark that thou wast really asking for love, light, and knowledge of the truth, since I have already told thee that by the increase of love grows grief and pain, wherefore he that grows in love grows in grief. Therefore, I say to you all, that you should ask, and it will be given you, for I deny nothing to him who asks of me in truth. Consider that the love of divine charity is so closely joined in the soul with perfect patience, that neither can leave the soul without the other. For this reason (if the soul elect to love me) she should elect to endure pains for me in whatever mode or circumstance I may send them to her. Patience cannot be proved in any other way than by suffering, and patience is united with love as has been said. Therefore bear yourselves with manly courage, for, unless you do so, you will not prove yourselves to be spouses of my truth, and faithful children, nor of the company of those who relish the taste of my honor, and the salvation of souls."

6. How Every Virtue and Every Defect Is Obtained by Means of Our Neighbor

"I wish also that thou shouldest know that every virtue is obtained by means of thy neighbor[28] and, likewise, every defect; he, therefore, who stands in hatred of me does an injury to his neighbor, and to himself, who is his own chief neighbor, and this injury is both general and particular. It is general because you are obliged to love your neighbor as yourself, and, loving him, you ought to help him spiritually, with prayer, counseling him with words, and assisting him both spiritually and temporally, according to the need in which he may be—at least with your good will if you have nothing else. A man, therefore, who does not love does not help him, and thereby does himself an injury; for he cuts off from himself grace, and injures his neighbor, by depriving him of the benefit of the prayers and of the sweet desires that he is bound to offer for him to me. Thus, every act of help that he performs should proceed from the charity which he has through love of me. And every evil, also, is done by means of his neighbor, for, if he do not love me, he cannot be in charity with his neighbor; and thus all evils derive from the soul's deprivation of love of me and her neighbor; whence, inasmuch as such a man does no good, it follows that he must do

28 *Col mezzo del Prossimo.*

evil. To whom does he evil? First of all to himself, and then to his neighbor—not against me, for no evil can touch me, except in so far as I count done to me that which he does to himself. To himself he does the injury of sin, which deprives him of grace, and worse than this he cannot do to his neighbor. Him he injures in not paying him the debt, which he owes him, of love, with which he ought to help him by means of prayer and holy desire offered to me for him. This is an assistance which is owed in general to every rational creature; but its usefulness is more particular when it is done to those who are close at hand, under your eyes, as to whom, I say, you are all obliged to help one another by word and doctrine, and the example of good works, and in every other respect in which your neighbor may be seen to be in need; counseling him exactly as you would yourselves, without any passion of self-love; and he (a man not loving God) does not do this, because he has no love toward his neighbor; and, by not doing it, he does him, as thou seest, a special injury. And he does him evil, not only by not doing him the good that he might do him, but by doing him a positive injury and a constant evil. In this way sin causes a physical and a mental injury. The mental injury is already done when the sinner has conceived pleasure in the idea of sin, and hatred of virtue, that is, pleasure from sensual self-love, which has deprived him of the affection of love which he ought to have toward me, and his neighbor, as has been said. And after he has conceived, he brings forth one sin after another against his neighbor, according to the diverse ways which may please his perverse sensual will. Sometimes it is seen that he brings forth cruelty, and that both in general and in particular.

"His general cruelty is to see himself and other creatures in danger of death and damnation through privation of grace, and so cruel is he that he reminds neither himself nor others of the love of virtue and hatred of vice. Being thus cruel, he may wish to extend his cruelty still farther, that is, not content with not giving an example of virtue, the villain also usurps the office of the demons, tempting, according to his power, his fellow creatures to abandon virtue for vice; that is cruelty toward his neighbors, for he makes himself an instrument to destroy life and to give death. Cruelty toward the body has its origin in cupidity, which not only prevents a man from helping his neighbor but causes him to seize the goods of others, robbing the poor creatures; sometimes this is done by the arbitrary use of power, and at other times by cheating and fraud, his neighbor being forced to redeem, to his own loss, his own goods, and often indeed his own person.

"Oh, miserable vice of cruelty, which will deprive the man who practices it of all mercy, unless he turn to kindness and benevolence toward his neighbor!

"Sometimes the sinner brings forth insults on which often follows murder; sometimes also impurity against the person of his neighbor, by which he becomes a brute beast full of stench, and in this case he does not poison one only, but whoever approaches him, with love or in conversation, is poisoned.

"Against whom does pride bring forth evils? Against the neighbor, through love of one's own reptuation, whence comes hatred of the neighbor, reputing one's self to be greater than he; and in this way is injury done to him. And if a man be in a position of authority, he produces also injustice and cruelty and becomes a retailer of the flesh of men. Oh, dearest daughter, grieve for the offense against me, and weep over these corpses, so that, by prayer, the bands of their death may be loosened!

"See now, that, in all places and in all kinds of people, sin is always produced against the neighbor, and through his medium; in no other way could sin ever be committed either secret or open. A secret sin is when you deprive your neighbor of that which you ought to give him; an open sin is where you perform positive acts of sin, as I have related to thee. It is, therefore, indeed the truth that every sin done against me is done through the medium of the neighbor."

7. *How Virtues Are Accomplished by Means of Our Neighbor, and How It Is that Virtues Differ to Such an Extent in Creatures*

"I have told thee how all sins are accomplished by means of thy neighbor, through the principles which I exposed to thee, that is, because men are deprived of the affection of love, which gives light to every virtue. In the same way self-love, which destroys charity and affection toward the neighbor, is the principle and foundation of every evil. All scandals, hatred, cruelty, and every sort of trouble proceed from this perverse root[29] of self-love, which has poisoned the entire world, and weakened the mystical body of the holy church, and the universal body of the believers in the Christian religion; and, therefore, I said to thee, that it was in the neighbor, that is to say, in the love of him,

29 *Perversa radice.*

that all virtues were founded; and, truly, indeed did I say to thee, that charity gives life to all the virtues, because no virtue can be obtained without charity, which is the pure love of me.

"Wherefore, when the soul knows herself, as we have said above, she finds humility and hatred of her own sensual passion, for she learns the perverse law, which is bound up in her members, and which ever fights against the spirit. And, therefore, arising with hatred of her own sensuality, crushing it under the heel of reason, with great earnestness, she discovers in herself the bounty of my goodness, through the many benefits which she has received from me, all of which she considers again in herself. She attributes to me, through humility, the knowledge which she has obtained of herself, knowing that, by my grace, I have drawn her out of darkness and lifted her up into the light of true knowledge. When she has recognized my goodness, she loves it without any medium, and yet at the same time with a medium, that is to say, without the medium of herself or of any advantage accruing to herself, and with the medium of virtue, which she has conceived through love of me, because she sees that in no other way can she become grateful and acceptable to me but by conceiving hatred of sin and love of virtue; and, when she has thus conceived by the affection of love, she immediately is delivered of fruit for her neighbor, because in no other way can she act out the truth she has conceived in herself, but, loving me in truth, in the same truth she serves her neighbor.[30]

"And it cannot be otherwise, because love of me and of her neighbor are one and the same thing,[31] and so far as the soul loves me she loves her neighbor, because love toward him issues from me. This is the means which I have given you, that you may exercise and prove your virtue therewith; because, inasmuch as you can do me no profit, you should do it to your neighbor. This proves that you possess me by grace in your soul, producing much fruit for your neighbor and making prayers to me, seeking with sweet and amorous desire my honor and the salvation of souls. The soul, enamored of my truth, never ceases to serve the whole world in general, and more or less in a particular case according to the disposition of the recipient and the ardent desire of the donor, as I have shown above, when I declared to thee that the endurance of suffering alone, without desire, was not sufficient to punish a fault.

---

30 Cf. *Dial.*, cap. 98; *Let.*, T. 56, 301; Guigues, *op. cit.*, pp. 278 ff.
31 *È una medesima cosa.* Cf. *Let.*, T. 242; *Dial.*, 64, 66.

"When she has discovered the advantage of this unitive love in me, by means of which she truly loves herself, extending her desire for the salvation of the whole world, thus coming to the aid of its neediness, she strives, inasmuch as she has done good to herself by the conception of virtue, from which she has drawn the life of grace, to fix her eye on the needs of her neighbor in particular. Wherefore, when she has discovered, through the affection of love, the state of all rational creatures in general, she helps those who are at hand, according to the various graces which I have entrusted to her to administer; one she helps with doctrine, that is, with words, giving sincere counsel without any respect of persons; another with the example of a good life, and this indeed all give to their neighbor, the edification of a holy and honorable life. These are the virtues, and many others, too many to enumerate, which are brought forth in the love of the neighbor; but, although I have given them in such a different way—that is to say, not all to one, but to one one virtue, and to another another—it so happens that it is impossible to have one, without having them all, because all the virtues are bound together. Wherefore, learn that in many cases I give one virtue, to be as it were the chief of the others; that is to say, to one I will give principally love, to another justice, to another humility, to one a lively faith, to another prudence or temperance or patience, to another fortitude. These, and many other virtues, I place, indifferently, in the souls of many creatures; it happens, therefore, that the particular one so placed in the soul becomes the principal object of its virtue; the soul disposing herself, for her chief conversation, to this rather than to other virtues, and, by the effect of this virtue, the soul draws to herself all the other virtues, which, as has been said, are all bound together in the affection of love; and so with many gifts and graces of virtue, and not only in the case of spiritual things but also of temporal. I use the word 'temporal' for the things necessary to the physical life of man; all these I have given indifferently, and I have not placed them all in one soul, in order that man should, perforce, have material for love of his fellow. I could easily have created men possessed of all that they should need both for body and soul, but I wish that one should have need of the other, and that they should be my ministers to administer the graces and the gifts that they have received from me. Whether man will or no, he cannot help making an act of love.[32] It is

---

[32] *Che voglia l'Uomo, o nò, non può fare, che per forza non usi l'atto della Carità.* Cf. *Let.*, T. 301, 304.

true, however, that that act, unless made through love of me, profits him nothing so far as grace is concerned. See, then, that I have made men my ministers, and placed them in diverse stations and various ranks, in order that they may make use of the virtue of love.

"Wherefore, I show you that in my house are many mansions, and that I wish for no other thing than love, for in the love of me is fulfilled and completed the love of the neighbor, and the law observed. For he only can be of use in his state of life who is bound to me with this love."

8. How Virtues Are Proved and Fortified by Their Contraries

"Up to the present, I have taught thee how a man may serve his neighbor, and manifest, by that service, the love which he has toward me.

"Now I wish to tell thee, further, that a man proves his patience on his neighbor when he receives injuries from him.

"Similarly, he proves his humility on a proud man, his faith on an infidel, his true hope on one who despairs, his justice on the unjust, his kindness on the cruel, his gentleness and benignity on the irascible. Good men produce and prove all their virtues on their neighbor, just as perverse men all their vices; thus, if thou consider well, humility is proved on pride in this way. The humble man extinguishes pride, because a proud man can do no harm to a humble one; neither can the infidelity of a wicked man, who neither loves me nor hopes in me, when brought forth against one who is faithful to me, do him any harm; his infidelity does not diminish the faith or the hope of him who has conceived his faith and hope through love of me; it rather fortifies it, and proves it in the love he feels for his neighbor. For he sees that the infidel is unfaithful because he is without hope in me, and in my servant, because he does not love me, placing his faith and hope rather in his own sensuality, which is all that he loves. My faithful servant does not leave him because he does not faithfully love me, or because he does not constantly seek, with hope in me, for his salvation, inasmuch as he sees clearly the causes of his infidelity and lack of hope. The virtue of faith is proved in these and other ways. Wherefore, to those who need the proof of it, my servant proves his faith in himself and in his neighbor, and so justice is not diminished by the wicked man's injustice, but is rather proved—that is to say, the justice of a just man. Similarly, the virtues of patience, benignity, and kindness manifest themselves in a time of wrath by the same sweet patience in my servants, and envy, vexation, and hatred demonstrate their love, and hunger, and desire for the salvation of souls. I say also to thee that not only is virtue proved in those who render good for evil, but that many times a good man gives back fiery coals of love which dispel the hatred and rancor of heart of the angry, and so from hatred often comes benevolence, and that this is by virtue of the love and perfect patience which is in him who sustains the anger of the wicked, bearing and supporting his defects. If thou wilt observe the virtues of fortitude and perseverance, these virtues are proved by the long endurance of the injuries and detractions of wicked men, who, whether by injuries or by flattery, constantly endeavor to turn a man aside from following the road and the doctrine of truth. Wherefore, in all these things, the virtue of fortitude, conceived within the soul, perseveres with strength, and in addition proves itself externally upon the neighbor, as I have said to thee; and, if fortitude were not able to make that good proof of itself, being tested by many contrarieties, it would not be a serious virtue founded in truth."

X

Jan Van Ruysbroeck (1293-1381)

INTRODUCTION

BIOGRAPHICAL NOTICE

RUYSBROECK, BORN IN 1293, WENT AT ELEVEN years of age to nearby Brussels, where he was assisted by his uncle, a canon of St. Gudule, in his early studies. These doubtless involved the medieval Latin and German mystics. Ordained around 1317, he received the title of vicar or chaplain to the clergy of St. Gudule, the collegial church. During some twenty-five years of such service, he came into conflict with the Brethren of the Free Spirit, the Beghards, Beguines, and other like groups, whom he was to challenge in later writings. In 1343, together with his uncle Jan Hinckaert, and a priest, Francis van Coudenberg, he helped to establish a community of contemplatives at Groenendael. This group, early in contact with the Victorines at Paris, eventually came under the rule of the Augustinian canons, with Coudenberg as provost and Ruysbroeck as prior. Here, until his death in 1381, Ruysbroeck fostered in his books and in his life the blending of contemplation and action, the union of canonical hours and working devotion. Poetic vision and service to others went hand in hand in this "God-seeing life." Not only to Gerard Groote, a founder of the Brethren of the Common Life, but to many others also, he gave the witness of Christian love "that cannot be lazy."

BIBLIOGRAPHICAL ESSAY

A critical study of MS. and printed sources concerning the life and works of Ruysbroeck is M. D'Asbeck, *Documents relatifs à Ruysbroeck*, Leroux, Paris, 1931. A pivotal work was W. De-Vreese, *De Handschriften van Jan van Ruusbroec's Werken*, 2 vols.,

Ghent, 1900–1902. The *Werken* were first critically set forth by J. B. David, in 6 vols., Ghent, 1858–1868. Ancient texts by H. Pomerius were edited as *De origine monasterii Viridisvallis una cum vitis B. Joannis Rusbrochii*, in *Analecta Bollandiana*, Vol. 4 (1885), pp. 257 ff. A famous Latin translation of the works by L. Surius, the *Opera omnia*, appeared at Cologne in four editions from 1552 to 1692. The fundamental study, *Jan Van Ruusbroec, Leven en Werken*, Antwerp, Amsterdam, and Malines, 1931, included studies of Ruysbroeck's mysticism by L. Reypens and an invaluable bibliography in all languages. The next year there began to appear the definitive *Ruusbroec Werken*, 4 vols., with key editing by Dr. J. B. Poukens, S. J., and Dr. L. Reypens, S. J.—revised 1944—. *Vanden Blinckenden Steen*, or *The Sparkling Stone*, is Vol. III, 1947, pp. 3–41. Modern translations include the *Œuvres de Ruysbroeck l'Admirable*, done from the Flemish by the Benedictines of Saint-Paul de Wisques, 1912—. Quite useful is J. A. Bizet, *Ruysbroeck, Œuvres choisies*, Aubier, Paris, 1946. Highly pertinent English translations from the Flemish are *The Adornment of the Spiritual Marriage; The Sparkling Stone; The Book of Supreme Truth*, translated by C. A. Wynschenk Dom, John M. Watkins, London, 1916, 1951; *The Seven Steps of the Ladder of Spiritual Love*, tr. by F. Sherwood Taylor, Dacre Press, Westminster, 1944, 1952; and *The Spiritual Espousals*, tr. by Eric Colledge, Faber & Faber, Ltd., London, 1952. Valuable studies are E. Underhill, *Ruysbroeck*, London, 1914; A. W. D'Aygalliers, *Ruysbroeck l'Admirable*, Paris, 1923; and, though perhaps exaggerating the Neoplatonic influences, M. D'Asbeck, *La mystique de Ruysbroeck l'Admirable*, Leroux, Paris, 1930. St. Axters, *La spiritualité des pays-bas*, J. Vrin, Paris, 1948, is suggestive, as is A. Hyma, *The Brethren of the Common Life*, Wm. B. Eerdmans Publishing Company, Grand Rapids, Michigan, 1950. On the Gerson issue, see A. Combes, *Essai sur la critique de Ruysbroeck par Gerson*, 2 vols., Paris, 1945, 1948. Of further significance are J. Stelzenberger, *Die Mystik des Johannes Gerson*, Breslau, 1928, and the references to source texts and literature in J. L. Connolly, *John Gerson, Reformer and Mystic*, B. Herder, St. Louis, 1928.

Synopsis

Ruysbroeck's mysticism shows intimate relationship, at certain points, with the Neoplatonists, Augustine, the Victorines, and the Rhenish school. However much he may have owed to the Eckhartian stimulus, he certainly qualified the more dangerous implications of his earlier writings in his later books. Some of his expressions in the third part of his *Adornment of the Spiritual Marriage* had provoked sincere, if not wholly justifiable, attacks by the redoubtable Jean Gerson. There had been relatively unguarded statements, for instance, concerning the possibility, and the face-to-face immediacy, of the unitive vision. This contemplative view of the divine essence in this present life had prompted various charges, that of pantheism included. To whatever extent modifications may have been elicited by the discussions of 1330–1336 and the intervention of Pope Benedict XII, these shifts of form and interpretation were introduced in *The Sparkling Stone* and in *The Book of Supreme Truth*. In the former (ch. 10), he stressed the necessity of man's remaining "eternally other than God, and distinct from him." In the latter (ch. 2), he asserted that "no creature is able to be or to become holy to the point of losing his created nature or to become God." *The Sparkling Stone*, for its part, summarizes in its first nine chapters the first two books of the *Spiritual Marriage*. Chapters 10–14 recapitulate the matter of the *Spiritual Marriage*'s third book, that is, contemplation as such.

Three traditional elements in Ruysbroeck that are placed in a distinctive synthesis are exemplarism, introversion, and the life of union.[1]

The basis of exemplarism is in Trinitarian doctrine. The divine life is a movement of flux and reflux, expansion and contraction, originating in the unity of nature from which there proceed the three Persons; theirs too is a return to unity in a common fruition. The eternal life of the creature, according to exemplarist ideas, participates in this flux and reflux.

Even the structure of the soul is calculated on the divine model. This is, of course, Augustinian doctrine. The three major faculties—memory, intelligence, and will—take their natural origin from the unity of the spirit. This unity must be possessed supernaturally. Man finally descends into himself. There he discovers in the ground of the soul the image of God. The soul must associate itself with the life of the three divine Persons until it attains, at the summit of contemplation, to "the union without difference," though not without otherness. Thus joined with the divine essence, it comes to "possession." This is the much emphasized "common life" which is not possible "without the exercise of love." By it the human life is led into

---

[1] DS II, 1999. Cf. Reypens, "Connaissance mystique de Dieu," DS, Fasc. 20–21 (1955), cols. 906–09.

the Trinitarian life itself. It is on this "common life" that *The Sparkling Stone* (ch. 14) and *The Seven Steps of the Ladder of Spiritual Love* have such eloquent résumés.[2]

Contemplation clearly constitutes for Ruysbroeck, then, as for the Rhineland school, the summit of an experience, the description of which is both dogmatically based and speculatively developed. Nor is it lacking in deeply affective elements. It is not quite so intellectualized as that of Eckhart. Perhaps Ruysbroeck is less concerned than Eckhart or Tauler with the technical aspects of spiritual detachment. He recalls for us the experiential qualities of Suso in a more rarefied form.[3]

As regards the role of introversion, it has been noted how the medieval world had lost the sense of introspective method inaugurated by Augustine and his *Confessions*; how, rather than observing in their empirical reality the successive transformations which mark the progress of the soul in its narrow way, many mystics had had progressive recourse to allegorical gradations. Such were the references to the ladder of Jacob, the degrees of Solomon's throne, the conventional appeal to the six degrees of charity, the seven virtues, and the three ways. Ruysbroeck did not disparage these; in fact he too utilized them as in his own *Ladder*. Yet in his personal experience, as in his capitalization of Catholic tradition, he recapitulated the Augustinian sense of interiority.[4]

One may anticipate in Augustine's *Confessions* (VII, x, 16), the introspective method later reapplied by Ruysbroeck. Presumably from his study of Platonist and Neoplatonist books, Augustine had learned the art of introversion. He had achieved with their help a fleeting intellectual contemplation of God; in his own words, "a hurried vision of That Which Is." Admonished to return into himself, he entered his own secret closet of the soul, guided by the Lord. There he beheld "the Light that never changes, above the eye of my soul, above the intelligence." Scattered but cumulative references to introversion in Ruysbroeck bear out this Augustinian emphasis in his own writings. Here the attention turns inward "from the distractions

---

2 *The Ladder*, 6th and 7th steps, pp. 55 ff.; Bizet, *op. cit.*, pp. 68 ff. On Ruysbroeck's synthesis of the soul's structure and of introversion in relation to Neoplatonist, Augustinian, and Rhenish currents, see Father Reypens, "Âme (Structure)," in DS I, 453–55.

3 DS II, 1999–2000.

4 Bizet, *op. cit.*, pp. 64 ff.; St. Axters, *op. cit.*, p. 53; *The Sparkling Stone*, chs. 1–3, 13.

of the sense world."[5] Consciousness enters "into the super-sensuous regions beyond thought." It retreats from the fringes of the sense world to the center of being and the souls' Ground "where human personality buds forth from the Essential world."[6]

Ruysbroeck's stages of mystical experience are readily identifiable. The active life presents the way of purgation and ethical purification. Here is the range of self-disciplined service and self-conquest. The interior life is one of illumination and intellectual purification as over against the ethical purification of the active life. The aim here is right vision and right thought, even as that of right conduct preponderates in the active way. The interior life in its more advanced stages opens up the route to union and contemplation. The apex of the unitive life, however, is found in what may be denominated the "superessential life."[7]

The emphasis on the "common" or "practical" life is found most beautifully stated in *The Sparkling Stone*, chapter 14. Hardly surpassable in Ruysbroeck's works are the first and second "Moments" of the contemplative life as they are set forth in *The Seven Steps*. Here also the divine-human respiration, flux, and reflux, as well as the "common life," have moving analysis. "Between action and rest live love and fruition," is only one of his choice lines. The character of the common, superessential life there depicted should be put alongside that of *The Spiritual Espousals* and *The Sparkling Stone*.[8]

Ruysbroeck, then, treats of mystical experience in terms of three unities, each facilitated through one of three ways.[9] The lower, corporeal unity, with its practice of external works, goes the way of the active life. The spiritual unity, expressing itself by the theological virtues and the imitation of Jesus Christ, follows in the way of the interior life. The sublime unity, which makes us to repose in God above all thought or intention, is the supernatural life with its end in contemplation. The active life,

---

[5] Underhill, *Ruysbroeck*, pp. 152, 80.   [6] *Ibid.*, p. 146.
[7] I.e., "more than being"—*Overwesen*. Cf. Underhill, *Ruysbroeck*, pp. 164 ff. On this "superessential contemplation," see *The Spiritual Espousals*, Book III, p. 179; *The Adornment of the Spiritual Marriage*, p. 167; *Werken*, Vol. I, p. 239, ll. 7–8: *eenen overweselijcken scouwene.* . . .
[8] See Colledge, *The Spiritual Espousals*, pp. 36, 48, 132, 158–60, on the "common life"; *The Ladder*, pp. 55–63, especially 58, etc.
[9] For the following, see the source references in Petry, "Social Responsibility," *Church History*, Vol. 21, pt. 1, pp. 12–13, 18–19. Cf. D'Aygalliers, *op. cit.*, pp. 286 ff.

19—L.M.M.

claiming virtuous men of God, will permit a foretaste of the divine union—the union of intermediary or with means. The interior life brings God and creature together in a union without intermediary or means. In the contemplative life there is consummated a union without distinction or differences, one such as Christ spoke of in his consecratory prayer. This is a time of ecstasy followed by knowledge, love, and jubilation. Still, it is no sheerly passive or quietist state. Between the writing of *The Adornment of the Spiritual Marriage* and that of *The Sparkling Stone*, Ruysbroeck has come to guard ever more closely against pantheistic encroachments and heretical "passivism." More and more he emphasizes "practical life." Those who multiply works, however, and lose themselves therein, belong in the same category with people who isolate themselves in contemplative repose, away from practical demands.

Invoking the spiritual law of aspiration and expiration, God draws us near to himself—beyond any holding back; but, after this God's Holy Spirit breathes us out again, for the practice of love and good works. As in nature, so here too, we exhale the old and inhale the fresh air. One enters inactive joys; then goes out to practice good works, remaining joined always to the Spirit of God.

Significantly enough, this practical life, distinguished by Ruysbroeck from the active, is denominated the "common." The active life, inspired by grace, is essentially the work of the human will. The common life, on the contrary, depends on God alone. The eloquent fourteenth chapter of *The Sparkling Stone* is entitled: "Of That Common Life That Comes from the Contemplation and Fruition of God." Here Ruysbroeck balances the active and the contemplative. As Underhill says, "His rapturous ascents toward divine Reality were compensated by the eager and loving interest with which he turned toward the world of men."[10]

Likewise, it is correct to say that Ruysbroeck's mysticism and ecclesiology support and clarify each other. He knows the human faults and schismatic shames of Mother Church. But he also knows her Petrine foundation, her apostolic power and order, and her ultimate invincibility. He believes in her hierarchy, her priesthood, and her sacraments. These last are the channels of God's love, the visible form of invisible grace. They are another coming of Christ the Bridegroom that takes place

[10] Underhill, introduction to *Spiritual Marriage*, pp. xv–xvi.

every day. To be desired with a loving heart, the sacrament is needful for him who would "remain steadfast and go forward in eternal life." From Mother Church, Ruysbroeck accepts his commission to serve world humanity. Such a man truly goes forth, after the fourfold way he sets down: namely, toward Christ and all saints; toward sinners and all perverted men; toward purgatory; toward himself and all good men.

Jan Van Ruysbroeck (1293-1381)

THE SPARKLING STONE [11]

The Text

Prologue

The man who would live in the most perfect state of holy church must be a good and zealous man; an inward and ghostly man; an uplifted and God-seeing man; and an outflowing man to all in common.[12] Whenever these four things are together in a man, then his state is perfect; and through the increase of grace he shall continually grow and progress in all virtues, and in the knowledge of truth, before God and before all men.

Chapter I

Through Three Things a Man Becomes Good

Hear now three things that constitute a good man. The first, which a good man must have, is a clean conscience without reproach of mortal sin. And therefore whosoever wishes to become a good man must examine and prove himself with due discernment, from that time onward when he could first have commited sin. And from all these sins he must purge himself, according to the precept and the custom of holy church.

The second thing that pertains to a good man is that he must in all things be obedient to God, and to holy church, and to his own proper convictions. And to each of these three he must be

---

[11] The translation from the Flemish is that of C. A. Wynschenk Dom, edited by Evelyn Underhill, *John of Ruysbroeck: The Adornment of the Spiritual Marriage . . . The Sparkling Stone . . . The Book of Supreme Truth*, London, 1916, 1951, pp. 181–221. Used by permission of the publisher, John Maurice Watkins. *The Sparkling Stone*, i.e., *Vanden Blinckenden Steen*, is Vol. III, pp. 3–41, in the *Werken*.

[12] The classification of *The Adornment of the Spiritual Marriage*, i.e., *Die Geestelike Brulocht*, in the *Werken*, Vol. I, pp. 103 ff.

equally obedient: so shall he live without care and doubt, and shall ever abide without inward reproach in all his deeds.

The third thing that behoves every good man is that in all his deeds he should have in mind, above all else, the glory of God. And if it happens that by reason of his business or the multiplicity of his works, he has not always God before his eyes, yet at least there should be established in him the intention and desire to live according to the dearest will of God.

Behold, these three things, when they are possessed in this way, make a man good. And whosoever lacks any one of these three is neither good nor in the grace of God; but whenever a man resolves in his heart to fulfill these three points, how wicked soever he may have been before, in that very instant he becomes good, and is susceptible of God, and filled with the grace of God.

Chapter II

Through Three Things a Man Becomes Inward

If, further, this good man would become an inward and ghostly man, he needs must have three further things. The first is a heart unencumbered with images[13]; the second is spiritual freedom in his desires; the third is the feeling of inward union with God.

Now let everyone who thinks himself to be ghostly observe himself. He who would have a heart void of images may not possess anything with affection, nor may he cling to anyone, or have intercourse with him with attachment of the will; for all intercourse and all affection which do not aim purely at the honor of God bring images into a man's heart, since they are born, not of God, but of the flesh. And so if a man would become spiritual, he must forsake all fleshly lusts and loves and must cleave with longing and love to God alone, and thus possess him. And through this, all imaginations and all inordinate love toward creatures are cast out. And this loving possession of God makes a man inwardly free from ungodly images; for God is a Spirit, of whom no one can make to himself a true image. Certainly in this exercise a man should lay hold of good images to help him; such as the Passion of our Lord and all those things that may stir him to greater devotion. But in the possession of God, the man must sink down to that imageless nudity which is

---

13 Cf. the *Spiritual Marriage*, Bk. II, chs. 1–4; *Werken*, Vol. I, pp. 144 ff.

God; and this is the first condition, and the foundation, of a ghostly life.

The second condition is inward freedom. Through this, the man should be able to raise himself toward God in all inward exercises, free from images and encumbrances; that is, in thanksgiving and praise, in worship, in devout prayer and fervent love, and in all those things that may be done by longing and love with the help of the grace of God and through inward zeal in all ghostly exercises.

Through this inward exercise, he reaches the third state; which is that he feels a ghostly union with God. Whosoever then has, in his inward exercise, an imageless and free ascent unto his God, and means nought else but the glory of God, must taste of the goodness of God; and he must feel from within a true union with God. And in this union the inward and spiritual life is made perfect; for in this union the desirous power is perpetually enticed anew and stirred to new inward activity. And by each act the spirit rises upward to a new union. And so activity and union perpetually renew themselves; and this perpetual renewal in activity and in union is a ghostly life. And so you are now able to see how a man becomes good through the moral virtues and an upright intention; and how he may become ghostly through the inward virtues and union with God. But without these said points he can neither be good nor ghostly.

Chapter III

Through Three Things a Man Becomes God-seeing

Further, you must know that if this ghostly man would now become a God-seeing man, he needs must have three other things. The first is the feeling that the foundation of his being is abysmal,[14] and he should possess it in this manner; the second is that his inward exercise should be wayless; the third is that his indwelling should be a divine fruition.

Now understand, you who would live in the spirit, for I am speaking to no one else. The union with God which a spiritual man feels, when the union is revealed to the spirit as being abysmal—that is, measureless depth, measureless height, measureless length, and measureless breadth—in this manifestation the spirit perceives that through love it has plunged itself into

---

[14] Cf. Eckhart, etc., on "desert" and "abyss."

the depth and has ascended into the height and escaped into the length; and it feels itself to be wandering in the breadth, and to dwell in a knowledge which is ignorance. And through this intimate feeling of union, it feels itself to be melting into the Unity; and, through dying to all things, into the life of God. And there it feels itself to be one life with God. And this is the foundation, and the first point, of the God-seeing life.

And from this there arises the second point, which is an exercise above reason and without condition: for the divine Unity, of which every God-seeing spirit has entered into possession in love, eternally draws and invites the divine Persons and all loving spirits into its Self. And this inward drawing is felt by each lover, more or less, according to the measure of his love and the manner of his exercise. And whosoever yields himself to this indrawing, and keeps himself therein, cannot fall into mortal sin. But the God-seeing man who has forsaken self and all things, and does not feel himself drawn away because he no longer possesses anything as his own, but stands empty of all, he can always enter, naked and unencumbered with images, into the inmost part of his spirit. There he finds revealed an eternal Light, and in this light, he feels the eternal demand of the divine Unity; and he feels himself to be an eternal fire of love, which craves above all else to be one with God. The more he yields to this indrawing or demand, the more he feels it. And the more he feels it, the more he craves to be one with God; for it urges him to pay the debt which is demanded of him by God. This eternal demand of the divine Unity kindles within the spirit an eternal fire of love; and though the spirit incessantly pays the debt, an eternal burning continues within it. For, in the transformation within the Unity, all spirits fail in their own activity, and feel nothing else but a burning up of themselves in the simple unity of God. This simple unity of God none can feel or possess save he who maintains himself in the immeasurable radiance, and in the love which is above reason and wayless. In this transcendent state the spirit feels in itself the eternal fire of love; and in this fire of love it finds neither beginning nor end, and it feels itself one with this fire of love. The spirit forever continues to burn in itself, for its love is eternal; and it feels itself ever more and more to be burned up in love, for it is drawn and transformed into the unity of God, where the spirit burns in love. If it observes itself, it finds a distinction and an otherness between itself and God; but where it is burned up it is undifferentiated and without distinction, and therefore it feels nothing but unity; for the flame of the love of God consumes and devours all that it can enfold in its Self.

And thus you may see that the indrawing unity of God is nought else than the fathomless love which lovingly draws inward, in eternal fruition, the Father and the Son and all that lives in them. And in this love we shall burn and be burned up without end, throughout eternity; for herein lies the blessedness of all spirits. And therefore we must all found our lives upon a fathomless abyss, that we may eternally plunge into love, and sink down in the fathomless depth. And with that same love we shall ascend, and transcend ourselves, in the incomprehensible height. And in that love which is wayless we shall wander and stray, and it shall lead us and lose us in the immeasurable breadth of the love of God. And herein we shall flee forth and flee out of ourselves, into the unknown raptures of the goodness and riches of God. And therein we shall melt and be melted away, and shall eternally wander and sojourn within the glory of God. Behold! by each of these images I show forth to God-seeing men their being and their exercise, but none else can understand them. For the contemplative life cannot be taught. But where the eternal Truth reveals itself within the spirit, all that is needful is taught and learned.

Chapter IV

Of the Sparkling Stone, and of the New Name Written in the Book of the Secrets of God

And therefore the Spirit of our Lord speaks thus in the Book of the Secrets of God, which Saint John wrote down: TO HIM THAT OVERCOMETH, He says, that is, to him who overcometh and conquereth himself and all else, WILL I GIVE TO EAT OF THE HIDDEN MANNA, that is, an inward and hidden savor and celestial joy; AND WILL GIVE HIM A SPARKLING STONE,[15] AND IN THE STONE A NEW

---

[15] *Werken*, Vol. III, p. 9, ll. 18 ff.: *ende Ic sal hem gheven . . . een blinckende steenken, ende in dien steenken eenen nuwen name ghescreven.* . . . Surius translates, *Op. om.* (1609), cap. IV, p. 514: *et dabo ei calculum candidum, & in calculo nomen novuum scriptum.* . . . Ruysbroeck went on to refer to this little stone as *een terdelinc*, "a tread-ling," thus suggesting on the Latin side a relationship "between *calculus* (pebble), from *calx* (stone), and *calcare* (to tread), from *calx* (knuckle, heel)." Underhill, ed., *The Sparkling Stone*, p. 187, note 1. *Œuvres*, III, p. 238, note 1. Cf. D'Asbeck, *La mystique*, p. 228.

NAME[16] WRITTEN, WHICH NO MAN KNOWETH
SAVING HE THAT RECEIVETH IT. This stone is called a
pebble, for it is so small that it does not hurt when one treads on
it. This stone is shining white and red like a flame of fire; and it
is small and round, and smooth all over, and very light. By this
sparkling stone we mean our Lord Christ Jesus, for he is, according to his Godhead, a shining forth of the eternal Light, and
an irradiation of the glory of God, and a flawless mirror in
which all things live. Now to him who overcomes and transcends all things, this sparkling stone is given; and with it he
receives light and truth and life. This stone is also like to a fiery
flame, for the fiery love of the Eternal Word has filled the whole
world with love and wills that all loving spirits be burned up to
nothingness in love. This stone is also so small that a man hardly
feels it, even though he treads it underfoot. And that is why it is
called *calculus*, that is, "treadling." And this is made clear to us
by Saint Paul, where he says that the Son of God EMPTIED
HIMSELF, AND HUMBLED HIMSELF, AND TOOK UP-
ON HIM THE FORM OF A SERVANT, AND BECAME
OBEDIENT UNTO DEATH, EVEN THE DEATH OF THE
CROSS. And He himself spoke through the mouth of the
prophet, saying: I AM A WORM, AND NO MAN; A RE-
PROACH OF MEN, AND DESPISED OF THE PEOPLE.
And he made himself so small in time that the Jews trod him
under their feet. But they felt him not; for, had they recognized
the Son of God, they had not dared to crucify him. He is still
little and despised in all men's hearts that do not love him well.
This noble stone of which I speak is wholly round and smooth
and even all over. That the stone is round teaches us that the
divine Truth has neither beginning nor end; that it is smooth
and even all over teaches us that the divine Truth shall weigh
all things evenly, and shall give to each according to his merits;
and that which he gives shall be with each throughout eternity.
The last property of this stone of which I will speak is that it is
particularly light; for the eternal Word of the Father has no
weight, nevertheless it bears heaven and earth by its strength.
And it is equally near to all things; yet none can attain it, for it
is set on high and goes before all creatures, and reveals itself
where it will and when it wills; and in its lightness our heavy

---

16 The first name is that given at baptism. The new name is that received in
   contemplation and is proportionate to the degree of perfection registered
   by each soul. *Œuvres*, p. 227.

human nature has climbed above all the heavens, and sits crowned at the right hand of the Father.

Behold, this is the sparkling stone which is given to the God-seeing man, and in this stone A NEW NAME IS WRITTEN, WHICH NO MAN KNOWETH SAVING HE THAT RECEIVETH IT. You should know that all spirits in their return toward God receive names; each one in particular, according to the nobleness of its service and the loftiness of its love. For only the first name of innocence, which we receive at baptism, is adorned with the merits of our Lord Jesus Christ. And when we have lost this name of innocence through sin, if we are willing still to follow God—especially in three works which he wishes to work in us—we are baptized once more in the Holy Ghost. And thereby we receive a new name which shall remain with us throughout eternity.

Chapter V

Of the Works Which God Works in All in Common and of Five Kinds of Sinners

Hear now what those three works are which our Lord works in all men if they will submit themselves thereto. The first work which God works in all men in common consists in his calling and inviting them all, without exception, to union with himself. And as long as a sinner does not follow this call, he must lack all the other gifts which would follow thereafter.

Now I have observed that all sinners may be divided into five kinds. To the first kind belong all those who are careless of good works, who through bodily ease and the lust of the senses prefer to live in worldly employments and in multiplicity of heart. All such are unfit to receive the grace of God, and even if they had received it, they would not be able to keep it.

To the second kind belong those who have willingly and wittingly fallen into mortal sin, yet also do good works, and dwell in the fear and awe of the Lord, and love the just, and desire their prayers, and put their trust therein. So long, however, as turning from God and love of sin vanquish and repulse love of God and turning to God, so long these remain unworthy of the grace of God.

The third kind of sinners consists in all unbelievers, and those who err in faith. What good works soever they do, or what lives soever they lead, without the true faith they cannot please

God; for true faith is the foundation of all holiness and all virtues.

To the fourth kind belong those who abide in mortal sin without fear and without shame, who care not for God and his gifts, and neglect all virtues. They hold all ghostly life to be hypocrisy and deceit; and they hardly listen to all that one may say to them of God or of the virtues, for they have established themselves as though there were no God, nor heaven, nor hell, and therefore they desire to know of nothing but that which they now perceive and have before them. Behold, all such are rejected and despised by God, for they sin against the Holy Ghost. Yet they may be converted; but this happens with difficulty and seldom.

The fifth kind of sinners are those hypocrites who do outward good works, not for the glory of God and their own salvation, but to acquire a name for holiness, or for the sake of some fleeting thing. Though they may appear holy and good from without, within they are false and turned away from God, and they lack the grace of God and every virtue.

See, I have shown to you five kinds of sinners, who have all been inwardly called to union with God. But so long as a sinner remains in the service of sin, so long he remains deaf and blind and unable to taste, or to feel, all the good that God wishes to work in him. But whenever a sinner enters into himself, and considers himself, if he be displeased by his sinful life, then he draws near to God. But if he would be obedient to the call and the words of God, he must of his own free will resolve to leave sin and to do penance. And so he becomes one aim and one will with God, and receives the grace of God.

And therefore we should all conceive of God in this way: First of all that, of his free goodness, he calls and invites all men, without distinction, to union with himself; both the good and the wicked, without exception. Secondly, we should thus comprehend the goodness of God; how he through grace flows forth toward all men who are obedient to the call of God. Thirdly, we should find and understand clearly in ourselves that we can become one life and one spirit with God when we renounce ourselves in every way, and follow the grace of God to the height whereto it would guide us. For the grace of God works according to order in every man, after the measure and the way in which he is able to receive it. And thereby, through the universal working of the grace of God, every sinner, if he desires it, receives the discernment and strength which are needful, that he may leave sin and turn toward virtue. And, through that hidden co-operation of the grace of God, every good man can overcome all sins, and can resist all temptations, and can fulfill all virtues, and can persevere in the highest perfection, if he be in all things submissive to the grace of God. For all that we are, and all that we have received, from without and from within, these are all the free gifts of God; for which we must thank and praise him, and with which we must serve him, if we are to please him. But there are many gifts of God which are for the good an aid to, and a source of, virtue; but for the wicked an aid to, and an occasion of, sin: such are health, beauty, wisdom, riches, and worldly dignity. These are the lowest and least precious gifts of God, which God gives for the benefit of all, to his friends and to his enemies, to the good and to the wicked. And with these the good serve God and his friends; but the wicked, their own flesh, and the devil, and the world.

Chapter VI [17]

Of the Difference Between the Hirelings and the Faithful Servants of God

Now you may mark this: that some men receive the gifts of God as hirelings, but others as faithful servants of God; and these differ one from another in all inward works, that is, in love and intention, in feeling, and in every exercise of the inward life.

Now understand this well: all those who love themselves so inordinately that they will not serve God, save for their own profit and because of their own reward, these separate themselves from God, and dwell in bondage and in their own selfhood; for they seek, and aim at, their own, in all that they do. And therefore, with all their prayers and with all their good works, they seek after temporal things, or maybe strive after eternal things for their own benefit and for their own profit. These men are bent upon themselves in an inordinate way; and that is why they ever abide alone with themselves, for they lack the true love which would unite them with God and with all his

---

[17] Background for the classification, finally, of "Faithful Servants," "Secret Friends," and "Hidden Sons," i.e., *Ghetrouwe knechte* (caps. 6 and 7, *Werken*, III, 14 ff.), *Heimelijcke vriende* (caps. 7 and 8, *Werken*, III, 16 ff.), and *Verborghene sonen* (caps. 8–9, *Werken*, III, 18 ff.). Cf. D'Asbeck, *La mystique*, pp. 229–32. Consult Bizet, *Œuvres*, pp. 64 ff., on the relation to purification, illumination, and contemplation.

beloved. And although these men seem to keep within the law and the commandments of God and of holy church, they do not keep within the law of love; for all that they do, they do, not out of love, but from sheer necessity, lest they shall be damned. And, because they are inwardly unfaithful, they dare not trust in God; but their whole inward life is doubt and fear, travail and misery. For they see on the right hand eternal life, and this they are afraid of losing; and they see on the left hand the eternal pains of hell, and these they are afraid of gaining. But all their prayers, all their labor and all the good works, whatsoever they do, to cast out this fear, help them not; for the more inordinately they love themselves, the more they fear hell. And from this you may learn that their fear of hell springs from self-love, which seeks its own.

Now the prophet, and also the preacher, say, THE FEAR OF THE LORD IS THE BEGINNING OF WISDOM; but by this is meant that fear which is exercised upon the right side, where one considers the loss of eternal blessedness; for this fear arises from the natural tendency which every man has in himself to be blessed, that is, to see God. And therefore, even though a man may be faithless to God, yet whenever he truly observes himself from within, he feels himself to be leaning out from himself toward that blessedness which is God. And this blessedness he fears to lose; for he loves himself better than God, and he loves blessedness wholly for his own sake. And therefore he dare not trust in God. And yet this is that FEAR OF THE LORD WHICH IS THE BEGINNING OF WISDOM, and is a law to the unfaithful servants of God: for it compels a man to leave sin, and to strive after virtue, and to do good deeds, and these things prepare a man from without to receive the grace of God and become a faithful servant.

But from that very hour in which, with God's help, he can overcome his selfhood—that is to say, when he is so detached from himself that he is able to leave in the keeping of God everything of which he has need—behold, through doing this he is so well-pleasing to God that God bestows upon him His grace. And through grace, he feels true love: and love casts out doubt and fear, and fills the man with hope and trust, and thus he becomes a faithful servant, and means and loves God in all that he does. Behold, this is the difference between the faithful servant and the hireling.

Chapter VII

Of the Difference Between the Faithful Servants and the Secret Friends of God

We must now observe the great difference which there is between the faithful servants and the inward friends of God. For through grace and the help of God, the faithful servants have chosen to keep the commandments of God, that is, to be obedient to God and holy church in all virtues and goodly behavior: and this is called the outward or active life. But the inward friends of God choose to follow, besides the commandments, the quickening counsels of God; and this is a loving and inward cleaving to God for the sake of his eternal glory, with a willing abandonment of all that one may possess outside God with lust and love. All such friends God calls and invites inward, and he teaches them the distinctions of inward exercises and many a hidden way of ghostly life. But he sends his servants outward, that they may be faithful to him and to his house in every service and in every kind of outward good works.

Behold, thus God gives his grace and his help to each man according to his fitness; that is, according to the way in which he is in tune with God, whether in outward good works or in the inward practice of love. But none can do and feel the inward exercises unless he be wholly turned inward to God. For as long as a man is divided of heart, so long he looks outward, and is unstable of mind, and is easily swayed by joy and grief in temporal things, for these are still alive within him. And though he may live according to the commandments of God, inwardly he abides in darkness, and knows not what inward exercises may be, nor how these should be practiced. But, since he knows and feels that he has God in mind, and in all his works desires to fulfill his dearest will, with this he may be content; for then he knows himself to be free from hypocrisy in his intention, and faithful in his service. And by these two things he contents himself; and it seems to him that outward good works done with a pure intention are more holy and more profitable than any inward exercise whatever, for by the help of God he has chosen an outward active way of virtue. And therefore he had rather exercise himself in the diversity of outward works than serve with inward love that same One for whom he works. And that is the cause why his mind is more filled with the works which he does than with God, for whom he does them. And through this tendency to images in his works he remains an outward man, and is not able to follow the counsels of God; for his exercise is more outward than inward, more of the senses than of the spirit. Though he is indeed a faithful servant of God in outward works, yet that which the secret friends of God experience remains hidden from, and unknown to, him. And this is why certain gross and outward men always condemn and blame the inward and contemplative men, because they have in mind that these are idle. And this was also the reason why Martha complained to our Lord of her sister Mary because she did not help her in serving; for she believed that she was doing much service and much usefulness, and that her sister was sitting idle and doing nothing. But our Lord gave his judgment and decided between them: he did not blame Martha for her diligence, for her service was good and useful; but he blamed her for her care, and because she was troubled and cast down by a multitude of outward things. And he praised Mary for her inward exercise, and said that one thing was needful, and that she had chosen the better part, which should not be taken away from her.

That one thing which is needful for all men is divine love. The better part is an inward life, with loving adherence to God. This Mary Magdalen had chosen, and this is chosen by the secret friends of God. But Martha chose an outward, unenclosed, and active life; and that is the other part, in which one may serve God, but which is neither so perfect nor so good. And this part is chosen out of love by the faithful servants of God.

But there are found some foolish men who would be so inward that they would neither act nor serve, even in those things of which their neighbor has need. Behold, these are neither secret friends nor faithful servants of God, but they are altogether false and deceived. For no man can follow the counsels of God who will not keep His commandments. And therefore all secret friends of God are also at the same time faithful servants, wherever this is needful; but all the faithful servants are not secret friends, for the exercise which belongs thereto is unknown to them.

This is the difference between the faithful servants and the secret friends of God.

Chapter VIII

Of the Difference Between the Secret Friends and the Hidden Sons of God

But further we find a more subtle and inward difference,

between the secret friends and the hidden sons of God; and yet both these alike by their inward exercise maintain themselves in the presence of God. But the friends possess their inwardness as an attribute, for they choose the loving adherence to God as best and highest of all that they ever can and will reach: and that is why they cannot with themselves and their own activity penetrate to the imageless nudity. For they have, as images and intermediaries between God and themselves, their own being and their own activity. And though in their loving adherence they feel united with God, yet, in this union, they always feel a difference and an otherness between God and themselves. For the simple passing into the bare and wayless, they do not know and love: and therefore their highest inward life ever remains in reason and in ways. And though they have clear understanding and discernment of all virtues that may be conceived, the simple staring with open heart into the divine Brightness remains unknown of them. And though they feel themselves uplifted to God in a mighty fire of love, yet they keep something of their own selfhood, and are not consumed and burned to nothingness in the unity of love. And though they may desire to live forevermore in the service of God and to please him eternally, they will not die in God to all the selfhood of their spirit, and receive from him a God-formed life. And even though they esteem little and count as nothing all consolation and all rest which may come from without, yet they greatly value the gifts of God, and also their own inward works, and the solace and sweetness which they feel within; and thus they rest upon the way, and do not so wholly die to themselves as to be able to attain the highest beatitude in bare and wayless love. And even if they could practice and apprehend with clear discernment the perfection of loving adherence to God, and all the inward and upward going ways by which one may pass into the presence of God, yet the wayless passing, and the glorious wandering, in the superessential Love, wherein neither end, nor beginning, nor way, nor manner, can ever be found, would remain hidden from, and unknown of, them.

And so there is great difference between the secret friends and the hidden sons of God. For the friends feel nought else but a loving and living ascent to God in some wise; but, above this, the sons experience a simple and deathlike passing which is in no wise.

The inward life of the friends of our Lord is an upward-striving exercise of love, wherein they desire to remain forever with

their own selfhood; but how one possesses God through bare
love above every exercise, in freedom from one's self, this they
do not feel. Hence they are always striving upward toward God
in true faith, and await God and eternal blessedness with sincere
hope, and are fastened and anchored to God through perfect
charity. And therefore good things have befallen them, for they
please God, and God is complaisant unto them: yet for all this,
they are not assured of eternal life, for they have not entirely
died to themselves and to all selfhood. But all those who abide
and endure in their exercise and in that turning to God which
they have chosen above all else, these God has chosen in eternity, and their names together with their works are written
from eternity in the living book of the providence of God. But
those who choose other things, and turn their inward faces away
from God toward sin, and endure therein (even though their
names were written and known of God because of the temporal
righteousness which they had practiced before), their names
shall be blotted out and erased from the Book of Life because
they did not persevere unto death, and they shall nevermore be
able to taste of God, nor of any fruit which springs from virtue.
And therefore we must needs observe ourselves with diligence,
and adorn our turning toward God, from within with inward
love, and from without with good works: thus we can await in
hope and joy the judgment of God and the coming of our Lord
Jesus Christ. But could we renounce ourselves, and all selfhood
in our works, we should, with our bare and imageless spirit,
transcend all things; and, without intermediary, should be led
of the Spirit of God into the Nudity. And then we should feel
the certainty that we are indeed the sons of God: for AS MANY
AS ARE LED BY THE SPIRIT OF GOD, THEY ARE THE
SONS OF GOD, says the apostle Saint Paul.

Nevertheless, you should know that all good and faithful men
are the sons of God; for they are all born of the Spirit of God,
and the Spirit of God lives in them. And he moves and stirs
them—each according to his own capacity—to virtues and
good works, wherein they are well-pleasing to God. But because
of the inequality of their adherence and their exercises, I call
some the faithful servants of God, and others I call his secret
friends, and others again his hidden sons: nevertheless, they are
all servants, friends, and sons, for they all serve and love and
mean one God, and they live and work only by the free Spirit of
God. And God permits and allows that his friends do and
leave undone all those things which are not contrary to his

commandments; and for those who are bound by the counsels of God, then this bond also is a commandment. And so no one is disobedient or contrary to God save he who does not keep His commandments; but all those things which God commands and forbids in Scripture, or by holy church, or in our conscience, all these things we must do and leave undone, or else be disobedient to God, and lose his grace. But if we fall into venial sins, this is suffered both by God and by our reason, for we cannot wholly guard against them. And therefore such failings do not make us disobedient, for they do not drive out the grace of God nor our inward peace; nevertheless, we should always lament such lapses, how small soever they may be, and guard against them with all our might.

And by these words I have explained to you what I said at the beginning, namely, that every man must needs be obedient in all things to God and to holy church and to his own conscience; for I do not wish that any should be unjustly offended by my words. And herewith I leave it even as I have said it.

Chapter IX

How We May Become Hidden Sons of God, and Attain to the God-seeing Life

But I still longed to know how we may become hidden sons of God, and may attain to the God-seeing life. And as to this I have apprehended the following. As it has been said before, we must always live and be watchful in all virtues, and beyond all virtues must forsake this life and die in God; for we must die to sin and be born of God into a life of virtue, and we must renounce ourselves and die in God into an eternal life. And as to this ensues the following instruction:

If we are born of the Spirit of God, we are the sons of grace; and so our whole life is adorned with virtues. Thereby we overcome all that is contrary to God; for Saint John says, WHAT-SOEVER IS BORN OF GOD OVERCOMETH THE WORLD. In this birth all good men are sons of God. And the Spirit of God kindles and stirs each one of them in particular to those virtues and to those good works for which he is in readiness, and of which he is capable. And so they please God all in common, and each in particular, according to the measure of his love and the nobleness of his exercise; nevertheless, they do not feel established nor possessed of God, nor assured of eternal life, for they may still turn away and fall into sin. And that is why I call them rather servants and friends than sons. But when we transcend ourselves, and become, in our ascent toward God, so simple that the naked love in the height can lay hold of us, where love enfolds love, above every exercise of virtue—that is, in our Origin, of which we are spiritually born—then we cease, and we and all our selfhood die in God. And in this death we become hidden sons of God, and find a new life within us: and that is eternal life. And of these sons, Saint Paul says, YOU ARE DEAD, AND YOUR LIFE IS HID WITH CHRIST IN GOD.

Now understand, the explanation of this is as follows. In our approach to God we must carry with us ourselves and all our works, as a perpetual sacrifice to God; and in the presence of God, we must forsake ourselves and all our works, and, dying in love, go forth from all creatureliness into the superessential richness of God: there we shall possess God in an eternal death to ourselves. And that is why the Spirit of God says in the Book of the Divine Secrets, BLESSED ARE THE DEAD WHICH DIE IN THE LORD. Justly he calls them the blessed dead, for they remain eternally dead and lost to themselves in the fruitive unity of God. And they die in love ever anew, through the indrawing transformation of that same unity. Further, the Spirit of God says, THEY MAY REST FROM THEIR LABORS, AND THEIR WORKS DO FOLLOW THEM. In the ordinary state of grace, when we are born of God into a ghostly and virtuous life, we carry our works before us, as an offering to God; but in the wayless state, where we die back into God in an eternal and blessed life, there our good works follow us, for they are one life with us. When we go toward God by means of the virtues, God dwells in us; but when we go out from ourselves and from all else, then we dwell in God. So soon as we have faith, hope, and charity, we have received God, and he dwells in us with his grace, and he sends us out as his faithful servants, to keep his commandments. And he calls us in again as his secret friends, so soon as we are willing to follow his counsels; and he names us openly as his sons so soon as we live in opposition to the world. But if above all things we would taste God, and feel eternal life in ourselves, we must go forth into God with our feeling, above reason; and there we must abide, onefold, empty of ourselves, and free from images, lifted up by love into the simple bareness of our intelligence. For when we go out in love beyond and above all things, and die to all observation in

ignorance and in darkness, then we are wrought and transformed through the eternal Word, who is the image of the
Father. In this idleness of our spirit we receive the incomprehensible Light, which enwraps us and penetrates us, as the air
is penetrated by the light of the sun. And this Light is nothing
else than a fathomless staring and seeing. What we are, that we
behold; and what we behold, that we are: for our thought, our
life, and our being are uplifted in simplicity, and made one with
the Truth which is God. And therefore in this simple staring we
are one life and one spirit with God: and this I call a contemplative life.[18] As soon as we cleave to God through love, we
practice the better part; but when we gaze thus into our superessence, we possess God utterly.[19] With this contemplation there
is bound up an exercise which is wayless, that is to say, a
noughting of life; for, where we go forth out of ourselves into
darkness and the abysmal waylessness, there shines perpetually
the simple ray of the splendor of God, in which we are grounded,
and which draws us out of ourselves into the superessence, and
into the immersion of love. And with this sinking into love there
is always bound up a practice of love which is wayless; for love
cannot be lazy,[20] but would search through and through and
taste through and through the fathomless richness which lives in
the ground of her being, and this is a hunger which cannot be
appeased. But a perpetual striving after the unattainable—this
is swimming against the stream. One can neither leave it nor
grasp it, neither do without it nor attain it, neither be silent on
it nor speak of it, for it is above reason and understanding, and
it transcends all creatures; and therefore we can never reach
nor overtake it. But we should abide within ourselves: there we
feel that the Spirit of God is driving us and enkindling us in this
restlessness of love. And we should abide above ourselves. And
then we feel that the Spirit of God is drawing us out of ourselves
and burning us to nothingness in his Selfhood; that is, in the
superessential Love[21] with which we are one, and which we
possess more deeply and more widely than all else.

This possession is a simple and abysmal tasting of all good and
of eternal life; and in this tasting we are swallowed up above

---

[18] I.e., *een scouwende leven. Werken*, III, 24, ll. 31–32. Cf. Augustine, *De quant.
animae*, cap. 33.
[19] *Daer wij met minnen ane Gode cleven . . . maer daer wij aldus in overwesene
staren, daer besitten wij Gode gheheel. Ibid.*, p. 24, ll. 32–35.
[20] *Want minne en mach niet ledich sijn. . . . Werken*, III, 25, l. 12.
[21] *In die overweselijcke Minne. . . . Ibid.*, l. 25.

reason and without reason, in the deep quiet of the Godhead,[22] which is never moved. That this is true we can only know by our own feeling, and in no other way. For how this is, or where, or what, neither reason nor practice can come to know; and therefore our ensuing exercise always remains wayless, that is, without manner. For that abysmal Good which we taste and possess, we can neither grasp nor understand; neither can we enter into it by ourselves or by means of our exercises. And so we are poor in ourselves, but rich in God; hungry and thirsty in ourselves, drunken and fulfilled in God; busy in ourselves, idle in God. And thus we shall remain throughout eternity. But without the exercise of love, we can never possess God; and whosoever thinks or feels otherwise is deceived. And thus we live wholly in God, where we possess our blessedness; and we live wholly in ourselves, where we exercise ourselves in love toward God. And though we live wholly in God and wholly in ourselves, yet it is but one life; but it is twofold and opposite according to our feeling, for poor and rich, hungry and satisfied, busy and idle, these things are wholly contrary to one another. Yet with this our highest honor is bound up, now and in eternity: for we cannot wholly become God and lose our created being—this is impossible.[23] Did we, however, remain wholly in ourselves, sundered from God, we should be miserable and unblest. And therefore we should feel ourselves living wholly in God and wholly in ourselves; and between these two feelings we should find nothing else but the grace of God and the exercise of our love. For out of our highest feeling the brightness of God shines into us, which teaches us truth, and moves us toward every virtue and in eternal love toward God. If we follow this brightness without pause, back into that Source from whence it comes forth, there we feel nothing but a quenching of our spirit and an irretrievable downsinking into simple and fathomless love. Could we continue to dwell there with our simple gaze, we should always so feel it; for our immersion and transformation in God continues without ceasing in eternity, if we have gone forth from ourselves, and God is ours in the immersion of love. For if we possess God in the immersion of love—that is, if we are lost to ourselves—God is our own and we are his own; and we sink ourselves eternally and irretrievably in our own possession,

---

[22] *Boven redene ende sonder redene in die diepe stilheit der Godheit.* . . . *Ibid.*, ll. 30–31.
[23] *Niet God werden ende onse ghescapenheit verliesen, dat es ommoghelijc. Ibid.*, p. 26, ll. 19–20.

which is God. This immersion is essential, and is closely bound up with the state of love: and so it continues whether we sleep or whether we wake, whether we know it or whether we know it not. And so it does not earn for us any new degree of reward, but it maintains us in the possession of God and of all that good which we have received. And this downsinking is like a river, which without pause or turning back ever pours into the sea; since this is its proper resting place. So likewise when we possess God alone, the downsinking of our being, with the love that belongs to it, flows forth, without return, into a fathomless experience which we possess, and which is our proper resting place. Were we always simple, and could we always contemplate with the same recollection, we should always have the same experience. Now this immersion is above all virtues, and above every exercise of love; for it is nothing else than an eternal going out from ourselves, with a clear looking forward, into an otherness or difference toward which, outside ourselves, we tend as toward our blessedness. For we feel an eternal yearning toward something other than what we are ourselves. And this is the most inward and hidden distinction which we can feel between God and ourselves, and beyond it there is no difference any more. But our reason abides here with open eyes in the darkness, that is, in an abysmal ignorance; and in this darkness, the abysmal splendor remains covered and hidden from us, for its overwhelming unfathomableness blinds our reason. But it enwraps us in simplicity, and transforms us through its selfhood: and thus we are brought forth by God, out of our selfhood, into the immersion of love, in which we possess blessedness, and are one with God.

When we are thus made one with God, there abides within us a quickening knowledge and an active love; for without our own knowledge we cannot possess God; and without the practice of love we cannot be united with God, nor remain one with him. For if we could be blessed without our knowledge, then a stone, which has no knowledge, could also be blessed. Were I lord over all the world and knew it not, how would it profit me? And therefore we shall ever know and feel that we taste and possess; and this is testified by Christ himself, where he speaks thus of us to his Father: THIS, he says, IS LIFE ETERNAL THAT THEY SHOULD KNOW THEE, THE ONLY TRUE GOD, AND JESUS CHRIST, WHOM THOU HAST SENT. And by this you may understand that our eternal life consists in knowledge with discernment.

Chapter X

How We, Though One with God, Must Eternally Remain Other than God

Though I have said before that we are one with God, and this is taught us by Holy Writ, yet now I will say that we must eternally remain other than God, and distinct from Him,[24] and this too is taught us by Holy Writ. And we must understand and feel both within us, if all is to be right with us.

And therefore I say further: that from the Face of God, or from our highest feeling, a brightness shines upon the face of our inward being, which teaches us the truth of love and of all virtues; and especially are we taught in this brightness to feel God and ourselves in four ways. First, we feel God in his grace; and when we apprehend this, we cannot remain idle. For like as the sun, by its splendor and its heat, enlightens and gladdens and makes fruitful the whole world, so God does to us through his grace: he enlightens and gladdens and makes fruitful all men who desire to obey him. If, however, we would feel God within us, and have the fire of his love evermore burning within us, we must, of our own free will, help to kindle it in four ways: We must abide within ourselves, united with the fire through inwardness. And we must go forth from ourselves toward all good men with loyalty and brotherly love. And we must go beneath ourselves in penance, betaking ourselves to all good works, and resisting our inordinate lusts. And we must ascend above ourselves with the flame of this fire, through devotion, and thanksgiving, and praise, and fervent prayer, and must ever cleave to God with an upright intention and with sensible love. And thereby God continues to dwell in us with his grace; for in these four ways is comprehended every exercise which we can do with the reason, and in some wise, but without this exercise no one can please God. And he who is most perfect in this exercise is nearest to God. And therefore it is needful for all men; and above it none can rise save the contemplative men.[25] And thus, in this first way, we feel God within us through his grace, if we wish to belong to him.

Secondly, when we possess the God-seeing life, we feel ourselves to be living *in* God; and from out of that life in which we feel God in ourselves there shines forth upon the face of our in-

---

24 *Wij een ander van Gode eewelijc bliven moeten.* . . . *Ibid.*, p. 28, ll. 29–30.
25 *Scouwende menschen. Ibid.*, p. 30, l. 1.

ward being a brightness which enlightens our reason, and is an intermediary between ourselves and God. And if we with our enlightened reason abide within ourselves in this brightness, we feel that our created life incessantly immerses itself in its eternal life. But when we follow the brightness above reason with a simple sight, and with a willing leaning out of ourselves, toward our highest life, there we experience the transformation of our whole selves in God; and thereby we feel ourselves to be wholly enwrapped in God.

And, after this, there follows the third way of feeling: namely, that we feel ourselves to be one *with* God; for, through the transformation in God, we feel ourselves to be swallowed up in the fathomless abyss of our eternal blessedness, wherein we can nevermore find any distinction between ourselves and God. And this is our highest feeling, which we cannot experience in any other way than in the immersion in love. And therefore, so soon as we are uplifted and drawn into our highest feeling, all our powers stand idle in an essential fruition; but our powers do not pass away into nothingness, for then we should lose our created being. And as long as we stand idle, with an inclined spirit, and with open eyes, but without reflection, so long we can contemplate and have fruition. But, at the very moment in which we seek to prove and to comprehend what it is that we feel, we fall back into reason, and there we find a distinction and an otherness between ourselves and God, and find God outside ourselves in incomprehensibility.

And hence the fourth way of distinction, which is, that we feel God *and* ourselves. Hereby we now find ourselves standing in the presence of God; and the truth which we receive from the Face of God teaches us that God would be wholly ours and that he wills us to be wholly his. And in that same moment in which we feel that God would be wholly ours, there arises within us a gaping and eager craving which is so hungry and so deep and so empty that, even though God gave all that he could give, if he gave not himself, we should not be appeased. For, whilst we feel that he has given himself and yielded himself to our untrammeled craving, that we may taste of him in every way that we can desire—and of this we learn the truth in his sight—yet all that we taste, against all that we lack, is but like a single drop of water against the whole sea: and this makes our spirit burst forth in fury and in the heat and the restlessness of love. For the more we taste, the greater our craving and our hunger; for the one is the cause of the other. And thus it comes about that we struggle

in vain. For we feed upon his immensity, which we cannot
devour, and we yearn after his infinity, which we cannot attain:
and so we cannot enter into God nor can God enter into us, for
in the untamed fury of love we are not able to renounce ourselves. And therefore the heat is so unmeasured that the exercise of love between ourselves and God flashes to and fro like the
lightning in the sky; and yet we cannot be consumed in its
ardor. And in this storm of love our activity is above reason and
wayless; for love longs for that which is impossible to it, and
reason teaches that love is in the right, but reason can neither
counsel love nor dissuade her. For as long as we inwardly perceive that God would be ours, the goodness of God touches our
eager craving: and therefrom springs the wildness of love, for
the touch which pours forth from God stirs up this wildness, and
demands our activity, that is, that we should love eternal love.
But the inward-drawing touch draws us out of ourselves, and
calls us to be melted and noughted in the Unity. And in this
inward-drawing touch, we feel that God wills us to be his; and,
therefore, we must renounce ourselves and leave him to work
our blessedness. But where he touches us by the outpouring
touch, he leaves us to ourselves, and makes us free, and sets us
in his presence, and teaches us to pray in the spirit and to ask in
freedom, and shows us his incomprehensible riches in such
manifold ways as we are able to grasp. For everything that we
can conceive, wherein is consolation and joy, this we find in him
without measure. And therefore, when our feeling shows us that
he with all these riches would be ours and dwell in us forevermore, then all the powers of the soul open themselves, and
especially the desirous power; for all the rivers of the grace of
God pour forth, and the more we taste of them, the more we
long to taste; and the more we long to taste, the more deeply we
press into contact with him; and the more deeply we press into
contact with God, the more the flood of his sweetness flows
through us and over us; and the more we are thus drenched and
flooded, the better we feel and know that the sweetness of God
is incomprehensible and unfathomable. And therefore the
prophet says: O TASTE, AND SEE THAT THE LORD IS
SWEET. But he does not say how sweet He is, for God's sweetness is without measure; and therefore we can neither grasp it
nor swallow it. And this is also testified by the bride of God in
The Song of Songs, where she says: I SAT DOWN UNDER
HIS SHADOW, WITH GREAT DELIGHT, AND HIS
FRUIT WAS SWEET TO MY TASTE.

Chapter XI

Of the Great Difference Between the Brightness of the Saints and the Highest Brightness to Which We Can Attain in This Life

There is a great difference between the brightness of the saints and the highest brightness or enlightenment to which we may attain in this life. For it is only the shadow of God which enlightens our inward wilderness, but on the high mountains of the Promised Land there is no shadow; and yet it is one and the same Sun, and one radiance, which enlightens both our wilderness and the high mountains. But the state of the saints is transparent and shining, and therefore they receive the brightness without intermediary; but our state is still mortal and gross, and this sets up an obstacle which causes the shadow, which so darkens our understanding that we cannot know God and heavenly things so clearly as the saints can and do. For as long as we dwell in the shadow, we cannot see the Sun in itself; but NOW WE SEE THROUGH A GLASS DARKLY, says Saint Paul. Yet the shadow is so enlightened by the sunshine that we can perceive the distinctions between all the virtues, and all the truth that is profitable to our mortal state. But if we would become one with the brightness of the Sun, we must follow love, and go out of ourselves into the Wayless, and then the Sun will draw us with our blinded eyes into its own brightness, in which we shall possess unity with God. So soon as we feel and understand ourselves thus, we are in that contemplative life which is within reach of our mortal state.

The state of the Jews, according to the Old Testament, was cold and in the night, and they walked in darkness. And they DWELT IN THE LAND OF THE SHADOW OF DEATH, says the prophet Isaias. The shadow of death came forth from original sin; and therefore they had all to endure the lack of God. But though our state in the Christian faith is but still in the cool and morning hour, yet for us the day has dawned. And therefore we shall walk in the light, and shall sit down in the shadow, of God; and his grace shall be an intermediary between ourselves and God. And, through it, we shall overcome all things, and shall die to all things, and shall pass without hindrance into the unity of God. But the state of the saints is warm and bright; for they live and walk in the noontide, and see with open and enlightened eyes the brightness of the Sun, for the glory of God flows through them and overflows in them. And each one, according to the degree of his enlightenment, tastes and knows the fruits of all the virtues which have there been gathered together by all spirits. But that they taste and know the Trinity in the Unity, and the Unity in the Trinity, and know themselves united therewith, this is the highest and all-surpassing food which makes them drunken, and causes them to rest in its Selfhood. And this it was that the bride in the Book of Love desired, when she said unto Christ: TELL ME, O THOU WHOM MY SOUL LOVETH, WHERE THOU FEEDEST, WHERE THOU MAKEST THY FLOCK TO REST AT NOON, that is in the light of glory, as Saint Bernard says; for all the food that is given to us here, in the morning hour and in the shadow, is but a foretaste of the food that is to come in the noontide of the glory of God.

Yet the bride of our Lord gloried in having sat under the shadow of God, and that his fruit was sweet to her taste. Whenever we feel that God touches us from within, we taste of his fruit and his food: for his touch is his food. And his touch is both indrawing and outpouring,[26] as I have said before. In his indrawing, we must be wholly his: thereby we learn to die and to behold. But in his outpouring, he wills to be wholly ours: and then he teaches us to live in the riches of the virtues. In his indrawing touch all our powers forsake us, and then we sit under his shadow, and his fruit is sweet to our taste, for the Fruit of God is the Son of God, whom the Father brings forth in our spirit. This Fruit is so infinitely sweet to our taste that we can neither swallow it nor assimilate it, but it rather absorbs us into itself and assimilates us with itself. And whenever this Fruit draws us inward and touches us, we abandon, forsake, and overcome all other things. And in this overcoming of all things, we taste of the hidden manna, which shall give us eternal life; for we receive the sparkling stone, of which I have spoken heretofore, in which our new names were written before the beginning of the world.

This is the NEW NAME WHICH NO MAN KNOWETH BUT HE THAT RECEIVETH IT. And whosoever feels himself to be forever united with God, he possesses his name according to the measure of his virtues, and of his introversion, and of his union. And, that every one may obtain his name and possess it in eternity, the Lamb of God, that is, the manhood of our Lord, has delivered itself up to death; and has opened for us the Book of Life, wherein are written all the names of the elect. And

---

26 *Intreckende ochte uutvloevende.* . . . *Ibid.,* p. 35, l. 15.

these names cannot be blotted out, for they are one with the Living Book, which is the Son of God. And that same death has broken for us the seals of the Book, so that all virtues may be fulfilled according to the eternal providence of God. And so, in the measure in which each man can overcome himself, and can die to all things, he feels the touch of the Father drawing him inward; and then he tastes the sweetness of the inborn Fruit, which is the Son; and in this tasting the Holy Ghost teaches him that he is the heir of God. But in these three points no one is like to another in every respect. And therefore each one has been named separately, and his name is continually made new through new graces and new works of virtue. And therefore every knee shall bow before the name of Jesus, for he has fought for our sake, and has conquered. And he has enlightened our darkness, and has fulfilled all the virtues in the highest degree. And so his name is lifted up above all other names, for he is the King and the Prince over all the elect. And in his name we are called and chosen, and adorned with grace and with virtues, and look for the glory of God.

Chapter XII

Of the Transfiguration of Christ on Mount Thabor

And so, that the name of Christ may be exalted and glorified in us, we should follow him up the mountain of our bare intelligence, even as Peter, James, and John followed him on to Mount Thabor. Thabor means in our tongue "an increase of light." So soon as we are like Peter in knowledge of truth, and like James in the overcoming of the world, and like John in fullness of grace possessing the virtues in righteousness, then Jesus brings us up onto the mountain of our bare intelligence to a hidden solitude, and reveals himself to us in glory and in divine brightness. And, in his name, his Father in heaven opens to us the living book of his eternal Wisdom. And the Wisdom of God enfolds our bare vision and the simplicity of our spirit in a wayless, simple fruition of all good without distinction; and here there are indeed seeing and knowing, tasting and feeling, essence and life, having and being: and all this is one in our transcendence in God. And before this transcendence we are all set, each in his own particular way; and our Heavenly Father, of his wisdom and goodness, endows each one in particular according to the nobility of his life and his practice. And therefore, if we ever remained with Jesus on Mount Thabor, that is, upon the mountain of our bare thought, we should continually experience a growth of new light and new truth; for we should ever hear the voice of the Father, who touches us, pouring forth with grace, and drawing us inward into the unity. The voice of the Father is heard by all who follow our Lord Jesus Christ, for he says of them all, "These are my chosen sons, in whom I am well pleased." And, through this good pleasure, each one receives grace, according to the measure and the way in which God is well-pleasing unto him. And therefrom, between our pleasure in God, and God's pleasure in us, there arises the practice of true love. And so each one tastes of his name and his office and the fruit of his exercise. And here all good men abide, hidden from those who live in the world; for these are dead before God and have no name, and therefore they can neither feel nor taste that which belongs to those who live indeed.

The outpouring touch of God quickens us with life in the spirit, and fulfills us with grace, and enlightens our reason, and teaches us to know truth and to discern the virtues, and keeps us stable in the presence of God, with such a great strength that we are able to endure all the tasting, all the feeling, and all the outpouring gifts of God without our spirits failing us. But the indrawing touch of God demands of us that we should be one with God, and go forth from ourselves, and die into blessedness, that is, into the eternal Love which embraces the Father and the Son in one fruition. And therefore when we have climbed with Jesus onto the mountain of our bare thought, and if, then, we follow him with a single and simple gaze, with inward pleasure, and with fruitive inclination, we feel the fierce heat of the Holy Ghost, burning and melting us into the unity of God. For when we are one with the Son, and lovingly return toward our Beginning, then we hear the voice of the Father, touching us and drawing us inward; for he says to all his chosen in his eternal Word, THIS IS MY BELOVED SON, IN WHOM I AM WELL PLEASED. For you should know that the Father with the Son, and the Son with the Father, have conceived an eternal satisfaction in regard to this: that the Son should take upon himself our manhood, and die, and bring back all the chosen to their Beginning.

And so soon as we are uplifted through the Son into our Origin, we hear the voice of the Father, which draws us inward, and enlightens us with eternal truth. And truth shows to us the wide-opened good pleasure of God, in which all good pleasure begins and ends. There all our powers fail us, and we fall from ourselves into our wide-opened contemplation, and become all One and one All, in the loving embrace of the three-fold Unity. Whenever we feel this union, we are one being and one life and one blessedness with God. And there all things are fulfilled and all things are made new; for when we are baptized into the wide embrace of the love of God, the joy of each one of us becomes so great and so special that he can neither think of nor care for the joy of anyone else; for then each one is himself a fruition of love, and he cannot and dare not seek for anything beyond his own.

Chapter XIII

How We Ought to Have Fruition of God

If a man would have fruition of God, three things are needful thereto; these are: true peace, inward silence, and loving adherence.

Whosoever would find true peace between himself and God must love God in such a way that he can, with a free heart, renounce for the glory of God everything which he does or loves inordinately, or which he possesses, or can possess, contrary to the glory of God. This is the first thing which is needful to all men.

The second thing is an inward silence; that is, that a man should be empty and free from images of all things which he ever saw or of which he ever heard.

The third thing is a loving adherence to God, and this adherence is itself fruition; for whosoever cleaves to God out of pure love, and not for his own profit, he enjoys God in truth, and feels that he loves God and that God loves him.

There are still three other points, which are higher still, and which establish a man and make him able to enjoy and to feel God continually, if it be His good will to have it so.

The first of these points is to rest in Him whom one enjoys; that is, where love is overcome by the lover, and love is taken possession of by the lover, in bare essential love. There love has fallen in love with the lover, and each is all to the other, in possession and in rest.

From this there follows the second: and this is called a falling asleep in God; that is, when the spirit immerses itself, and knows not how, nor where, nor in what it is.

And therefrom follows the last point that can be put into

words, that is, when the spirit beholds a Darkness into which it cannot enter with the reason. And there it feels itself dead and lost to itself, and one with God without difference and without distinction. And when it feels itself one with God, then God himself is its peace and its enjoyment and its rest. And this is an unfathomable abyss wherein man must die to himself in blessedness, and must live again in virtues, whenever love and its stirring demand it. Lo! if you feel these six points within you, then you feel all that I have, or could have, said before. And introversion [27] is as easy to you, and contemplation and fruition are as ready to you, as your life according to nature. And from these riches there comes that common life of which I promised to speak to you at the beginning.

Chapter XIV

Of That Common Life Which Comes from the Contemplation and Fruition of God

The man who is sent down by God from these heights into the world is full of truth and rich in all virtues. And he seeks not his own but the glory of Him who has sent him. And hence he is just and truthful in all things, and he possesses a rich and a generous ground, which is set in the richness of God, and therefore he must always spend himself on those who have need of him; for the living fount of the Holy Ghost, which is his wealth, can never be spent. And he is a living and willing instrument of God, with which God works whatsoever he wills and howsoever he wills; and these works he reckons not as his own, but gives all the glory to God. And so he remains ready and willing to do in the virtues all that God commands, and strong and courageous in suffering and enduring all that God allows to befall him. And by this he possesses a universal life, for he is ready alike for contemplation and for action, and is perfect in both of them. [28] And none can have this universal life save the God-seeing man; and none can contemplate and enjoy God save he who has

---

[27] *Ende in uwen inkeere. . . . Ibid.*, p. 40, ll. 31–32.

[28] *Ende hier-omime heeft hi een ghemeyn leven; want hem es scouwen ende werken even ghereet, ende in beyden es hi volcomen. Ibid.*, p. 41, ll. 17–19. On the further ambivalence of the "common life" and the "common," i.e., truly "noble," man as serving both the active and the contemplative, see Bizet, ed., *Le royaume des amants*, pt. 5, sec. 5, pp. 176–78; *Dat Rijake der Ghelieven*, V, 5, *Werken*, I, pp. 99–100. Apropos of the relation to Richard of St. Victor's fourth grade of *Violent Love*, see D'Asbeck, *La mystique*.

within himself the six points, ordered as I have described heretofore. And therefore, all those are deceived who fancy themselves to be contemplative, and yet inordinately love, practice, or possess some creaturely thing; or who fancy that they enjoy God before they are empty of images, or that they rest before they enjoy. All such are deceived; for we must make ourselves fit for God with an open heart, with a peaceful conscience, with naked contemplation, without hypocrisy, in sincerity and truth. And then we shall mount up from virtue unto virtue, and shall see God, and shall enjoy him, and in him shall become one with him, in the way which I have shown to you. That this be done in all of us, so help us God. Amen.

XI

German Theology (Theologia Germanica) [Late Fourteenth Century]

INTRODUCTION

Bio- Bibliographical Essay

THIS WORK WAS PROBABLY WRITTEN IN THE LATTER half of the fourteenth century. Tauler, who died in 1361, is appreciatively recognized by the author. The anonymous work is referred to by a later editor as *The Frankfurter*. The book may not be the product of concerted authorship on a given occasion. It may be a later collection of an earlier set of spiritual "collations" or "colloquies." Whether or not by "a Teutonic Knight, a priest, and a warden in the House of the Teutonic Knights at Frankfurt," the book has an abiding appeal.

There are introductory materials in Wentzlaff-Eggebert, *Deutsch Mystik*, pp. 160 ff., 324–325, with literature and primary editions. Oriented to the 1518 edition of Luther and the MS. of 1497 are the texts of H. Mandel, Leipzig, 1908, and *Der Franckforter (Eyn deutsch Theologia)*, ed. by Willo Uhl, Bonn, 1912. The last becomes the basis for the modern editions of Jos. Bernhart, *Der Frankfurter, Eine deutsche Theologie*, Hermann Rinn, 1922 and 1947. A valuable modern utilization of the 1497 Bronnbacher MS., following the edition of Dr. Franz Pfeiffer (Stuttgart, 1851, and Gütersloh, 1923), is *Das Buch vom vollkommenen Leben: die Theologia Deutsch, Thalwil-Zürich*, 1947, by K. F. Riedler. This includes the *Urtext*, pp. 183–316, and useful notes, as well as a modern text, pp. 7–152. See, especially, Luther's 1518 edition of *Eyn deutsch Theologia*, with a *Vorrede*. Note that Susanna Winkworth's translation, brought into accord with Bernhart's text, and with introduction and notes by Willard R. Trask, has been issued by Pantheon, New York, 1949, as *Theologia Germanica*.

Synopsis

The initial chapters deal with the goal of spiritual perfection and the way to it. Having established the claims of the contemplative vocation, there is a statement of the three ways: purification (*Reinigung*), illumination (*Erleuchtung*), and union (*Vereinigung*) [Ch. 14].[1]

The ensuing chapters declare the way to union and the character of *Vergottung*, that is, of "deification," or "apotheosis." But this is not the fleeting rise of the soul during this life into the *unio mystica* described earlier (in Ch. 8). Here is the turning of the life of man into the kind of existence in the present that is laid down by the Christ ideal. This Christiformity is only approximately realizable, to be sure. Christ and his following is, nonetheless, the preoccupation of the book (cf. Chs. 7–14).

Over and beyond the mystical stages of purification, illumination, and union, looms the teaching on the following of Christ, the *Nachfolge Christi*, with its more speculative and quietistic overtones. This is an orientation that never banishes the more active, daily participation of man in worldly life, though it does leave this in the background at times. There is a balancing of the active and the passive in a context which doubtless appealed to Luther (Ch. 26). It is a call to true righteousness without vain accent on works. The author is clearly not disparaging rules and order. Perfect men, however, live higher than the law. They will, work, and desire no end but the good. The writer reminds us that "blessedness lies not in any creature or working of the creatures, but it lies alone in God and in his working" (Ch. 9).

A central point of the *German Theology* is the problem of will and its freedom. Here a double concept is involved. There is the conception of self-will (*Eigenwille*), which in its independent strivings is opposed to God. But in the inmost power of man's will (*Willenskraft*), God himself works and wills (Ch. 51). This latter concept of a freedom of the will resting in God is one that gets its deepening in God and in the self preserved in him. There is a basic admonition against the hindering of God's working by the possessive will of the "I." The soul that will not let God do and perform all things in it, being wholly possessed by its own

---

1 Bernhart edition, pp. 157–58. See the *Urtext,* cap. XIV (Lat. XIII), p. 211. Cf. Dionysius, *Hiér. Cél.,* ch. III, and references to the Areopagite in the introduction of this anthology. Consult chs. I and V of the *Mystical Theology* and Riedler's notes, pp. 160–62 and 166, on Dionysius and the Neoplatonists in relation to chs. 8 and 14 of *Die Theologia Deutsch.*

existence, thus hinders God. He cannot "perform a work" in the soul, "alone and without hindrance" (Chs. 3, 4, 51).

God gives man full freedom of decision. He forces no one. He lets man do what he will, be it good or evil. He has to decide between good and evil, between his own self-will and God's will. God, speaking to the soul, reminds it that all is lawful which comes to pass from the divine Will. All, however, that springs from the possessive human will is against the eternal Will (Ch. 50). Why, then, if self-will is so contrary to God and the eternal Will, has God created it? (Cf. Chs. 4, 15, 16, etc.) Answering this question, the author first disavows for the truly humble and enlightened man any desire to force God's secrets (Ch. 51). He then proceeds to the analysis of the second kind of will; that is, not self-will but the original form (*die Urform, die "Idee"*) of will as godly power (*göttliche Kraft*). Reason (or cognition) and will raise man above the creature. These are among the immediate gifts of God. The purpose of the godly *Willenschaffung*, the creation of the will in the creature by God, is that God's own will may do its perfect work. Man's duty is to see to it that, prompted by the human negation of its own self-will, this godly power is increasingly freed in him. Man may then conform himself to God and let him work unmediated in the human soul.

The consideration of the eternal Will in man, of man's part in it, and, chiefly, of its proper origin and working in God is beautifully dealt with (Ch. 51). The will that springs up from God and back to him is of all earthly freedoms the most truly free. It is the nobility (*Adel*) of the soul. Manifestly the thing that is truly free cannot be arrogated to anyone as his own. The man striving to make it his own errs grievously. But among all free things, none is as free as the Will. One trying to possess it for himself, and thus wresting it from its own free nobility and nature, does wrong. This is precisely what the devil, Adam, and all their followers do. "But he who leaves the Will in its noble freedom does right, and this is what Christ and all his followers do" (Ch. 51).[2] The penalty for robbing the Will of this noble freedom and selfishly expropriating it is dire indeed. One who does this becomes laden with cares, discontent, and strife. But he who leaves the Will in its free estate knows contentment, peace, rest, and blessedness, both temporal and eternal.

The *Theologia Deutsch* places man, during this present life, in a world between heaven and hell. He may turn to either of these

2 *Theologia Germanica* (Bernhart-Trask), p. 213.

that he wills. The more of his own possessiveness he invokes, the more of hell and balefulness he will have. The less of self-will he exemplifies, the farther from hell and the nearer to heaven he will be (Ch. 51).

But the real deification (*Vergottung*) of man is the life in imitation of Christ. This has its freight of sorrow and renunciation, its life in suffering passivity (*in leidender Weise*), and in the doing, active way (*in tuender, diender Weise*) (Ch. 26).[3] A whole series of chapters[4] stresses Christ's life and its imitation by the one in process of deification. The life of the Master is in every way most bitter to nature, to selfhood, and to "I-hood" (Ch. 20). There is consistent emphasis upon the way that leads from selfhood and I-hood. It stresses the desired working according to the working of Christ; this being prepared by him to work as he works. Man must, of course, do something of himself toward this preparation. Active, as well as passive, qualities are called for (Chs. 22–23).

Obedience, poverty, and living under the law are necessary, as well as going beyond it with Christ (Ch. 26). A steady refrain is the deifying of man through Christ's drawing him to divine reunion with God (Chs. 52–54). Everywhere is the double warning against despising outer works and being limited to them. The author adverts repeatedly to the manner in which one may keep the balance; the way in which one may live beyond rules, order, and laws without committing the shameful antinomianism of the "false free spirits."[5]

The writer always tries to keep the balance between suffering passivity and active working (Chs. 23–39). He notes, realistically, that Christ never rose above pain before his death (Ch. 29). His followers too may expect to suffer unto the end. So, too, they may not expect to come fully to a life that lies beyond all laws, works, and good deeds. There is a sense in which one may come through these to something that lies beyond them. But Christ did not despise them, nor may his followers do so.[6]

The Frankfurter, like Eckhart and the Rhenish school, knows the need of rising above creaturely affections and vain workings. It also knows the necessity of combining adherence to God's will and a positive share in the active duties of life. There is sober warning against casting "imagery" aside too soon (Ch. 13). The

---

[3] Uhl's text reads: "*yn leydender weyss und ettwan yn thónder weyss und auch yn diender weyss*" (p. 29).

[4] Caps. 51–54, also 18–20, 26, etc.

[5] Cf. caps. 26, 30, 39, and 43.   [6] Especially caps. 25 and 30.

life of Christ is held up as both the bitterest and the sweetest, the most precious and the best (Chs. 18, 20). *The Frankfurter* reminds us of the doing of certain outward things that must be (Ch. 21). It tells how to be still under God's hand and obedient in all things "both passively and sometimes actively as well" (Ch. 23).[7] The writer also teaches how man must think of himself as being nothing in himself (Ch. 26). From this it follows that man finds himself wholly unworthy of all that God has done or will do for him and all other creatures. He finds himself "indebted to God and also to all creatures in God's stead, passively, and sometimes also actively, and as one who should serve them" (Ch. 26).[8] Farther on he recalls how the life of poverty and humility, which Christ exemplified, did not rule out works of true humility and virtue. Christ did not despise or set at nought the commandments. Yet, to keep them is not enough; we must press forward to what is higher and better, the righteousness that will exceed that of scribes and Pharisees.

Chapter 27 admonishes against man's thinking that he has nothing to do, for a man must always have work to do as long as he lives. But we are not to think that union with God lies in any man's powers, in his working or in his abstaining, learning or knowing. Neither in conjunction with creatures does union exist (Ch. 27; Lat. 25).

The matter of order, rule, and measure in creatures is a recurring theme. Four different classes of men react differently to this; among them the "Free Spirits." The writer ranges over a wide field, including the "False Light" and its tokens (Chs. 39–40). Developing the theme of love, begun earlier, he shows how that love comes to its fruition in the truly deified man; how it is in Christ and is to be matched, therefore in his followers (Chs. 43, 41). This order and law-abidingness lived in love, Christward, never ceases to claim part of man's attention while he lives in this world (Ch. 27). True, one must remember that no works, words, or any creaturely thing or observance can save us. Nevertheless, life must go on, and we must both do and refrain. "In particular, we must sleep and wake, walk and stand still, speak and be silent, eat and drink, and much more of the like. These must go on so long as we live" (Ch. 27).[9]

---

7 *Theologia Germanica*, pp. 152–53.
8 *Ibid.*, p. 157. *Eine deutsche Theologie*, p. 183: *auf leidende und bisweilen auf tätige und auch auf dienende Weise.* Cf. Riedler, *Urtext*, p. 236: *in lidender wise und etwan in tünder wise und ouch in diender wise.*
9 *Theologia Germanica*, p. 163.

In perspective, here, the author, like Tauler, strikes out at the "False Lights," "Free Spirits," and others. He attacks these antinomians who hold themselves above Scripture, teaching, sacraments, and all the rest of Catholic life and lore (Ch. 25). This "rank spiritual pride" disregards "wise order, the laws and precepts of the holy Christian church, . . . [and] the sacraments; yea, mocks at them. . . ." [10] *The Frankfurter* also attacks those who think themselves "raised above all works and words, above rule, law, and order . . ." (Ch. 40).[11] Of course, there is a sense in which we ought and are able to get beyond all rule and order. There is real danger of misunderstanding at this point, however. Christ "stood above" the Christ life and above all virtues, rules, and order, in the sense of his having them all to perfection. The author admits with Paul that those driven of the Spirit, the sons of God, are not under the law in the sense of having to wait and let it tell them what to do. Christ has already done this. So should each seek to be a follower of Christ (*Nachfolger Christi*) in his daily life (Chs. 19, 26, 30).

Furthermore, the role of love before indicated has large implications for the outworkings of fellow feeling. The love of the good, of God, demonstrates the necessity of love for all things, also of neighbors. If man did nothing but acts of love to his neighbor, all men would be one. However, the author knows the realistic limits of human love and co-operation in this life. The "False Lights" arrogate to themselves in prideful self-love that which belongs to God alone. This is the role of Lucifer and Antichrist, rising against God and his unique place. The true imitators of Christ know that he who loves his own soul shall lose it; the true, perfect lover finds all good, comfort, love, and joy in the Lord (Ch. 40).

The writer warns against the deceptiveness of self-reasoning, self-will (Ch. 20); also against undue freedom. Man has not in this life a full participation in the Christ of grace (Ch. 16). No man may attain to the perfect obedience of Christ. Yet every man may approach so near it as to be called, and to be, "indeed, godlike and deified."[12]

---

[10] *Ibid.*, p. 156.   [11] *Ibid.*, p. 186.
[12] *Ibid.*, p. 143. Bernhart, *op. cit.*, p. 165: *dass er göttlich und vergottet heisst und ist.*

German Theology (Theologia Germanica)
[Late Fourteenth Century]

GERMAN THEOLOGY

THE TEXT

Chapter VII [13]

Of the Two Eyes of the Spirit with Which Man Looks Into Eternity and Into Time, and How the One Is Hindered by the Other

Let us remember how it is written and said that the soul of Christ had two eyes, a right and a left eye.[14] In the beginning, when the soul of Christ was created, she fixed her right eye upon eternity and the Godhead, and remained in perfect enjoyment and intuition of the divine Essence and eternal Perfection, immovably; and continued thus unmoved and undisturbed by all the accidents and travail, suffering, torment, and pain that ever befell the outward man. But with her left eye she beheld the creature, and perceived all things therein, and took note of the difference between the creatures, which were better or worse, nobler or meaner; and thereafter was the outward man of Christ ordered. Thus the inner man of Christ, according to the right eye of his soul, stood in perfect enjoyment of his divine nature, in perfect bliss, joy, and eternal peace. But the outward man and the left eye of Christ's soul stood in perfect suffering, in all tribulation, affliction, and travail. And this befell in such sort that the inward and right eye remained unmoved, unhindered, and untouched by all the travail, suffering, grief, and anguish that ever befell the outward man. It has been said that when Christ was scourged at the pillar, and when he hung upon the holy cross, according to his outward man, yet his soul, or

---

[13] The translation utilized is that of Susanna Winkworth revised in accord with J. Bernhart's modern German version and issued with introduction and notes translated by Willard R. Trask, New York, 1949, pp. 123–37, 201–25. Used by permission of Pantheon Books, Inc., New York, and Victor Gollancz, Ltd., London.

[14] Signifying the soul's versatile regard, inward and outward, upward and downward; or, with Eckhart, denoting its capacity to face God, above, and the sense world, below. Cf. Riedler, *op. cit.*, note 18, p. 158; Bernhart-Trask, *Theologia Germanica*, p. 232.

327

inner man according to the right eye, stood in as full possession of divine joy and bliss as it did after his ascension, or as it does now. In like manner, his outward man, or soul according to the left eye, was never hindered or disturbed or troubled by the inward eye in its work, in all that it had outwardly to accomplish.

Now the created soul of man has also two eyes. The one is the power of seeing into eternity, the other of seeing into time and the creatures, of perceiving how they differ from each other as aforesaid, of giving life and needful things to the body, and ordering and governing it for the best. But these two eyes of the soul of man cannot perform their work at once; but if the soul shall see with the right eye into eternity, then the left eye must cease and refrain from all its working, and be as though it were dead. If now the left eye shall perform its outward work, that is, shall work with time and the creature, then the right eye must be hindered in its work, that is, in its contemplation. Therefore whosoever will have the one must let the other go. For no man can serve two masters.

Chapter VIII

How the Soul of Man, While It Is Yet in the Body, May Obtain a Foretaste of Eternal Bliss

It has been asked whether it be possible for the soul, while it is yet in the body, to reach so high as to cast a glance into eternity, and there receive a foretaste of eternal life and eternal bliss. This is commonly denied; and truly so, in a sense. For it indeed cannot be, so long as the soul is looking upon the body, and the things which minister and appertain thereto, and upon time and the creature, and is darkened and preoccupied and distracted thereby. For if the soul shall rise to such a state, she must be quite pure, wholly stripped and bare of all images,[15] and be entirely separate from all creatures, and above all from herself. Now many think this is not to be done and is impossible in this temporal world. But Saint Dionysius maintains that it is possible, as we find from his words in his Epistle to Timothy, where he says:[16] "For the beholding of the hidden things of God, shalt thou forsake sense and the things of the flesh, and all that the

[15] All religious media used by the intellect, imagination, and senses. *Theologia Germanica*, pp. 233, 89, 100.
[16] *Mystical Theology*, I, 1.

senses can apprehend, and that reason of her own power can bring forth, and all that the intellect can comprehend and know, both created and uncreated things, and shalt take thy stand upon an utter abandonment of thyself, forgetting all of the aforesaid things, and enter into union with Him who is, and who is above all essence and all knowledge." Now if he did not hold this to be possible in time, why should he teach it and enjoin it upon us in this temporal world? Know too that a master, commenting on this passage of Saint Dionysius, has said that it is wholly possible, and may indeed befall a man so often, that he will grow so far accustomed to it as to be able to look into eternity whenever he will. For when a thing is at first very hard to a man, and strange and seemingly quite impossible, if he put all his strength and striving into it, and persevere therein, that will afterward grow quite light and easy which he at first thought impossible; for there is no use in a beginning save it have a good end.

And a single one of these noble glances[17] is incomparably better, worthier, higher, and more pleasing to God than all that the creature can perform as a creature. As soon as a man turns back, heartily and with his whole will, and, rising above time, sinks his spirit into the spirit of God,[18] then all that ever has departed from him is restored in a moment. And if a man would do this a thousand times in a day, each time a fresh and true union would come about; and in this sweet and divine work stands the truest and purest union that may be in this temporal world. For he who has attained thereto asks nothing further: he has found the Kingdom of Heaven and eternal life on earth.

Chapter IX

How It Is Better and More Profitable for a Man that He Should Know What God Will Do with Him, or to What End He Will Make Use of Him, than If He Knew All That God Had Ever Wrought, or Would Ever Work Through All Creatures; and How Blessedness Lies Alone in God, and Not in Any Work, Nor Yet in Creatures

We should mark and know in very truth that all virtue and

---

[17] *Ein einziger dieser edlen Blicke.* . . . (Riedler, *op. cit.*, pp. 24, 162), referring to the *cognitio matutina* (*Morgenschau*) of the mystics, i.e., the knowledge of the world in its ideal existence in God vs. *die cognitio vespertina* (*Abendschau*), dealing with the creation in which man seeks God.

[18] *Einsenkt in Gottes Geist.* Bernhart, *op. cit.*, p. 144.

goodness, and even that eternal Good which is God himself, can never make a man virtuous, good, or blessed, so long as he is outside of his soul; that is, so long as he casts about outwardly with his senses and reason, and does not withdraw into himself and learn to know his own life, who and what he is. And the like is true of sin and evil. For all manner of sin and wickedness do not make us wicked, so long as they are outside of us; that is, so long as we do not commit them or do not give consent to them. Therefore, although it be good and profitable that we should ask and learn and know what good and holy men have wrought and suffered, and likewise how God has willed and wrought in and through them, yet were it a thousand times better that we should in ourselves learn and perceive and understand who we are, how and what our life is, what God is in us and works in us, what he will have from us, and to what ends he will or will not make use of us. For wholly to know oneself in the truth is above all learning: it is the highest learning;[19] if you know yourself well, you are better and more praiseworthy before God than if you did not know yourself, but knew the course of the heavens and of all the planets and stars, the virtue of all herbs, and the bodily and intellectual frame of all mankind, the nature of all beasts, and had further all the arts of all who are in heaven and on earth. For it is said, there came a voice from heaven, saying, "Man, know thyself." Therefore there is this saying too: "Never was there a going out so good but that an indwelling had not been far better."[20]

Further, you should learn that eternal bliss lies in one thing alone, and in nought else. And if ever man or the soul is to be made blessed, that one thing alone shall and must be in the soul. "But what is that one thing?" I answer: It is the Good—or that which has become good—and yet neither this good nor that, which we can name, or know, or show; but it is all good, and above all good. Moreover, it needs not to enter the soul, for it is there already, only it is unperceived. When we say we should come to it, we mean that we should seek it, feel it, and taste it. And now since it is One, unity and singleness is better than manifoldness. For blessedness lies not in much and manifoldness, but in One and oneness. And in short, blessedness lies not in any creature or working of the creatures, but it lies alone in God and in his working. Therefore should I wait only on God

[19] . . . *in der Wahrheit, das ist über alle Wissenschaft: es ist die höchste Wissenschaft.* Bernhart, *op. cit.*, p. 146.
[20] See *Von Abegescheidenheit* in F. Pfeiffer, *Meister Eckhart*, p. 485, ll. 13–14.

and his work, and let go all creatures with their works, and first of all myself. And all the works and wonders that God has ever wrought or shall ever work in or through all creatures, yea, God himself with all the good that is his—so far as these things exist or are done outside of me, they can never make me blessed. But only in so far as they exist and are done in me, are loved, known, tasted, and felt in me.

Chapter X

How Perfect Men Have No Other Desire than that They May Be to the Eternal Good What His Hand Is to a Man; and How They Have Lost the Fear of Hell and Desire of Heaven

Now let us mark: Where there are enlightened men, men with the True Light,[21] they perceive that all which they might desire or choose is nothing to that which all creatures, as creatures, ever desired or chose or knew. Therefore they renounce all desire and choice, and commit and resign themselves and all things to the eternal Good. Nevertheless, there remains in them a desire which helps their progress and their approach to the eternal Good, namely, a desire to come to a closer knowledge and warmer love, a pure readiness and entire obedience and subjection; so that every enlightened man could say, "I would fain be to the eternal Good what his own hand is to a man"; and they always fear that they fall short of it, and they wish for the salvation of all men. But they stand far above this one remaining desire, nor take it to themselves, for they know well that this desire is not man's affair, but belongs to the eternal Good. Nay, nothing of what is good shall any man arrogate to himself as his own, for it belongs to the eternal Good only.

Moreover, these men are in a state of such freedom that they have lost the fear of punishment, or hell, and the hope of reward, or heaven; nay, they live in pure submission and obedience to the eternal Good, in love freely given and intensely felt. This was in Christ in perfection, and also in his followers, in some more and in some less. And it is a sorrow and shame that the eternal Good is ever guiding us toward what is most noble, and we will have none of it! What is better and more precious than true poorness in spirit? And when that is held up before us, we will have none of it, and are always seeking ourselves, and our own things. We would always have our mouths daubed

21 Cf. cap. 40 on the "True" vs. the "False" Light.

with sugar, and relish a pleasant taste and delight and sweetness in ourselves. When this is so, we are well pleased, and think it stands not amiss with us. But we are yet a long way off from a perfect life. For when God will draw us up to something higher, that is, to an utter loss and forsaking of our own things, spiritual and natural, and withdraws his comfort and all sweetness from us, we faint and are troubled, and can in no way bring our minds to it; and we forget God and cease our practice, and imagine that we are quite lost. This is great frailty and a bad sign. For a true lover loves God, or the eternal Good, alike in having and in not having, in sweetness and in bitterness, in joy and sorrow; for he seeks alone the glory of God and of that which is God's, and he seeks it in neither spiritual nor natural things, and therefore he stands alike unshaken in all things, at all seasons. Hereby let every man judge how he stands toward God, his Creator and Lord. Amen.

Chapter XI

How a Righteous Man in This Temporal World Is Brought Into Hell, and There Cannot Be Comforted; and How He Is Taken Out of Hell and Brought Into Heaven, and There Can No More Be Troubled

Christ's soul must needs descend into hell before it ascended into heaven. So must also the soul of man. But mark you in what manner this comes to pass. When a man truly perceives and marks himself, who and what he is, and finds himself, so utterly vile and wicked, and unworthy of all the comfort and kindness that he has ever received or can receive from God and from the creatures, he falls into such a deep discouragement and despising of himself that he thinks himself unworthy the earth should bear him, and it seems to him just that all creatures in heaven and on earth should rise up against him and avenge their Creator on him, and should punish and torment him; and that he were unworthy even of that. And it seems to him that he shall be eternally lost and damned, and a footstool to all the evil spirits in hell, and that this is right and just, and all too little compared to his sins, so often and in so many ways has he committed sin against God his Creator. And therefore also he will not and dare not desire any consolation or release, either from God or from any creature that is in heaven or on earth; but he is willing and glad to be unconsoled and unreleased, and he does

not grieve over his condemnation and sufferings; for thus it is
right and just, and not contrary to God, but according to the
will of God. Therefore it is pleasing to him, and he has nothing
to say against it. Nothing grieves him but his own guilt and
wickedness; for these are unrighteousness and contrary to God,
and therefore is he sorrowful and troubled in spirit. This is
what is meant by true repentance for sin. And he who in this
temporal world enters into hell in this wise enters afterward
into the Kingdom of Heaven, and obtains a foretaste thereof
which excels all the delight and joy that ever came or could
come in this temporal world from temporal things. And while a
man is thus in hell, none may console him, neither God nor the
creature, as it is written, "In hell there is no redemption." Of
this state one has said:

> "Wasting, dying,
> I live uncomforted;
> Damned am I
> Without, within:
> Let no one pray
> I be redeemed!"

Now God does not leave a man in this hell; but he takes him
to himself, that the man no longer desires nor regards anything
but the eternal Good only, and comes to know that the eternal
Good is so precious, and more than good, that none can fathom
or express its bliss, consolation, and joy, its peace, rest, and
satisfaction. And then, when the man neither cares for nor seeks
nor desires anything but the eternal Good alone, and seeks not
himself, nor his own things, but only the honor of God in all
things, he is made a partaker of the joy, bliss, peace, rest, and
consolation of the eternal Good—and than this there is nothing
more—and so the man is thenceforth in the Kingdom of
Heaven. This hell and this heaven are two good, safe ways for a
man in this temporal world, and happy is he who travels them
to the end.

> For this hell shall pass away
> But heaven shall endure for aye.

Yet let a man mark: When he is in this hell, nothing may console him, and he cannot believe that he shall ever be released
and comforted. But when he is in heaven, nothing can trouble
him; he believes also that none will ever be able to offend or
trouble him. Yet it is indeed true that after this hell he may be

comforted and released, and after this heaven he may be troubled and left without consolation. Often this hell or this heaven come over a man in such sort that he knows not whence it comes, and whether it come to him or depart from him he can of himself do nothing toward it. Neither the heaven nor the hell can he give to himself or take from himself, can he of himself make or banish; but as it is written, "The spirit bloweth where it listeth, and thou hearest the voice thereof"; that is to say, it is present, but thou knowest not whence it comes, nor whither it goes. And when a man is in one of these two states, it is well with him, and he can be as safe in hell as in heaven, and so long as a man is on earth, it is possible for him to pass ofttimes from the one into the other; yea, many times in the space of a day and night, and all without his own doing. But when a man is in neither of these two, he holds converse with the creature, and wavers hither and thither, and knows not where he is. Therefore let him never forget either of them in his heart.

Chapter XII

What That True Inward Peace Is, Which Christ Left to His Disciples

Many say they have not peace and rest; they have so many crosses and trials, afflictions and sorrows, that they know not how they shall ever get through them. Now he who will consider and weigh this rightly will clearly perceive that true peace and rest lie not in outward things. For if it were so, the Evil Spirit also would have peace when things go according to his will and liking, which is nowise the case. For the Lord declares through the prophet, "There is no peace to the wicked and the faithless." And therefore we must consider and see what is that peace which Christ left to his beloved disciples, when he said, "My peace I leave with you, my peace I give unto you." We may perceive that by these words Christ did not mean a bodily and outward peace; for his beloved disciples, with all his lovers and followers, have ever from the first suffered great affliction, persecution, and martyrdom, as Christ himself said, "In this world ye shall have tribulation." But Christ means that true, inward peace of the heart, which begins here and endures forever hereafter. Therefore he said, "Not as the world gives it," for the world is false, and deceives in her gifts. She promises much, and performs little. Moreover, there lives no man on earth who may always have rest and peace without troubles and crosses, with whom things go always according to his will. There is always something to be suffered here, consider it as you will. And as soon as you are free of one adversity, perhaps two others come in its place. Therefore yield yourself willingly to them, and seek only that true peace of the heart which none can take away from you, that you may overcome all adversity; the peace that breaks through all adversities and crosses, all oppression, suffering, misery, humiliation, and what more there may be of the like, so that a man may be joyful and patient therein, as were the beloved disciples and followers of Christ. Now if a man were lovingly to give his whole diligence and might thereto, he would very soon come to know that true eternal peace which is God himself, as far as it is possible to a creature; insomuch that what was bitter to him before, would become sweet, and his heart would remain ever unmoved among all things, and after this life he would attain everlasting peace. Amen.

Chapter XIII

How a Man Often Casts Aside Imagery too Soon

Tauler says, There be some men at the present time who take leave of imagery too soon,[22] before truth and knowledge have shown them the way thence; hence they are scarcely or perhaps never after able to understand the Truth aright. For such men will follow no one, hold fast to their own understandings, and desire to fly before they are fledged. They would fain mount up to heaven in one flight, albeit Christ did not so, for after his resurrection he remained full forty days with his beloved disciples. No one can become perfect in a day. A man must first wholly deny himself, and willingly forsake all things for God's sake, and must give up his own will, and all his natural inclinations, and purge and cleanse himself thoroughly from all sins and evil ways. After this let him humbly take up the cross and follow Christ. Also let him accept example and instruction, wise counsel and teaching, and permit devout and perfect servants of God to advise him, and not follow his own guidance; thus shall the work be established and come to a good end. And

---

[22] I.e., "It is dangerous too soon to abandon the world of mediating images which the Church offers to devotion." Bernhart-Trask, *Theologia Germanica*, p. 235. Cf. Riedler, *op. cit.*, p. 165, note 37, on Eckhart's injunction, *alle Bilder zu lassen und in den Grund einzugehen.*

when a man has thus broken loose from and overleaped all temporal things and creatures, he may afterward come to perfection
in a life of contemplation. For he who will have the one must let
the other go. There is no other way.

Chapter XIV

Of Three Stages Which Lead and Bring a Man to True Perfection

Now be assured that no one can be enlightened unless he has
first cleansed and purified and freed himself. And further, no
one can be united with God unless he has first been enlightened.
And so correspondingly there are three ways: first, purification,
secondly, enlightening, thirdly, union. Purification belongs to
such as are beginning and repenting, and takes place in three
ways: by contrition and sorrow for sin, by full and free confession, by perfect penitence. Enlightening belongs to such as are
growing, and likewise takes place in three ways, to wit: by the
rejection of sin, by the practice of virtue and good works, and
by the willing endurance of adversity and tribulations. Union
belongs to such as are perfect, and also is brought to pass in three
ways, to wit: by pureness and singleness of heart, by godly love,
and by the contemplation of God,[23] the Creator of all things.

Chapter XLIV

How Nothing Is Against God but Self-will,[24] and How He Who Seeks His Best as His Own Finds It Not; and How a Man of Himself Neither Knows Nor Can Do Any Good Thing

If now it should be asked, "Is there, then, something that is
against God and the true Good?" the answer must be, "No."
Likewise there is nothing without God, except to will otherwise
than is willed by the eternal Will; that is, against the eternal
Will. Now, the eternal Will wills that nothing be willed or loved
but the eternal Good; and where it is otherwise, there is something against Him; and in this sense it is true that he who is
without God is against God. But in truth there is nothing
against God or the true Good.

We must understand it as though God said: "He who wills

---

23 Bernhart (p. 158) reads: *in göttlicher Liebe und in Betrachtung Gottes.* . . .
   Riedler's *Urtext* (p. 211): *in götlicher liebe und in beschowunge gotes.* . . .
24 *Eigenwille.*

without me, or wills not as I will, or otherwise than as I will, he wills against me; for my will is that no one should will otherwise than I, and that there should be no will without me, and without my will, even as without me there is neither being nor life, nor this, nor that. So also there should be no will without me and my will." And even as in truth all essences are one in essence in the perfect Essence, and all goods are one in the One, and cannot exist without that One; so likewise shall all wills be one in the one perfect Will, and there shall be no will without that One. And whatever is otherwise is wrong, and against God and his will, and therefore it is sin. Therefore, all will without God's will (that is, all self-will) is sin, and so is all that comes of self-will. So long as a man seeks his self-will and his best as his, and for his own sake, he will never find it. For so long as he does this, he is not seeking his best, and how, then, should he find it? For so long as he does this, he seeks himself, and imagines that he is himself the best; and seeing that he is not the best, he seeks not the best so long as he seeks himself. But whosoever seeks, loves, and pursues the Good for the sake of the Good and for nothing but the love of the Good, not as from the me, or as the I, me, mine, or for the sake of the me, he will find it, for he seeks it aright. And they who seek it otherwise err. Truly it is in this wise that the true and perfect Good seeks and loves and pursues itself, and therefore it finds itself.

It is a great folly when a man or any creature conceives that it knows or can accomplish aught of itself, and above all when it imagines that it knows or can accomplish any good thing, whereby it may deserve much at God's hands and prevail with him. Rightly considered, this is to put a great affront upon God. But the true and perfect Good overlooks it in the foolish, simple man who knows no better, and orders things for the best for him, and God gladly gives him as many good things as he is able to receive. But as we have said before, he finds and receives it not so long as he remains unchanged; for I-hood and selfhood must depart,[25] otherwise he will never find and receive it.

Chapter XLV

How that Where There Is the Christ Life, There Christ Is Also, and How the Christ Life Is the Best and Most Precious Life That Ever Has Been or Can Be

He who knows and recognizes the Christ life, knows and

[25] Bernhart, p. 239: *denn die Ichheit und Selbstheit muss hineweg.* . . .

22—L.M.M.

recognizes Christ also. And in like manner, he who knows not that life, knows not Christ either. He who believes in Christ believes that his life is the best and most precious life that ever was; and if a man believe not this, neither does he believe in Christ. And in so far as the Christ life is in a man, Christ is in him, and the less of the one, the less of the other. For where there is the Christ life, there is Christ also, and where his life is not, Christ is not. But where the Christ life is, the man must say with Saint Paul, "I live, yet not I, but Christ lives in me."[26] And this is the most precious and best life; for in him who has it, God himself is and dwells, with all goodness. How could there be a better life? When we speak of obedience, of the new man, of the true Light, the true Love, or the Christ life, it is all the same thing. And where one of these is, there are they all, and where one is wanting or lacking, there is none of them, for they are all one in truth and essence. The means whereby a man may bring it about that all these are born and come to life in him, to those let us cleave with all our might and to nought else. And let us forswear and flee all that hinders it. He who has received it in the Holy Sacrament, has verily and indeed received Christ; and the more of it he has received, the more he has received Christ, and the less, the less of Christ.

Chapter XLVI

How Entire Satisfaction and True Rest Are to Be Found in God Alone, and Not in Any Creature; and How He Who Will Be Obedient to God Must Also Be Passively Obedient to All Creatures, and He Who Would Love God Must Also Love All Things

It is said, "He who is content to find his satisfaction in God, has enough," and this is true. And he who finds satisfaction in aught which is this or that, finds it not in God; and he who finds it in God finds it in nought else, save in that which is neither this nor that, but is All. For God is the One and must be the One, and God is All and must be All. Therefore, what is, and is not the One, is not God; and what is, and is not All and above All, is also not God. For God is the One and above the One, and is All and above All. Therefore he who finds satisfaction in God, his satisfaction is the One, and is all in the One. And he to whom the One is not all and all not the One, and to whom something and nothing are not one and the same, cannot find

[26] Gal. 2:20.

satisfaction in God. But where it should be thus, there would be true satisfaction, and not else.

Indeed, he who will wholly commit himself to God and be obedient to him, must also resign himself to all things passively, and be obedient to them, without resisting or defending himself or any evasion. And he who is not thus resigned, and obedient to all things in the One, and as the One, is not resigned and obedient to God. This we may see in Christ. He who will suffer God must suffer all in the One, and in no wise resist any suffering. But this is to be Christ. He who resists suffering and refuses to endure it will not and cannot suffer God. That is to say, we may not withstand any creature or thing by force or fighting, either in will or in works. But we may indeed without sin prevent affliction, or avoid it and evade it.

Now, he who will hold to God loves all things in the One which is One and All, and the One in All, because All is in the One; and he who loves somewhat, this or that, otherwise than in the One, and for the sake of the One, loves not God; for he loves somewhat which is not God, therefore he loves it more than God. But he who loves somewhat more than God, or equally with God, loves not God; for God must be and will be alone loved, and in truth nothing ought to be loved but God alone. And when the true Light and the true divine Love dwell in a man, he loves nothing else but God alone. For he loves God as the Good and for the sake of the Good, and all goods as One, and One as All. For, verily, All is One and One is All in God.

Chapter XLVII

A Question: Whether, If We Ought to Love All Things, We Ought to Love Sin Also?

Some may put a question here and say, "If we are to love all things, must we then love sin also?" I answer, "No." When we say "all things," we mean the good. And all that is, is good, in virtue of having being. The devil is good in virtue of having being. In this sense nothing is evil, or not good. But sin is to will, desire, or love otherwise than as God does. And willing is not essence, therefore it is not good. A thing is good only in so far as it is in God and with God. Now all things have their essence in God, and more truly in God than in themselves, and therefore all things are good in their essence. And if there were anything that had not its essence in God, it would not be good.

Now behold, the willing or desiring which is against God is not in God. For God cannot will or desire against God, or otherwise than God. Therefore it is evil, or not good, or merely nought. God loves also works, but not all works. Which then? Such as follow from the teaching and guidance of the true Light and from the true Love. What comes to pass from these comes to pass in the spirit and in the truth, and what is thereof is God's, and pleases him well. But what comes to pass from false light and false love is all evil. And especially what comes to pass and is done or left undone, wrought or suffered, from any other will and desire and from any other love than God's will, and his love. This is, and comes to pass, without God and against God, is contrary to God's work, and is altogether sin.

Chapter XLVIII

How We Must Believe Certain Things of Divine Truth Beforehand, Ere We Can Come to a True Knowledge and Experience of Divine Truth

Christ said, "He that believes not, and will not or cannot believe, is lost and shall be damned."[27] It is so in truth. For a man who is come into this temporal world, has not knowledge; and he cannot come to knowledge unless he first believe. And he who would know before he believes comes never to true knowledge. We speak not here of the articles of the blessed faith, for everyone believes them, and they are common to every Christian man, whether he be sinful or saved, wicked or good. That we must first believe, for without first believing we cannot come to knowledge, applies to Truth; that which it is possible to know and learn, must be believed before it is known or learned, else you will never come to true knowledge. This is the faith that Christ means.

Chapter XLIX

Of Self-will, and How Lucifer and Adam Fell from God Through Self-will

It has been said that there is of nothing so much in hell as of self-will. For hell is nothing but self-will, and if there were no self-will there would be no devil and no hell. When it is said that

27 Cf. Mark 16:16.

Lucifer fell from heaven, and turned away from God and the like, it means nothing else than that he would have his own will, and would not be of one will with the eternal Will. So was it likewise with Adam in Paradise. And when we say "self-will," we mean: "to will otherwise than as the One and eternal Will of God wills."

Chapter L

How This Temporal World Is a Paradise and Outer Court of Heaven, and How Therein There Is Only One Tree Forbidden, That Is, Self-will

But what is Paradise? All things that are; for all that is, is good and joyous. Therefore it is called a Paradise, and is so indeed. It is said also that Paradise is an outer court of heaven. Even so, all there is, is verily an outer court of the Eternal and of eternity, and especially what we may recognize and know of God and eternity, in time and in temporal things and in creatures. For the creatures are a guide and a way to God and to eternity. Thus all this is an outer court or forecourt of eternity; and therefore it may well be called a Paradise, and be so in truth. And in this Paradise all things are lawful that are therein, save one tree and the fruits thereof. That is to say, in all that is there is nothing forbidden and nothing contrary to God but one thing only, that is, self-will, or to will otherwise than as the eternal Will wills. Take this to heart! For God says to Adam, that is, to every man, "Whatever thou art, or doest, or leavest undone, or whatever cometh to pass, is all lawful and not forbidden if it come not to pass from thy will but from mine."[28] But all that comes to pass from thine own will is against the eternal Will. It is not that all works which come to pass are against the eternal Will, but when they come to pass from a different will, or otherwise than from the eternal and divine Will.

Chapter LI

Wherefore God Has Created Self-will, Seeing that It Is So Contrary to Him

Now some may ask: "Since this tree, to wit, self-will, is so contrary to God and the eternal Will, wherefore has God created it, and set it in Paradise?" *Answer:* Whatever man or

[28] Gen. 2:16 ff.

creature desires to understand and know the secret counsel and will of God, so that he would fain know wherefore God does this, or does not that, and the like, desires the same as Adam did and the devil. And so long as this desire persists, the truth will never be known to him, and the man is even as Adam or the devil. For this desire is seldom from aught else than that the man takes delight in knowing and glories therein, and this is sheer pride. A truly humble and enlightened man does not desire of God that he should reveal his secrets to him, nor ask wherefore God does this or that, or hinders or allows such a thing, and so forth; but all his care is to please God only, and to become as nought in himself, having no will, and that the eternal Will may live in him, and have full possession of him, unhindered by any other will, and how its due may be rendered to the eternal Will, by him and through him.

However, there is yet another answer to this question, for we may say: The most precious and joyful thing that is in any creature is cognition, or reason, and will, and these two are bound together; where the one is, there the other is also. And were there not these two, there would be no reasonable creatures, but only brutes and brutishness. And that were a great loss, for then God could not have his due nor put his properties, of which we have before spoken, to work, which yet is necessary and requisite for his perfection. Now, behold, cognition and reason is created and bestowed along with will; and it must teach the will, and also itself, that neither cognition nor will is of itself, and that neither of them may belong to itself or demand and will of itself, that neither of them may employ itself or profit itself for its own sake; nay, that His they are from whom they proceed, and to him shall they submit, and flow back into him, and become nought in themselves, that is, in their selfhood.

But here you must consider more particularly somewhat concerning the will. There is an eternal Will, which is in God originally and essentially, apart from all works and working, and the same Will is in man, or the creature, working and willing,[29] for it belongs to the Will and is its property that it shall will. Were this not so, what else should it do? For it were in vain, unless it had some work to do. And this cannot come to pass without the creature. Therefore there must be creatures, and God will have them, to the end that the Will may have and work its proper work in them, which Will in God is and must be

---

[29] Cf. cap. 31 and the typical Eckhartian distinction between the acting *Gott* and the nonacting *Gottheit*. Riedler, *op. cit.*, p. 173, note 76.

apart from working. Therefore the Will in the creature, which
we call a created will, is as truly God's as the eternal Will, and
is not a property of the creature. Since God cannot will works
and changes without the creature, therefore it pleases him to do
this in and with the creature. Therefore the creature should not
will with this same Will, but God alone should will works with
this Will, which is in man and yet belongs to God alone. And in
whatever man or creature it should be purely and wholly thus,
the Will would be exerted, not by the man but by God, and
thus it would not be self-will, and the man would not will otherwise than as God wills. For God himself would will in him, and
not the man, and that Will would be one with the eternal Will,
and have flowed out into it.

But the man would still keep his sense of loving and loathing,
pleasure and pain, and the like. For wherever the Will wills
works, there must be that which is loved or that which is
loathed; for if things go according to His Will, the man loves it,
and if they do not, he loathes it, and this loving and loathing
likewise is not of the man, but of God. Now the Will comes not
of man but of God, therefore loving and loathing is also His,
and nothing is complained of, save only what is contrary to God.
So also there is no joy but from God alone, and from that which
is God's. Now, as it is with the will, so it is also with cognition,
reason, resources, love, and whatever is in man; they are all of
God, and not of man. And wherever the Will should be altogether surrendered to God, the rest would of a certainty be surrendered likewise, and God would have his right, and the man's
will would not be self-will. Behold, therefore has God created
the Will, but not that it should be self-will.

Now comes the devil or Adam, that is to say, false nature, and
takes this Will into itself and makes the same its own, and uses it
for itself and its own ends. And this is the ruin and wrong, and
the bite that Adam took of the apple, and this is forbidden, because it is against God. And therefore, how long soever, and
wheresoever there is any self-will, there true love, true peace,
true rest will never come. This we see both in man and in the
devil. And so never will true blessedness arise, either in time or
in eternity, there where this self-will rules, that is to say, where
man is the usurper, arrogating the Will to himself and making
it his own. And if self-will be not surrendered in time, but a man
carry it over with him out of time, it may be foreseen that it can
never be vanquished. So it is true that, there also, neither content nor peace, rest nor blessedness, will ever come to growth.

This we may see by the devil. If there were no reason or will in the creatures, God were, and must remain, unknown, unloved, unpraised, and unhonored, and all the creatures were worth nothing, and were of no avail to God. Behold, thus the question is answered. And were there any who might be led to amend their ways by these many words and long considerations (which yet are short and profitable before God), this were well-pleasing to God.

That which is free none may call his own, and he who makes it his own does wrong. Now, among all free things, none is freer than, or so free as, the Will, and he who makes it his own, and suffers it not to remain in its noble freedom, in its free nobility and free nature, does a grievous wrong. This is what the devil and Adam and all their followers do. But he who leaves the Will in its noble freedom does right, and this is what Christ and all his followers do. Whoso robs the Will of its noble freedom and makes it his own, must of necessity as his reward, be laden with cares and trouble, with discontent, disquiet, strife, unrest, and all manner of wretchedness, and this will remain and endure in time and in eternity. But he who leaves the Will in its free nature has content, peace, rest, and blessedness in time and in eternity. Wherever there is a man in whom the Will is not usurped but continues in its noble freedom, there is the true freeman, knowing no bondage, of whom Christ said, "The truth shall make you free"; and immediately after, "If the Son shall make you free, ye shall be free indeed."

And now mark: In whatever man the Will enjoys its freedom it does its proper work, that is, willing; and if now it may choose as it will, unhindered, it chooses always the noblest and best in all things, and all that is not noble and good is contrary to it and makes it suffer and complain. And the more free and unhindered the Will is, the more is it pained by that which is not good, and unrighteousness, and vice, and in short all manner of wickedness and all that is called and is sin, and the more do they make it suffer and complain. This we see in Christ. The Will in him was free and unhindered and unusurped as it was never in any man, nor ever will be. So likewise was Christ's human nature the most free and single of all creatures, and yet suffered the deepest grief, pain, and indignation at sin (that is, at all that is against God) that any creature ever felt.

But when men arrogate freedom to themselves, so as to feel no sorrow or indignation at sin and what is against God, but say that we must heed nothing and care for nothing, but even now, in time, be as Christ was after his resurrection—there is no true and divine freedom springing from true divine Light, but a natural, unrighteous, false, and deceived freedom, springing from natural, false, and deceived light.

Were there not this self-will, this will of the creature's own, there were likewise no property, nothing owned. In heaven there is nothing owned, wherefore in heaven there reign content, true peace, and all bliss. Were there one in heaven who presumed to own aught, he would instantly be cast out into hell, and would become a devil. But in hell each will have his own will, therefore in hell there reign pure wretchedness and bale. So it is also in the temporal world. But were there one in hell who were without self-will, owning neither will nor aught else, he would come out of hell into heaven. Now, in this temporal world, man stands between heaven and hell, and can turn himself to which of them he will. For the more of own, the more of hell and bale, and the less of own self-will, the less of hell and the nearer to heaven. And could a man in this temporal world be wholly without self-will or aught else of his own, and stand up quit and free, being lightened by the true divine Light and Love, his were indeed the Kingdom of Heaven.[30] He who has or wills or wishes aught of his own is himself owned, and he who has and wills naught of his own, and desires to have naught, is quit and free and owned of naught.

All that has been here said Christ taught in words and fulfilled in works for three and thirty years. And he teaches it to us very briefly when he says, "Follow me." But he who will follow him must forsake all things, for in Him all things were so wholly forsaken as never in any creature else they were or will be. Moreover, he who will follow Him, must take up the cross, and the cross is nothing else than the Christ life, for that is a bitter cross to all nature. Therefore he says, "He that renounces not all things and takes not up the cross is not worthy of me, and cannot be my disciple, and follows me not."[31] But false, free nature imagines that it has forsaken all things; yet it will have none of the cross, and says it has had enough of it already, and needs it no longer; and thus is it deceived. For had it ever tasted the cross, it would never forsake it. He that believes in Christ must believe all that is here written.

---

[30] . . . *ihm wäre das Himmelreich gewiss.* Bernhart, *op. cit.*, p. 255.
[31] Matt. 10:38; Luke 14:27.

Chapter LII

How We Must Take Those Two Sayings of Christ: "No Man Cometh Unto the Father, but by Me," and "No Man Cometh Unto Me, Except the Father Draw Him"

Christ says: "No man cometh unto the Father, but by me."[32] Now mark how we must have come unto the Father through Christ. Over himself, and all that belongs to him, within and without, the man shall set a watch, and shall so govern, and guard himself, as far as in him lies, that neither will nor desire, love nor longing, wish nor thought, shall spring up in his heart, or have any abiding place in him, save such as belong to God and would be meet for Him, if God himself were that man. And whenever he becomes aware of aught rising up within him that does not belong to God and is not meet for Him, he must resist it and root it out, as thoroughly and as speedily as he may. And even so shall it be with his outward behavior also, whether he do or refrain, speak or keep silence, wake or sleep, go or stand still, in short, in all his ways and walks, whether touching his own business or his dealings with other men: to the end that he shall watch over all these, lest in him he suffer aught to spring up or dwell, inwardly or outwardly, or lest aught be done in him or through him other than what would belong to God, and would be possible and meet for Him, if God himself were that man.

Behold! he in whom it should be thus, whatever he had within, or did without, would be all of God, and the man would be a follower of Christ in His life, as we understand it and set it forth. And he who led such a life would go in and out through Christ, for he would be a follower of Christ. Therefore also he would come with Christ unto the Father, and through Christ. And he would be also a servant of Christ, for he who follows him is his servant, as he himself also says, "If any man serve me, let him follow me"[33] (as if he said, "He who follows me not, neither does he serve me"). And he who is thus a servant and follower of Christ, comes even to that place where Christ is; that is, unto the Father. So Christ himself says: "Father, I will that my servants be with me where I am."[34] Behold, he who walks in this way, "entereth in by the door into the sheepfold," that is, into eternal life, "and to him the porter openeth."[35] But he who walks in some other way, or imagines that he can

[32] John 14:6.   [33] John 12:26.
[34] John 17:24.   [35] John 10:1, 3.

come to the Father or to eternal blessedness otherwise than through Christ, is deceived; for he walks not in the right Way, nor enters in by the right Door. Therefore to him the porter opens not, for he is a thief and a murderer, as Christ names him. Lo, now consider whether a man may live in lawless freedom and license, disregarding virtue and vice, order and disorder, and the like; consider well whether, so living, he walks in the right Way and enters in by the right Door! Such heedlessness was not in Christ, neither is it in any of his true followers.

Chapter LIII

Considers That Other Saying: "No Man Cometh Unto Me, Except the Father Draw Him"

Christ says further: "No man cometh unto me, except the Father draw him."[36] Now mark: By the Father, I understand the perfect, simple Good, which is All and above All, and without which and besides which there is no true Essence nor true Good, and without which no good work ever was or will be done. And in that it is All, it must be in All and above All. And it cannot be any one of those things which the creature, as creature, can comprehend and understand. For whatever the creature, as creature, can comprehend and understand, conforms with its creature nature; it is something, this or that, and therefore is likewise all creature. Now if the simple perfect Good were a something, this or that, which the creature understands, it would not be All, and in All, and therefore also not perfect. Therefore we name it also "Nothing";[37] meaning thereby that it is none of all the things which the creature can comprehend, know, conceive, or name, in virtue of its creature nature. Now behold, when this Perfect and Unnamable flows into a person able to bring forth, and brings forth the only-begotten Son in that person, and itself in him, we call it the Father.

Now hear how the Father draws men to Christ. When somewhat of this perfect Good is discovered and revealed to the soul of man, as it were in a vision or an ecstasy, there is born in the man a longing to draw near to the perfect Goodness, and unite himself with the Father. And the stronger this longing grows, the more is revealed to the man; and the more is revealed to

---

[36] John 6:44.
[37] *Darum nennt man es auch Nichts* (Bernhart, p. 259). Cf. Riedler, *op. cit.*, p. 143 and p. 154, in relation to cap. 1. Cf. Bernhart-Trask, *Theologia Germanica*, p. 114 and Introduction, pp. 96 ff.

him, the more he longs and is drawn. In such wise is a man drawn and called to a union with the eternal Goodness. And this is the drawing of the Father, and thus the man is taught of Him who draws him, that he cannot come to that union except he come by the Christ life. Behold! now he puts on that life, of which I have spoken before.

Now consider again those two sayings of Christ's. The one: "No man cometh unto the Father, but by me"; that is, through my life, as set forth above. The other saying: "No man cometh unto me," that is, he does not take my life upon him and follow me, "except he be moved and drawn of my Father"; that is, of the simple and perfect Good, of which Saint Paul says: "When that which is perfect is come, then, that which is in part shall be done away." That is to say: In whatever man this Perfect is known, felt, and tasted, so far as may be in this temporal world, to that man all created things seem as nought compared with the Perfect, as in truth they are. For beside or without the Perfect is neither true Good nor true Essence. Whosoever, then, has, recognizes, and loves the Perfect, has and recognizes all that is good. What more or else, then, should he want, or what is all that "is in part" to him, seeing that all the parts are united in the Perfect, in the one Essence.

What has here been said wholly concerns the outward life; it is the way or access to the true inward life. But the inward life begins in this wise: Once a man has tasted the Perfect as far as is possible in this temporal world, all created things, and even himself, become as nought to him. And when he recognizes in truth that the Perfect alone is All and above All, it needs must follow that he ascribes all that is good, such as essence, life, cognition, knowledge, power, and the like, to the Perfect alone, and to no creature. Hence it follows that the man arrogates nothing to himself, neither Essence nor Life, Knowledge nor Power, Doing nor Refraining, nor anything that we can call good. And thus the man comes wholly to poorness, and indeed he becomes nought to himself, and in him becomes nought all that is somewhat, that is, all created things. Such is the first beginning of his true inward life; and, thereafter, God himself becomes the man, so that nothing is left that is not God or of God, and nothing is left that arrogates anything to itself. And thus God himself, that is, the one eternal Perfect alone, is, lives, knows, works, loves, wills, does, and refrains in the man. And thus should it be in truth, and where it is otherwise, let it be improved and rectified.

And the good way or access is to look to it that the best be always the most loved, and to choose the best, and cleave to it, and unite oneself to it. First: In the creatures. But what is best in the creatures? Be assured: That, in which the eternal perfect Goodness and what is thereof, that is, all which belongs thereto, is most manifested and works, and is best recognized and loved. But what is that which is of God, and belongs to him? I answer: Whatever with justice and truth we may call good. When therefore among the creatures a man cleaves to that which is the best that he can recognize, and keeps steadfastly to that, and does not backslide, he comes time after time to a better, until at last he recognizes and tastes that the eternal Good is a perfect Good, immeasurably and numberlessly above all created good.

Now, if what is best is to be most loved by us, and we are to follow after it, the one eternal Good must be loved above all and alone, and we must cleave to it alone, and unite ourselves with it as much as we may. And, now, if we must ascribe all good things to the one eternal Good, as of right and truth we ought, so must we also of right and truth ascribe to it our beginning, progress, and perfection, so that nothing remain to man or the creature. So it should be in truth, let men write and rhyme what they will. On this wise we should attain to a true inward life. And what then further befalls, what is revealed to us, and what our life is thenceforward, none can rhyme or write. It has never been uttered by man's lips, nor has it entered into the heart of man to conceive, the manner thereof in truth.

This our long discourse, briefly recapitulated, declares: In right and truth there should be in a man nought which would arrogate aught to itself, or desire, will, love, or strive after aught in all things, save only God and what is divine, that is: the one, eternal, perfect Goodness.

But if there be aught else in a man, so that he arrogates somewhat to himself, or wills, strives after, and desires this or that, whatever it may be, beside or more than the eternal and perfect Good, which is God himself, this is all too much and a great fault, and hinders the man from a perfect life; wherefore he can never reach the perfect Good, unless he first forsake all things and himself first of all. For no man can serve two masters who are contrary the one to the other. He who will have the one must let the other go. Therefore, if the Creator shall enter in, all creature must depart. Of this be assured.

Chapter LIV

How a Man Shall Not Seek His Own in Aught, Either in Things Spiritual or Natural, but the Honor of God Only; and How He Must Enter in by the Right Door, to Wit, by Christ, Into Eternal Life

If a man may attain thereunto, to be unto God as his hand is to a man, let him be therewith content, and not seek further; this is my faithful counsel, and here I take my stand. That is to say, let him exercise and accustom himself to obey God and His commandments so thoroughly at all times and in all things that, neither in his spirit nor his nature, shall he find aught of resistance remaining, so that his whole soul and body with all their members may stand ready and willing for that to which God has created them; as ready and willing as his hand is to a man. For a man's hand is so wholly in his power that in the twinkling of an eye he moves and turns it as he will. And when we find it otherwise with us, we must give our whole diligence to amend our state; and this must come to pass from love and not from fear, and in all things whatsoever, we must fix our aim upon God and seek his glory and praise alone. We must not seek our own, neither in things spiritual nor in things natural. And it must needs be thus, if indeed it is to stand well with us. And every creature owes this of right and truth to God, and especially man, to whom, by the ordinance of God, all creatures are made subject, and are servants, that he may be subject to and serve God only.

Take this, too, to heart: When a man has climbed so high that he imagines and is persuaded that he has attained his goal, then is the time for him to beware, lest the devil be strewing ashes and sowing his seed, and nature seek and take comfort and rest, peace and delight, therein, and thus he fall into that foolish, lawless freedom and heedlessness which is so wholly a stranger to, and at war with, a truly godly life. And this will happen to that man who has not entered in, or refuses to enter in, by the right Way and the right Door (which is Christ, as we have said), and imagines that he could come by another door and another way to the highest truth. Perhaps he even thinks that he has attained thereto, but verily he has not. And our witness is Christ, who declares, "He that will enter otherwise than through me, comes not in, nor comes to the highest truth, but is a thief and a murderer."[38] A thief, for he robs God of His

[38] John 10:1.

honor and glory, which belong to God alone; he arrogates them to himself, and seeks and purposes himself. He is a murderer, for he slays his own soul, and takes away her life, which is God himself. For as the body lives by the soul, even so the soul lives by God. Moreover, he murders all those who follow him, by his doctrine and example. For Christ says, "I came not to do my own will, but the will of my Father in heaven that sent me."[39] And again: "Why call ye me Lord, Lord, and do not the things which I say?"[40] as if he would say, "It will avail you nothing to eternal life." And again, "Not every one that says unto me, Lord, Lord, shall enter into the Kingdom of Heaven; but he that does the will of my Father which is in heaven."[41] And he says also, "If thou wilt enter into eternal life, keep God's commandments."[42] But what are God's commandments? They are this: "Love God in all things with all thy heart, and thy neighbor as thyself. In these two commandments lie all other commandments."[43] There is nothing dearer to God, and more profitable to man, than humble obedience. To him, one good work wrought from true obedience is dearer than a hundred thousand wrought from self-will, contrary to obedience. Therefore he who has this obedience need fear nothing, for he is in the right way, and follows after Christ.

That we may thus deny and renounce ourselves, and forsake all things through God, and die to our own self-will, and live unto God alone and to his Will, may he help us, who gave up his Will to his Heavenly Father—Jesus Christ, our dear Lord, who is blessed above all things forever. Amen.

HERE ENDS THE FRANKFURTER.
TO THE LORD BE PRAISE AND HONOR
AND TO THE NOBLE QUEEN AND VIRGIN,
MARY, MOTHER OF GOD. AMEN.
1497 ON THE DAY
OF THE BLESSED MARTYRS
COSMAS AND DAMIAN.
1497

Sit laus vitam humilianti in semetipso.

---

[39] John 6:38.   [40] Luke 6:46.   [41] Matt. 7:21.
[42] Matt. 19:17.   [43] Luke 10:27; Matt. 22:37 ff.

XII

Nicholas of Cusa (1401-1464)

INTRODUCTION

BIOGRAPHICAL NOTICE

NICHOLAS KREBS, SON OF A MOSELLE SHIP'S MASTER, was born at Cusa in 1401. With instruction begun at Deventer under the Brethren of the Common Life in 1413, he studied successively at Heidelberg (1416–1417), Padua (1417–1423), Rome (1423), and Cologne (1425). In 1426 he became secretary of the papal legate, Cardinal Orsini. Elevated to the priesthood, he was made dean of St. Florin in Coblenz about 1430. Commissioned in 1431 to represent Ulrich von Manderscheid's interests at Basel, he was admitted to the Conciliar college in 1432. Here he participated in negotiations with the Hussites and wrote his *Catholic Concordance*, 1433. He was a member of the legation to Constantinople seeking East–West union in 1437. Having gone over to the papal party in 1438, he served until 1448 as envoy of Eugenius IV in the Imperial Diet. Between his writing *On Learned Ignorance* in 1440 and *The Vision of God* in 1453, he was in 1448 made a cardinal, with St. Peter in Chains as his titular church. He was declared bishop of Brixen in 1450. He made sweeping trips throughout Germany (1451–52) as papal legate for reform. In Brixen after 1457 he collided with Duke Sigismund of Tirol over episcopal rights and spent his last years in exile employed in scholarly pursuits. He died in Todi, 1464.

BIBLIOGRAPHICAL ESSAY

E. Vansteenberghe has an excellent article in the *Dictionnaire de théologie catholique*, Vol. 11, pt. 1 (1931), cols. 601–612. Compare with this his biography, *Le cardinal Nicolas de Cues*, Paris, 1920. H. Bett, *Nicholas of Cusa*, London, 1932, is useful. The

INTRODUCTION 353

Opera omnia in the three-volume edition of J. Lefèvre d'Étaples
of Paris, 1514, was reissued, 3 vols. in 1, by Henri Petrus in
Basel, 1565. In the critical *Opera omnia* of E. Hoffmann-R.
Klibansky-G. Kallen, published by F. Meiner, at Leipzig, *De
docta ignorantia* is Vol. I (1932), the *Apologia doctae ignorantiae* is
Vol. II (1932). Of basic worth are P. Rotta, *De docta ignorantia*
. . . Bari, 1913, and A. Petzelt, *Nicolaus von Cues, Texte seiner
philosophischen Schriften* (based on the 1514 and 1565 editions),
W. Kohlhammer, Stuttgart, 1949, with Vol. I, including both
the *De docta* and the *Apologia*. Modern translations are L.
Moulinier, *De la docte ignorance*, Felix Alcan, Paris, 1930, Fr. G.
Heron, *Of Learned Ignorance*, Routledge & Kegan Paul, London,
1954, and M. de Gandillac, *Œuvres choisies*, Paris, 1942. Good
translations of *The Vision of God* are Vansteenberghe's *La vision
de Dieu*, Paris, 1925, and, largely based on this and the Basel
text, E. G. Salter's *Nicholas of Cusa: The Vision of God*, J. M.
Dent & Sons, Ltd., London, and E. P. Dutton & Co., Inc., New
York, 1928. A good German text with full notes is E. Bohnenstaedt, *Von Gottes Sehen*, F. Meiner, Leipzig, 1942, 1944. Indispensable studies with literature include M. de Gandillac's *La
philosophie de Nicolas de Cues*, Aubier, Paris, 1941, revised edition,
Nikolaus von Cues, L. Schwann, Düsseldorf, 1953, and E. Hoff-
mann, *Das Universum des Nicolaus von Cues*, Heidelberg, 1930. See
articles by Bohnenstaedt and P. Wilpert on mysticism and the
coincidentia oppositorum in J. Koch, *Humanismus, Mystik und Kunst
in der Welt des Mittelalters*, Cologne, 1953. See Wentzlaff-Eggebert, *op. cit.*, pp. 150–160, 320–323.

On the relation of *On Learned Ignorance* and the Dionysian
theology to *The Vision of God*, see E. Underhill's introduction to
Salter's translation above, pp. xi ff.; and pp. xxv ff., on the
"complication" and the "explication." Gilson, *History*, pp.
534–40, is enlightening. Consult the "Correspondance" of Cusa
and his friends in Vansteenberghe, "Autour de la docte ignorance," *Beiträge*, Vol. 14, pt. 2, pp. 107 ff. Regarding the coincidence of knowledge and ignorance as learned ignorance and the
relation of the vision of God to love and faith, see Letter 4
(1452), pp. 111–113. For the mystical theology of Dionysius as
surpassing both affirmative and negative theology, and the impossibility of seeing God mystically except by "copulative
theology" and in the cloud of coincidence that blots out all
contradiction, see Letter 5 (1453), pp. 113–117; also Vansteenberghe, *Vision*, pp. xvi–xvii. Cusa interprets this whole mystical theology, this vision of God, as an entering into absolute

infinity itself, inasmuch as infinity is the coincidence of contradiction and "end without end." No one is able to see God mystically except in the cloud or fog of coincidence, which is infinity (*et nemo potest Deum mistice videre nisi in caligine coincidencie, que est infinitas*), p. 116. The little book on mystical theology, this practical treatise (*hanc praxim experimentalem*), Cusa was about to send the Benedictines of Tegernsee, was *The Vision of God*. This little booklet, far from propounding speculative subtleties, was frankly calculated to whet the taste for spiritual research, to inculcate an experiential knowledge of mystical theology (*omnia scibilia quodam experimento venari poteritis, maxime in mistica theologia*). Vansteenberghe, "Correspondance," *Beiträge*, Vol. 14, pt. 2, p. 116; *Vision*, pp. xvii ff.

SYNOPSIS

Cusa has been sympathetically assessed by his biographer as a metaphysician by temperament, a theologian by task, an apostle by vocation. Nicholas' *On Learned Ignorance* constitutes a remarkable synthesis of his thought and method. He surmounts sheer dialectic and nominalist assumptions alike. He subscribes to the reality sought by metaphysics and theology. Nevertheless, he places sharp limitations upon the mind's attempt to reach it. Man's very knowledge of his impotence to command the full truth about anything constitutes the highest science of which humanity is capable. This is the "learned ignorance" upon which Cusa comes to rely so heavily in his preparation for the mystic vision—his *Vision of God*.

Cusa concurs in the Socratic conviction that the thing we know best is the fact that we know nothing. This paradox stems from the disjunction between truth on the one hand and knowledge on the other. In humiliating contrast with truth which is absolute, one, and infinitely simple, knowledge presents itself as necessarily relative, complex, and finite. Among the things we cannot know perfectly is God himself, who is the absolute maximum and the irreducible unity. Elusive, also, is the quiddity of things, that is, their essence, of which the truth is in God. All knowledge is circumscribed and approximate. All science is, at last, conjectural.[1]

It is necessary, then, to seek the truth beyond reason. This simple, absolute maximum, this infinite truth, is beyond our comprehension. Rational knowledge is manifestly superior to

[1] *Doct. ign.*, I, 1–3.

sensible knowledge. Yet the understanding finds itself thwarted by the inability of any rational process to resolve contradictions, just as it experiences frustration before the multiplicity of distinct sensations. All things apprehended by the interplay of sense, reason, and intellect are so diverse as to preclude any precise equality therein. The maximum equality, which is the very antithesis of diversity, is completely beyond our understanding.[2] For man to get at truth, therefore—to apprehend the unique maximum which is absolutely simple—he must, somehow, transcend discursive reason and the imagination, even as he raises himself above the confusing ramifications of sense. Man is compelled to eject or spew out all things attained by sense, imagination, or reason with its natural additions. He is forced to grasp the maximum in a simple intuition. Intelligence adequate to the laying hold upon absolute, intelligent Being will enable man to attain simplicity or "the coincidence of contraries." The intellect is thus enabled to rise by simple intuition above differences, diversities, and mathematical figures.[3]

The philosophy that seeks to understand why the maximum unity must be a trinity can obviously expect no help from the imagination or the reason. Cusa's appeal to the coincidence of the maximum and the minimum, to the coincidence of contradictions, will be, then, at base, less a matter of ordinary reason than of mystical speculation or contemplation. It will be constituted essentially by an outlook on ultrarational realities that basically exploits the fundamental idea of faith. Faith comprises or enfolds everything intelligible. Understanding explicates or unfolds what was complicated or enfolded. The intelligence gets direction from faith. Faith itself is extended by understanding, which is impossible without faith. The most perfect faith will be founded on Jesus, who is the Truth itself.[4]

Such speculations will presume less to be true than to be beautiful and beneficent. They will open up before the spirit charming vistas which will invite the soul to adhere, by faith and love, to the truth glimpsed in the obscurity of mystery. The humblest people, living daily by their faith in Jesus, who is God's Word and Power, can be caught up into that simplicity beyond reason and intelligence which is the third heaven of pure, simple intellection.

Naturally, this simple intellection will not find adequate expression in rational language. Cusa will revert to comparisons

---

[2] *Ibid.*, I, 4.   [3] *Ibid.*, I, 10.   [4] *Ibid.*, III, 11.

and symbols. He will appeal to geometric figures, however inadequate.[5] It is beyond contraries that the simple eye of the intelligence must seek God. This is because God is the being to which nonbeing does not oppose itself, the one against which the multiple does not set itself. It is at once the infinitely great and the infinitely small; the maximum with which the minimum coincides.[6] This is the power with which there coincides the act, the *possest*. The divine attributes, multiple to our eyes, coincide in the divine essence. The circle is the perfect figure of unity and simplicity. All theology is, then, circular as it were.[7] Negative theology is superior to affirmative theology.[8] Better than either is that which unites the two. They coincide in copulative theology.[9] God is neither one nor trine. He is the unity with which the trinity coincides; he is *unitrine* or *triune*.[10]

All is in God. He complicates, comprises, or *enfolds* all things in his infinite simplicity and, at the same time, he is in all things. He explicates or *unfolds* all. The *complicatio* coincides with the *explicatio*.[11]

God's providence unites contraries, and, by consequence, nothing is able to escape him. This *providence* is at once the center and circumference of the world. It is everywhere and nowhere. In a word, it is *non aliud*.[12]

John Wenck, professor of theology at Heidelberg, tries to make Cusa out a pantheist in his *De ignota litteratura*. Cusa answers him directly in his *Apologia doctae ignorantiae*. Because all things are in God as things caused are in the cause, it hardly follows that what is caused is itself the cause.[13] What, then, of all this as it affects Cusa's immediately mystical experience? What of Christ, of the church, of faith, and the rest?

At the summit of the creatures, if one excepts the angels, there is found human nature, which "complicates" in itself the intellectual nature and the sensible nature. By sin the upward movement of the universe found itself thwarted and driven back. It was unable to eventuate except as a superior being

---

[5] *Ibid.*, I, 1, 12.   [6] *Ibid.*, I, 4.   [7] *Ibid.*, I, 21.
[8] *Ibid.*, I, 24, on the "Positive" and I, 26, on the "Negative."
[9] *De filiatione Dei*, Petzelt, *op. cit.*, I, 235.
[10] *Doct. ign.*, I, 19.
[11] *Ibid.*, II, 3. The Latin *complicatio* plays upon "folding up," hence "*enfold-ing*," enveloping, comprising, implicating. *Explicatio* means "*unfolding*," developing, explaining, explicating.
[12] *Doct. ign.*, I, 22; II, 11–12.
[13] *Per hoc enim, quod omnia sunt in Deo ut causata in causa, non sequitur causatum esse causam. Apol. D. I.*, fol. 37 v., Petzelt, *op. cit.*, I, 285.

reattached it to God. This being was Christ, who was at once the maximum absolute and the maximum contracted. He was creator and creature, in the person of whom there coincide divinity and humanity as well as nature and grace. His humanity was not merely individual like that of other men. Jesus was the perfect man, the "maximum" man, in whom human nature implicated all the power of the species. As maximal man, therefore, he was unable to be born in a purely natural way. The Father "clothed his Son in human nature by means of the Holy Spirit," with the aid of the virgin mother. In his Passion and death, the sins of all men were concentrated and mortified. His maximal humanity made possible a triumphant destiny for all those adhering to him in the meritorious union of faith founded in love. To attain his own proper end, therefore, man must unite himself as closely as possible to Christ, by faith and works. The faithful, circumcised, baptized, and brought to death in him, are likewise resurrected to new life in him. Christ appeared, therefore, in the proper order of things and in the fullness of time as a *natura media*, "complicating" or "enfolding" in himself all natures and thus leading the entire universe to the highest possible degree of perfection. In him maximum and minimum coincide; maximum humiliation is joined to supreme exaltation.[14]

As to mystical theology itself, Nicholas saw in the "learned ignorance" the point of departure. He identified the "coincidence of contraries" with the threshold of paradise where God hides himself in the cloud. Beyond this, there stretches out the domain of faith and of vision, says Cusa. Faith must there serve as guide. It is the beginning of intelligence because it "complicates" or "enfolds" all intelligence. Desire must there impel one with ardor until the moment when one is raised to "simple intellectuality" where one passes, so to speak, from slumber to the state of vigil, from audition to vision. Here one is, like Paul, ravished in ecstasy and admitted to the intuition of the ineffable.[15]

The faith of which Cusa speaks was already a faith formed by love. But, to the extent that he meditates on the mystic way, he understands better how, in order to raise the soul beyond the wall of coincidence, the way of love is the easiest and the surest; because God makes himself known to those whom he loves, to those who love him.

[14] *Doct. ign.*, III, 2–6. [15] *Ibid.*, III, 11.

Questioned by his monastic friends as to whether the mystic ascent was to be prosecuted solely by love to the exclusion of all knowledge, he said, No! He thus ranged himself on the side of Gerson against the Chartreux Vincent d'Aggsbach. God is beyond all coincidence of the true and the good. On the other hand, perfect charity is above the coincidence of containing and contents. According to Scripture, "The one remaining in love remains in me and I in him." Therefore, the love of God and the knowledge of God do not proceed, the one without the other. At the limit they blend to become one, only.[16]

The experience of God found in the *Vision* and *On Learned Ignorance* is that of ineffable sweetness and intellectually ordered delight. The theme of these works, as of the *Sermons* and many tracts, is the translatability of God's love revealed in Christ to the sober work of the world.[17] The need and the power of Christiformity constitute the passionate refrain of his sermonic exhortations. The joyous burden of his efforts as scholar, teacher, writer, preacher, scientist, philosopher, conciliarist, bishop, and cardinal was the application of the contemplative way opened *through* Christ to the active way pursued *with* Christ. In him, who was the Mediator between God and man, the life of contemplation has already become the way of action.

The way of faith that is the beginning of understanding, the learned ignorance by which Paul saw the Christ formerly hidden to him, the verities revealing themselves to him who raises himself to Christ by faith—all these are a part of the vision that unites the believer to Christ and the holy wisdom with which contemplation invests itself in action.

Cusa followed the vision celestial into the harvest field of the world. This is best proved in his works that celebrate the church, her sacraments, her hierarchy, and her preached gospel as the servants of the eternal Kingdom in the temporal world. Here in the Eucharist, Christ the Head, united to the Father, spiritually vivifies the faithful in a redemptive work in, and for, the world. Here, then, is the bread of life—Christ the bread-giving life—bread obtainable only by faith, faith that calls alike

---

16 Consult the invaluable work of Vansteenberghe, "Autour de la docte ignorance," in *Beiträge*, Vol. 14, pts. 2–4 (Münster i/W, 1915), pp. 1–220, and especially the "Documents," i.e., "Correspondance," pp. 107 ff. See particularly "Corresp.," nos. 4, 5, 9, 16.

17 See convenient materials in F. U. Scharpff, *Wichtigste Schriften*, Freiburg, i/B, 1862, and the *Excitationum ex sermonibus*, in the Basel *Opera*. Note, also, the sermons in this anthology.

for the preaching of the gospel and the justifying host. The "love of your neighbor is not enough, unless it is also in God, and the existence of the sacrament is necessary for salvation, so that you may be incorporated in the unity of the body of Christ and the head of Christ, for otherwise you cannot live."

Nicholas of Cusa (1401-1464)

ON LEARNED IGNORANCE [18]

The Text

Book I, Chapter 1

How "To Know" Is "Not to Know"

We see that, by divine grace, there is within all things a certain natural desire to be better, in the manner which the natural condition of each one permits, and that those beings in whom judgment is innate act toward this end and have the necessary instruments; this is in accord with the goal of knowledge so that the longing for it may not be vain, and that it may be able to reach repose in the desired equilibrium of its own nature. If, by chance, it happens otherwise, that comes necessarily from an accident, as when sickness warps the taste or simple opinion warps reasoning. For this reason we say that the sound and free intellect, which insatiably, from an innate quest, longs to attain the true by examining all, knows the true when it apprehends it in an amorous embrace, for we do not doubt the perfect truth of that which all sound minds are unable to reject.

Now all those who investigate judge of the uncertain by comparing it to a reliable presupposition by a system of proportion. All inquiry, therefore, is comparative, using the means of proportion so that as long as the objects of inquiry can be compared to the presupposition by a close proportional reduction, the judgment of apprehension is easy; but if we have need of many intermediaries, then difficulty and trouble arise. This is well known in mathematics, where the first propositions are easily referred to the first principles which are very well known, but

---

18 The translation, based on the text of P. Rotta, Bari, 1913, is that of James Bruce Ross, who, with Mary Martin McLaughlin, edits *The Portable Medieval Reader*, New York (Copyright, 1949, by The Viking Press). The passages, used by permission of The Viking Press, are pp. 667–75. In order, they are from Book I, Chapters 1, 2, and 3, and Book III, Chapter 11.

the later ones, since they need the intermediary of the first, present much more difficulty. All inquiry, therefore, consists in comparative proportion, easy or difficult, and that is why the infinite, which as infinite escapes all proportion, is unknown.

Now proportion, since in anything it expresses agreement together with difference, cannot be understood without number. Number, consequently, includes all that is susceptible to proportion. Number, therefore, does not create proportion in quantity only, but in all those things which in any way, by substance or accident, can agree or differ. Hence Pythagoras judged with vigor that everything was constituted and understood through the force of numbers. But the precision of combinations in material things and the exact adaptation of the known to the unknown so far surpass human reason that it seemed to Socrates that he knew nothing except his ignorance,[19] and the very wise Solomon affirmed that all things are difficult and inexplicable in language. And another man of divine spirit says that wisdom is hidden, and also the seat of intelligence, from the eyes of the living. If, therefore, it is true, as likewise the very profound Aristotle affirms in his *First Philosophy*, that such a difficulty befalls us in the things most manifest in nature, like owls trying to see the sun, since the divine in us is certainly not vain, we need to know that we are ignorant. If we can attain this end completely, we shall attain "learned ignorance."[20] For nothing becomes a man, even the most zealous, more perfectly in learning that to be found very learned in ignorance itself, which is his characteristic, and anyone will be the more learned the more he knows his own ignorance. On this goal of learned ignorance I have assumed the labor of writing a few words.

Book I, Chapter 2

Preliminary Explanation of What Follows

Before treating the greatest doctrine, that of ignorance, I consider it necessary to take up the nature of "the quality of being maximum" [*maximitas*]. Now I call "maximum" a thing than which nothing can be greater. Plenitude, in truth, is appropriate to one; that is why unity coincides with "the quality of being maximum," and it is also entity. Now if such unity is absolute universally, beyond all relation and all concreteness, it is clear,

19 *Nihil scire, nisi quod ignoraret.* . . .
20 *Doctam ignorantiam assequemur.*

since it is the absolute "quality of being maximum," that nothing is opposed to it. And so the absolute maximum is one, which is all, in which all is, because it is the maximum. And since nothing is opposed to it, with it at the same time coincides the minimum; wherefore it is thus in everything. And because it is absolute, then it is actually all possible being, undergoing no restrictions from things and imposing them on all.

This maximum, which by the indubitable faith of all nations is accepted also as God, I shall, in my first book on human reason, labor to seek, though incomprehensibly, led by that One who, alone, lives in inaccessible light.

In the second place, as the absolute quality of being maximum is absolute entity, by which all things are what they are, so universal unity of being comes from that which is called absolute maximum, and therefore exists concretely as universe, whose unity, indeed, is restricted in plurality without which it cannot be. This maximum, indeed, although in its universal unity it embraces everything, so that all which comes from the absolute is in it and it is in all, does not, however, have subsistence outside of plurality, in which it is, because it does not exist without concreteness from which it cannot be freed. Concerning this maximum, which appears as the universe, I shall add some remarks in my second book.

In the third place, the maximum will show the necessity of a third order of consideration. For, as the universe subsists concretely only in plurality, we shall seek in the multiple things themselves, the maximum one, in whom the universe subsists most greatly and most perfectly both in its realization and in its end. And since this universe unites itself with the absolute, which is the universal goal, because it is the end which is most perfect and beyond all our capacities, I shall add below on this maximum, at the same time concrete and absolute, which we call by the name forever blessed of Jesus, some words as Jesus himself shall inspire. He who wishes to attain the meaning of what I am going to say must raise the intelligence above the force of the words themselves, rather than insist on the properties of words, which cannot be adapted properly to such great intellectual mysteries. It is necessary to use in a transcendental fashion the examples which my hand will trace, so that the reader, leaving aside sensible things, should rise easily to simple intellectuality. I have applied myself to seeking this way with ordinary talents, as clearly as I could, avoiding any roughness of style, to lay bare the root of learned ignorance, making it manifest at once although not with the comprehensible precision of truth.

Book I, Chapter 3

That Precise Truth Is Incomprehensible

Because it is clear in itself that there is no proportion of the infinite to the finite, from this it is most clear that where one finds something which exceeds and something which is exceeded, one does not arrive at the simple maximum, since what exceeds and what is exceeded are finite objects while the simple maximum is necessarily infinite. No matter what has been given, if it is not the simple maximum itself, it is clear that a greater one can be given.

And because we find that equality permits degrees, so that a certain thing is more equal to one than to another, according to the points of agreement and difference, in genus, in species, of place, of influence, and of time, with similar things, it is clear that one cannot find two or more objects similar and equal to such a point that objects more similar still can not exist in infinite number. Let the measures and the objects measured be as equal as can be, there will always be differences. Therefore, our finite intellect cannot, by means of similitude, understand with precision the truth of things. For truth, existing in a certain indivisible nature, is not either more or less, and all that is not true itself is not able to measure it with precision; thus what is not circle cannot measure the circle whose being consists in something indivisible. Therefore the understanding, which is not truth, never attains truth with such precision that it cannot be attained more precisely by the infinite: for it is to truth as the polygon is to the circle; the greater the number of angles inscribed in the polygon, the more it will be like the circle, but nevertheless it is never made equal to the circle, even if one multiplies the angles infinitely, unless it breaks down into identity with the circle. It is clear, therefore, that we know nothing concerning the true except that we know it to be incomprehensible precisely as it is; for truth, being absolute necessity, which cannot be more or less than it is, presents itself to our understanding as possibility. Therefore, the quiddity of things, which is the truth of beings, is unattainable in its purity; all philosophers have sought it, none has found it, such as it is; and the more we shall be profoundly learned in this ignorance, the more we shall approach truth itself.

Book III, Chapter 11

The Mysteries of Faith

Our ancestors assert with one voice that faith is the beginning of understanding. For in every discipline certain things are presupposed as first principles, which are apprehended by faith alone and from which springs the comprehension of the matters treated. Every man who wishes to raise himself to knowledge must necessarily believe in the things without which he cannot raise himself. As Isaiah says, "Unless you believe, you will not understand." Faith, therefore, comprises in herself all that is intelligible. Understanding is the explication of faith. Understanding is, therefore, directed by faith, and faith is developed by understanding. Where there is no sound faith, there is no true understanding. It is clear to what conclusion error in principle and fragility in foundations lead. There is no faith more perfect than the truth itself, which is Jesus.[21] Who does not understand that the most excellent gift of God is perfect faith? The apostle John says that faith in the incarnation of the Word of God leads us to truth, in order that we may become sons of God; that is what he shows simply in his exordium, and then he recounts numerous works of Christ consonant with this belief that understanding is illuminated by faith. Therefore he comes finally to this conclusion, saying: "These things were written so that you might believe that Jesus is the Son of God."

Now that sweetest faith in Christ, firmly sustained in simplicity, may by stages of ascent be extended and developed according to the aforesaid doctrine, that of ignorance. For the greatest and most profound mysteries of God, hidden from those who go about in the world, however wise they may be, have been revealed to the small and humble in the faith of Jesus, because Jesus is the one in whom all the treasures of wisdom and science are enclosed, and without whom no one can do anything. For he is the Word and the Power by whom God created the very ages, alone, the highest, having power over all things in heaven and on earth. This One, since he is not knowable in this world, where reason, opinion, and knowledge lead us by symbols through the better known to the unknown, can be grasped only there where proofs cease and faith begins, by which we are ravished in simplicity so that beyond all reason and intelligence,

---

21 *Ubi igitur non est sana fides, nullus est verus intellectus. . . . Nulla autem perfectiori fides quam ipsamet veritas, quae Iesus est. Doct. ign.,* III, 11, *Opera omnia,* I, 152 (Kallen).

in the third heaven of the most simple intellectuality, we may contemplate him in his body incorporeally, because in spirit, and in the world but not of the world, but celestially and incomprehensibly in order that it may be understood that he is incomprehensible by reason of his infinite excellence.

And this is that learned ignorance by which the most blessed Paul himself, arising, saw that Christ whom he formerly only had knowledge of; he did not know when he was raised higher up to him. We are led, therefore, we faithful in Christ, in learned ignorance to that mountain which is Christ, which the nature of our animality prevents us from attaining, and when we try to perceive it with the intellectual eye, we fall down in the fog, knowing only that this fog hides us from the mountain, on which only those may live who flourish in understanding.[22] If we approach this with a greater firmness in our faith, we are snatched away from the eyes of those who wander in the world of the senses, so that with internal hearing we perceive the voices, the thunder, and the terrible signs of the majesty of God, easily perceiving the Lord himself, whom all things obey, advancing by stages in the imperishable traces of his steps, like I do not know what divine creatures; and hearing the voice, not of mortal creatures, but of God himself in the holy organs and in the signs of his prophets and saints, we contemplate him more clearly, as if through the cloud of reason. Then the believers, with more burning desire, rising continually, are carried up to intellectuality in its simplicity, passing beyond all sensible things, as if from sleep to waking, from hearing to sight, where those things are seen which cannot be revealed, because they are beyond all hearing and the teaching of the voice. For if what is revealed there had to be expressed, then the inexpressible would be expressed and the inaudible would be heard, just as the invisible is seen there. For Jesus, blessed throughout the ages, end of all intellection, since he is truth; end of all sensibility since he is life; end ultimately of all being, because he is entity; perfection of every created being as God and man, is incomprehensibly heard there as the limit of every word. For from him proceeds, to him returns every word; all that is true in the word comes from him. Every word has as its goal edification, therefore him, who is wisdom itself. All that has been written has been for our edification. The words are represented in the

---

[22] Cf. *Doct. ign.*, I, 24, 26, and Vansteenberghe, in *Beiträge*, Vol. 14, pt. 2, "Correspondance," no. 5, pp. 113–17. Cf. Dionysius, *Mystical Theology*, I, 1 ff.

Scriptures, the heavens are sustained by the Word of God. Therefore, all created things are signs of the Word of God. Every corporeal word is the sign of the spiritual Word. The cause of every spiritual corruptible word is the incorruptible Word, which is reason. Christ is the incarnate reason of all reasons, because the Word was made flesh. Jesus therefore is the end of everything.

Such are the verities which reveal themselves by degrees to him who raises himself to Christ by faith. The divine efficacy of this faith is inexplicable for, if it is great, it unites the believer to Jesus, so that he is above all that is not in unity with Jesus himself.

THE VISION OF GOD [23]

Chapter XIX

How Jesus Is the Union of God and Man

I render unto thee thanks unspeakable, O God, light and life of my soul. For I now perceive the faith which, by the teaching of the apostles, the Catholic Church holdeth, to wit, how thou, a loving God, dost beget of thyself a lovable God, and how thou, the lovable God-begotten, art the absolute mediator. For 'tis through thee that all existeth which doth exist or can exist, since thou, the loving or willing God, enfoldest them all in thee, the lovable God. For all that thou, O God, willest or conceivest is enfolded in thee, the lovable God. Nought can exist except thou will it to be. Wherefore all things have their cause or reason for being in thy lovable concept, and the sole cause of them all is that it so pleaseth thee; nought pleaseth a lover, as a lover, save the lovable. Thou, O lovable God, art the Son of God the loving Father, since in thee is all the Father's delight. Thus all creatable being is enfolded in thee, the lovable God.

Thou too, O loving God—since from thee cometh the lovable God, as a son from a father—art the Father of all beings by reason that thou art God, the loving Father of the lovable God thy Son. For thy concept is a Son, in whom are all things, and thy union and thy concept is act and operation arising therefrom—the act and operation wherein existeth the actuality and unfolding of all things. As therefore of thee, the loving God, there is begotten the lovable God, and this generation is a concept, even so there proceedeth from thee, the loving God, and from thy concept, the lovable God begotten of thee, thine act and concept, to wit, the bond knitting together and the God

23 The translation is that of E. G. Salter, *Nicholas of Cusa: The Vision of God*, 1928, pp. 92–130, used by permission of J. M. Dent & Co., London (E. P. Dutton & Co., New York).

uniting thee and thy concept, even as the act of loving uniteth in love the lover and the beloved. And this bond is called Spirit; for spirit is like motion, proceeding from that which moveth and that which is moved. Thus motion is the unfolding of the concept of him that moveth. Wherefore in thee, God the Holy Spirit, all things are unfolded, even as they are conceived in thee, God the Son.[24]

I perceive, then—thou, God, enlightening me—how all things of God the Father are in thee, God the Son, as in his reason, concept, cause, or exemplar, and how the Son mediateth all things because he is the reason. For 'tis by means of reason and wisdom that thou, God the Father, workest all things, and the spirit or motion giveth effect unto the concept of reason, as we learn from the craftsman who, by the motive power in his hands, giveth effect unto the coffer which he hath in his mind. Thus, my God, I perceive how thy Son mediateth the union of all things, that all may find rest in thee by the mediation of thy Son. And I see that blessed Jesus, Son of Man, is most closely united unto thy Son, and that the son of man could not be united unto thee, God the Father, save by mediation of thy Son, the absolute mediator.

Who would not be ravished to the highest in the attentive consideration of these things? Thou, my God, disclosest unto me, a poor wretch, this so great secret that I may perceive that man cannot apprehend thee, the Father, save in thy Son, who may be apprehended and who is the mediator, and that to apprehend thee is to be united unto thee. Man, then, can be united unto thee through thy Son, who is the means of union; and human nature most closely knit unto thee, in whatsoever man it be, cannot be more united unto the intermediary than it is, for without an intermediary it cannot be united unto thee. Thus it is united in the closest degree unto the intermediary, yet it doth not become the intermediary: wherefore, albeit it cannot become the intermediary (since it cannot be united unto thee without an intermediary), 'tis yet so joined unto the absolute intermediary that nought can mediate between it and thy Son, the absolute mediator. For if aught could mediate between human nature and the absolute mediator, human nature would not then be united unto thee in the closest degree.

O good Jesu, I perceive that in thee human nature is linked most closely unto God the Father, by that most exalted union

[24] Cf. *Doct. ign.*, II, 3, and the works of M. de Gandillac, Koch, etc., already cited on *complicatio* and *explicatio*, "enfolding" and "unfolding."

through which it is linked unto God the Son, the absolute mediator. Since thou art Son of Man, human sonship is in the highest degree united in thee, Jesu, unto the divine Sonship, so that thou art rightly called Son of God and Son of Man, for in thee nought mediateth between those twain. In that absolute Sonship, which is the Son of God, is enfolded all sonship, and thereunto thy human sonship, Jesu, is supremely united. Accordingly, thy human sonship subsisteth in the divine, not only as enfolded therein, but as that which is attracted in that which attracteth, and that which is united in that which uniteth, and that which is substantiated in that which giveth substance. Thus in thee, Jesu, there can be no possible separation between Son of Man and Son of God. Possibility of separation ariseth from the fact that a union is not of the closest, but, where a union is of the closest possible, there no intermediary can exist. Separation, then, can have no place where nought can mediate between the things united. But where that which is united subsisteth not in that which uniteth, the union is not the closest possible; for 'tis a closer union where the united subsisteth in the uniter than where it subsisteth separately, separation being a withdrawal from perfect union.

Thus in thee, my Jesu, I see how the human sonship whereby thou art Son of Man subsisteth in the divine Sonship whereby thou art Son of God, as in the most perfect union that which is united subsisteth in that which uniteth. Glory be to thee, O God, throughout all ages!

Chapter XX

How Jesus Is Understood to Be the Union of the Divine Nature and the Human Nature

Thou showest me, O Light unfailing, that the perfect union whereby human nature is united through my Jesus with thy divine nature is not in any wise like unto infinite union. The union whereby thou, God the Father, art united unto God thy Son is God the Holy Spirit, and thus 'tis an infinite union, seeing that it attaineth unto absolute and essential identity. 'Tis not so when human nature is united unto the divine, for human nature cannot pass over into essential union with the divine, even as the finite cannot be infinitely united unto the infinite, because it would pass into identity with the infinite, and thus would cease to be finite when the infinite were verified in it. Wherefore this union, whereby human nature is united unto the divine nature, is nought else than the attraction in the highest degree of the human nature unto the divine, in such wise that human nature, as such, could not be attracted to greater heights. This union, then, of human nature, as such, with the divine is the greatest, in the sense of being the greatest possible, but it is not purely and simply the greatest, and infinite, as is the divine union.

Thus through the bounty of thy grace I see in thee, Jesu, Son of Man, the Son of God, and in the Son of God, the Father. Now, in thee, the Son of Man, I see the Son of God, because thou art both of these alike, and in thy finite nature which is attracted I perceive the infinite nature which attracteth; in the absolute Son I behold the absolute Father, for the Son cannot be seen as Son unless the Father be seen. I behold in thee, Jesu, the divine Sonship which is the truth of all sonship, and equally with it the highest human sonship, which is the most approximate image of the absolute Sonship. Just as the image, between which and the exemplar no more perfect image can be interposed, hath an existence nearest in truth to the object whereof it is the image, even so I perceive thy human nature subsisting in the divine nature.

Accordingly, I see in thy human nature all that I see in the divine, but I see that in thy human nature those attributes exist in human guise which in the divine nature are divine truth itself. That which I see to exist in human guise in thee, Jesu, is a likeness unto the divine nature, but the likeness is united unto the exemplar without a medium, in such wise that no greater likeness can exist or be imagined. In thy human or rational nature I see the rational human spirit most closely united unto the divine Spirit, which is absolute reason, and so the human intelligence and all things in thine intelligence, Jesu, united unto the divine intelligence. For thou, Jesu, as God, dost understand all, and to understand in this sense is to be all. As Man, thou understandest all, and to understand in this sense is to be a likeness of all. For man only comprehendeth things by a likeness; a stone existeth not in human understanding as in its proper cause or nature, but as in its specific idea and likeness. Thus in thee, Jesu, human intelligence is united unto the divine intelligence itself, even as a most perfect image unto the truth of its pattern. If I consider the ideal form of the coffer in the craftsman's mind and the species of coffer made by that master most perfectly carrying out his idea, I learn how the ideal form is the truth of the species, and that only in this one master is it united unto it as truth is unto the image. So in thee, Jesu, Master of masters, I see that the absolute idea of all things, and with it what resembles it in species, is united in the highest degree.

I see thee, good Jesu, within the wall of paradise, since thine intelligence is alike truth and image, and thou art alike God and creature, alike infinite and finite. And 'tis not possible that thou shouldst be seen this side of the wall, for thou art the bond between the divine nature that createth and the human nature that is created.

Howbeit, between thy human intellect and that of any other man soever I perceive a difference: for no one man knoweth all things that may be known by man, since no man's intellect is so joined unto the exemplar of all things, as the image unto the truth, but that it could not be more nearly joined, and more actually set therein, and so it doth not understand so much but that it could understand yet more, had it access unto the exemplar of things whence every thing actually existent deriveth its actuality. But thine intellect actually understandeth all that may be apprehended of men, because in thee human nature is in full perfection, and most entirely joined unto its exemplar. By means of this union, thy human intelligence exceedeth all created intelligence in perfection of understanding. Wherefore, all rational spirits are far beneath thee, and thou, Jesu, art the Master and Light of them all, and thou art perfection, and the fullness of all things, and by thee they attain unto absolute truth, as by their mediator. For thou art alike the way unto truth, and the truth itself; thou art alike the way unto the life of the intellect and that life itself; thou art alike the fragrance of the food of joy and the taste that maketh joyful. Be thou, then, more sweet Jesu, blessed forever!

Chapter XXI

That Bliss Is Not Possible Without Jesus

O Jesu, thou end of the universe, in whom resteth, as in the final degree of perfection, every creature, thou art utterly unknown to the wise of this world. For of thee we affirm many antitheses that are yet most true, since thou art alike Creator and creature, alike he that attracteth and he that is attracted, alike finite and infinite. They pronounce it folly to believe this possible, and because of it they flee from thy name, and do not receive thy light whereby thou hast illumined us. But, esteeming themselves wise, they remain forever foolish, and ignorant, and blind. Yet if they would believe that thou art Christ, God and Man, and would receive and handle the words of the gospel as being those of so great a Master, then at last they would see most clearly that, in comparison with that light there hidden in the simplicity of thy words, all things else are nought but thickest shadows, and ignorance. Thus 'tis only humble believers who attain unto this most gracious and life-giving revelation. There is hidden in thy most holy gospel, which is heavenly food, as there was in the manna, sweetness to satisfy all desire, which can only be tasted by him that believeth and eateth. If any believeth and receiveth it, he shall prove and find the truth, because thou didst come down from heaven and thou alone art the Master of truth.

O good Jesu, thou art the Tree of Life, in the paradise of delights, and none may feed upon that desirable life save from thy fruit. Thou art, O Jesu, the food forbidden to all sons of Adam who, expelled from paradise, seek their sustenance from the earth whereon they toil. Wherefore it behoveth every man to put off the old man of presumption and to put on the new man of humility, which is after thy pattern, if he hope to taste the food of life within the paradise of delights. The nature of the new and of the old Adam is one, but in the old Adam it is animal; in thee, the new Adam, it is spiritual, for in thee, Jesu, it is united unto God, who is Spirit. Wherefore, every man must needs be united in one spirit unto thee, Jesu, even as he is by the human nature that is common to himself and to thee, to the end that thus in his own nature, which thou, Jesu, dost share, he may be able to draw near unto God the Father, who is in paradise. Now to behold God the Father, and thee, Jesu, his Son, is to be in paradise, and is glory everlasting. For he that stayeth outside paradise cannot have such a vision, since neither God the Father nor thou, Jesu, are to be found outside paradise.

Every man, then, hath attained bliss who is united unto thee, Jesu, as a limb unto the head. None can come unto the Father unless he be drawn by the Father. The Father drew thy humanity, Jesu, by his Son, and by thee, Jesu, the Father draweth all men. Just as thy humanity, Jesu, is united unto the Son of God the Father, as unto the means whereby the Father drew it, even so the humanity of every man soever is united unto thee, Jesu, as unto the one and only means whereby the Father draweth all men. Therefore without thee, Jesu, 'tis impossible for any man to attain bliss. Thou art, Jesu, the revelation of the Father. For the Father is invisible to all, and visible only to thee, his Son, and, after thee, to him who through thee and thy revelation shall be found worthy to behold Him. Thou art, therefore, he that uniteth each of the blessed, and each of the blessed subsisteth in thee, as that which is united in that which uniteth.

None of the wise men of this world can attain true bliss while he knoweth thee not. None of the blessed can see the Father in paradise save with thee, Jesu. Antitheses are made true in the blessed, even as in thee, Jesu, since he is united unto thee in a rational, natural, and single spirit. For every blissful spirit subsisteth in thine, as that which is quickened in the life-giver. Every blissful spirit beholdeth the invisible God and is united in thee, Jesu, unto God the unapproachable and immortal. And thus in thee the finite is united unto the infinite, and unto that which is beyond union, and the incomprehensible is possessed in an eternal fruition which is bliss most joyous and inexhaustible. Be merciful unto me, Jesu, be merciful, and grant me to behold thee unveiled, and my soul is healed!

Chapter XXII

How Jesus Seeth and How He Hath Worked

The mind's eye cannot be sated in beholding thee, Jesu, because thou art the fulfillment of all beauty the mind can picture, and in this icon I conjecture thy right marvelous and astounding sight, Jesu blessed above all. For thou, Jesu, whilst thou didst walk this world of sense, didst use eyes of flesh like unto ours. With them thou didst see, even as we men do, one object and another, for there was in thine eyes a certain spirit which informed the organ, like the sensitive mind in an animal's body. In that spirit there was a noble power of discernment whereby thou, Lord, didst see and distinguish between one object of one color and another of another. And, yet more, from the aspect of the face and eyes of the men whom thou sawest thou didst judge truly of the passions of the soul—anger, joy, sorrow. And more subtly still thou didst comprehend from few tokens what was hidden in a man's mind (for nothing is conceived in the mind that is not in some way shown in the face, which is the heart's herald, and especially in the eyes). By all these tokens thou didst much more truly reach the inmost places of the soul than any created spirit can. From any one sign, albeit of the slightest,

thou didst perceive the man's whole thought, even as understanding men grasp from a few words an idea that requireth a
whole long discourse to set it forth, and even as the learned,
from running their eye hastily over a book, can narrate the
writer's whole intent as though they had read it through.

Thou, Jesu, didst excel in this manner of vision all the perfection, swiftness, and keenness of all men past, present, and to
come, and yet this sight was human because it was not perfected
without the eye of flesh. Howbeit, it was stupendous and marvelous. For if there be men who, after prolonged and subtle examining, can read the mind of a writer, under characters and
signs newly devised at the time, and unseen before, thou, Jesu,
didst perceive all things under every sign and figure.

If, as we read, there was once a man who, by certain tokens
in the eye, knew the thoughts of an interrogator, even the verses
that he might be repeating to himself, thou, Jesu, hadst more
skill than all in grasping all the mind's thought from each glance
of the eye. I myself have seen a deaf woman who read everything from the movement of her daughter's lips, and understood it as if she had heard it. If such a thing is possible by long
practice among deaf and dumb persons, and Religious who
converse by signs, thou, Jesu, who, as a Master of masters,
actually knewest all that is to be known, didst more perfectly
form a true judgment of the heart and its thoughts from the
slightest glances and signs invisible to us.

But unto this thy human sight, most perfect albeit finite and
limited unto an organ, there was united an absolute and infinite
sight—the sight whereby thou, as God, didst see alike all things
and each, absent as well as present, past as well as future. Thus,
Jesu, with thy human eye thou sawest such accidentals as are
visible, but with thy divine, absolute sight the substance of
things. None save thee, Jesu, ever in the flesh beheld the substance or essence of things. Thou alone sawest most truly the
soul and spirit and whatsoever there was in man. For as in man
the faculty of understanding is linked with the animal faculty of
sight, so that a man not only seeth like an animal but also, as a
man, discerneth and judgeth, so in thee, Jesu, the absolute
sight was united unto the human faculty of understanding,
which, in the animal sight, is discernment. In man, the faculty
of animal sight subsisteth, not in itself, but in the reasoning soul,
as in the form of the whole: in thee, Jesu, the intellectual faculty
of sight subsisteth, not in itself, but in the faculty of absolute
sight. O most sweet Jesu, how marvelous is thy sight!

Sometimes it befalleth us to fix our gaze on a passer-by without giving heed to recognize who he was; so we cannot tell the name of that passer-by to any that asketh it, albeit it is a man we know, and we are aware that someone hath passed by. We have seen him as an animal might, not like a man, because we have not applied our faculty of discernment. Whence we learn that the natures of our faculties, though they be bound up in one human form, do yet abide distinct, and have distinct workings. Even so in thee, the one Jesus, I perceive that the human intellectual nature was united after somewhat the same fashion unto the divine nature, and that in like manner thou didst many works as Man, and, as God, many marvelous works beyond what man could do. I see, most loving Jesu, that the intellectual nature is absolute in regard to that of the senses, and not, as is the sensible nature, finite and tied to an organ, as the seeing faculty of the senses is tied to the eye; but the divine faculty is immeasurably more absolute, beyond the intellectual. For the human intellect, if it is to find expression in action, requireth images, and images cannot be had without the senses, and senses subsist not without a body; and by reason of this the faculty of human intelligence is limited, and slight, requiring the things aforesaid. Now the divine intelligence is necessity itself, independent, requiring nought—nay, rather do all things require it, since without it they cannot exist.

I consider more attentively how the discursive faculty which, in the process of reasoning, runneth hither and thither, and seeketh, is another thing from the faculty which judgeth and understandeth.[25] We see a dog run hither and thither, and seek his master, and recognize him and hear his call. This running about is natural to an animal, and in the dog is found in a degree of specific perfection. There are other animals that are even keener in this pursuit, according to their more perfect species, and in man this pursuit most nearly approacheth the intellectual faculty, so that it is the summit of perfection in the senses, embracing many, nay, innumerable degrees of perfection, on a lower level than the intellectual, as the different species of animals reveal unto us. For there is no species which shareth not the degree of perfection proper unto itself. Each of the degrees hath a wide space within whose limits we see individuals of the species partaking of the species in divers ways. In like manner the intellectual nature hath, on a lower level than

25 *Doct. ign.*, I, 2–4.

the divine, innumerable degrees. Whence, just as in the intellectual nature all degrees of perfection of the senses are implied, so in the divine are implied all degrees of perfection, alike of the intellect and of the senses, and all others. Thus in thee, my Jesu, I behold all perfection.

Since thou art all-perfect Man, I see in thee an intellect united unto a rational or discursive faculty, which is the supreme faculty of the senses. And thus I see that thine intellect was set in thy reason as in its own place, like unto a candle placed in a room, which illumineth the room, and all the walls, and the whole building, howbeit by more or less according to the degree of its distance from them. Finally, I see that in thee the divine Word is united unto a sovran intellect, and that the place where the Word is received is that intellect itself, just as in ourselves we prove that the intellect is the place where the word of a master is received, as if the sun's light should be joined unto the candle afore chosen. For the Word of God illumineth the intellect as the sun's light illumineth this world. Wherefore in thee, my Jesu, I perceive the life of the senses illumined by the light of the intellect; the life of the intellect as a light that illumineth and that is illumined; and the divine life, which illumineth alone. For I see in thine intellectual light the very Fount of light, to wit, the Word of God which is truth, illumining every intellect. Thou only, then, art the highest of all creatures, since thou art thus at once creature and blessed Creator.

Chapter XXIII

How that When Jesus Died His Union with Life Persisted

O Jesu, the mind's most delectable food, when I look upon thee within the wall of paradise, how marvelous dost thou appear unto me! For thou art the Word of God humanified, and thou art man deified. Yet art not thou as it were compounded of God and man? Between component parts some proportion is necessary, without which there can be no composition, but there is no proportion between the finite and infinite. Nor art thou the coincidence of the creature and Creator, in the sense in which coincidence maketh one thing to be another. For human nature is not divine, nor divine nature human. The divine nature is not mutable, nor can it be changed into another nature, since it is eternity itself. Nor can any nature by reason of its union with the divine pass over into another nature: as is illustrated in the case of the image, when united unto its truth. For an image cannot be said to become other when thus united, but rather to withdraw itself from otherness, because it is united unto its own truth, which is unchangeableness itself.

Neither, most sweet Jesu, canst thou be said to be of an intermediate nature, between divine and human, for between these twain it is not possible for any intermediate nature to be set, partaking of both. For the divine nature may not be shared, since it is entirely and absolutely onefold, nor in that wise wouldst thou, blessed Jesu, be either God or man. But I see thee, Lord Jesu, to be One Person beyond all understanding, because thou art One Christ, in the same manner that I see thy human soul to be one, albeit therein, as in any human soul, I see there was a nature of the senses liable to corruption, subsisting in an intellectual and incorruptible nature.

That soul was not composite of corruptible and incorruptible, nor is the nature of the senses one with that of the intellect; but I perceive the intellectual soul to be united through the sentient faculty with the body, which it quickeneth. If a man's intellectual soul should stay from quickening the body without being separated from the body, that man would be dead, because life would cease; and yet his body would not be separated from life since the intellect is his life. 'Tis as when a man who had attentively sought by means of his sight to discern someone approaching becometh rapt in other thoughts and so withdraweth his attention from that pursuit, though his eyes are none the less directed toward it—that man's eye is not then separated from his mind, although it existeth in separation from the mind's discerning attention. But if that state of being rapt should not only cease quickening his discernment but should also cease quickening his senses, his eye would be dead because it would not be quickened. Howbeit, for all that, it would not be separated from the intellectual form, which is the form that giveth being, just as a withered hand remaineth united unto the form which maketh the whole body one.

There are men, so Saint Austin saith, who have skill to withdraw the life-giving spirit from their body, and appear dead and without feeling. In such a case, the intellectual nature would remain united unto the body, because that body would not exist under another form than afore; nay more, it would not only have the same form and remain the same body, while the quickening power would not cease to exist, but it would remain in union with the intellectual nature, albeit that did not actually extend itself unto the body. I perceive a man in such a case as one truly dead because he lacketh the quickening life (death being the lack of that which quickeneth), and yet he would not be a dead body separated from its life, which is its soul.

'Tis thus, Jesu most merciful, that I look upon the absolute life, which is God, inseparably united unto thy human intellect and thereby unto thy body. For that union is such that none can be closer. Every union that can be disparted is far inferior to that than which none can be closer. Wherefore it never was true, nor can it ever be, that thy divine nature was separated from thy human nature, nor yet from thy mind, nor thy body, the parts without which human nature cannot exist. Although it be most true that thy soul did cease from quickening thy body and that thou didst truly undergo death, yet wast thou never separated from true life. If that priest of whom Austin telleth had some kind of power of withdrawing from the body that which quickeneth, and attracting it into the soul—as if a candle illumining a room were a living thing, and should attract to the center of its light the beams whereby it illumined the room, without being separated from the room, and this attraction were nought else than ceasing to shed forth those beams—what marvel, then, if thou, Jesu, hadst the power (since thou art the most free of living lights), of assuming and of laying down thy quickening soul? When thou willedst to lay it down thou didst suffer death, and when thou willedst to resume it thou didst rise again in thine own might.

Now the intellectual nature, when it quickeneth or animateth the body, is called the human soul. And the soul is said to be removed when the human intellect ceaseth to quicken it. For when the intellect ceaseth from its function of quickening, and, with regard to that, separateth itself from the body, it is not therefore separated purely and simply.

These thoughts thou inspirest, Jesu, that thou mayest show thyself unto me, most unworthy, in so far as I can receive it, and that I may contemplate how in thee mortal human nature put on immortality, so that all men sharing that same human nature may in thee attain to resurrection and divine life. What can be sweeter, what more delightsome, than to know that in thee, Jesu, we find all things that be in our nature—in thee, who alone canst do all things, and givest most liberally and upbraidest not? O ineffable loving-kindness and mercy! Thou, God, who art goodness' self, couldest not satisfy thine infinite clemency and bounty unless thou gavest us thyself! Nor could this be done more beseemingly, more possibly, for us recipients than in thy taking on thee our nature, because we could not approach unto thine. Thus thou camest unto us, and art called Jesus, our Saviour ever blessed.[26]

Chapter XXIV

How Jesus Is the Word of Life

Of thine own best and greatest gift, my Jesus, I contemplate thee preaching words of life, and plentifully sowing the seed divine in the hearts of them that hear thee. I see those depart from thee who have not perceived the things that are of the Spirit. But I see the disciples remaining, who have already begun to taste the sweetness of the doctrine that quickeneth the soul. On behalf of all these, that prince and leader of all the apostles, Peter, confessed how thou, Jesu, hadst the words of life, and marveled that seekers after life should depart from thee. Paul in ecstasy heard from thee, Jesu, the words of life, and thereafter neither persecution nor sword nor bodily hunger could separate him from thee. None could depart from thee who had tasted the words of life. Who can separate a bear from honey after he hath once tasted the sweetness thereof? How great is the sweetness of truth which maketh life delightsome to the full! It surpasseth all bodily sweetness, for 'tis absolute sweetness, whence floweth all that is desired by every taste! What is stronger than love, whence all that is lovable hath that for which it is loved? If the bond of love in limitation be sometimes so strong that the fear of death cannot sever it, how strong is the bond when that love is tasted whence all love springeth? I wonder not that their cruel torments were accounted as nought by other of thy soldiers, Jesu, to whom thou hadst afforded a foretaste of thyself, the Life. O Jesu my Love, thou hast sowed the seed of life in the field of the faithful, and hast watered it by the witness of thy blood, and hast shown by bodily death that truth is the life of the rational spirit; the seed grew in good soil and bore fruit.

Thou showest me, Lord, how my soul is the breath of life in regard to my body, whereinto it breatheth and infuseth life, but 'tis not life in regard to thee, O God, but as it were a potentiality of life. Now, thou canst not but grant our petitions if they

[26] *Ibid.*, III, 4–8, 11.

be made in most expectant faith. And so thou dost inspire me with the thought that there is a soul in the child which hath vegetative power in actual exercise, since the child groweth; he hath also a percipient power in actual exercise, since the child feeleth; he hath moreover an imaginative power, but not as yet in actual exercise; and a reasoning power, the exercise whereof is as yet still more remote; he hath, too, an intellectual power, but that is even more delayed in developing. Thus we find that one and the same soul hath the lower powers in actual exercise first, and afterward the higher, as if man were animal before he is spiritual.

In the same way, we find that a certain mineral power, which can also be called spirit, existeth in the bowels of the earth, and hath the power to become a mineral of stone, or hath the power to become salt, or, again, the power to become a metal, and that there are divers such spirits in that stones, salts, and metals are diverse. Howbeit, there is but one spirit of the mineral of gold, which, being ever more and more refined through the influence of the sun or sky, is at last fashioned into gold of such a nature that it may not be corrupted by any element. And 'tis in it most chiefly that the heavenly incorruptible light shineth forth, for it much resembleth the sun's corporeal light. We find the same of the vegetative spirit and of the percipient spirit. The percipient spirit, in man, conformeth itself closely unto the motive and influential power of the heavens, under which influence it receiveth one increase after another, until it is set in perfect act. But as 'tis drawn out from the power of the body, its perfection ceaseth with the failing of the bodily perfection whereon it dependeth.

There is, finally, an intellectual spirit which, in the act of its perfection, is independent of the body, but is united thereunto by means of the percipient power; this spirit, being independent of the body, is not subject unto the influence of the heavenly bodies; 'tis independent of the percipient spirit, and thus of the motive power of the heavens. But, just as the motive forces of the heavenly bodies are subject unto the First Mover, so too is this moving force, which is the intellect. Howbeit, since 'tis united unto the body by means of the percipient power, it cometh not to perfection without the senses, since all that reacheth it from the world of sense doth so by the medium of the senses. Whence nought of this kind can exist in the intellect that hath not first existed in the senses, but the more the senses are pure and perfect, the imagination clear, and discursive reason in good state, the more the intellect in its intellectual operations is unhampered, and clear-sighted.

But the intellect feedeth on the Word of life, under whose influence it is stablished, like the motive forces of the orbs; howbeit in other fashion, as even the spirits which are subject unto the influences of the heavens come to perfection in divers ways. And the intellect is not perfected, save, incidentally, by the percipient spirit, just as an image maketh not perfect, albeit it stirreth up an inquiry after the truth of the exemplar. The image of the Crucified, for example, doth not inspire devotion, but kindleth the memory that devotion may be inspired. Since the intellectual spirit is not constrained by the influence of the heavens, but is absolutely free, it cometh not to perfection unless it submit itself through faith unto the Word of God, like a free disciple, under no control, who is not perfected unless by faith he submit himself unto the word of a master: he needs must have confidence in the master and listen unto him. The intellect is perfected by the Word of God, and groweth, and becometh continually more receptive and apt, and liker unto the Word.

This perfection, which thus cometh from the Word whence it had being, is not a corruptible perfection, but Godlike. Like the perfection of gold, 'tis not corruptible, but of heavenly form. But it behoveth every intellect to submit itself by faith unto the Word of God, and to hear with closest attention that inward teaching of the supreme Master, and, by hearing what the Lord saith in it, it shall be made perfect. 'Twas for this that thou, Jesu, one and only Master, didst preach the necessity of faith for all approaching the fount of life, and didst show that the inflowing of divine power was according unto the measure of faith.

Two things only hast thou taught, O Saviour Christ—faith and love.[27] By faith the intellect hath access unto the Word; by love 'tis united thereunto; the nearer it approacheth, the more it waxeth in power; the more it loveth, the more it stablisheth itself in its light. And the Word of God is within it; it needeth not to seek outside itself, since it will find him within, and shall have access unto him by faith. And by prayer it shall obtain a nearer approach unto him, for the Word will increase faith by communication of his light.

I render thee thanks, Jesu, that by thy light I have come thus far. In thy light I see the light of my life. I see how thou, the

[27] *Ibid.*, III, 9, 11; also the sermons from Cusa in this anthology.

Word, infusest life into all believers, and makest perfect all that love thee. What teaching, good Jesu, was ever briefer and more effectual than thine? Thou persuadest us but to believe; thou biddest us but to love. What is easier than to believe in God? What is sweeter than to love him? How pleasant is thy yoke, how light is thy burden, thou one and only Teacher! To them that obey this teaching thou dost promise all their desires, for thou requirest nought difficult to a believer, and nought that a lover can refuse. Such are the promises that thou makest unto thy disciples, and they are entirely true, for thou art the Truth, who canst promise nought but truth. Nay more, 'tis nought other than thyself that thou dost promise, who art the perfection of all that may be made perfect. To thee be praise, to thee be glory, to thee the rendering of thanks through endless ages! Amen.

Chapter XXV

How Jesus Is the Consummation

What is it, Lord, that thou conveyest to the spirit of the man whom thou makest perfect? Is it not thy good Spirit, who in his Being is consummately the power of all powers and the perfection of the perfect, since it is he that worketh all things? 'Tis as when the sun's strength, descending on the spirit of growing things, moveth it toward perfection, so that by the right pleasant and natural mellowing of the heavenly heat it may become good fruit on a good tree: even so thy Spirit, O God, cometh upon the intellectual spirit of a good man, and, by the heat of divine love, melloweth its latent power toward perfection, that it may become fruit most acceptable unto Him.

Lord, we find that thy one Spirit, infinite in power, is received in manifold ways, for it is received in one way by one, in whom it produceth the spirit of prophecy, and in another way by another, in whom it produceth skill in interpretation, and by yet another, to whom it teacheth knowledge, and so in divers ways in others. For His gifts are diverse, and they are perfections of the intellectual spirit, even as that same heat of the sun bringeth to perfection divers fruits on divers trees.

I perceive, Lord, that thy Spirit cannot be lacking unto any spirit, because it is the Spirit of spirits, and motion of motions, and it filleth the whole world: but it directeth all such things as have not an intellectual spirit by means of intellectual nature which moveth the heavens and, by their motion, all things that exist thereunder. But the disposition and distribution of intellectual nature he reserved for himself alone. For he hath espoused unto himself this nature, wherein he chose to rest as in an house of abiding and in the heaven of truth: since 'tis intellectual nature alone that can grasp truth of itself.

Thou, Lord, who makest all things for thine own sake, hast created this whole world for the sake of intellectual nature. Even so a painter mixeth divers colors that at length he may be able to paint himself, so that he may possess his own likeness, wherein his art may rest and take pleasure, and so that, his single self being not to be multiplied, he may at least be multiplied in the one way possible, to wit, in a likeness most resembling himself. But the Spirit maketh many figures, because the likeness of his infinite power can only be perfectly set forth in many, and they are all intellectual spirits, serviceable to every spirit. For, were they not innumerable, thou, infinite God, couldst not be known in the best fashion. For every intellectual spirit perceiveth in thee, my God, somewhat which must be revealed unto others in order that they may attain unto thee, their God, in the best possible fashion. Wherefore these spirits, full of love, reveal one unto another their secrets, and thereby the knowledge of the Beloved is increased, and yearning toward him is aflame, and sweetness of joy.

Yet, O Lord God, thou couldst not have brought thy work to perfect consummation without thy Son, Jesus, whom thou hast anointed above his fellows, who is the Christ. In his intellect the perfection of creatable nature is at rest, for he is the final and entirely perfect Image of God who cannot be multiplied, and there can be but one such supreme Image. Howbeit, all other intellectual spirits are, through the medium of that Spirit, likenesses, and the more perfect the more they resemble it. And all rest in that Spirit as in the final perfection of the Image of God, of whose Image they have attained the likeness, and some degree of perfection.

Wherefore of thy giving, O my God, I possess this whole visible world and all the Scripture, and all ministering spirits to aid me to advance in knowledge of thee. Yea, all things stir me up to turn unto thee: all Scriptures strive only to set thee forth, and all intellectual spirits exercise themselves only in seeking thee and in revealing as much of thee as they have found. Thou hast above all given me Jesus as Master, as the Way, the Truth, and the Life, so that absolutely nothing may be lacking unto me. Thou dost strengthen me by thy Holy Spirit; through him thou dost inspire the choice of life, holy yearnings. Thou dost draw me, by a foretaste of the sweetness of the life in glory, to love thee, O infinite Good! Thou dost ravish me above myself that I may foresee the glorious place whereunto thou callest me. For thou showest me many dainties, most delectable, that allure me by their excellent savor: thou grantest me to behold the treasury of riches, of life, of joy, of beauty. Thou uncoverest the fountain whence floweth all that is desirable alike in nature and in art. Thou keepest nought secret. Thou hidest not the channel of love, of peace, and of rest. All things dost thou set before me, a miserable creature whom thou didst create from nothing.

Why, then, do I delay, why do I not run, in the sweet smell of the unguents of my Christ? Why do I not enter into the joy of my Lord? What restraineth me? If ignorance of thee, Lord, hath held me back, and the empty delight of the world of sense, they shall restrain me no longer. For I desire, Lord (since thou grantest me so to desire) to leave the things of this world, because the world desireth to leave me. I hasten toward the goal. I have all but finished my course, I will be beforehand with it in taking farewell, I who pant for my crown. Draw me, Lord, for none can come unto thee save he be drawn by thee; grant that, thus drawn, I may be set free from this world and may be united unto thee, the absolute God, in an eternity of glorious life.

AMEN.

A SERMON ON THE EUCHARIST [28]

The Text

Since Christ is life-giving life, and since our life cannot be preserved without food, he who is the giver of life is also its preserver. Wherefore he is the Bread of Life. And because he is the Bread or food of life, this Bread cannot be attained except by faith;[29] for that which gives life is Spirit. The Spirit, moreover, cannot be known, whence it comes or whither it goes, as the doctrine of Christ teaches. It cannot be attained, therefore, by knowledge. But since we must come to the Spirit of life, if we strive to gain life; and since we cannot achieve this by knowledge, it is fitting that this should be accomplished by that virtue which is above knowledge, namely, faith. This faith, moreover, which deserves to attain spiritual life should be triumphant and militant, and obedient to Christ. It should hold captive the intellect, that thus it may be victorious and virtuous.

Virtue, however, is not perfected except in adversity. Therefore, this faith, in order to be perfected in virtue and become strong, must endure difficulties, and the more numerous they are, the greater should be its virtue. But if it is necessary that faith be of such great virtue that it reaches, in the spirit, the eternal life of the spirit, it must be most virtuous, and hence most victorious. Therefore, the obstacles which ought to be

---

[28] The following sermons, both translated by Miss Dorothy Ann Freeman, from the *Excitationum ex sermonibus*, IV, 444–45, and *Cusanus Texte*, I, 2–5, *Vier Predigten in Geiste Eckharts . . .*, ed. by Koch, Winter, Heidelberg, 1937, pp. 92–98, respectively, are from R. C. Petry, *No Uncertain Sound*, Philadelphia, 1948, pp. 289–294. They are used by permission of The Westminster Press.

[29] Cf. the *Doct. ign.*, III, 11, the *Visio Dei* and the other sermon, here attached, on the role of faith.

overcome are necessarily most evident; and that which most obviously opposes faith is the certitude which abides in the senses. Because nothing exists in the intellect that does not exist first in sense, it is particularly the duty of the virtue of faith to hold captive the intellect, that it may believe the opposite of what sense shows. Thence it comes that Christ offers himself as the Bread of Life to those discerning spirits of ours, which, through victory over sensible things, deliver themselves captive through faith, and without doubt believe that to be true which sense denies. Such a result, indeed, proceeds from this alone, that [the spirit] believes him, whom it sees a man, to be the Son of God. In consequence of this faith, it believes all that the Son pronounces and preaches as the words of God, to whom nothing is impossible. But the more impossible anything seems according to the judgment of the senses, the more possible it is to God, for the manifestation of this omnipotence and great glory. This faith shows, moreover, that the bread of the gospel has the knowledge of life, since it is the word of eternal life and shows also, since it is the only food of life, the justification of the incarnate Word [in its two aspects] of preaching and of the justifying host. Therefore, for this purpose, to touch the Bread of Life in faith through victory over appearances, and in opposition to the sensible world, it has always been necessary to have this warfare. Since this nourishment is always necessary for us, so also the strongest faith is always requisite to attain it. For this reason, when he was about to depart from this world, Christ promised to abide with us until the end of time, in such way that his presence should contribute to our attainment of life. And because he saw that it was especially conducive to the attainment of life, he concealed himself, the food of spiritual life, under sensible semblance, having corporeal form, that is the bread and wine. In this same way he himself appeared corporeally, when he bore the true food of spiritual life hidden in a body nourished on bread and wine, that is, a body of flesh and blood. Hence, departing from this world, he left us the Eucharist, in which he who is the sustenance of the mind lies hidden under sensible sacramental signs. Just so, while he walked in body on this earth, he bore hidden in flesh and blood the food of life; so that in those very foods by which the physical body is fed, the spirit, when the refreshment of the corruptible manna is withdrawn, may through faith be nourished by the food of the incorruptible bread which comes down from heaven. And therefore, even as the stomach by its own heat extracts food from the

bread of the corruptible manna in order to restore itself, faith by
its own fire may infuse the living spirit into the bread in order
itself to live in life. Therefore, as he himself was sent by the
Father, minister of the word of life which he possessed, ministering the sustenance of life, and offering himself as that sustenance, just so he sent the apostles and disciples and their succes-
sors to the end of the ages in the same way as he himself was
sent by the Father, that they also, in the word of life, might
minister the food of life and might offer Christ himself as the
nutriment of life in the form of corporeal foods. And thus you
see how the sustenance of life should be ministered in preaching,
just as in oblation. And the preaching is so much the more perfect in proportion to the fruitfulness and the frequency in it of
that sweetest oblation, the mystical body of Christ.

Let us touch upon the cause of this institution. One purpose
was mentioned in the beginning, namely, that thus Christ may
be with us, so that through faith we may be able to partake of
the nutriment of life. And since he is with us as the justifying
host, given for the life of the world, intangible to the senses, we
are able to partake of life through strong faith, in the oblation
of the invisible host, contained under visible semblances. There
is another cause of the institution which we must especially remember: that Christ took bread and, giving thanks, broke it,
and gave it to his disciples, saying: "Take and eat; this is my
body which is given for you; this do in commemoration of me"
(cf. Matt. 26:26; Luke 22:19). [Thus] he wished to show that
his true body must be given for them, that he might give them
life. And just as the bread, which he made his body, was one and
was divided, and offered to all, and refreshed each one partaking of it, thus also was it with the wine. Just as Christ, the en-
livening life, unites the whole body of the faithful in the unity of
faith, since he himself is [both] the life and the body of faith,
just so he instituted this sacrament, that in it he himself might
be the food of life, and those sharing in this one bread, the one
body of Christ, by the one food of life should be refreshed.
Christ, therefore, wished that in memory of this, that he himself
was life and gave himself for the faithful, the bread should be
consecrated and given to the faithful. Of the faithful it is therefore required that he should participate in the body of Christ,
which is in the sacramental bread, that thus he may show himself to remember the sacrifice of Christ for him. This [he should
do] in unity with the mystical body of Christ, in whose existent
body he participates through the bread of faith. And, together

with the mystical body, he shares in the unity of Christ, who is partaken in the sacrament.

The love of your neighbor is not enough unless it is also in God, and the existence of the sacrament is necessary for salvation, so that you may be incorporated in the unity of the body of Christ and the head of Christ, for otherwise you cannot live. Therefore, it is fitting that you should receive the sacrament of this unity, so that you may openly show that you believe such an incorporation to be a necessity for salvation.

"WHERE IS HE WHO IS BORN KING OF THE JEWS?"

Matt. 2:2 (On the Epiphany: At Brixen, 1456)

THE TEXT

9. Paul said that we exist in God and move in him, for we are wayfarers. The wayfarer takes his name and his existence from the Way.[30] The wayfarer who walks or moves in the infinite Way, if he is asked where he is, says, "On the Way"; if asked where he moves, replies, "In the Way"; if asked why he moves, says, "Because of the Way"; and if asked whither he goes, says, "From the way to the Way." Accordingly, the infinite Way is called the place of the wayfarer, and this is God. Therefore, this Way, outside of which no wayfarer is to be found, is an existence without beginning or end, and from it the wayfarer takes all that he is or has, and through it he is a wayfarer. The fact that a farer begins to be a wayfarer on the Way adds nothing to the infinite Way itself, nor does it make any change in this Way, which is eternal and immovable.

10. Therefore, take note how the Word of God proclaims itself to be the Way; you are able to understand this, because the living intellect is a wayfarer on the Way or in the Word of life, from which Way he takes his being and his name, and in which he moves. If to move is to live, the moving Way is life, and thus it is the living Way of the living wayfarer. From the Way the wayfarer receives his life, and the living Way is his place, and he moves in it and from it, through it and to it. Rightly, therefore, did the Son of God call himself the Way and the Life.

11. But take note of this also: this Way, which is Life, is also Truth. The living wayfarer is a rational spirit who in his faring takes a living delight; for he knows whither he goes. He knows that he is in the Way of Life, and this Way is Truth, for Truth

---

[30] See the play on *Viator* and *Via* in the Latin and *Pilger* and *Wege* in the German. Koch, *Vierte Predigten*, cols. 92 Lat., and 93 Ger.

is the most delightful and the immortal food of his life; through which he has his being, and by which he is sustained. Therefore, this living Way, which is also Truth, is, in addition, the Word of God, itself God, and is "the light of men" walking on the Way; for the wayfarer, walking, needs no other light to prevent him from walking in darkness, as one not knowing where he wanders. But the Way, which is Life and Truth, is also illuminating light, and this light is living, because it shows itself to be "the light of life."

12. All men enter this world in the same way, but they do not all live after the same fashion, for although men, like other animals, are born naked, they clothe themselves, through the art of the tailor, in order that they may live more comfortably. Also, they make use of cooked foods, and houses, and horses, and many such things which art adds to nature for the betterment of life. These arts we receive as a great gift or favor from their discoverers. Therefore, although many live in much misery, grief, and oppression, suffering much, while others lead lives of luxury in joy and splendor, still we rightly assert that a man, by various arts or graces, can attain greater peace and joy in life than nature grants. Many, it is true, have discovered, through natural ability or divine inspiration, various arts for the improvement of living: some have invented the mechanical arts of sowing, planting, and doing business; others have written out the laws of politics and economics; and still others have discovered the ethic of habituating themselves through their manners and ways of life to delight in virtuous living, and thus to govern themselves peacefully. Yet, nevertheless, none of these arts serve the spirit, but rather they offer suggestions according to which one can, in this world, live a virtuous life of peace and quiet and praiseworthiness.

13. Therefore, to these arts religion was added, founded on divine authority and revelation, to bring man to obedience to God, through fear of him and love of him and our neighbor; in the hope of gaining the favor of God, the giver of life, that he may attain in the present world a long and tranquil life, and in heaven a life that is joyful and divine. In contrast to all other forms of religion which fail of true life, the Way to eternal life was revealed to us through Jesus, the Son of God, who made known to us the nature of the heavenly life which the sons of God enjoy, the assurance that we may achieve the sonship of God, and the means by which we may accomplish it.

But just as the art of living well in this world is variously revealed by various insights, and the clearer these are the more perfect it is, so also religion, which looks to the future life and orders the present for the sake of the future, has been variously revealed by prophets foreseeing the future from a distance. And because no one sees the future life except in imagination, therefore only He who came into our human nature from God and that heavenly life which is future for us could perfectly reveal religion or the way to it. This is our Jesus, who came from heaven that we might have life and live more abundantly through him than through nature, who "began to do and to teach" how this might be accomplished, and who said: *Whoever follows me, walks not in darkness, but he shall have the light of life* (John 8:12). He who was also the Way of nature was himself, therefore, the Way to the attainment of grace.

14. Jesus, therefore, is the place where every motion of nature or of grace comes to rest. The Word of Christ or the teaching, the command or the example of his motion, is the Way to the vision or the apprehension of eternal life, which is the life of God, who alone is immortal; and this life is more abundant than the life of created nature. But no one can enter into the way of grace, which leads to the Father, through himself; he must enter through a gate. Christ who proclaimed himself to be the gate is also the Way: the faithful Christian, by the work of faith through love, enters through the gate and finds himself in the Way. The gate is faith. The Way is love. Thus faith in Christ becomes both gate and Way. The Word of God the Father summons us out of nonexistence into existence, and finally to that sort of existence which the intellectual life enjoys, because it understands its own existence. The Word made flesh summons this intellectual life through grace to fellowship with the Word, through which it tastes, in the fountain of the Father, the sweetness of his divine life, which is imparted to the sons of God.[31]

---

[31] Cf. *Doct. ign.*, III, 4–11, and the *Visio Dei*, chs. XIX ff.

XIII

Catherine of Genoa (1447-1510)

INTRODUCTION

BIOGRAPHICAL NOTICE

CATHERINE WAS BORN IN 1447, AT GENOA, OF THE noble Fieschi family. These distinguished Guelphs had given a long line of popes, cardinals, bishops, and secular officials to society. Pious from the first, Catherine wished at thirteen to follow her sister's example and join a religious order. Owing, perhaps, to her youth and to family disinclination, she was not accepted. Several years afterward her father died, and her brother, through pressure for a diplomatic union of families, effected her marriage, in 1463, to Giuliano Adorni, a Ghibelline scion. After an unhappy union with this headstrong youth, she had an ecstatic experience of conversion in 1474, following which she secured his promise to release her from marital obligations. Her life was now devoted to strict austerities, long hours of prayerful, penitential vigil, and a ministry with the Ladies of Mercy to sick and poor. The hopelessly diseased at St. Lazarus came to know her loving services quite well. After twenty-five years without a spiritual director, she received the priest Cattaneo Marabotto as her confessor. Subsequent to her conversion, she kept periodic long fasts and enjoyed the rare privilege of daily communion. Her husband, received into the Franciscan Third Order shortly after her conversion, joined her in her vocation of mercy. It is probable that she herself became a Franciscan Tertiary. She served for years as superintendent of the sick and, later, as rector of the Genoese hospital. She and her husband lived their last years in humble, rented quarters near this institution. Here she nursed him in his last illness, 1497–1498. Given increasingly to burning love for God and sacrificial labors of love for her fellows, she died in 1510. She was canonized in 1737.

BIBLIOGRAPHICAL ESSAY

A good brief summation of the sources, life, doctrine, and influence of Catherine is by P. Debongnie in the *Dictionnaire d'histoire et de géographie ecclésiastiques*, ed., A. Baudrillart *et al.*, Vol. 11 (Paris, 1939), cols. 1506–1515. More intricately critical treatments are those by Umile da Genova, O. M. Cap., and M. Viller in DS II, 290–325, and, by the former, "L'opus Catharinianum et ses auteurs," in the *Revue d'ascétique et de mystique*, Vol. 16 (1935), pp. 351–380. The highly controversial work of Baron F. von Hügel, *The Mystical Element of Religion as Studied in Saint Catherine of Genoa and Her Friends*, 2 vols., J. M. Dent & Sons, London, and E. P. Dutton & Co., Inc., New York, 1908, 1923, is indispensable. The *editio princeps* of the so-called *Opus Catharinianum* is the *Libro de la Vita mirabile e Dottrina Santa de la Beata Caterinetta da Genova*, Antonio Bellono, Genoa, 1551. This contains the *Life* in fifty-two chapters, the *Purgatory*, undivided, and the *Dialogue* in two parts. The *Vita di B. Catherina* in the edition of A. Maineri was published at Genoa, 1737. Not available to the present editor was the text of P. Valeriano da Finale (Finalmarina), *Trattato del Purgatorio di Santa Caterina da Genova*, Genoa, 1929 (divided into nineteen chapters as against the more usual seventeen customary with the 1666 French translation and thereafter). A useful selection of texts in German is L. Sertorius, *Katharina von Genua: Lebensbild und geistige Gestalt ihre Werke*, Kösel-Pustet, Munich, 1939. See Pourrat, *Christian Spirituality*, Vol. II, pp. 286 ff.

SYNOPSIS

Catherine's mystical doctrine finds its center in love. Thus the *Vita* and the *Dialogue* depict the purgative and the illuminative ways as conducing, finally, to the unitive life in the identification of pure love. She finds contemplative union with God through love's identification. This involves, for the soul, not merely certain acts of participation, but veritable annihilation of all self-love and genuine transformation in God. The soul, created for eternal beatitude, and turned aside from its end by love of self, needs three purifying stages so that God may reclaim it for himself and consume everything that holds him at bay. In the first, the soul participates with God through its progressive detachment from all obstacles, inner and outer, by which it nourishes self-love and feeds rebellion against the divine. In the

second, it enjoys numerous spiritual consolations. Fixing itself
in God, it rejoices constantly in him through readings, meditations, and contemplations. Therein it finds instruction in divine
secrets and sweet sustenance. Thus it undergoes transformation
in the divine through a steady preoccupation with God himself.
In the third stage, the soul is borne out of itself, interiorly and
exteriorly. It transcends knowing, finding, or doing, and becomes like an inert instrument of the divine, fully attentive to
that which God works in it. The Lord now vouchsafes to the
soul the key to all his treasures, the preoccupation with his all-
surrounding presence. Burning rays of the divine love emanate
from him in such penetrating power as, seemingly, to destroy
everything in its path—actually to remove all hindrance to
union with him. This last stage, in its fullest development, constitutes that purgatory of which Catherine writes. Here she
lends her conscious states in mystic trust to divinely wrought
sufferings in herself, by which she is identified, now, with the
pains of those souls already in purgatorial cleansing.[1] The form
of purgation, seen by her in the souls of purgatory, she feels in
her own mind. She sees her own soul within its present body "as
in a purgatory." It is "formed as is the true purgatory and like
it, but so measured that the body can bear with it and not die;
yet little by little it grows until the body die."[2]

One senses in Catherine's account of this ultimate purgation
the lacerations produced in the soul by the stress between two
opposing forces: the one attracting it to God, which is the object
of its beatitude, the other setting up the conflicting pull of its
own imperfections. In the give-and-take of Catherine's tension
between God's purity and her own impurity—in the realistic
attribution of her own sufferings to the condition of purgational
sufferers—we discover Catherine's spiritual doctrine already in
full play.

The souls in purgatory suffer pain so great as to be beyond
the descriptive power of any language, or the comprehension of
any intellect (Chs. 2, 8). The mind could not understand its least
pang were God not disposed, by his special grace, to make this
possible. Manifestly, the soul undergoing purification for its re-

---

1 See the *Purgatory*, chs. 1, 9, 17 (19); *Dialogue* (*Dial.*), pt. II, chs. 2, 6, 8, 10,
and III, 13; *Vita*, ch. 30. The *Purgatory* will be referenced subsequently in
the body of the Introduction as ch. 1, etc., without title. Variant numberings for 17–(and 19–), chapter editions are indicated. See Hügel, *Mystical
Element*, on purgatory, Vol. I, pp. 283–94; Vol. II, pp. 230–46.
2 *Purgatory*, 17 (19).

turn to the state in which it was created finds itself unable to quench its desire for complete cleansing. With its beatific instinct growing unceasingly, it presses forward with "fierce charity," impetuous of any hindrance put in the way of its final purification. Obstacles to this seem unendurable. "The more it sees, the more extreme is its pain" (Ch. 3).

For Catherine the exquisite anguish of those in purgatory consists in the violent contrast between the knowledge of the soul's intended beatitude with God and the realization of the delay in attaining thereto which is imposed on it because of the pains it has yet to undergo (Ch. 3). It is this which excites in the soul an insatiable hunger for the divine. This the saint describes under the symbolism of the one, all-satisfying loaf that is ardently desired by every man (Ch. 6).

God is, for the soul, like the light or sun of her life. He exercises upon the soul an irresistible action and attracts her by rays of love so ardent as seemingly to destroy her, immortal though she be (Ch. 9(11). This "causes it to be so transformed in God that it sees itself as though it were none other than God." Catherine sees rays and shafts of light proceeding from the divine love toward the soul with such strength and penetration as seemingly to destroy not only the body but the soul too, were that possible. The soul, in so far as it is in God, is, of course, indestructible. To the extent that it is centered in itself, it can be obliterated (Ch. 10(12).

Catherine reveals how sin's rust is the real hindrance to God's entry into the soul. The rust of the body prevents the full reflection of the sun's rays. A thing thus covered cannot respond to these rays, not because of the sun's fault, for it goes right on shining, but because the cover interposes a difficulty. The cover, once burned away, leaves all open to the sun's penetrating influence. The more the obstacle is consumed, the greater is the response to the sun's rays (Ch. 2).

Obviously, the pains of purgatory are extremely distressing. Catherine's psychology of the souls in purgatory is perhaps the most personal part of this "poem of purgatory." Joy and sorrow are inextricably joined. Catherine cannot presume to fathom or to describe the intensity of such suffering (Ch. 2(3). There is a triple cause for these terrible pains. The first is the sight that these souls have of those things in them that are displeasing to God (Ch. 9 (10). Second is the sight of the divine Love, calling souls to it, and the knowledge of the obstacle opposed by sin to this divine Love (Chs. 12 (11, 14). The love of these souls as it experiences hindrance gives rise to pain. The more perfect the love of which God makes them capable, the more exquisite does their suffering become (Ch. 12). Third is the delay in pursuing the destiny which is the soul's birthright. The grievousness of thus being frustrated in its panting desire for its end, this hindrance put in its way, is what occasions pain unbearable for the soul (Ch. 17 (19).

Catherine denies that the intensity of pain diminishes in the course of purgatorial suffering. Pain does not lessen, merely the time for which it is endured (Ch. 2 (3). With time and the progress of purification, the nearer the soul approaches heaven, its end, the more the intensity of its grief mounts. Naturally, then, the last days and hours of purgatory, just before the soul's liberation, are the most harrowing of all (Ch. 17).

The reason for this increase of pain is twofold. The greater knowledge of God augments the desire and the pain (Ch. 3). The more it perceives, the greater is its suffering. The delay of union with God, while developing the perfection, increases the pain (Chs. 12, 13 (14). Joy and sadness coexist in the souls in purgatory. They know the greatest happiness even as they endure the greatest anguish. One does not hinder the other (Ch. 12 (14). The explanation of this coexistence lies in the fact that the soul makes more of the divine will than of its own pain, however great that may be (Ch. 17 (19). "As the man who would let himself be killed rather than offend God feels death and its pain, but is given by the light of God a zeal which causes him to rate divine honor above bodily death, so the soul who knows God's ordinance rates it above all possible inner and outer torments, terrible though they may be, for this is a work of God who surpasses all that can be felt or imagined" (Ch. 17 (19). In effect, these souls know a very great joy (Chs. 12 (14), 2) that increases steadily (Chs. 16 (18), 17), because the rust of sin diminishes little by little, and because God unveils himself in the measure that the soul purifies itself (Ch. 2).

The soul in purgatory loves God intensely. The loving God attracts the loving soul to him with a sweet violence. He it is who is the mysterious force that "ignites, feeds, and stimulates the amorous fire which liquefies the soul" (Chs. 9-11 (12, 11). To repeat, Love transforms the soul so as to recall it to the state of its first creation. "Unceasingly he draws it to himself and breathes fire into it, never letting it go until he has led it to the state whence it came forth, that is, to the pure cleanliness in which it was created" (Ch. 9 (12). He causes it to ache with the desire for this transformation that consumes it like fire. He ennobles and purifies it by delivering it (without its having perceived it) from its imperfections, not showing the soul this until he has destroyed these imperfections. He prostrates it by suppressing in it all vestiges of egotism, by producing in it, through himself alone, "this last act of love by which he purifies it. . . . A last act of love is done by God without help from man." So many are the imperfections of the soul that if these were disclosed to it, it would recoil in despair. But having been burned away, these defects are then shown by God to the soul. Thus it may behold the divine operation that kindles the fire of love in which its imperfections have been consumed (Ch. 11). It rejoices even as it continues to sorrow (Ch. 12).

The principle is clearly posited that Christian perfection is won by total self-abnegation. This done, Catherine describes for us the soul which knows itself all unworthy of the divine graciousness and entirely incapable of giving itself to the work of unifying love. It now rises spontaneously to the transforming and purifying love. Purgatory ceases to be an imposed prison. It becomes, rather, a desired purification, one that is willed and amorously sought (Chs. 16–17, 9 (18, 9). This self-abnegation of souls in purgatory manifests itself by their perfect conformity to God's own will (Ch. 5 (6–7).

Certain and predictable are the happy results that spring from this perfect renunciation and conformity of the soul's will with that of the Divine. The soul fixes its gaze on the working of the divine goodness. It sloughs off the final remnants of earthly egoism. Its sole occupation is in God. Purification itself is, as it were, unconscious. The soul does not rejoice in it as if it were her own doing. That would be to cancel her own abnegation. She rejoices in purification in order to experience fuller union with God (Ch. 12 (15). Following the total destruction of egoistic pride, the soul voluntarily suffers these pains, knowing that it is the divine will, so that it would not diminish them if it had the power (Chs. 16–17 (18). This purificatory self-abandon leads the soul to complete forgetfulness of itself. Also, it is unable to consider how it suffers these pains for its own sins. It has seen, once and for all, in the divine judgment the meaning of its sins and the necessity for their purification. By consequence, it completely forgets itself, abandoning itself entirely to God. Happy to accomplish his will in everything, it knows only that because of its lack of dispatch, pain retards union with the eternal love (Ch. 1 (1).

As a result of the perfect degree of charity attained by the soul, as also of the complete renunciation of self, it does not desire to be freed from the prison of purgatory (Ch. 17 (15). The last fruit of abnegation is the purification from every last vestige of guilt-laden temporal besmirchment that corrupts the soul, rendering it unworthy of the blessed life.

What may be said as to the comparison of pains suffered by those in purgatory and by those doomed to hell? The sense of unworthiness that the soul feels in God's presence means for the one in purgatory a deeply harrowing sorrow. For the one in hell a sense of guilt ensues in a malignant will ever opposed to the will of God. The pains of hell and purgatory differ less in their intensity and violence than in the duration of the suffering and the matter of guilt. Those in hell suffer eternal pain and with guilt. Those in purgatory suffer finite pain without guilt. Furthermore, the pain of the souls in purgatory is tempered by the desire for satisfaction that animates them, as also by their perfect conformity to the divine will that makes them appreciate the necessity and rightness of their sufferings. On the other hand, the sentiment of Satanic rebellion characteristic of the damned blinds all such with fury and further anguish (Chs. 3, 4).

Catherine of Genoa (1447-1510)

TREATISE ON PURGATORY[3]

THE TEXT

How by Comparing it to the Divine Fire which she Felt in Herself, this Soul Understood what Purgatory was like and how the Souls there were Tormented.

Chapter I

The State of the Souls Who Are in Purgatory, How They Are Exempt from All Self-love

This holy soul[4] found herself, while still in the flesh, placed by the fiery love of God in purgatory, which burned her, cleansing whatever in her needed cleansing, to the end that when she passed from this life she might be presented to the sight of God, her dear Love. By means of this loving fire, she understood in her soul the state of the souls of the faithful who are placed in purgatory to purge them of all the rust and stains of sin of which they have not rid themselves in this life. And since this soul, placed by the divine fire in this loving purgatory, was united to that divine love and content with all that was wrought in her, she understood the state of the souls who are in purgatory. And she said:

The souls who are in purgatory cannot, as I understand, choose but be there, and this is by God's ordinance who therein

---

[3] The translation, based on the edition of 1737, is that of Charlotte Balfour and Helen Douglas Irvine, *Saint Catherine of Genoa: Treatise on Purgatory; The Dialogue*, 1946, pp. 17–35. Used by permission of publisher, Sheed & Ward, Inc., New York and London.

[4] This reference and the chapter headings of 4 and 9 are obviously from other hands, as, indeed, the final form of the *Trattato* itself is.

has done justly. They cannot turn their thoughts back to themselves, nor can they say, "Such sins I have committed for which I deserve to be here," nor, "I would that I had not committed them for then I would go now to paradise," nor, "That one will leave sooner than I," nor, "I will leave sooner than he." They can have neither of themselves nor of others any memory, whether of good or evil, whence they would have greater pain than they suffer ordinarily. So happy are they to be within God's ordinance, and that he should do all which pleases him as it pleases him that in their greatest pain they cannot think of themselves. They see only the working of the divine goodness, which leads man to itself mercifully, so that he no longer sees aught of the pain or good which may befall him. Nor would these souls be in pure charity if they could see that pain or good. They cannot see that they are in pain because of their sins; that sight they cannot hold in their minds because in it there would be an active imperfection, which cannot be where no actual sin can be.

Only once, as they pass from this life, do they see the cause of the purgatory they endure; never again do they see it for in another sight of it there would be self.[5] Being, then, in charity, from which they cannot now depart by any actual fault, they can no longer will, nor desire, save with the pure will of pure charity. Being in that fire of purgatory, they are within the divine ordinance, which is pure charity, and in nothing can they depart thence for they are deprived of the power to sin as of the power to merit.

Chapter II

What Is the Joy of the Souls in Purgatory. A Comparison to Show How They See God Ever More and More. The Difficulty of Speaking of This State

I believe no happiness can be found worthy to be compared with that of a soul in purgatory except that of the saints in paradise; and day by day this happiness grows as God flows into these souls, more and more as the hindrance to his entrance is consumed. Sin's rust is the hindrance, and the fire burns the rust away[6] so that more and more the soul opens itself up to the

---

5 "Otherwise self would come in (*vi saria una proprietà*)." Hügel, *op. cit.*, Vol. I, p. 283.
6 Sertorius, *op. cit.*, p. 122: *Der Rost der Sünde bildet diesen Widerstand;* cf. Hügel, *op. cit.*, Vol. I, pp. 290 ff.

divine inflowing. A thing which is covered cannot respond to
the sun's rays, not because of any defect in the sun, which is
shining all the time, but because the cover is an obstacle;[7] if
the cover be burned away, this thing is open to the sun; more
and more as the cover is consumed does it respond to the rays
of the sun.

It is in this way that rust, which is sin, covers souls, and in
purgatory is burned away by fire; the more it is consumed, the
more do the souls respond to God, the true sun. As the rust
lessens and the soul is opened up to the divine ray, happiness
grows; until the time be accomplished the one wanes and the
other waxes. Pain, however, does not lessen, but only the time
for which pain is endured. As for will: never can the souls say
these pains are pains, so contented are they with God's ordain-
ing with which, in pure charity, their will is united.

But, on the other hand, they endure a pain so extreme that no
tongue can be found to tell it, nor could the mind understand
its least pang if God by special grace did not show so much.
Which least pang God of his grace showed to this soul, but with
her tongue she cannot say what it is. This sight which the Lord
revealed to me has never since left my mind and I will tell what
I can of it. They will understand whose mind God deigns to
open.

Chapter III

Separation from God Is the Chief Punishment of Purgatory. Wherein
Purgatory Differs from Hell

All the pains of purgatory arise from original or actual sin.
God created the soul pure, simple, and clean of all stain of sin,
with a certain beatific instinct toward Himself whence original
sin, which the soul finds in itself, draws it away, and when
actual is added to original sin the soul is drawn yet farther
away. The farther it departs from its beatific instinct, the more
malignant it becomes because it corresponds less to God.

There can be no good save by participation in God, who
meets the needs of irrational creatures as he wills and has ordained, never failing them, and answers to a rational soul in the
measure in which he finds it cleansed of sin's hindrance. When
therefore a soul has come near to the pure and clear state in
which it was created, its beatific instinct discovers itself and

---

7 Hügel, *op. cit.*, Vol. I, pp. 290–91: "but because the covering intervenes
(*opposizione*)."

grows unceasingly, so impetuously and with such fierce charity (drawing it to its last end) that any hindrance seems to this soul a thing past bearing. The more it sees, the more extreme is its pain.

Because the souls in purgatory are without the guilt of sin, there is no hindrance between them and God except their pain, which holds them back so that they cannot reach perfection. Clearly they see the grievousness of every least hindrance in their way, and see too that their instinct is hindered by a necessity of justice: thence is born a raging fire, like that of hell save that guilt is lacking to it.[8] Guilt it is that makes the will of the damned in hell malignant, on whom God does not bestow his goodness and who remain therefore in desperate ill will, opposed to the will of God.

Chapter IV

Of the State of the Souls in Hell and of the Difference Between Them and Those in Purgatory. Reflections of This Saint on Those Who Are Careless of Their Salvation

Hence it is manifest that there is perversity of will, contrary to the will of God, where the guilt is known and ill will persists, and that the guilt of those who have passed with ill will from this life to hell is not remitted, nor can be, since they may no longer change the will with which they have passed out of this life, in which passage the soul is made stable in good or evil in accordance with its deliberate will. As it is written, *Ubi te invenero*, that is in the hour of death, with the will to sin or dissatisfaction with sin or repentance for sin, *Ibi te judicabo*. Of which judgment there is afterward no remission, as I will show:

After death free will can never return, for the will is fixed as it was at the moment of death. Because the souls in hell were found at the moment of death to have in them the will to sin, they bear the guilt throughout eternity, suffering not indeed the pains they merit but such pains as they endure, and these without end. But the souls in purgatory bear only pain, for their guilt was wiped away at the moment of their death when they were found to be ill content with their sins and repentant for their offenses against divine goodness. Therefore their pain is finite and its time ever lessening, as has been said.

O misery beyond all other misery, the greater that human blindness takes it not into account!

---

[8] Sertorius, *op. cit.*, p. 124: *nur frei von der Schuld.* . . .

The pain of the damned is not infinite in quantity because the dear goodness of God sheds the ray of his mercy even in hell. For man dead in sin merits infinite pain for an infinite time, but God's mercy has allotted infinity to him only in time and has determined the quantity of his pain; in justice God could have given him more pain.

O how dangerous is sin committed in malice! Hardly does a man repent him thereof, and without repentance he will bear its guilt for as long as he perseveres, that is for as long as he wills a sin committed or wills to sin again.

Chapter V

Of the Peace and the Joy There Are in Purgatory

The souls in purgatory have wills accordant in all things with the will of God, who therefore sheds on them his goodness, and they, as far as their will goes, are happy and cleansed of all their sin. As for guilt, these cleansed souls are as they were when God created them, for God forgives their guilt immediately who have passed from this life ill content with their sins, having confessed all they have committed and having the will to commit no more. Only the rust of sin is left them and from this they cleanse themselves by pain in the fire. Thus cleansed of all guilt and united in will to God, they see him clearly in the degree in which he makes himself known to them, and see too how much it imports to enjoy him and that souls have been created for this end. Moreover, they are brought to so uniting a conformity with God, and are drawn to him in such wise, his natural instinct toward souls working in them, that neither arguments nor figures nor examples can make the thing clear as the mind knows it to be in effect and as by inner feeling it is understood to be. I will, however, make one comparison which comes to my mind.

Chapter VI

A Comparison to Show with What Violence and What Love the Souls in Purgatory Desire to Enjoy God

If in all the world there were but one loaf of bread to feed the hunger of all creatures, and if they were satisfied by the sight of it alone, then since man, if he be healthy, has an instinct to eat, his hunger, if he neither ate nor sickened nor died, would grow unceasingly for his instinct to eat would not lessen. Knowing

that there was only that loaf to satisfy him and that without it
he must still be hungry, he would be in unbearable pain. All the
more if he went near that loaf and could not see it would his
natural craving for it be strengthened; his instinct would fix his
desire wholly on that loaf which held all that could content him;
at this point, if he were sure he would never see the loaf again,
he would be in hell. Thus are the souls of the damned from
whom any hope of ever seeing their Bread, which is God, the
true Saviour, has been taken away. But the souls in purgatory
have the hope of seeing their Bread and wholly satisfying themselves therewith. Therefore they suffer hunger and endure pain
in that measure in which they will be able to satisfy themselves
with the Bread which is Jesus Christ, true God and Saviour and
our Love.[9]

Chapter VII

Of God's Admirable Wisdom in Making Purgatory and Hell [10]

As the clean and purified spirit can find rest only in God, having been created for this end, so there is no place save hell for
the soul in sin, for whose end hell was ordained by God. When
the soul as it leaves the body is in mortal sin, then, in the instant
in which spirit and body are separated, the soul goes to the
place ordained for it, unguided save by the nature of its sin.
And if at that moment the soul were bound by no ordinance
proceeding from God's justice, it would go to a yet greater hell
than that in which it abides, for it would be outside his ordinance, in which divine mercy has part so that God gives the
soul less pain than it deserves. The soul, finding no other place
to hand nor any holding less evil for it, casts itself by God's
ordinance into hell as into its proper place.

To return to our matter which is the purgatory of the soul
separated from the body when it is no longer clean as it was
created: seeing in itself the impediment which can be taken
away only by means of purgatory, it casts itself therein swiftly
and willingly. Were there not the ordinance it thus obeys, one
fit to rid it of its encumbrance, it would in that instant beget
within itself a hell worse than purgatory, for it would see that
because of that impediment it could not draw near to God, its
end. So much does God import that purgatory in comparison

---

[9] Cf. Hügel, *op. cit.*, Vol. I, pp. 288 ff.
[10] Cf. *Dial.*, III, 13, on purgatory, hell, etc.; cf. *Vita*, 12, 14, 30.

counts not at all, for all that it is, as has been said, like hell. But compared to God it appears almost nothing.

Chapter VIII

Of the Necessity of Purgatory. How Terrible It Is

When I look at God, I see no gate to paradise, and yet because God is all mercy he who wills enters there. God stands before us with open arms to receive us into his glory.[11] But well I see the divine essence to be of such purity, greater far than can be imagined, that the soul in which there is even the least note of imperfection would rather cast itself into a thousand hells than find itself thus stained in the presence of the divine Majesty.[12] Therefore the soul, understanding that purgatory has been ordained to take away those stains, casts itself therein, and seems to itself to have found great mercy in that it can rid itself there of the impediment which is the stain of sin.

No tongue can tell or explain, no mind understand, the grievousness of purgatory. But I, though I see that there is in purgatory as much pain as in hell, yet see the soul which has the least stain of imperfection accepting purgatory, as I have said, as though it were a mercy, and holding its pains of no account as compared with the least stain which hinders a soul in its love. I seem to see that the pain which souls in purgatory endure because of whatever in them displeases God—that is, what they have willfully done against his so great goodness—is greater than any other pain they feel in purgatory. And this is because, being in grace, they see the truth and the grievousness of the hindrance which stays them from drawing near to God.

Chapter IX

How God and the Souls in Purgatory Look at Each Other. The Saint Acknowledges that in Speaking of These Matters She Cannot Express Herself

All these things which I have surely in mind, in so much as in this life I have been able to understand them, are, as compared with what I have said, extreme in their greatness. Beside them all the sights and sounds and justice and truths of this world

[11] *Vita*, 30.
[12] Cf. *Dial.*, III, 6; Hügel, *op. cit.*, Vol. I, p. 284: "the least mote (*minimo chè*)." Sertorius, *op. cit.*, p. 130 reads: "*Nur ein Splitterchen Unvollkommenheit in sic hat. . . .*"

seem to me lies and nothingness. I am left confused because I cannot find words extreme enough for these things.

I perceive there to be so much conformity between God and the soul that when he sees it in the purity in which his divine Majesty created it he gives it a burning love, which draws it to himself, which is strong enough to destroy it, immortal though it be, and which causes it to be so transformed in God that it sees itself as though it were none other than God. Unceasingly he draws it to himself and breathes fire into it, never letting it go until he has led it to the state whence it came forth, that is, to the pure cleanliness in which it was created.

When with its inner sight the soul sees itself drawn by God with such loving fire, then it is melted by the heat of the glowing love for God, its most dear Lord, which it feels overflowing it. And it sees by the divine light that God does not cease from drawing it, nor from leading it, lovingly and with much care and unfailing foresight, to its full perfection, doing this of his pure love. But the soul, being hindered by sin, cannot go whither God draws it; it cannot follow the uniting look with which he would draw it to himself. Again the soul perceives the grievousness of being held back from seeing the divine light; the soul's instinct too, being drawn by that uniting look, craves to be unhindered. I say that it is the sight of these things that begets in the souls the pain they feel in purgatory. Not that they make account of their pain; most great though it be, they deem it a far less evil than to find themselves going against the will of God, whom they clearly see to be on fire with extreme and pure love for them.

Strongly and unceasingly this love draws the soul with that uniting look, as though it had nought else than this to do. Could the soul who understood find a worse purgatory in which to rid itself sooner of all the hindrance in its way, it would swiftly fling itself therein, driven by the conforming love between itself and God.[13]

Chapter X

How God Uses Purgatory to Make the Soul Wholly Pure. The Soul Acquires in Purgatory a Purity So Great that Were It Well for It Still to Stay There After It Had Been Purged of Sin, It Would No Longer Suffer

I see, too, certain rays and shafts of light which go out from

[13] Hügel, *op. cit.*, Vol. I, p. 284.

that divine love toward the soul and are penetrating and strong enough to seem as though they must destroy not only the body but the soul too, were that possible. Two works are wrought by these rays: the first, purification, and the second, destruction.

Look at gold: the more you melt it, the better it becomes; you could melt it until you had destroyed in it every imperfection. Thus does fire work on material things. The soul cannot be destroyed in so far as it is in God, but in so far as it is in itself it can be destroyed; the more it is purified, the more is self destroyed within it, until at last it is pure in God.

When gold has been purified up to twenty-four carats, it can no longer be consumed by any fire; not gold itself but only dross can be burned away. Thus the divine fire works in the soul: God holds the soul in the fire until its every imperfection is burned away and it is brought to perfection, as it were to the purity of twenty-four carats, each soul however according to its own degree. When the soul has been purified, it stays wholly in God, having nothing of self in it; its being is in God who has led this cleansed soul to himself; it can suffer no more, for nothing is left in it to be burned away; were it held in the fire when it has thus been cleansed, it would feel no pain. Rather, the fire of divine love would be to it like eternal life and in no way contrary to it.[14]

Chapter XI

Of the Desire of Souls in Purgatory to Be Wholly Cleansed of the Stains of Their Sins. The Wisdom of God Who Suddenly Hides Their Faults from These Souls

The soul was created as well conditioned as it is capable of being for reaching perfection, if it live as God has ordained and do not foul itself with any stain of sin. But, having fouled itself by original sin, it loses its gifts and graces and lies dead, nor can it rise again save by God's means. And when God, by baptism, has raised it from the dead, it is still prone to evil, inclining and being led to actual sin unless it resist. And thus it dies again.

Then God by another special grace raises it again, yet it stays so sullied and so turned to self that all the divine workings of which we have spoken are needed to recall it to its first state in which God created it; without them it could never get back thither. And when the soul finds itself on the road back to its first state, its need to be transformed in God kindles in it a fire

[14] See, further, on the divine, vivifying light and flaming rays of love, *Purgatory*, chs. 2, 9, etc.; *Dial.*, III, 12; *Vita*, 21, 31.

so great that this is its purgatory. Not that it can look upon this as purgatory, but its instinct to God, aflame and thwarted, makes purgatory.

A last act of love is done by God without help from man.[15] So many hidden imperfections are in the soul that, did it see them, it would live in despair. But in the state of which we have spoken they are all burned away, and only when they have gone does God show them to the soul, so that it may see that divine working which kindles the fire of love in which its imperfections have been burned away.

Chapter XII

How Suffering in Purgatory Is Coupled with Joy

Know that what man deems perfection in himself is in God's sight faulty, for all the things a man does which he sees or feels or means or wills or remembers to have a perfect seeming are wholly fouled and sullied unless he acknowledge them to be from God. If a work is to be perfect it must be wrought in us, but not chiefly by us, for God's works must be done in him and not wrought chiefly by man.

Such works are those last wrought in us by God of his pure and clean love, by him alone without merit of ours, and so penetrating are they and such fire do they kindle in the soul, that the body which wraps it seems to be consumed as in a furnace never to be quenched until death. It is true that love for God which fills the soul to overflowing gives it, so I see it, a happiness beyond what can be told, but this happiness takes not one pang from the pain of the souls in purgatory. Rather the love of these souls, finding itself hindered, causes their pain; and the more perfect is the love of which God has made them capable, the greater is their pain.

So that the souls in purgatory enjoy the greatest happiness and endure the greatest pain; the one does not hinder the other.

Chapter XIII

The Souls in Purgatory Are No Longer in a State to Acquire Merit. How These Souls Look on the Charity Exercised for Them in the World

If the souls in purgatory could purge themselves by contri-

15 *Vita*, 31; cf. *Vita*, 41.

tion, they would pay all their debt in one instant, such blazing vehemence would their contrition have in the clear light shed for them on the grievousness of being hindered from reaching their end and the love of God.

Know surely that not the least farthing of payment is remitted to those souls, for thus has it been determined by God's justice. So much for what God does; as for what the souls do, they can no longer choose for themselves, nor can they see or will, save as God wills, for thus has it been determined for them.

And if any alms be done them by those who are in the world to lessen the time of their pain, they cannot turn with affection to contemplate the deed, saving as it is weighed in the most just scales of the divine will. They leave all in God's hands who pays himself as his infinite goodness pleases. If they could turn to contemplate the alms except as it is within the divine will, there would be self in what they did and they would lose sight of God's will, which would make a hell for them. Therefore they await immovably all that God gives them, whether pleasure and happiness or pain, and never more can they turn their eyes back to themselves.

Chapter XIV

Of the Submission of the Souls in Purgatory to God's Will

So intimate with God are the souls in purgatory, and so changed to his will, that in all things they are content with his most holy ordinance. And if a soul were brought to see God when it had still a trifle of which to purge itself, a great injury would be done it. For since pure love and supreme justice could not brook that stained soul, and to bear with its presence would not befit God, it would suffer a torment worse than ten purgatories. To see God when full satisfaction had not yet been made him, even if the time of purgation lacked but the twinkling of an eye, would be unbearable to that soul. It would sooner go to a thousand hells, to rid itself of the little rust still clinging to it, than stand in the divine presence when it was not yet wholly cleansed.

Chapter XV

Reproaches Which the Souls in Purgatory Make to People in the World

And so that blessed soul,[16] seeing the aforesaid things by the

16 An obvious editorial insertion.

divine light, said: "I would fain send up a cry so loud that it would put fear in all men on the earth. I would say to them, 'Wretches, why do you let yourselves be thus blinded by the world, you whose need is so great and grievous, as you will know at the moment of death, and who make no provision for it whatsoever?'

"You have all taken shelter beneath hope in God's mercy, which is, you say, very great, but you see not that this great goodness of God will judge you for having gone against the will of so good a Lord. His goodness should constrain you to do all his will, not give you hope in ill-doing, for his justice cannot fail but in one way or another must needs be fully satisfied.

"Cease to hug yourselves, saying, 'I will confess my sins and then receive plenary indulgence, and at that moment I shall be purged of all my sins and thus shall be saved.' Think of the confession and the contrition needed for that plenary indulgence, so hardly come by that, if you knew, you would tremble in great fear, more sure you would never win it than that you ever could."

Chapter XVI

This Soul Shows Again How the Sufferings of the Souls in Purgatory Are No Hindrance at All to Their Peace and Their Joy

I see the souls suffer the pains of purgatory having before their eyes two works of God.

First, they see themselves suffering pain willingly, and as they consider their own deserts and acknowledge how they have grieved God, it seems to them that he has shown them great mercy, for if his goodness had not tempered justice with mercy, making satisfaction with the precious blood of Jesus Christ, one sin would deserve a thousand perpetual hells. And therefore the souls suffer pain willingly, and would not lighten it by one pang, knowing that they most fully deserve it and that it has been well ordained, and they no more complain of God, as far as their will goes, than if they were in eternal life.

The second work they see is the happiness they feel as they contemplate God's ordinance and the love and mercy with which he works on the soul.

In one instant God imprints these two sights on their minds, and because they are in grace they are aware of these sights and understand them as they are, in the measure of their capacity.

Thus a great happiness is granted them which never fails; rather, it grows as they draw nearer God. These souls see these sights neither in nor of themselves but in God, on whom they are far more intent than on the pains they suffer, and of whom they make far greater account, beyond all comparison, than of their pains. For every glimpse which can be had of God exceeds any pain or joy a man can feel. Albeit, however, it exceeds the pain and joy of these souls, it lessens them by not a little.

Chapter XVII

She Concludes by Applying All She Has Said of the Souls in Purgatory to What She Feels and Has Proved in Her Own Soul

This form of purgation, which I see in the souls in purgatory, I feel in my own mind. In the last two years I have felt it most; every day I feel and see it more clearly. I see my soul within this body as in a purgatory, formed as is the true purgatory and like it, but so measured that the body can bear with it and not die; yet little by little it grows until the body die.

I see my spirit estranged from all things, even things spiritual, which can feed it, such as gaiety, delight, and consolation, and without the power so to enjoy anything, spiritual or temporal, by will or mind or memory, as to let me say one thing contents me more than another.

Inwardly I find myself, as it were, besieged. All things by which spiritual or bodily life is refreshed have, little by little, been taken from my inner self, which knows, now they are gone, that they fed and comforted. But so hateful and abhorrent are these things, as they are known to the spirit, that they all go never to return. This is because of the spirit's instinct to rid itself of whatever hinders its perfection; so ruthless is it that to fulfill its purpose it would all but cast itself into hell. Therefore it ever deprives the inner man of all on which it can feed, besieging it so cunningly that it lets not the least atom of imperfection pass unseen and unabhorred.

As for my outer man, it too, since the spirit does not respond to it, is so besieged that it finds nothing to refresh it on the earth if it follow its human instinct. No comfort is left it save God, who works all this by love and very mercifully in satisfaction of his justice. To perceive this gives my outer man great peace and happiness, but happiness which neither lessens my pain nor weakens the siege. Yet no pain could ever be inflicted on me so great that I would wish to depart from the divine ordinance. I neither leave my prison nor seek to go forth from it: let God do what is needed! My happiness is that God be satisfied, nor could I suffer a worse pain that that of going outside God's ordinance, so just I see him to be and so very merciful.

All these things of which I have spoken are what I see and, as it were, touch, but I cannot find fit words to say as much as I would of them. Nor can I say rightly what I have told of the work done in me, which I have felt spiritually. I have told it, however.

The prison in which I seem to myself to be is the world, my chains the body, and it is my soul enlightened by grace which knows the grievousness of being held down or kept back and thus hindered from pursuing its end.[17] This gives my soul great pain, for it is very tender. By God's grace it receives a certain dignity which makes it like unto God; nay, rather he lets it share his goodness so that it becomes one with him. And since it is impossible that God suffer pain, this immunity too befalls the souls who draw near him; the nearer they come to him, the more they partake of what is his.

Therefore to be hindered on its way, as it is, causes the soul unbearable pain. The pain and the hindrance wrest it from its first natural state, which by grace is revealed to it, and, finding itself deprived of what it is able to receive, it suffers a pain more or less great according to the measure of its esteem for God. The more the soul knows God, the more it esteems him and the more sinless it becomes, so that the hindrance in its way grows yet more terrible to it, above all because the soul which is unhindered and wholly recollected in God knows him as he truly is.

As the man who would let himself be killed rather than offend God feels death and its pain, but is given by the light of God a zeal which causes him to rate divine honor above bodily death, so the soul who knows God's ordinance rates it above all possible inner and outer torments, terrible though they may be, for this is a work of God who surpasses all that can be felt or imagined. Moreover, God when he occupies a soul, in however small a degree, keeps it wholly busied over his Majesty so that nothing else counts for it. Thus it loses all which is its own, and can of itself neither see nor speak nor know loss or pain. But, as

---

17 Cf. *Dial.*, *passim*, especially pt. II, chs. 2, 6, 8, 10, 11, on soul, body, and purgatory.

I have already said clearly, it knows all in one instant when it leaves this life.

Finally and in conclusion, let us understand that God who is best and greatest causes all that is of man to be lost, and that purgatory cleanses it away.

END OF THE TREATISE ON PURGATORY

INDEXES

GENERAL INDEX

Modern Authors

BIBLICAL REFERENCES